The Norton

Field Guide to Speaking

The Norton
Field Guide
to Speaking

Isa N. Engleberg
EMERITA, PRINCE GEORGE'S COMMUNITY COLLEGE

John A. Daly
UNIVERSITY OF TEXAS, AUSTIN

W. W. NORTON & COMPANY
Independent Publishers Since 1923

W. W. NORTON & COMPANY has been independent since its founding in 1923, when William Warder Norton and Mary D. Herter Norton first published lectures delivered at the People's Institute, the adult education division of New York City's Cooper Union. The firm soon expanded its program beyond the Institute, publishing books by celebrated academics from America and abroad. By midcentury, the two major pillars of Norton's publishing program—trade books and college texts—were firmly established. In the 1950s, the Norton family transferred control of the company to its employees, and today—with a staff of five hundred and hundreds of trade, college, and professional titles published each year—W. W. Norton & Company stands as the largest and oldest publishing house owned wholly by its employees.

Editor: Pete Simon
Developmental Editor and Project Editor: Michael Fauver
Associate Editor: Katie Pak
Editorial Assistant: Olivia Atmore
Media Editor: Joy Cranshaw
Media Project Editor: Cooper Wilhelm
Assistant Media Editor: Katie Bolger
Managing Editor, College: Marian Johnson
Director of Production, College: Jane Searle
Managing Editor, College Digital Media: Kim Yi
Ebook Production Manager: Sophia Purut
Market Research and Strategy Manager, Communication & Media: Trevor Penland

Sales and Market Development Specialists, Humanities: Heidi Balas, Kim Bowers, Elizabeth Pieslor, and Emily Rowin
Design Director: Rubina Yeh
Designers: Anna Palchik and Jen Montgomery
Director of College Permissions: Megan Schindel
Permissions Associate: Patricia Wong
Photo Editor: Thomas Persano
Copyeditor: Jude Grant
Proofreader: Alice Gribbin
Indexer: Caryn Sobel
Composition: MPS Limited
Manufacturing: Transcontinental—Beauceville

Library of Congress Cataloging-in-Publication Data
Names: Engleberg, Isa N., author. | Daly, John A. (John Augustine), 1952- author.
Title: The Norton field guide to speaking / Isa Engleberg, John Daly.
Description: First edition. | New York : W. W. Norton & Company, 2021. | Includes bibliographical references and index.
Identifiers: LCCN 2021022397 | ISBN 9780393442120 (paperback) | ISBN 9780393442175 (epub)
Subjects: LCSH: Public speaking.
Classification: LCC PN4129.15 E53 2021 | DDC 808.5/1--dc23
LC record available at https://lccn.loc.gov/2021022397

W. W. Norton & Company, Inc., 500 Fifth Avenue, New York, NY 10110
    wwnorton.com
W. W. Norton & Company, Ltd., 15 Carlisle Street, London W1D 3BS

1 2 3 4 5 6 7 8 9 0

Preface

The Norton Field Guide to Speaking began as an attempt to offer the sort of guidance found in the leading full-length textbooks in a format as user-friendly and referenceable as the best brief speakers' handbooks. We wanted to create a handy guide to help college students with all their presentations—both in public speaking courses and beyond. Just as there are field guides for bird-watchers, for gardeners, and for accountants, this would be one for speakers.

The Norton Field Guide offers practical guidance new instructors and their students need as well as the flexibility many experienced faculty members want. From our own experience as communication instructors, we've seen how explicit speaking guides can work for students and novice teachers. We've also observed that most public speaking textbooks provide a format that assumes students will read the book in a certain order, and at great length. The result is books that are bigger, less flexible, and more expensive than they should be. So, with the *Norton Field Guide* format, we have tried to provide enough structure to make the book familiar to any instructor who has taught from the leading textbooks while also dividing the book's contents into smaller, more referenceable chunks that can be taught in whatever order suits the instructor and that can be quickly accessed by students looking for particular information. Our overriding goal is to give college speakers all the information they *need* to know while resisting the temptation to tell them everything there is to know. That said, because of the unique flexibility of the *Norton Field Guide* format, we provide more, and more useful, guidance on key topics that are especially important in contemporary communication courses.

Most of all, we have tried to make the book easy to use. To that end, *The Norton Field Guide* includes menus, directories, a glossary/index, and color-coded links to make it simple for students to find what they're looking for and navigate the parts. These links are also the key to keeping the book brief: chapters are short, but the links send students to pages elsewhere in the book if they need more detail.

What's in the Book

The Norton Field Guide to Speaking covers all major types of speeches assigned in college courses. Much of the book is in the form of practical how-and-why guidelines, designed to help students make informed decisions as they prepare and deliver presentations in a variety of contexts. The book is organized into nine parts:

1. **GETTING STARTED**. The first four chapters in part 1 set the stage for the course and for any speaking occasion. The first chapter provides a capsule overview of the full scope of what we call the *rhetorical speechmaking process*. It introduces students to the fundamental steps in miniature they should follow as they approach any speaking situation. The next three chapters cover topics that are often on students' minds (such as speaking anxiety) and subjects that instructors ask students to think about throughout the course (the importance of good listening habits and the indispensable role of communication ethics).

2. **FUNDAMENTALS**. Part 2 focuses on the three essential elements that form the core of every speaking occasion: the *speaker*, the *audience*, and the speaker's *purpose*. These fundamentals represent the beating heart of the speechmaking process. Color-coded links throughout the book refer back to these crucial components of an effective presentation.

3. **CONTENT**. The four chapters in part 3 provide students with core guidelines for choosing their topic (if the choice is up to them), developing and shaping it, researching and selecting good supporting material, and organizing their presentations, including guidance on how to begin and end them.

4. **DELIVERY**. In an especially handy and easy-to-reference way, part 4 covers the essential principles of effective vocal and physical delivery. We recommended how-to tips and techniques that are concrete and specific and that go well beyond the advice typically provided in competing texts. This part concludes with a chapter emphasizing the importance of preparation and practice.

5. **ENGAGING YOUR AUDIENCE**. "How can I be *interesting*?" It's a question we've often heard from students in our classes. We also

know from conversations with hundreds of instructors that it's something of great concern to most students. The four chapters in part 5 provide concrete advice about using language, stories, presentation aids, and other strategies (for example, humor and audience participation) to generate an audience's interest and keep them engaged.

6. **SPEAKING TO INFORM**. The three chapters in part 6 cover one of the essential speaking assignments in most communication courses: the informative speech. An opening chapter offers a short overview of general principles to consider when speaking to inform. The next two chapters split our coverage of informative speaking into two parts: (1) how to plan, prepare, and deliver an informative presentation that reports new information to an audience and (2) how to explain complex and frequently misunderstood concepts.

7. **SPEAKING TO PERSUADE**. Persuasive speaking, another requisite speaking assignment in most courses, is covered extensively in the three chapters in part 7. These chapters recommend strategies for developing, structuring, and delivering effective persuasive presentations that adapt to audience characteristics, beliefs, and attitudes. We place a major emphasis on critical thinking when developing a persuasive presentation as well as when listening to or reading other people's arguments.

8. **SPECIAL SPEAKING OCCASIONS**. Part 8 features ten short chapters, each of which describes the key features of a common speaking situation—from introducing a speaker to making a toast; from online speaking to question-and-answer sessions. Each chapter provides brief just-in-time advice that is specific to each occasion.

9. **RESOURCES**. Part 9 offers additional and more extensive advice on two topics: (1) tools and techniques to use if there is time to conduct detailed audience analysis and (2) an extensive guide to outlining, including the construction of full-sentence outlines (often a requirement in speaking courses). Both of these topics are covered in parts 2 and 3 in what we believe is sufficient detail for most speaking situations. Part 9 provides the sort of additional information some instructors require in their courses.

Notable Speakers

Throughout the book, in addition to the advice and guidance, the tips and techniques, and the prompts and questions to consider, we include seventeen Notable Speaker features. These features highlight recorded presentations, easily found online, by a diverse variety of skilled speakers. These presentations exemplify the principles covered in the text and provide students with models of effective presentational speaking. They also offer time-stamped commentaries—rhetorical analysis in miniature—that help students appreciate and understand what works and what (occasionally) doesn't work in these presentations.

What's Online

Ebook

The Norton Field Guide to Speaking is available as an ebook—readable on all computers and mobile devices—and is included with all new print copies of the text. All the content featured in the print book is enhanced throughout by dynamic hyperlinks that make the book's color-coded linking format even more convenient for quick referencing. Students can also quickly access relevant pages of the ebook from within InQuizitive activities (see below). Offered at less than half the price of the print book, the ebook provides an active reading experience, enabling students to take notes, bookmark, search, highlight, and read offline. Instructors can even add notes that students can see as they are reading the text.

InQuizitive

Norton's award-winning, easy-to-use adaptive learning tool personalizes the learning experience for students, helping them master—and retain—key learning objectives. Premade activities for each of the major chapters in the book start with questions about key concepts, proceed to application questions, and even include questions about speeches included in the Speech Library (see below). Offering a variety of question types, answer-specific feedback, and interactive gamelike features, InQuizitive motivates students to carefully read and engage with course content.

As a result, students arrive better prepared for class, giving instructors more time for lecture, discussion, and activities and providing students a more solid foundation for working on their own presentations.

A robust activity report makes it easy to identify challenging concepts and allows for just-in-time intervention when students are struggling, and the convenience of Learning Management System (LMS) integration saves time by allowing InQuizitive scores to report directly to the LMS gradebook.

Speech Library

This curated collection of links to additional sample speeches, openly available online and keyed to relevant chapters, supplements the Notable Speaker features in the text itself.

What's Available for Instructors

Norton Teaching Tools

Created by Susan Ward (Delaware County Community College), with special contributions from the authors and instructors across the country, Norton Teaching Tools for *The Norton Field Guide to Speaking* provide support for teaching every chapter in the text, including tips for tackling difficult concepts, PowerPoint lecture slides, and suggested activities and assignments for both in-person and online classes. In addition, a comprehensive guide to teaching the introductory speaking course offers syllabus and course design models, strategies for dealing with communication apprehension, and an introduction to culturally responsive teaching. A set of common presentation assignments is accompanied by rubric templates and student models and a curated Speech Library. The Norton Teaching Tools site is searchable and can be filtered by chapter or by resource type, making it easy to find exactly what you need for your course.

Resources for Your Learning Management System

Digital resources provided by Norton—including InQuizitive—can be integrated with your online, hybrid, or lecture courses so that all activities can be accessed within your existing LMS. Instructors can also add customizable multiple-choice and short-answer questions to their LMS using Norton Testmaker.

Test Bank

Norton uses evidence-based models to deliver high-quality and pedagogically effective testing materials. The framework used to develop our test banks is the result of a collaboration with leading academic researchers and advisers. More than 750 questions for *The Norton Field Guide to Speaking* can be searched and filtered by chapter, type, difficulty, learning objective, and other criteria in Norton Testmaker, making it easy to construct tests and quizzes that are meaningful and diagnostic. Available online, without the need for specialized software, Testmaker allows easy export of tests to Microsoft Word or Common Cartridge files for the course LMS.

Your Norton representative can provide more information about all these resources. Visit wwnorton.com/find-your-rep to find your representative.

Acknowledgments

When traveling around the country—as active conference presenters, book authors, consultants, representatives of our institutions, and National Communication Association (NCA) officers—we've met hundreds of instructors and students who helped us identify what students need to know to improve their speaking skills. That plus new research led us to what has become *The Norton Field Guide for Speaking*.

Two insightful projects inspired us to embrace a more contemporary, needs-based approach to the art and practice of speaking in a variety of contexts. The first, in which one of the authors participated, was the NCA's Core Communication Competencies (CCC) project. The project team sought input from a series of focus groups in which more than 125 participants rated and responded to a set of proposed core competencies (based on a literature search and team expertise) that constitute the basis for introductory communication courses, including public speaking. The project identified seven core competencies, two of which are often neglected or given short shrift in many textbooks and courses: communication ethics and effective listening. The importance of these two topics prompted us to write chapters about them and to place those topics in the first part of the book. We thank the CCC team: Susan Ward (Delaware County Community College), Scott A. Myers (West Virginia University), Patricia O'Keefe (College of Marin), Lynn Disbrow (Huntingdon College), and James Katt (University of Central Florida), as well as the 125 focus group participants.[1]

The second project was conducted by the authors. We asked hundreds of individual participants, representing two distinct groups—professionals who frequently speak to public audiences and introductory public speaking students—to rate twenty-four commonly identified skills an effective speaker should possess. Both groups rated the ability to keep an audience interested as the *most important*. This result was a revelation for both of us. Inspired by this response, we prepared a special section, Part 5: Engaging your Audience, that addresses this topic. We know of no other book that devotes as much attention to this skill area as *The Norton Field Guide to Speaking*. We thank the hundreds of anonymous individuals who helped us refocus our attention on what matters most to speakers.

We extend very special thanks to Susan Ward, who served as our spirited and invincible super reviewer and our astute investigator who found and helped write commentaries for the Notable Speaker features. She is also a recognized online teaching expert and primary writer of this textbook's supplemental Norton Teaching Tools. Everyone needs a Susan Ward in their life.

Thanks, too, to the instructors across the country who reviewed *The Norton Field Guide to Speaking* in various draft stages:

Jaye Atkinson, Georgia State University
Ferald Bryan, Northern Illinois University
Deanna Fassett, San Jose State University
Tonya Forsythe, Ohio State University
Brandi Frisby, University of Kentucky
Brandon Gainer, De Anza College
Liliana Herakova, University of Maine
Brittany Hochstaetter, Wake Technical Community College

Emily Holler, Kennesaw State University

Angela Hosek, Ohio University

Jennifer Mellow, California State University–San Marcos

Shellie Michael, Volunteer State Community College

Elizabeth Nelson, North Carolina State University

Leslie Pace, University of Louisiana–Monroe

Dennis Porch, Wake Technical Community College

Kendra Rand, University of Maine

Toni Shields, Ivy Tech Community College

David Simon, Northern Illinois University

Shelly Stein, Hillsborough Community College

Ruth Stokes, Trident Technical College

Dudley Turner, University of Akron

Victor Viser, Texas A&M University–Galveston

Kylene Wesner, Texas A&M University–College Station

To all the scholars and communication educators who have advised us over the years: your feedback and critiques have been invaluable in helping us create a book that best suits the needs of both instructors and students. This book is in many ways yours as much as ours. We thank you all.

Finally, we thank the thousands of students who have taken our courses in person and, more recently, online. You are the reason we do what we do and the measure of all things.

We would be remiss if we didn't thank our gifted teammates at W. W. Norton & Company for taking an idea in the minds of two faculty members and transforming it into *The Norton Field Guide to Speaking*, an innovative contribution to the communication discipline.

It all began with Pete Simon, our editor. From our first meeting, Pete inspired, nurtured, and built on our initial ideas, and he demonstrated an unfailing drive and resolve to make *The Norton Field Guide to Speaking* a breakthrough resource for students and instructors—and for anyone seeking to become a more engaging, effective, and ethical speaker. Pete was our constant companion throughout the process, offering valuable insights and counsel and never hesitating to challenge our assumptions or look at conventional topic treatments with new eyes. In the course of our academic careers, we have worked with dozens of editors for academic journals, book chapters, university press books, and textbooks. Pete stands above the rest as a model of professionalism, hands-on collaboration, and conscientiousness. His marketing expertise and exceptional writing and editing skills kept us focused on the mantra that informed our thinking from the start: "Tell students what they need to know, not everything there is to know." Writing a book can be both tense and exhausting, but Pete made it a joy.

In the early days of development, Lib Triplett, field editor, was our eyes and ears on college campuses. Her insights let us know what was "going on" from a marketing perspective, and she provided valuable feedback from faculty members as we wrote our first drafts. Many of the people she met along the way had never heard of Norton before Lib showed up at their door. By the time she left their offices, they were Norton fans. We couldn't have asked for a livelier, more personable, or more insightful early advocate.

Michael Fauver, our indefatigable developmental editor *and* project editor, was a twofold gift. He read every word we wrote and did so many times as we passed multiple revisions back and forth. He analyzed the ideas, research, and claims we made to ensure they were clear, accurate, appropriate, and consistent with other content. He questioned—with amazing restraint and patience—apparent errors, debatable conclusions, the relevance and timeliness of the research and examples we used, and the specificity and style of our language. And, as project editor, he was the conscientious "traffic manager" between Norton's editorial and production departments. His exceptional contributions have made *The Norton Field Guide to Speaking* clearer, more helpful, and more beautifully stitched together than it otherwise would have been.

We also worked with what Michael Fauver rightly described as our "rock star" copyeditor and proofreader. Jude Grant and Alice Gribbin did more than find errors no one else had seen; they asked questions that changed entire sentences, paragraphs, and chapters as well as identified inconsistencies from one chapter to another. We also thank them for often suggesting the perfect word we'd been searching for. The result is a brighter (in every sense of the word) book.

Katie Pak, who began as Pete Simon's editorial assistant (and has since been deservedly promoted—twice!) ran the review programs of our draft chapters and provided crucial editorial support behind the scenes.

Our media editor, Joy Cranshaw, and her predecessor, Erica Wnek, were with us from the very start of our work on *The Norton Field Guide to Speaking*. Rather than waiting until the authors completed writing, Erica, Joy, and other members of the Norton media team began working closely with Susan Ward to develop the media program in tandem with our efforts. The ebook, the innovative InQuizitive platform, and all the other resources that accompany this book reflect the Norton media team's forethought and professionalism.

The Norton Field Guide for Speaking looks the way it does—with color-coded links and icons, its distinctive typeface and trim size, and more—because it is based on the original design for *The Norton Field Guide to Writing*. We thank the designer, Anna Palchik, and the legendary Norton editor, Marilyn Moller, for their original vision and execution of the *Norton Field Guide* model. The designer of *our* book, Jen Montgomery, guided by design director Rubina Yeh, transformed and adapted the original design to make it fresh and attractive for speaking courses. We also extend our deep gratitude to Jane Searle who managed the book's production even as she also manages Norton's entire production department. The design and production team "pulled out all the stops" by enlisting their best efforts and available resources to create this beautiful book.

Although we've often dreaded the rigorous permission and photo research process, we welcomed the gentle professionalism of Patricia Wong, who cleared text permissions, and Tommy Persano, who researched and secured permissions for our photos and illustrations. And special thanks to Danny Vargo who swooped in from the Norton science team to help us with frame captures for our Notable Speaker features.

Knowing how challenging persuasion is in almost any context, both of us hold the marketing and sales team in great esteem. In addition to Lib Triplett, we thank Trevor Penland, our diligent marketing research and strategy manager, as well as the sales and marketing development specialists who work closely with Norton's traveling sales reps: Kim Bowers,

Elizabeth Pieslor, and Emily Rowin. We trust you all will enjoy meeting these folks and will come to realize, through them, that Norton is a perfect fit with the communication discipline.

And that leads us to our final, special note of gratitude. We join our editor, Pete Simon, to thank Norton's leadership team for taking a leap of faith by entering the communication market at a time of extreme uncertainty throughout higher education. The support of Julia Reidhead, president of Norton; Roby Harrington, former director of the college department; Mike Wright, the current director of the college department; and Ann Shin, editorial director of the college department, made this book, and Norton's entry into the communication discipline, possible. Norton's leaders chose to do so at a time when effective speaking is more important than ever. We hope that they look back on that decision fondly in the years to come, as we know we will.

How to Use This Book

There is more than one way to do most things, and speaking is no exception. *The Norton Field Guide to Speaking* is designed to allow you to chart your own course as a speaker, offering practical guidelines that suit your needs and your particular speaking situation. It is organized in nine parts:

1. **GETTING STARTED**. Whether it is assigned by your instructor or not, we urge you to read and refer to 1.1, The Rhetorical Speech-making Process, throughout your course and your speaking life outside of college. This chapter maps out the essential elements of any successful presentation. It is a springboard into the rest of the book that is linked to subsequent chapters through the *Norton Field Guide*'s distinctive color-coded linking system. Also, if you are nervous or anxious about making a presentation, read 1.2, Speaking Anxiety. There's a lot of good advice there about how to manage your apprehension. Your listening (1.3) and ethical (1.4) responsibilities as a speaker *and* as an audience member are critical considerations in all presentations.

2. **FUNDAMENTALS**. Every presentation must have a speaker and an audience, and successful ones always have a purpose. The chapters in part 2 lay out these three fundamental elements of every presentation. The color-coded links found throughout the rest of the text often refer back to the principles covered here, so even if you jump straight to a specific speaking topic later in the book, you will probably find your way back to these important chapters. If you're not sure where to turn after reading 1.1, these three chapters are the best next stop.

3. **CONTENT**. Use the advice in part 3 to help you choose a worthy topic (if the choice is up to you) that links your interests, abilities, and values to your audience's needs and expectations. This part also provides advice for selecting appropriate,

reliable, and interesting supporting material, as well as several methods for organizing the content of your presentation. The all-important topic of how to begin and end your presentation is discussed in 3.4.

4. **DELIVERY**. The chapters in part 4 focus on how to improve your vocal and physical delivery. The advice in this part is concrete and precise, and with practice, these techniques will help you become a more confident and expressive speaker.

5. **ENGAGING YOUR AUDIENCE**. "How can I be *interesting?*" It's a common concern of students taking their first speech class. Use the advice in part 5 to help you capture your audience's interest and keep them engaged.

6. **SPEAKING TO INFORM**. These chapters are your guide to giving an effective informative speech—a common assignment in communication courses and a common speaking task in the world outside of the college classroom. In addition to providing several general tips, part 6 also examines the ways that informative presentations differ. If the presentation you're working on will report information *new* to your audience, 6.2 will help you. If, instead, your presentation focuses on a concept that is difficult to understand, complex, or frequently misunderstood, 6.3 offers advice specific to that situation.

7. **SPEAKING TO PERSUADE**. Persuasive speaking, another essential assignment in most speech courses, is covered extensively in the three chapters of part 7. Use the advice found here to structure and deliver persuasive presentations of your own and to think critically about other people's arguments.

8. **SPECIAL SPEAKING OCCASIONS**. If your instructor assigns an impromptu speech, if you are asked to introduce a speaker on campus or to present an award, or if you need specific advice for giving a toast or a eulogy, part 8 is the place for you. It offers short, concise guides to ten common (but special) speaking occasions you will encounter in college and beyond.

9. **RESOURCES**. If your instructor asks you to do a detailed audience analysis (such as a pre-speech survey or a series of interviews), or if you are asked to produce a detailed outline of your presentation, the two chapters in part 9 provide the information you will need to complete these assignments.

Ways into the Book

The Norton Field Guide to Speaking gives you the practical advice you need to become an effective speaker, along with the flexibility to find specific advice that works best for you. Here are some of the ways you can find what you need in the book.

Brief Menus

Inside the front cover of the print book you'll find a list of all the chapters. Start here if you are looking for a chapter on a certain topic. You can also access the brief menu in the ebook, or you can use the table of contents feature within your ebook reader.

Complete Contents

Pages xx–xxvii contain a detailed table of contents. Look here if you need to find a specific section in a chapter, or use the table of contents feature in your ebook reader.

Color Coding

The parts of this book are color coded for easy reference. You'll find a key to the colors inside the front cover of the print book and also at the foot of each even-numbered page. The color of a highlighted word tells you where you can find additional detail on the topic, or you can click the word to go directly to that section in the ebook.

Glossary / Index

At the back of the book is a combined glossary and index, where you'll find full definitions of key terms and topics, along with a list of the pages where everything is covered in detail. You can read the glossary entries for key terms wherever they appear in the text of the ebook by hovering your cursor over them.

The Ebook

Even if you're using a print copy of *The Norton Field Guide*, you may wish to access the ebook by registering the code inside the front cover or purchasing at digital.wwnorton.com/nfgspeaking. Reference the *Norton Field Guide* ebook on your phone whenever you need it, or download sections for offline reading. The ebook is fully searchable and its color-coded cross-references are hyperlinked, so the process of moving from one topic to another is even easier than with the print text. And you can highlight, take notes, and bookmark pages for easy reference later, accessing them from any device with an internet connection.

InQuizitive

This adaptive learning tool helps you practice your own understanding of core concepts from each chapter and includes direct links to relevant pages in the ebook. Your instructor may assign InQuizitive activities for a grade, but you can also use InQuizitive on your own to review course material. See if you can reach the target score for each chapter, and then refer to the Activity Report to determine which Learning Objectives you already have a firm grasp of and which you might want to read again (or for the first time). Like the ebook, you can access InQuizitive by registering the code inside the front cover of your print book or by purchasing at digital.wwnorton.com/nfgspeaking.

Whatever path you follow into and throughout *The Norton Field Guide to Speaking*, we hope you find it a useful and reassuring resource as you build your speaking skills. If you have suggestions about how we might make the book even more useful, please write to us at communication@wwnorton.com.

Contents

● Part 1   Getting Started   1

★ Part 8   Special Speaking Occasions   405

❋ Part 9 Resources 491

Notable Speakers

Introduction: Your Voice Matters

If you remember nothing else from this book, please remember this: the question you should always know the answer to as you get ready to speak in the front of the room, at the head of the table, or on camera is:

Why am I here?

Not here on this earth—that's too big of a question for this book. (If that sort of thing concerns you, and if your campus still has a philosophy department, you might take a course or two from them. They've come up with some interesting responses to that question.)

No, what we're talking about is a question of smaller scope but of the utmost importance to your success in life. Here's a slightly different way of framing it:

Why am I here, speaking to these people?

Knowing the answer to this question each and every time you speak to an audience is the most important thing you can do as a speaker. If you don't know the answer, neither will anyone else.

So, is that it? Have we saved the best for first? Is there no more to say? Should you close this book, return it for a refund, and save your time and money? Well, no. We've got a little more advice to offer. The rest of this book unpacks the various ways you can answer this all-important *why* question and, more important, helps you *use that answer* to plan, prepare, and deliver strong and effective presentations.

For some of us, the answer is that we feel compelled to speak—we feel we have no choice but to say something. Consider Greta Thunberg, a Swedish teenager who was moved by the enormity of the global climate crisis to become in late 2018 a public voice for her generation—sounding an alarm on behalf of all the children whose futures were being "stolen" by older generations who, in her words, "didn't do anything while there was still time to act."[1] Despite her youth (she was fifteen years old), despite the fact that she is on the autism spectrum and finds many aspects of social interaction difficult, Ms. Thunberg made a commitment to speak out, to become a public figure, to persuade the powerful adults of the world—and all of us, really—that "our house is falling apart, and our leaders need to start acting accordingly, because at the moment they are not."[2] That was (and still is) Greta Thunberg's powerful answer to the *why* question.

During your lifetime, you will say many things that matter to many people: things that teach, things that persuade, and things that inspire, entertain, and touch emotions. If you hope to convince other people that a brilliant idea you have is worthy of their consideration, if you want to demonstrate your knowledge and expertise to an employer, if you want to ensure your perspective is considered when important decisions are being made, or even if you want to publicly express something important about a dear friend, colleague, or family member, you will need to speak up.

Sometimes there's a fine line between feeling compelled to speak (as Greta Thunberg was) and feeling *forced* to do so. If you're reading this book, it's safe to assume you're taking a course in public speaking (or, as the authors of this book prefer to call it, presentation speaking). We know you might not be here—in this course—because you want to be. For some people—perhaps for you, certainly for Greta Thunberg—speaking in front of an audience is an anxiety-inducing prospect that is best avoided. But no matter how much you may want to avoid speaking, there will be occasions in school, work, and life when you will be called to speak before groups of people. If you believe you can succeed in the world of work or have a significant impact in your community without knowing how to speak to audiences, think again. Regardless of your goals in life, the lack of effective speaking skills is the ultimate glass ceiling, holding back people of all genders, races, ages, and abilities. We live in a highly complex, competitive age. Your ability to develop and deliver compelling presentations will mark you as both competent and interesting. Even more important, being an effective speaker will help you change the world—make it a better place. You will have a *voice* in the world. You will matter. You will shape the future.

Whether you are reading this book because you chose to or are required to, whether you are feeling ambivalent or confident about the course or your speaking ability, whether you are excited about what lies ahead or a bit anxious, we want you to hear the same thing: this book and this course are about you and your voice. And your voice matters. If you start there, with the presumption that "my voice matters," then you can walk into this class with a perspective beyond any individual speaking assignments. Yes, in the speeches you give in this course, your voice matters. But just as important, outside of this course, in all the other speaking you do in other courses and on your campus generally, your voice matters. And finally, beyond your time in college, in your community and the world at large, your voice matters.

How?

Well, your ability to speak well can make the difference between getting a job, or not; convincing a friend to take you on as a roommate, or not; persuading your parents to loan you money for a fabulous summer adventure, or not. Speaking well, simply put, helps you get what you want and need.

Yet speaking well does more than get you what you want in daily interactions and relationships. Speaking well can also make a difference to others. You'll have many opportunities to speak in ways that reach large audiences. Social media influencers have figured this out. They use various communication modes to spread a message, sell an idea, and establish a brand for themselves with followers. Outside of social media, there are countless opportunities to make your voice heard in ways that matter. From the residence hall meeting to the student government forum to the campus-wide town hall, you may have the opportunity to speak on important issues in ways that change minds and spark action. How you speak can make a difference—in what you achieve for yourself and for others who hear you speak.

In fact, some of the best-known speeches in history are famous because they have had a profound impact far beyond their first audiences. These speeches—like Abraham Lincoln's Gettysburg Address, Sojourner Truth's "Ain't I a Woman?," John F. Kennedy's first inaugural address, Martin Luther King Jr.'s "I Have a Dream," Michelle Obama's "When They Go Low, We Go High" speech at the 2016 Democratic National Convention, and many others—have shaped the world we live in. They consoled and unified a nation ripped apart by a terrible war (Lincoln), they galvanized half of humanity to advocate for their equality with the other half (Truth), they inspired their generations to strive for goals that had previously seemed unattainable (Kennedy, King), and they spurred young people to speak their minds with authority and confidence even in the face of put-downs, insults, and bitter resistance (Obama). Although you may not match the achievements of the greatest speakers, you can study the principles that explain their power and apply those principles to presentations you will deliver.

It is important to remember, though, that your voice can make a difference in positive and negative ways. Anyone reading this can probably think of an example of someone who, by the virtue of what they have said and how they have said it, harmed others. Perhaps you've been on the receiving end of an experience like this, having been hurt in one way or another by someone else's words. Yes, it goes both ways—your voice matters and there is the potential it can matter in negative, hurtful ways. Making your voice matter for good isn't automatic. Just because you can speak and do speak doesn't mean you will get what you want in a way that is constructive. Just because you can speak and do speak doesn't mean you will influence others in a respectful way. Just because you can speak and do speak doesn't mean your words will be kind. You can speak destructively, inhumanely. We hope you don't.

Your ability to speak effectively and ethically about difficult issues epitomizes democratic ideals. Knowing how to present yourself in a positive light, to adapt to the characteristics and attitudes of diverse audiences, and to seek a just and meaningful purpose are the first steps in making sure the messages you share with others result in collaboration and cooperation rather than opposition and antagonism.

Your voice matters. We want you to use your voice to get what you want, to influence others, and to make a difference. We want you to leave this course more confident in your voice. We want you to leave this experience more eager to go out there and find opportunities to make your voice matter. So whatever brought you here, and regardless of the path you take from here forward, we hope you'll seize this opportunity—with your classmates and teacher—to find ways to use your voice for good.

—Isa Engleberg and John Daly,
with Deanna Dannels (North Carolina State University)[3]

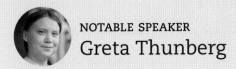

NOTABLE SPEAKER
Greta Thunberg

Search Terms

To locate a video of this presentation online, enter the following key words into a search engine: Greta Thunberg The Disarming Case to Act Right Now on Climate Change Stockholm November 2018. The video is approximately 11:12 in length.

Speaking Matters

Greta Thunberg was born in January 2003. At the age of fifteen, she skipped school for three weeks to protest in front of the Swedish Parliament building with a black-and-white sign reading "Skolstrejk för Klimatet" (School Strike for Climate). Her efforts grabbed the world's attention. Since then, Thunberg has received numerous honors, including *Time*'s Person of the Year (she was the youngest person to receive that honor), *Forbes*' list of the World's Most Powerful Women, and three consecutive nominations for the Nobel Peace Prize.

Why, you may ask, did Greta Thunberg become so famous so fast? Many climate activists before her have publicly called for action.

What brought her to the world's attention, however, was her young age, her personal courage, and her direct, clear, principled manner of speaking to students, public audiences, politicians, and world assemblies. Imagine standing in front the UN Climate Change Conference and passionately saying to the assembled delegates, "You have stolen my dreams and my childhood with your empty words. . . . We are in the beginning of a mass extinction, and all you can talk about is money and fairy tales of eternal economic growth. How dare you!"[4]

The following excerpt comes from a speech Thunberg delivered in Stockholm, Sweden, in 2018. Without question, Thunberg knows why she is speaking—and she does so with poise rather than dramatics, with simple language rather than fancy words, and with absolute assurance that what she has to say must be said.

> When I was about eight years old, I first heard about something called climate change or global warming. Apparently, that was something humans had created by our way of living. I was told to turn off the lights to save energy and to recycle paper to save

resources. I remember thinking that it was very strange that humans, who are an animal species among others, could be capable of changing the Earth's climate. Because if we were, and if it was really happening, we wouldn't be talking about anything else. As soon as you'd turn on the TV, everything would be about that. Headlines, radio, newspapers, you would never read or hear about anything else, as if there was a world war going on. But no one ever talked about it. . . .

To me, that did not add up. It was too unreal. So when I was 11, I became ill. I fell into depression, I stopped talking, and I stopped eating. In two months, I lost about 10 kilos of weight. Later on, I was diagnosed with Asperger syndrome, OCD and selective mutism. That basically means I only speak when I think it's necessary—now is one of those moments."[5]

Part 1
Getting Started

Beginnings can be a challenge, and that's as true of speaking to an audience as it is for any other activity. The chapters in this section will help you take your first steps as a speaker. We'll start with a big-picture overview of the entire **RHETORICAL SPEECHMAKING PROCESS**, which gives you a roadmap for everything else in the book; we'll address the perfectly understandable—and manageable—phenomenon of **SPEAKING ANXIETY**; and we'll help you understand your **ETHICAL OBLIGATIONS** as a speaker and audience member, including active **LISTENING**.

Getting Started

1.1 The Rhetorical Speechmaking Process

Successful speechmaking is a dynamic process, not the result of a step-by-step recipe or a list of rigid rules. Unlike scripted or programmed processes that follow a predictable set of instructions in a particular order, speechmaking is a complex psychological process where strategic and adaptive decision making is the only constant. Speechmaking is complex not because its principles are difficult to comprehend (as calculus or organic chemistry can be for many people), but because each speaking situation is uniquely challenging. Like other complex human activities—playing chess, learning a new sport, writing a sonnet—the process of speechmaking is relatively easy to learn, but difficult to master.

Effective speaking is the ability to think critically about yourself as a speaker as well as about your audience and to make appropriate, strategic decisions before and while you speak. This chapter presents a short introduction to the components of the speechmaking process, all of which are covered in more detail throughout the rest of the book. Familiarizing yourself with the big picture now will help you make sense of the particular advice we provide in later chapters, and it will help you keep your sights on the ultimate goal: delivering effective presentations.

Why *Presentations*?

Throughout this book, we use the phrase *presentation speaking* to describe the activity of speaking to an audience. You may wonder why we use this phrase more often than *public speaking*, a phrase that is more common and may even be the name of the course you're taking.

When you hear *public speaking*, what do you envision? A manager leading a staff meeting? A programmer describing a new app to salespeople?

● getting started　　　▶ delivery　　　　　　　◆ speaking to persuade

▲ fundamentals　　　　∴ engaging your audience　★ speaking occasions

▮ content　　　　　　　♥ speaking to inform　　　✳ resources

A teacher leading a class lesson? Probably not. Instead, you likely picture a lone figure standing on a stage inspiring a large audience.

As we see it, **public speaking** occurs when speakers address public audiences in community, government, or organizational settings. Public speeches are usually open and accessible to the public and have the potential, if not the purpose, of affecting people beyond the immediate audience. They are used to campaign for votes, give sermons, dedicate monuments, and deliver public lectures. In contrast, **presentation speaking** refers to any time speakers create meaning with verbal and nonverbal messages and establish relationships with audience members in a variety of contexts.[1] Presentation speaking encompasses everything from small, intimate talks in private settings to major public speeches—either live or MEDIATED—in front of large audiences.

479–89 ★

In all likelihood, you will make more presentations than public speeches over the course of your life. Presentations are used to teach classes, brief colleagues, summarize sales strategies, and coach middle-school soccer teams. When employers are asked about the skills they seek in new employees, the ability to present ideas and information to colleagues and clients is near the top of the list. What they're looking for are good *presenters*—not necessarily dazzling public orators. Of course, if you decide to run for public office or become active in community issues, or if you become famous—as either an expert or a celebrity—you will give many public speeches. Rest assured, the principles and skills described in this book will be useful to you if such a future awaits. But most of us, most of the time, will make presentations in smaller, less public settings.

Throughout this book, we still use the phrase *public speaking* and the word *speech* when the situation warrants those terms. No matter the term or phrase, in all these cases what we are talking about is *speaking to an audience*, and the guiding principles and crucial skills involved in doing this effectively are the same.

The Rhetorical Situation

The speechmaking process begins with understanding the context in which you'll be speaking. We call this the *rhetorical situation*. At the heart of this phrase is the word *rhetoric*. Let's start by defining what that word means.

● getting started	▶ delivery	◆ speaking to persuade
▲ fundamentals	⁂ engaging your audience	★ speaking occasions
■ content	◤ speaking to inform	✳ resources

What Is Rhetoric?

Rhetoric is the art of influencing the thinking, feelings, and behavior of an audience. Thousands of years ago, long before writing had been invented, speaking was the only means by which a person could practice rhetoric. Today, writing, visual media, and speaking are all options available to us when we seek to influence, inform, or motivate other people.

In the late fourth century BCE, Aristotle, one of the most notable philosophers in classical Greece, wrote *Rhetoric*, a treatise that described many of the strategies that successful speakers employ to express their views clearly and persuasively. *Rhetoric* formed the basis for many of the speaking strategies we use today.

Our cultural context has changed considerably since Aristotle's time. For example, the only people who could practice rhetoric in public in ancient Athens were free adult men—not women, not the many enslaved people, not minors. And yet, as different as Aristotle's world was from ours, the observations he made and strategies he recommended nearly twenty-five hundred years ago are still relevant. Of course, neither Aristotle nor the cultures of the so-called West have a monopoly on good ideas about effective communication. The practice of rhetoric has always been valued by people all over the world. The best ideas about the art of speaking well—wherever and whenever they come from—help us do so today, when the need is greater than ever.

Elements of the Rhetorical Situation

A **rhetorical situation** is the particular circumstance in which we speak to influence what our listeners know, believe, feel, and/or do. Every rhetorical situation involves six primary elements: *occasion*, *speaker*, *audience*, *purpose*, *content*, and *delivery*. Let's briefly look at each of these.

OCCASION   Every presentation occurs for a particular *reason*. It also happens at a specific *time* and in a particular *place* (we sometimes refer to time and place together as the **setting**) using a particular *medium*. These four factors—reason, time, place, and medium—constitute the presentation's **occasion**.

★ 405–89

Your audience will have certain expectations about what you will say and how you will say it based on the occasion. The norms and protocols of a **TOAST**

★ 442–48

449–55 ★

will be quite different, for example, from those of a **EULOGY**. Being aware of and adapting your presentation to the occasion is essential to your success as a speaker.

Here are some questions to ask about occasion:

- What is the reason for this presentation? Why are people gathering to hear it?
- Why am I speaking on this particular occasion?
- What media will I use? Will this be a face-to-face event? Will I speak via Zoom, FaceTime, Teams, or another medium?
- What is generally considered appropriate behavior for this occasion?
- What does this particular audience expect for this occasion?
- Has something happened recently or nearby—a natural disaster, for example, or a national news story—that I can assume my audience will be thinking about during my presentation?
- How will the logistics of the setting affect my speech? Will the time or time limit of my presentation affect what I say? Will I be speaking alone or as one among several speakers? How can I adapt to or modify the physical setting to make sure I am seen and heard by the audience?

If you need more help

405–89 ★

See Part 8, **SPECIAL SPEAKING OCCASIONS**, for more detailed advice about preparing for and adapting to various occasions.

55–69 ▲

SPEAKER   All presentations require a speaker. This is self-evident. But what isn't as obvious is how essential it is to know *what kind* of speaker you are and *what sorts of things* you'll do. As you think about a particular speaking occasion, consider what it calls for in a speaker.

Just as no two people are exactly alike, no two speakers communicate identically. Your personal characteristics, attitudes, and skills affect the way you speak to others and how others react to you. Understanding yourself—your strengths and your weaknesses—and assessing this understanding in light of what the occasion may require of you as a speaker are important aspects of the rhetorical speechmaking process.

● getting started ▶ delivery ◆ speaking to persuade
▲ fundamentals ∴ engaging your audience ★ speaking occasions
■ content ▼ speaking to inform ✳ resources

Here are some questions to ask about speaker:

- How do my personal characteristics, traits, skills, attitudes, values, and confidence level influence my speaking goals and style?
- How can I adapt my personal strengths and style to the audience's expectations for this particular occasion?
- How can I present myself as knowledgeable, experienced, qualified, and well prepared—in other words, as a **COMPETENT** speaker?
- What can I do to show that I am worthy of the audience's trust?
- How can I project **CONFIDENCE** and commitment?
- How can I demonstrate my integrity as an **ETHICAL SPEAKER**?

▲ 58–61

▶ 184–85

● 42

If you need more help

See 2.1, **SPEAKER**, for more guidance on how to be a competent, confident, credible, and ethical speaker.

▲ 55–69

AUDIENCE When you speak, the members of your audience—the people whose knowledge, beliefs, feelings, or actions you seek to influence—are not passive. They will react in a variety of ways to what you say, and their reactions will be shaped by the unique mix of attitudes, values, and characteristics they bring with them. No two audiences are exactly alike, so thinking critically about who your listeners are in every rhetorical situation is an essential step in the presentation process.

▲ 70–86

Here are some questions to ask about audience:

- What are the characteristics of my audience, and how will their demographics, backgrounds, interests, and attitudes affect my purpose?
- How can I **LEARN MORE ABOUT MY AUDIENCE**?
- How can I **ADAPT TO MY AUDIENCE** and, as a result, improve my presentation and achieve my purpose?
- How can I adapt to the ways in which **CULTURAL DIFFERENCES** may affect how audience members interpret my message?
- How is my audience likely to react to what I say?
- How do I craft my message for audience members who agree or disagree with me, as well as those who are **UNINFORMED OR UNDECIDED**?

▲ 72–80

▲ 80–82

◆ 391–92

◆ 390–91

70–86 ▲

If you need more help

See 2.2, **AUDIENCE**, for more on how to be an audience-centered speaker.

87–101 ▲

PURPOSE At its most fundamental level, your purpose is the outcome you are seeking as the result of making a presentation. It answers the question *What do I want my audience to know, think, believe, or do as a result of my presentation?* Purpose is not the same as **TOPIC**, which is simply another name for the subject matter of your presentation.

105–13 ◼
307–46 ◤
347–404 ◆
94 ▲
93–94 ▲

A speaker's purpose has an overarching goal: to **INFORM** and explain, **PERSUADE** and influence, **INSPIRE** and motivate, and/or **ENTERTAIN** and please. Effective speakers identify and focus on a clear, relevant, and achievable purpose, and they use it to guide all other major decisions.

Here are some questions to ask about purpose:

- What do I want my audience to know, think, believe, or do as a result of my presentation?
95–97 ▲
- Is my purpose **SPECIFIC, ACHIEVABLE, AND RELEVANT**?
- What are the key points I want to make to achieve my purpose?
- How can I focus my message to achieve my purpose in the time I've been allotted?
- Are there obstacles to achieving my purpose? If so, how can I overcome or minimize them?
405–89 ★
- Is my purpose appropriate for the **OCCASION** as well as for my audience, content, and delivery?
43–44 ●
- Is my purpose **ETHICAL**? Will achieving my purpose benefit both me and my audience?

If you need more help

87–101 ▲

See 2.3, **PURPOSE**, for more detailed advice about determining and achieving your purpose.

103–79 ◼

CONTENT Every presentation conveys a **message**—the synthesis of ideas and information communicated verbally and nonverbally to an audience.

● getting started ▶ delivery ◆ speaking to persuade
▲ fundamentals ⁘ engaging your audience ★ speaking occasions
◼ content ◤ speaking to inform ✳ resources

The rhetorical decisions you make about a particular occasion will result in a message that is different from the one that would emerge from another set of rhetorical decisions, even if the general topic of your presentation is the same in both cases.

Your presentation's content should reflect two indispensable actions on your part:

1. Selecting ideas and information that support your purpose and that are appropriate for the occasion and your audience
2. Strategically organizing your ideas and information into a coherent and compelling message

If you don't know your purpose and haven't chosen an appropriate topic, you cannot select the best and most appropriate ideas and information. If you have not analyzed and adapted to your listeners, your ideas and information may fail to achieve your purpose. And if you don't strategically organize your content, your audience may not understand or appreciate your presentation.

Here are some questions to ask about content:

- Where and how can I find good ideas and information for my presentation?
- How much and what kind of **SUPPORTING MATERIAL** do I need? 114–20
- Does my supporting material come from reputable and credible **SOURCES**? 120–30
- Are my ideas and information valid, appropriate, and believable? 138–48
- What are the most effective ways to **ORGANIZE** my presentation? 137–38
- Do I have a clear **CENTRAL IDEA** and relevant **KEY POINTS**? 133–36
- What should I say in the **INTRODUCTION** and **CONCLUSION** of my presentation? 161–69 169–75

If you need more help

See Part 3, **CONTENT**, for more specific advice about choosing a topic, finding and using appropriate supporting material, and organizing your presentation effectively. 103–79

181–233 **DELIVERY** Delivery is what audience members see and hear when you speak. Delivery focuses on how you use your voice, face, body, notes, and presentation aids to convey your message to an audience.

As you think about how you want to deliver your presentation, the first question you need to answer is this: What channel or channels will I use? **Channel** refers to the medium or media you use to transmit a message. Messages can be sent via all five senses as well as electronically. Most presentations use sight and sound with or without mediated assistance. Speaking 479–89 to a live audience is different from delivering an **ONLINE PRESENTATION**. Recording and posting a presentation for later viewing requires different strategies and delivery decisions than giving a real-time, face-to-face speech.

Here are some questions to ask about delivery:

- Which channels will I use, and how will I adapt my presentation to them?
- Should I speak in an informal style, a conversational style, or a more formal style?
- 152–55 How should I **PREPARE** and use any speaking **NOTES**?
- 225–28 How should I design and handle **PRESENTATION AIDS**?
- 282–305 What delivery techniques will make my presentation more effective?
- 194–209 Are my **VOCAL** and **PHYSICAL DELIVERY** skills appropriate and effective?
- 210–19 228–33 Have I practiced enough? Have I incorporated my presentation aids into most of my **PRACTICE** sessions?

If you need more help

181–233 282–305 See Part 4, **DELIVERY**, and 5.4, **PRESENTATION AIDS**, for more specific advice about how to improve your vocal and physical delivery.

Putting It All Together: An Impromptu Speech

Decisions about the six elements of the rhetorical situation are interconnected. To illustrate, let's consider one example of one type of presentation: 407–13 the **IMPROMPTU SPEECH**.

---

getting started   ▷ delivery   ◆ speaking to persuade
▲ fundamentals   ⁘ engaging your audience   ★ speaking occasions
■ content   ♥ speaking to inform   ✳ resources

An **impromptu speech** presents a coherent message with little or no preparation and no time to practice. You may be called on to do an impromptu speech in a communication class, asked to summarize a report at a meeting with no advance warning, moved to speak at a public forum, or prompted during a job interview to react to a hypothetical situation.

It may seem that by definition, it's impossible to prepare for an impromptu presentation. There are, however, ways to think critically about the six elements in this on-the-spot rhetorical situation. In some impromptu speaking situations, speakers are given a minute to collect their thoughts and jot down a few ideas before speaking.

The best impromptu speakers use what little time they have to think ahead. As they get up to speak, they're deciding on their two or three **KEY POINTS** and which **ORGANIZATIONAL PATTERN** they will use. As they reach the place where they will stand, they're formulating an attention-getting **BEGINNING**. They may stretch those precious seconds by pausing thoughtfully before they begin, rephrasing the question to make sure they understand it, and/or considering the relevant facts, examples, stories, or quotations they might use. (Most of us know a few quotations by heart—a verse from a holy book, a poem, a song lyric, a line from a movie, or the moral at the end of a folktale or children's story.) As they start talking, they're thinking ahead to their first key point. They trust that the words will come out right, even though their thinking is divided between what they are saying now and what they want to say in the next few seconds. No wonder impromptu speakers feel exhausted after a successful presentation!

133–36
138–48
161–69

Suppose your instructor gives you the following instructions for a first-day-of-class introductory speech:

> Select one letter of the alphabet and think of three words beginning with the same letter that describes who you are, your beliefs, your behavior, and/or something you like to do. Examples: *M* for *mountains*, *motorcycling*, and *motivated*; *T* for *teaching*, *traveling*, and *talking*. After choosing a letter and three words, prepare a brief presentation to the class in which you
> - State your name (and anything interesting they should know about your name)

- Share the letter and the three words you chose, and briefly explain why you selected those words; you may write your three words on a small piece of paper to make sure you don't forget them

The following table illustrates how decisions about occasion, speaker, audience, purpose, content, and delivery form a basis for making a presentation in this rhetorical situation.

Occasion	This presentation is occurring on the first day of class. You're in a twenty-five-student classroom, so you'll be heard as long as you speak at a normal volume. The protocols of this occasion are determined by your instructor's directions. Your classmates don't expect you to have rehearsed, and they won't expect your delivery to be superlative.
Speaker	What is it about you that "describes who you are"? Can you think of three words that accurately and memorably capture your uniqueness?
Audience	Given what you know about your classmates, what three words will they find interesting, unusual, and memorable? Are there any words that you should avoid using with this audience?
Purpose	Your purpose has been determined for you by your instructor, and it is the same for you and all your classmates: to help your classmates become acquainted with and remember you.
Content	The three words you've chosen—and the explanations you give for each—generate the content of your speech. You decide to talk about each word in turn, not all together, and to give an explanation of each word before moving to the next one. This decision makes your presentation clear and well organized.
Delivery	Given the classroom setting, you should use a conversational voice that is loud enough for everyone to hear and make sure to look at your audience and smile while delivering your presentation.

● getting started   ▶ delivery   ◆ speaking to persuade
▲ fundamentals   ⁝ engaging your audience   ★ speaking occasions
■ content   ▼ speaking to inform   ✳ resources

Here are two examples of this impromptu speech. Notice how decisions about all six elements are reflected in each talk.

Hi. My name is Mike Johnson. Did you know that Johnson is the most popular last name in the United States after Smith? Anyway, the letter I chose is *R*: *rap*, *Rachel*, and *reading*.

My first word is *rap*. Not only do I like most rap music, I like writing rap music and lyrics. Here's a short verse from one. [He performs the verse.]

My second word is *Rachel*. She's my girlfriend and we've been together since our junior year in high school. If you met Rachel, you'd say, "Mike's a lucky guy."

My third word is *reading*. I'll read just about anything. Online news and blogs, social media sites, and books about music and history.

Good morning. My name is Jessica Nevins. It was hard to choose a letter, but I went for *N*. The three words are *Natovitz*, *nursing*, and *nature*.

Natovitz. When my grandfather emigrated from Russia in 1909, his last name was Natovitz. Because Natovitz was hard to spell, difficult to say clearly, and not very American sounding, he changed it to Nevins.

Nursing. I'm a nursing major hoping to become a registered nurse and then a nurse practitioner. A lot of friends and family members think I should become a doctor, but I think nursing suits my personality and lifestyle better.

Nature. I love nature. Walking in the woods. Working in a garden. Watching wild birds at the feeder in my backyard. I also think we should do everything we can to preserve natural wonders and animal habitats. Someday, I'll go on a safari.

For an example of a speaker applying the six elements of the rhetorical situation to create an effective and memorable presentation, see Notable Speaker: Yassmin Abdel-Magied, page 189.

Conclusion

Throughout your lifetime, you will make many different kinds of presentations. Your ability to succeed in any speaking situation depends on how well you think critically and make strategic decisions about the essential elements of the rhetorical situation: occasion, speaker, audience, purpose, content, and delivery. As these strategies and skills become second nature, you will improve your speaking ability and become a more confident, polished, and effective presenter.

Reading this book can help you become a better speaker. Speaking will help even more. Like many skills, presentation speaking requires knowledge and practice. Everyone benefits from the time and effort spent learning the strategies and skills of any task—planning, preparing, and delivering effective presentations is no different.

1.2 Speaking Anxiety

You may be required to give a presentation during the first week of your communication course. It may be a brief speech introducing yourself (or another student) to the class. You might be asked to draw a random topic out of an envelope and speak about it for a minute or two. You might have to speak about your dream job, the place you'd most like to live, or your opinion about an issue on campus or in the news.

No matter what the assignment, you will probably feel some anxiety. After all, it will be the first time you have stood in front of your classmates and instructor to speak. It may be the first time you have *ever* been asked to speak to an audience. You know that first impressions matter. What if you look awkward and uncomfortable or say something that makes no sense?

Many people believe that this kind of nervousness (also called **speaking anxiety**, **stage fright**, and **communication apprehension**) is a rare, uncommon experience and that other speakers, especially speakers who seem poised and confident, don't feel nervous when they're speaking. That is a myth.

Speaking Anxiety Is Common

Speaking anxiety is one of the most common personal fears. Surveys consistently show that fear of speaking in front of a group is among people's most intense fears—sometimes ranked higher than their fear of death![1]

If you believe that you're the only person feeling apprehensive about speaking, you may wrongly blame your nervousness for a poor presentation. "I was nervous; therefore, my talk went badly." But nervousness doesn't predict whether a presentation succeeds or fails. Many nervous speakers develop and deliver outstanding presentations. And even the most experienced and successful speakers feel tense or uneasy before and as they begin speaking.

Speaking anxiety is the common ground on which nearly all speakers stand. In fact, 75 to 85 percent of the US population experience some form of anxiety when faced with the prospect of making a presentation.

The difference in the relative success of speakers' presentations comes down to how well they understand and manage their anxiety. The fact that you are nervous doesn't necessarily matter to your success. Your *level* of nervousness doesn't matter either. What matters is how you handle it. Successful speakers use their nervousness to make their presentations better.[2]

Sources of Speaking Anxiety (and How to Respond to Them)

The process of managing speaking anxiety begins with recognizing and understanding why you feel anxious. Speakers cite many reasons for their nervousness, such as "I could forget what I want to say," "My audience won't like me," or "I'll make a huge, embarrassing mistake." The probability of any of these things happening is very small. But *imagining* them happening can create anxiety.

Although all of us have personal reasons for feeling nervous, those reasons generally cluster into six categories. What follows are the most common sources of speaking anxiety, along with strategies for dealing with each one.

Novelty

Doing anything new can cause anxiety. Meeting new people, for example, can be both exciting and challenging. Performing in an unfamiliar or unexpected role can transform a usually confident person into a nervous wreck. One reality of speaking to an audience is that each presentation will be new to you in important ways. The topic may require you to learn new content. Or you might be asked to speak in a location or in front of an audience that is very different from what you're used to. That's probably the case with an "icebreaker" speech in class—you may not know your classmates very well, if at all.

So how can you reduce the anxiety that arises from novelty? The answer shouldn't be a surprise: find ways to make the new and unfamiliar

● getting started   ▶ delivery   ◆ speaking to persuade
▲ fundamentals   ∴ engaging your audience   ★ speaking occasions
■ content   ♥ speaking to inform   ✳ resources

feel familiar to you. The more familiar you are with the **AUDIENCE**, the setting, and the **OCCASION**, the less anxious you will feel. Prior to any presentation, get to know some of the people in your audience. Connecting with even a few audience members before you speak can help take the edge off your anxiety. It may even give you some new content—a relevant story or an interesting fact—to share with the audience during your presentation. At the very least, figure out the similarities between people in your audience and other people you know.

Likewise, if the setting of your talk is new to you, take the time to acquaint yourself with it beforehand. Familiarity and comfort with the setting can settle your nerves and boost presentation confidence. If you know you are going to be speaking in an unfamiliar setting, get there early. Check it out. Notice what might distract you or your audience. Is there a flickering light? A column that blocks the view of some listeners? Is the room too warm or too cool? Figure out a way to minimize or eliminate those distractions. Speak a few sentences of your presentation at the volume you intend to use in that room. Also, make sure any equipment you need is set up properly and working.

Consider whether the new setting reminds you of another one that is familiar to you. In the classic movie *Hoosiers*, the basketball team from a small Indiana high school makes it to the state championship game. When the players enter the arena, they are awed by the size of the place. They've never played in such a huge venue, and that fact makes them anxious. The coach has them walk the court to measure the width and length. This simple exercise confirms an important fact: this court is the same size as every other court they have played on during every other game in every other town. This realization helps the team face their fear and get down to the business of winning the championship.

If your presentation will be an **ONLINE** event, make sure that you are familiar with the technology you'll use. For example, if you're using Zoom, practice with the camera and software ahead of time to determine whether you can comfortably address your audience while simultaneously scanning their chats. Be prepared for people entering the "room" as you speak. If you'll be using **PRESENTATION AIDS**, make sure they are well done—most eyes will be on your slides, not on you, while you show them.

▲ 72–80

● 5–6

★ 479–89

∴ 282–305

Physiological Symptoms

When you make a presentation, your palms may sweat, your pulse may speed up, and your hands may shake. These physical responses are not only the initial *symptoms* of stage fright but also some of the most common *sources* of the ongoing anxiety that some speakers—and certainly most inexperienced speakers—feel during their presentations.

The reason for this feedback loop is simple: inexperienced and highly anxious speakers often assume that their audience (or at least the people in the first few rows) can see the physical symptoms of nervousness. As a result, they become preoccupied with what audience members might think of them. Fortunately and despite what you may think, most symptoms of speaking anxiety are not visible. Audience members cannot see or hear your fear. They cannot see a pounding heart, an upset stomach, or worried thoughts. They do not notice small changes in your voice or remember occasional mistakes. Even experienced communication instructors, when asked about how anxious a student is, seldom accurately estimate the speaker's level of anxiety.[3] So the first thing to remember about these symptoms is simply this: they're rarely obvious to your listeners.

Nonetheless, the symptoms of speaking anxiety aren't an illusion. You really are feeling them. So what can you do to reduce this response? Effective speakers learn how to relax their bodies. Before the presentation, they take some deep breaths, relax tight muscles, and move around if they can. These physical pre-presentation rituals, whatever they may be, can relax your body and mind. Nearly all performers—actors, musicians, dancers, and athletes of all kinds—enact rituals designed to relax their bodies prior to a high-stakes challenge. Do the same for a presentation: find a ritual that helps you relax, and make sure you do it before every presentation.

Here's a technique that has worked for many speakers: Right before you speak, repeat a two-syllable word or phrase silently to yourself, syllable by syllable, deeply inhaling and exhaling each time. Use, for example, the word *relax*. Breathe in slowly while saying the sound "re" silently to yourself, holding the long "e" sound all the while you are inhaling. This should take two or three seconds. Then breathe out slowly, also for two or three seconds, as you say the sound "lax" silently to yourself. Hold the "a" sound while exhaling. Inhale and exhale, thinking "reee-laaax" four or five times.

By the time you finish this thirty-second relaxation exercise, your pulse should be slower, and, ideally, you will also feel calmer.

If repeating a word or phrase doesn't work for you, try something simpler. A small yawn or quiet sigh right before you speak can relax your neck and throat muscles. Tensing and relaxing your stomach muscles before speaking can release stress from your body. Find the tension-reducing exercise that works for you, and you'll be rewarded with a calmer body, a calmer mind, and a more confident **STAGE PRESENCE**. Although you may still feel nervous, a ritual will help you get through it, and it will help you look poised and relaxed.

▶ 185–86

What should you do with the anxious feelings that remain? Consider this thought: Aren't these feelings the same ones that occur when you are watching an action sequence of a suspenseful movie or when you are buckling into your seat on a notorious roller coaster? There are few physiological differences between the arousal you feel when you are anxious and when you are excited. When symptoms of nervousness set in, effective speakers enlist those feelings as extra energy and enthusiasm. When they feel that rush of adrenaline and their hearts beat faster and stronger, they take those feelings as signs that they're revved up, eager, and ready to go. They think to themselves, "Let's get this show on the road!"

Adopting a ritual of relaxation and harnessing nervous feelings to energize your presentation will help you ride out the physiological symptoms of speaking anxiety and get to the business of connecting with your audience.

Unrealistic Beliefs

Many speakers worry that their nervousness dooms them to failure. When we've asked students to share their goals for taking a speaking course—other than passing it with a good grade—an overwhelming number give answers related to fear of speaking. They want to "overcome anxiety," "stop being nervous," and "totally calm down." Professional speakers have a very different attitude and expectation. They acknowledge that they're probably just as nervous as other speakers, and they accept that it's unlikely they will stop being nervous or totally calm down. Instead they transform worrisome, irrational, and nonproductive thoughts into positive statements.

Psychologists call this technique **cognitive restructuring**, a method that challenges and changes unrealistic thinking into realistic expectations. Rather than thinking, "I'll make mistakes," "I might be laughed at," or "I'll forget what I want to say," experienced speakers focus on their role or message, remind themselves that they will calm down as they start to speak (as research clearly shows[4]), and tell themselves positive things, such as "I'm going to do great," "I'm a well-prepared, skilled speaker," "My message is important," or "Apprehension makes me work hard and do a better job."

Can positive statements like this help? Sure! Positive self-talk helps you become more realistic about what you need to do and what will happen when you make a presentation. The speaking experience won't be as bad as you expect. You will survive, particularly if you banish the negative beliefs and unrealistic expectations that get in the way of speaking success.

Fear of the Spotlight

Most of us experience some anxiety when we are the focus of other people's attention. When all eyes are on you, the attention can make you more self-conscious than you otherwise might be. Psychologists call this reaction the **spotlight effect**, a tendency to overestimate the extent to which our behavior and appearance are noticed and assessed by others.[5]

If you mispronounce a word, discover your shirt is unbuttoned a bit more than intended, or make a clumsy gesture during your presentation, you may feel uncomfortable, awkward, or embarrassed. And during that time, your attention will be diverted from your message and your audience, which should be your primary focus.

So how do you reduce this sense of conspicuousness? Start by reminding yourself that most speakers significantly overestimate the extent to which audience members are criticizing their appearance or their speaking skills. Your audience is more concerned with whether you **ADDRESS THEIR NEEDS** and engage their attention and **INTEREST**. If they're absorbed in what you're saying and see how it affects their lives, they won't pay as much attention to your posture or pronunciation. This isn't to say that your words, delivery, and appearance aren't important. Of course they are. And

77 ▲
268–79 ⁘

● getting started   ▶ delivery   ◆ speaking to persuade
▲ fundamentals   ⁘ engaging your audience   ★ speaking occasions
■ content   ◤ speaking to inform   ✹ resources

obviously, you should do what you can before your presentation to ensure that you're as polished and professional as you can be when you speak. But if you find yourself dwelling on these things in a self-conscious way *during* your presentation, that's the moment to remember that these things are not as noticeable to your audience as they are to you.

One specific strategy for both addressing your own anxiety about conspicuousness and connecting with your audience is to literally shift attention away from yourself and toward them. Put the spotlight on your listeners. Comedians often do this. When they're nervous, they'll address people sitting near the stage. Why? Because while they're doing that, audience members are craning their necks, trying to get a look at the person they're talking to. And during that time, the comedian is getting more comfortable by no longer being the focus of everyone's attention.

We are not recommending that you act like a comedian. But shifting attention away from yourself and toward an audience member or two may be all that's needed to take the edge off your anxiety. Look at an audience member and nod your head at them. In many cases, they're likely to nod back. Pick someone else and smile at them. They're likely to smile back. Engage your audience with a quick activity or question. With each of these actions, and others like them, you are mentally shifting your attention from yourself to others and reducing your anxiety in the process.

"Rigid Rules"

Although this book is filled with recommendations about how to become a more effective speaker, they are not rigid rules—as in strict, inflexible, or hard-and-fast—that must be adhered to in every presentation.

Unfortunately, some speakers become very anxious when they believe they are violating a "rule" of presentation speaking. *Never*, they were once told, *put your hands in your pockets or sit on the corner of a desk when you are speaking.* Or *Banish every filler phrase like "um," "uh," "you know," and "really" from your presentation.* While advice like this may be generally true, always remember that finding a way to connect and communicate with your audience matters much more than whether or not you follow a set of rules. An occasional "um" or "uh" is natural and common in everyday speech. It can also make the speaker sound thoughtful and relaxed.

Rigid rules trap us. When we think we have made a mistake or broken a rule, we may become more nervous. Our advice: Focus instead on your audience and your purpose. Know the rules, but don't let them control every decision you make.

Fear of Evaluation

Fear of evaluation is a leading source of speaker anxiety. It is true that whenever you make a presentation, you are being judged by your audience. While you speak, members of your audience may be thinking to themselves, "Is this topic interesting?" or "Is this talk relevant to my own life?" or "Is this speaker believable? Likable? Persuasive?" Knowing that your listeners may be asking these questions during your talk can make you nervous. After all, very few of us like to be evaluated by others, particularly if they have more status, power, or influence than we do. So how can you overcome this fear of evaluation? Two words: *preparation* and *practice*.

Researchers note that speaking anxiety affects the way speakers prepare presentations. Some anxious speakers don't prepare effectively because they don't know how to prepare. Rather than making orderly and well-informed decisions about a presentation, nervous speakers become lost in the process.[6] Consequently, they end up focusing on their fears rather than on what they need to say and do.

All performers have stage fright to some extent. To counter these fears, they spend hours preparing and practicing. It should be no different for speakers. Giving yourself adequate time to prepare for your talk (**DOING RESEARCH**, choosing strong **SUPPORTING MATERIALS**, **ORGANIZING** your content) and to **PRACTICE YOUR DELIVERY** will reduce your speaking anxiety. Novice speakers often report that a symptom of their nervousness is a feeling of being lost and confused as they speak. Preparation and practice can replace this sense of confusion with confidence.

111–12 ■
115–19 ■
133–59 ■
228–33 ▶

Just Do It!

Experience is a great teacher. One of the best ways to change presentation anxiety into presentation confidence is simply to speak as often as you can.

●　getting started　　▶　delivery　　◆　speaking to persuade
▲　fundamentals　　∴　engaging your audience　　★　speaking occasions
■　content　　▼　speaking to inform　　✳　resources

Many students and experienced speakers report that the more they speak and improve their speaking skills, the less nervous they feel.

Speaking apprehension is a complex phenomenon. There are no easy answers or magic bullets that guarantee a "cure." Effective speakers can, however, manage their anxiety by identifying its sources and choosing appropriate strategies to deal with them. Here's a summary of the most common sources and recommended responses to each one:

Source	Response
Novelty	Make the unfamiliar feel familiar. Learn more about the audience, setting, and occasion. Practice your presentation until you feel comfortable and more confident.
Physiological symptoms	Adopt a ritual of relaxation to reduce the physical symptoms of speaking anxiety. Avoid overestimating the extent to which your internal feelings are detectable by the audience. Use nervousness to create positive energy and excitement. Remember that nervousness tends to decrease once you've begun speaking.
Unrealistic beliefs	Convert worrisome, irrational, and nonproductive beliefs into positive statements. Focus on your message and audience, and count on calming down as you speak.
Fear of the spotlight	Shift attention (both yours and the audience's) away from yourself to your audience's needs and interests.
"Rigid rules"	Do not let rigid rules control you. Regardless of the rule, make sure your presentation is appropriate for you, your purpose, your audience, and the occasion.
Fear of evaluation	Devote adequate time to preparing your message and to practicing your delivery.

NOTABLE SPEAKER
Monica Lewinsky

In 1995—at the age of 22—Monica Lewinsky spent more than a year working as a White House intern, during which time she had an affair with President Bill Clinton. Lewinsky faced intense media scrutiny when the affair became national news in January 1998. Although social media websites such as Twitter and Facebook did not exist at the time, the internet provided a platform for the public shaming of Lewinsky. By 2005, she decided to escape the spotlight and move to London to pursue a master's degree in psychology. She maintained a relatively private life until October 2014, when she spoke about cyberbullying and internet shaming at a *Forbes* magazine "30 under 30" summit. Since her presentation at the summit and subsequent TED talk in 2015, Lewinsky has served as an ambassador for the antibullying organization Bystander Revolution, participated in a number of antibullying campaigns, and written about the #MeToo movement.

Search Terms
To locate videos of these presentations online, enter the following key words into a search engine: Monica Lewinsky first public speech Forbes; and, Lewinsky the price of shame. The videos are approximately 25:31 and 22:31 in length.

What to Watch For
First speech: October 2014
[0:00–0:35] At the outset of the presentation, Lewinsky tells the audience that this is only her fourth time delivering a speech in public. She asks them to forgive her because she is nervous and emotional. Since anxiety is a common experience for most speakers, especially for those who don't have much experience speaking in public, it's not surprising that she is nervous.

[0:35–0:40] Likely a physiological manifestation of her anxiety, Lewinsky takes a deep breath before beginning the formal introduction of her presentation. In the absence of her telling the audience that she is nervous and taking a deep breath, it's likely that the audience wouldn't be able to observe any outward signs of the internal anxiety she was experiencing.

[1:30–2:05] As a way of introducing herself to an audience who may know who she is but not know much else about her personal life, Lewinsky makes a humorous reference to all the rap songs she is mentioned in. The audience laughs at the reference, and Lewinsky pauses and thanks them for doing so. Recognizing the audience is an effective way of shifting the attention away from herself. This may help her feel less conspicuous.

[12:15–25:00] As Lewinsky reaches the midpoint of her speech, she appears more comfortable. While she may still be experiencing some anxiety, it is difficult from the audience's point of view to see her symptoms of nervousness.

(NOTABLE SPEAKER CONTINUED)

Second speech: March 2015

[0:14–1:00] In March 2015, Lewinsky delivered a similar presentation at a TED talk event in Vancouver, British Columbia. Unlike her previous presentation, she begins this one without any mention of her nervousness. There is no way to know if she was experiencing the same level of anxiety as she did in October 2014.

[4:00–4:30] As the speech progresses, Lewinsky projects confidence by maintaining eye contact with audience members, using purposeful gestures, and speaking clearly. She mirrors the content of her message by using a kind and compassionate tone throughout the presentation. If she is experiencing any nervousness internally, it is not visible to the audience. The audience gives her a standing ovation at the conclusion of her presentation—a sign that her message and presentation achieved her purpose.

EXERCISE

After viewing both of Lewinsky's speeches, reflect on these questions:

1. In her 2014 speech, would you have known that Lewinsky was nervous if she hadn't told you?

2. Do you think it's useful for speakers to tell an audience that they are nervous? How might doing so affect a speaker's credibility?

3. If at all, how did Lewinsky appear to use her nervousness to make the first speech better?

4. Describe your reaction to Lewinsky's display of emotion about the possibility of her mother being prosecuted (7:20–7:30 in the first speech). Do you think it was appropriate? Did she need to say "sorry" before moving on?

5. How might preparation and practice have helped Lewinsky manage her anxiety between her first public address and her TED talk? What might account for a noticeable increase in her comfort level?

Conclusion

Whether you call it speaking anxiety, communication apprehension, or stage fright, you wouldn't be human if the thought of giving a presentation didn't make you a bit nervous. Understanding why you experience speaking anxiety and using a few of the techniques recommended in this chapter to respond to it can help you manage this common fear.

But speaking anxiety doesn't disappear overnight. Managing it becomes easier only with practice and experience. Over time, as you speak in a variety of rhetorical situations, your skills will improve and even become second nature, and eventually you will find it much easier to project confidence in yourself and your message as a result.

No matter how nervous you are now, rest assured that you can do this. So take a deep breath, focus on your goals, and start speaking!

1.3 Listening

This book addresses the strategies and skills of effective speaking. So what is a chapter on *listening* doing here? If you have not made many presentations, you may feel as though all you've ever done is listen to other people speak. Do you really need to be told how to do it? What can you possibly learn that you don't already know? As it turns out, the answer is quite a lot.

There is a large body of knowledge in the discipline of communication studies about the need for better listening. Communication experts recognize that without responsible, skilled listening, any attempt to communicate is likely to fail. They also know that many of us overestimate the extent to which we listen to, understand, and remember what other people say.

What Is Listening?

Listening is the process of receiving, constructing meaning from, remembering, and responding to spoken and/or nonverbal messages. Listening helps both speakers and audience members interact more effectively. As a speaker, if you watch for and understand your audience's reactions, you can adjust how you speak and motivate them to listen more attentively and remember what you've said. As an audience member, your ability to listen affects how you respond to a speaker's message. Communication is more successful and meaningful when both speakers *and* audiences commit themselves to listening attentively and responsibly.

Listening may appear to be as easy and natural as breathing. After all, doesn't everyone listen? In fact, the answer to this question is often no. What most of us do is *hear*. Hearing is merely a physical capability, whereas listening is a skill. It involves focused attention and purposeful, critical thinking. And, like any skill, listening requires effort, and some people are better at it than others. The first step in improving your own listening skills is identifying and avoiding bad listening habits.

Poor Listening

In a world filled with constant physical and psychological distractions, it's amazing that anyone listens effectively. In the much smaller world of presentation speaking, loud and annoying sounds, uncomfortable room temperature and seating, and disruptive outside activities can be distracting, as can a speaker's **DELIVERY**. It's difficult and annoying to listen to a speaker who talks too softly, too rapidly or too slowly, or who speaks in a monotone voice. Even a speaker's mannerisms and appearance can be distracting. Similarly, a noisy, fidgeting, nonresponsive, or noticeably critical audience can disturb and sidetrack a speaker. All these things can make it difficult to listen well.

▶ 183–84

External distractions and competing pressures are generally beyond our control. But within our control are the habits we adopt when we listen. Unfortunately, many of us have acquired poor listening habits over the course of our lives. Here are some of the most common ones:

- **Pseudolistening** happens when you fake attention or pretend to listen, particularly when your mind is elsewhere, you are bored, or you think it pleases the speaker. It can be especially frustrating because it communicates a false message of interest and attention to the speaker, misleading them into thinking that they've been heard and understood.
- **Selective listening** happens when you listen only to messages that you like and agree with or when you avoid listening to complex, unfamiliar information or messages that contradict or challenge your opinions. A selective listener often listens not only to confirm prior beliefs but also to identify flaws in what a speaker says.
- **Superficial listening** happens when you pay more attention to how a speaker looks and sounds than to what they say, or when you draw hasty conclusions about what a speaker means before they have finished expressing a thought.
- If you assume that a speaker's controversial or critical remarks are personal or unjust attacks, you may be engaging in **defensive listening**. Defensive listeners often focus only on how to respond to or challenge a speaker rather than listening objectively and seeking to understand the speaker's message.

- If you interrupt a speaker, exaggerate your nonverbal responses, make distracting movements or noise, or noticeably withhold your attention during a presentation, you are engaging in **disruptive listening**. Both the speaker and other audience members may become irritated or offended by your behavior.

290–92

- **Multitask listening** involves doing two things at the same time, such as listening while texting someone, whispering to someone next to you, or reading a document (even a **HANDOUT** distributed by the speaker!) while a speaker is talking about something else.
- The **next-in-line effect** means that instead of listening attentively and accurately to what a speaker is saying, you are thinking about why you disagree or are silently rehearsing how you will challenge the speaker's claims as soon as you have the opportunity.

The first step in becoming a more effective listener is being aware of and doing your best to avoid these poor listening habits.

The Components of Effective Listening

Of course, there's more to listening well than simply avoiding bad habits. Judi Brownell, a leading listening researcher, has identified six separate but interrelated skills that together constitute **effective listening**. Brownell's "HURIER" model—the name is an acronym created by the first letter of each of the six skills: hearing, understanding, remembering, interpreting, evaluating, and responding[1]—provides a clear and memorable definition of effective listening. The following are brief descriptions of the six listening skills and what you can do to improve each one.

- **Hearing** is your ability to make clear, aural distinctions among the sounds and words being spoken. To hear properly, make sure that you're in the proper state of mind, that you minimize as many distractions as you can, and that you position yourself close enough to the speaker. If necessary, ask the speaker to repeat themselves or speak in a louder voice.
- **Understanding** is your ability to accurately grasp the intended meaning of a speaker's message. To make sure you understand, you may

● getting started   ▶ delivery   ◆ speaking to persuade
▲ fundamentals   ∴ engaging your audience   ★ speaking occasions
■ content   ◤ speaking to inform   ✳ resources

need to ask the speaker to clarify, to provide an example or definition, or to rephrase what's been said in more precise terms. You can also ask for a perception check by stating what *you* think the speaker is saying and then asking whether your understanding is correct.

- **Remembering** is your ability to store, retain, and recall information you have heard. One of the best ways to remember what a speaker says and means is to identify good reasons to care about what you're hearing. We remember things that are **PERSONALLY RELEVANT** and **EMOTIONALLY ENGAGING** much better than things that we perceive as disconnected from our lives. In addition to identifying good reasons to listen, write down essential ideas and/or information, and repeat them silently to yourself as you record them.

76–77
357–61

- **Interpreting** is your ability to understand the meaning of what's being communicated beyond the literal, verbal message. Interpret the speaker's nonverbal communication: **EYE CONTACT, FACIAL EXPRESSIONS, AND GESTURES**, as well as **VOCAL QUALITY**. Empathize with the emotions, values, and attitudes that the speaker is expressing through nonverbal cues.

210–15
196–206

- **Evaluating** is your ability to analyze and make a judgment about someone's message. It requires you to think critically about the validity of the speaker's **CLAIMS** before criticizing, to distinguish logical from **ILLOGICAL APPEALS**, and to monitor your own emotions and attitudes that could interfere with reasonable judgment.

352–54
374–80

- **Responding** is your ability to provide appropriate and meaningful feedback that signals you have or have not heard and understood the speaker. This response needn't be in words. Just as you can read a speaker's intention and meaning from nonverbal cues, you can communicate your understanding or confusion nonverbally just as clearly as you could verbally.

The Audience's Listening Responsibilities

What does it feel like to be a responsible listener in an audience? Ralph Nichols, the pioneer listening researcher, puts it this way:

> Good listening is not relaxed and passive at all. It's dynamic; it's constructive; it's characterized by a slightly increased heart rate, quicker

circulation of the blood, and a small rise in bodily temperature. It's energy consuming; it's plain hard work.[2]

Although effective listening is neither easy nor instinctive, it is half the equation that constitutes effective communication. That alone makes it worth the effort. The following are some strategies help you listen more effectively and responsibly to a presentation.

Understand before Criticizing

48–50

Good listeners are open minded and support a speaker's **FREEDOM OF SPEECH** rights. They make sure that they understand a speaker before reacting to what they've heard. As a responsible listener, you should acknowledge that your feelings about and responses to other speakers are at least partly determined by your beliefs and related biases. Recognizing this perfectly human tendency will help you listen more thoughtfully and will put you in the right frame of mind to understand a speaker's message on its own terms.

There are times when you may be offended or angered by what you hear. What should you do? If you are committed to being an effective listener, you should pause, maintain your concentration, and make sure that you accurately comprehend the speaker's message. In other words: *listen before you leap*. When you listen before you leap, you are not approving of or condoning what someone says. Rather, you are deciding whether and how to react and taking time to determine if you've accurately understood the speaker's intended message.

Use Your Thinking Time Responsibly

Thought speed is the speed at which most people can think, compared to the speed at which they speak. Most speakers talk at a rate of 150 to 175 words per minute. If thoughts were measured in words per minute, most of us can think at three or four times the rate at which we speak.[3] Thus, we have about 400 words' worth of spare thinking time for every minute we listen to another person's presentation.

So what do you do with all that extra thinking time? Poor listeners use their extra thought speed to daydream, engage in side conversations, take unnecessary notes, or plan how to confront a speaker. An effective listener, however, will do some of the following:

- Assess the speaker's **CREDIBILITY**, qualifications, and potential biases.
- Identify and summarize the presentation's **KEY POINTS** and **CENTRAL IDEA**.
- Analyze the strengths and weaknesses of the speaker's **ARGUMENTS**.
- Weigh the relevance and practicality of the speaker's comments.

▲ 57–66

▇ 133–36

▇ 137–38

◆ 363–81

Take Useful Notes

Skilled notetakers recall messages better than non-notetakers. The key word in the previous sentence is *skilled*. If you spend all your time taking notes or writing down almost every word you hear, you can't observe the speaker's nonverbal behavior or devote thinking time to assessing and responding to what the speaker says. Skilled notetakers select key words and phrases they want to remember or challenge. If speakers foolishly put everything they say on **SLIDES**, don't be seduced into copying what's on the screen. Instead, listen to the speaker, read the slide (if you're given enough time to do that), and write down a short phrase to summarize the message in that portion of the talk. Finally, take notes by hand, not on a digital device. Research demonstrates that we remember what we write more than what we type.[4]

⁘ 296–302

The Speaker's Listening Responsibilities

Listening to members of your audience goes beyond hearing and seeing their reactions before and after your presentation. It also requires watching, listening, and adapting yourself and your message to their feedback and listening behavior *during* your presentation.

Ask for and Respond to Audience Feedback

All audiences react to a presentation. In face-to-face presentations, speakers can usually see, hear, and adapt to what is known as **feedback**, the verbal and nonverbal responses made by audience members as they interpret and evaluate the meaning and delivery of a presentation. In the case of televised, recorded, or time-delayed presentations, speakers may have to wait until afterward for feedback.

If listener reactions are difficult to see, hear, or interpret, ask the audience questions, such as "Let me make sure I'm explaining the new features of our new accounting system clearly. How could these features benefit your department or office?" Not only do questions help you **ADAPT TO YOUR AUDIENCE**, they also tell listeners that you are interested in their reactions. There is nothing wrong with pausing in the middle of a presentation to ask for audience reactions or questions.

80–82

In addition to questions, you can also adapt to problems and pleasures. If you hear audience members talking to one another rather than listening to you, stop and ask those members whether they need clarification or examples. If audience members are squirming in their seats, perhaps it's time to shorten your presentation or move on to a more interesting section. And if audience members are leaning forward and are highly focused, you may delight in how well you are doing—and carry on with more confidence.

Honor the Audience Bill of Rights

Effective speakers believe that every audience member has the right to understand and evaluate their presentation, and that this right depends on the speaker's attention to a number of individual rights. The following Audience Bill of Rights applies to the six components of the **RHETORICAL SITUATION**.

5–10

THE AUDIENCE BILL OF RIGHTS[5]

405–89

OCCASION	Listeners have the right to know why this speaker and topic have been chosen for this particular occasion. They also have the right to know, in advance, how long the presentation or session will last.
SPEAKER	Listeners have the right to know enough information about the speaker's background, experiences, and expertise to decide whether the speaker is **COMPETENT** and **CREDIBLE**.

55–69
58–61
57–66

● getting started   ▶ delivery   ◆ speaking to persuade
▲ fundamentals   ∴ engaging your audience   ★ speaking occasions
■ content   ◤ speaking to inform   ✳ resources

THE AUDIENCE BILL OF RIGHTS

AUDIENCE	Listeners have the right to be spoken to with respect for their experiences, background, intelligence, knowledge, attitudes, beliefs, and **CULTURE**. They also have the right to ask questions and expect substantive answers.	▲ 70–86 ◆ 391–92
PURPOSE	Listeners have the right to know the speaker's purpose—what the speaker wants them to think or do as a result of a presentation. They also have a right to know the reasons why the speaker has chosen this purpose and how they can **BENEFIT** from its achievement.	▲ 87–101 ◆ 384
CONTENT	Listeners have the right to understand and evaluate the ideas and information used to support the speaker's message. They also have the right to expect a clear, **WELL-ORGANIZED PRESENTATION**.	■ 103–79 ■ 133–59
DELIVERY	Listeners have the right to see and hear a speaker and to be able to see every **PRESENTATION AID** used by the speaker, no matter where the aids are located.	▶ 181–233 ⁙ 282–305

Shared Listening Responsibilities

Audiences and speakers also share certain listening responsibilities. When and how you use these strategies depends on whether you are the speaker or an audience member, whether you are speaking to a large or small group, whether the topic is controversial or not, and whether you have the flexibility to interact with the speaker or audience members during or after a presentation.

Overcome Distractions

Distractions take many forms and can be caused by a speaker, an audience member, or outside interference. Depending on the circumstances and setting of a presentation, you may be able to take direct action to reduce behavioral noise. If an audience member's behavior is distracting, a speaker should ask that person to stop talking or moving around. After all, if side conversations are distracting you, they are probably distracting others. If a presenter speaks too softly or uses visual aids that are too small, a conscientious audience member may ask the speaker to use more volume or further explain what is being shown.

When distractions are environmental, you are well within your rights as a speaker or audience member to shut a door, open a window, or turn on more lights. In large groups, you may need to ask permission to improve the group's surroundings.

"Listen" to Nonverbal Messages

Speakers and audience members don't put everything that is important into words. Very often, you can understand a speaker's meaning or gauge audience members' reactions by noting and interpreting their nonverbal behavior.

Good listeners pay attention to the combined meaning of verbal and nonverbal messages, and they notice any mismatch between the two, such as when a speaker says, "I'm delighted to see you here today" while slouching and speaking in a dull voice.

204–5
196–200
210–12
212–13

A change in a speaker's **INFLECTION** or **VOLUME** may be another way of saying, "Listen up; this is very important." A presenter's sustained **EYE CONTACT** may be a way of saying, "I'm talking to you!" **FACIAL EXPRESSIONS** can reveal whether a thought is painful, joyous, exciting, serious, or boring. Effective listeners pay attention to all aspects of a speaker's delivery.

In turn, effective speakers pay attention to audience members' nonverbal behaviors. Facial expressions, alert or laid-back postures, full attention to the speaker or preoccupation on cell phones, and positive or negative head nods send messages about whether the presentation is on track or if changes are necessary to recapture the audience's attention and interest.

If we fail to "listen" to one another's nonverbal behavior—either as listeners or as speakers—we may be missing the intended meaning of a message.

⬤ getting started   ▷ delivery   ◆ speaking to persuade
▲ fundamentals   ⸪ engaging your audience   ★ speaking occasions
■ content   ▼ speaking to inform   ✳ resources

Listen and Respond with Civility

Both speakers and audience members jeopardize the success of a presentation if they fail to listen and respond to one another with civility. In his book *Choosing Civility*, P. M. Forni defines **civility** as "being constantly aware of others and weaving restraint, respect, and consideration into the very fabric of this awareness."[6] Listening to others with concentration and empathy is a hallmark of civility. When someone listens to you patiently, politely, and thoughtfully, the result is pleasure and encouragement. In contrast, when you feel as though someone is not listening to you and is dismissing what you are saying, the result is frustration and discouragement.

In recent years, many news commentators, politicians, and citizens have bemoaned the lack of civility in both speakers and audience members discussing important social and political issues. Is it any wonder that so many people claim to hate politics?

We may not be able to do much about the incivility of political pronouncements and debate in the world at large, but we can adopt and abide by clear standards of civil behavior in most of the rhetorical situations we encounter. In classrooms, houses of worship, community centers, corporate or organizational meeting rooms, and many other settings, we can and should carve out spaces where civility and respectful dialogue are the norm. The responsibility falls on all of us, as speakers and listeners, to hold ourselves to these **ETHICAL COMMUNICATION** standards wherever possible. 40–41

As hard as it may be, we should listen to people with whom we disagree. And they should do the same when we speak. The best opportunity to advance a cause you believe in is by listening to an adversarial speaker and then crafting an intelligent, engaging, and persuasive response. You may be tempted to interrupt a speaker with whom you passionately disagree. Shutting down a presentation in which the ideas expressed seem to be factually inaccurate or morally wrong may seem in the moment to be a victory, but if your intention is to address, criticize, or correct what the speaker is saying, your best chance of doing so will come only if you listen in an attentive and civil manner.

In turn, as a speaker, it is your responsibility, even if you choose to speak about an issue that you know will be controversial, to treat your audience with respect and civility. You may argue for something that you know most of your listeners won't approve of at first, but if you hope to persuade them to change their minds, you must listen to them prior to, during, and after your presentation. Your presentation is more likely to achieve its purpose if you conscientiously strive to comprehend their point of view before you speak and then respectfully adapt to them as you speak.

Conclusion

We spend more time listening than we do speaking, reading, or writing. But most of us are not very good listeners and have never been taught to listen well. Effective listening is a complex process, requiring a variety of listening skills—hearing, understanding, remembering, interpreting, evaluating, and responding—and a conscientious commitment to avoid bad listening habits.

Regardless of whether you are a speaker or audience member, apply the golden listening rule: listen to others as you would have them listen to you. As an audience member, try to suspend your judgments and biases until you have understood the speaker's message. As a speaker, be aware of and adapt to the ways your audience is listening. The effort you devote to being a better listener will help you become a more effective, more engaging speaker.

1.4 Ethics and Freedom of Speech

More than two thousand years ago, the ancient Roman rhetorician Quintilian gave aspiring speakers this advice: "The orator must above all things study morality, and must obtain a thorough knowledge of all that is just and honorable, without which no one can either be a good man or an able speaker."[1] His enduring idea—that *a good speaker is a good person speaking well*—is as true today as it was then.

What Quintilian called morality we now more commonly refer to as *ethics*. **Ethics** is a system of principles about what is right or wrong, moral or immoral, and bad or good about a belief or action. Ethical questions arise in every rhetorical situation, whenever speakers make decisions about how they will present themselves, how they will treat and adapt to their audience, and how they select strategies that will achieve their presentation's purpose. Will you tell the truth and serve the needs of the people in your audience? Will you use speaking strategies that respect and appropriately adapt to audience members? Will your message serve your own interests *and* those of your listeners? How you answer these questions will determine whether or not you have chosen to be an ethical speaker.

Unfortunately, in recent years we have witnessed a significant deterioration in ethical communication standards and practices. In a world where people routinely spread misinformation, make unsubstantiated **CLAIMS**, and even tell outright lies, it's hard to know what to believe and whom to trust. And worse, the speed with which "fake news" seems to spread farther and wider than the truth can lead some people to conclude that it's better to fight fire with fire—to bend their own communication ethics in order to achieve what they believe is a noble end. This trend is alarming and runs counter to everything that makes a free and democratic society viable.

◆ 352–54

The very best speakers, the ones who have had and will have the most positive and enduring influence, are those who commit themselves to making ethical decisions as they develop and deliver their presentations and who speak honestly with the well-being of their audiences foremost in their minds.

 For an example of a strongly worded, principled speech that had worldwide impact about the need for human and government intervention to minimize climate change, see Notable Speaker: Greta Thunberg, page xxxiii.

A Credo for Ethical Communication

The National Communication Association (NCA)—the largest professional organization for communication scholars, educators, students, and practitioners—promotes its Credo for Ethical Communication, which describes what it means to be an ethical communicator, whether you're speaking with one other person, a small group, or an audience of thousands:

Preamble

Questions of right and wrong arise whenever people communicate. Ethical communication is fundamental to responsible thinking, decision making, and the development of relationships and communities within and across contexts, cultures, channels, and media. Moreover, ethical communication enhances human worth and dignity by fostering truthfulness, fairness, responsibility, personal integrity, and respect for self and others. We believe that unethical communication threatens the well-being of individuals and the society in which we live. Therefore we, the members of the National Communication Association, endorse and are committed to practicing the following principles of ethical communication.

Principles of Ethical Communication

- We advocate truthfulness, accuracy, honesty, and reason as essential to the integrity of communication.

- We endorse freedom of expression, diversity of perspective, and tolerance of dissent to achieve the informed and responsible decision making fundamental to a civil society.
- We strive to understand and respect other communicators before evaluating and responding to their messages.
- We promote access to communication resources and opportunities as necessary to fulfill human potential and contribute to the well-being of families, communities, and society.
- We promote communication climates of caring and mutual understanding that respect the unique needs and characteristics of individual communicators.
- We condemn communication that degrades individuals and humanity through distortion, intimidation, coercion, and violence, and through the expression of intolerance and hatred.
- We are committed to the courageous expression of personal conviction in pursuit of fairness and justice.
- We advocate sharing information, opinions, and feelings when facing significant choices while also respecting privacy and confidentiality.
- We accept responsibility for the short- and long-term consequences of our own communication and expect the same of others.[2]

Ethical Decision Making

Considering the ethical implications of strategic decision making at every stage of the **RHETORICAL SPEECHMAKING PROCESS** is the obligation of every good speaker. It can also enhance the value and success of your presentations. Let's look at how the above principles might affect how you think critically and make decisions about every rhetorical situation.

3–14

Ethical Decisions about the Occasion

Are you aware of and will you honor your audience's expectations about the occasion? Have you planned a presentation that honestly and respectfully conforms to the occasion's focus, setting, and logistics? If you are one of several speakers scheduled to speak, will you stick to your time limit and your assigned topic and not trespass on other speakers' territory?

If you do not honor your audience's expectations about an occasion, you may anger listeners who will judge you as dishonorable and arrogant. If your **LANGUAGE** style at a formal or public occasion is filled with incomprehensible jargon, inappropriate slang, and/or clichés, you will be seen as rhetorically insensitive to the occasion. If you impose on a fellow presenter's time or topic, you will have treated them and the audience unfairly. Regardless of whether the occasion is a classroom presentation, a work briefing, a wedding, an award ceremony, or testimony at a public meeting, ethical communicators respect and adapt to what makes every speaking occasion special and unique.

245–52

Most importantly, an ethical speaker should make sure to not misuse an occasion to suit only their private goals. Consider, for example, how an unethical political candidate might use the occasion of a military funeral—where they are expected only to speak with respect and gratitude for the deceased's sacrifice—to give a stump speech about how their political opponent's vote to limit defense spending is somehow to blame for the deaths of military personnel in general. Regardless of the **VALIDITY** of the claim that is being made, it is unethical for the speaker to use a solemn gathering to make this point and to bend the occasion to their own political purposes.

120–30

Ethical Decisions about Yourself

How do you present yourself to an audience? What will you do to demonstrate that you are **TRUSTWORTHY**? When they see and hear you, will they conclude that you are a good person speaking well? Have you done the work necessary to be knowledgeable about your topic so that whatever you say will genuinely benefit your audience as well as respect their time and attention? And when making an **ARGUMENT**, can you acknowledge honestly and accurately the best versions of other points of view, even as you make a strong case for your own? Cultivating these qualities in yourself, and making the decisions that flow from them, is key to being an ethical speaker. Happily, it also makes you much more likely to achieve your speaking goals.

61–62

363–81

● getting started   ▶ delivery   ◆ speaking to persuade
▲ fundamentals   ⁑ engaging your audience   ★ speaking occasions
■ content   ◣ speaking to inform   ✳ resources

Ethical Decisions about Your Audience

Are you committed to being an **AUDIENCE-CENTERED SPEAKER**? To being fair to your listeners? Will you use what you learn about your audience to help them or harm them? Will you use inclusive language that seeks your listeners' understanding, or will you instead speak in ways that may exclude or anger them?

▲ 70–72

Making ethical choices about your audience begins with learning as much as you can about them—their prior knowledge, their interests, their attitudes, and their values. But this knowledge can also be put to unethical uses too. The more you know about your listeners, the easier it is to tell them only what they want to hear—to pander to them. As an ethical speaker, your obligation is to resist this temptation and to use whatever you learn about your audience to deliver as effectively as possible a message that you believe will benefit them, even if it isn't what they initially want to hear.

For example, there is nothing wrong with a politician promising potential voters that the revenue from property tax increases will only be used to improve public education, provide medical care for children, and fight crime—policies that polls confirm are popular with most voters—if in fact that statement is true. There is something wrong and unethical, however, if the same politician also promises corporations that the revenue from the same property tax increases will be used to offset or reduce corporate taxes. Changing your message as you move from group to group may demonstrate that you are skilled at **AUDIENCE ANALYSIS** and **ADAPTATION**, but it is an unethical communication practice if the two messages conflict with each other.

▲ 72–80
▲ 80–82

Ethical Decisions about Your Purpose

Who will benefit if you achieve your **PURPOSE**—you, your audience, or you *and* your audience? Unfortunately, audiences are often deceived by speakers who appear to be honest but whose intentions are selfish and even harmful. It's fine to have **PRIVATE GOALS** when you speak—goals that benefit you, such as getting a good grade in your communication course or getting a promotion because you impressed your boss with your presentation—but

▲ 87–101

▲ 90–91

your private goals should always complement your overall purpose or at least *not conflict with* it. If your private agenda undermines or contradicts your purpose, you may be headed down an unethical path.

For instance, imagine you are a salesperson whose purpose is to tell people to "join the Superfit Health Spa because it has the best equipment and trainers." Your private goal is to earn a fifty-dollar bonus for every new member you recruit. That private goal may be just fine if the spa's equipment is at least as good as or arguably better than the competition's. But if you cannot truthfully make this claim because you know that the equipment is run down and the trainers are not certified, then you face an ethical crossroads. Your desire for the bonus needs to be weighed against your audience's right to know the truth. If you would be ashamed or embarrassed to reveal your private goal to an audience, you should question the honesty and fairness of your purpose.

Ethical Decisions about Your Content

352–54 ◆
120–30 ■

126–30 ■

You will also face many ethical choices about the content of what you say in a presentation. Are your CLAIMS well founded and reasonable? Have you made sure that your SUPPORTING MATERIAL is up to date and accurate? If most experts disagree with you, can you support and justify your position with valid evidence? Are you using STATISTICS in a manner that is honest, clear, and relevant? By making ethical decisions about content, you ensure that your presentation will be truthful and fair.

The Perils of Plagiarism One of the most important ethical decisions you can make about the content of your presentation is to always and explicitly acknowledge the sources of the words and ideas you use while speaking. **Plagiarism**—the word comes from the Latin *plagium*, which

130–32 ■

means "kidnapping"—occurs when you fail to DOCUMENT or give credit to the sources of your information and/or present their statements as your own. If you plagiarize, you are stealing something that belongs to someone else.

Changing a few words of someone else's work is not enough to avoid plagiarism. If they're not your original ideas and most of the words are not yours, you are ethically obligated to tell your audience who wrote or said

● getting started ▶ delivery ◆ speaking to persuade
▲ fundamentals ⸪ engaging your audience ★ speaking occasions
■ content ◣ speaking to inform ❋ resources

them and where they came from. The following guidelines are criteria for avoiding plagiarism:

- If your presentation includes an identifiable phrase or an idea that appears in someone else's work, always provide an **ORAL FOOTNOTE** of the source in your presentation. 131–32
- Also, provide an oral citation of the source of any information that is not widely known or widely available or about which there is ongoing debate. This clearly signals to your audience whose interpretation of contested facts you are relying on.
- Do not use someone else's sequence of ideas and organization without acknowledging and citing the similarities in structure.
- In a classroom setting, if you use any visual aid or other supporting material that was not created by you—for instance, if you display data from someone else's research as a chart, table, or graph, or if you display a photograph, video clip, or animation that was produced by someone else—you should orally cite the source, and if you're displaying that material on a screen, include a written citation alongside that material.
- When you speak in public settings, you should exercise extreme caution when using visual aids or supporting materials that were not created by you. Many such materials are protected by copyright laws, and as such, if you use them without first seeking the explicit permission of the copyright holder, you could be legally liable for violating copyright laws.
- Even if you secure permission to use material (of any sort) from the person who created it, always give proper credit in your presentation, and never claim that material as your own original work.

Although most speakers don't intend to commit plagiarism, it occurs more frequently than it should, often with serious consequences. In colleges, students have failed classes, been expelled, or been denied a degree when caught plagiarizing. In the publishing business, authors have been sued by writers who claimed that their ideas and words were plagiarized.

In 2016, plagiarism took center stage at the Republican National Convention in Cleveland, Ohio, where Melania Trump gave a speech to support her husband's candidacy for president. Although it was initially praised, the speech soon came under suspicion because key passages resembled portions of a speech that Michelle Obama gave at the Democratic National Convention eight years earlier. Review the two passages comparing Michelle Obama's 2008 speech and the one delivered by Melania Trump in 2016. What you are reading is a definitive example of plagiarism.

Michelle Obama's 2008 speech	Melania Trump's 2016 speech
"And Barack and I were raised with so many of the same <u>values: that you work hard for what you want in life; that your word is your bond and you do what you say</u> you're going to do; <u>that you treat people with</u> dignity and <u>respect</u>, even if you don't know them, and even if you don't agree with them.	"From a young age, my parents impressed on me the <u>values that you work hard for what you want in life, that your word is your bond and you do what you say</u> and keep your promise, <u>that you treat people with respect</u>.
"<u>Because we want our children</u>—and all children <u>in this nation</u>—<u>to know that the only limit to</u> the height of <u>your achievements is the</u> reach <u>of your dreams and your willingness to work for them</u>."	"<u>Because we want our children in this nation to know that the only limit to your achievements is the</u> strength <u>of your dreams and your willingness to work for them</u>."

Republican officials initially denied that the speech included plagiarized material, but those claims collapsed when Mrs. Trump's speechwriter, Meredith McIver, took the blame. This plagiarism overshadowed whatever positive impact Mrs. Trump's presentation had at the time she delivered it, and it ensured that the speech will be remembered for all the wrong reasons. But more important, it was simply unethical.

Here's the bottom line: plagiarism is wrong. It is unfair to your audience and to the person whose ideas and words you're stealing, and it is also a betrayal of your personal integrity. Plagiarizing a portion of a presentation,

● getting started   ▶ delivery   ◆ speaking to persuade
▲ fundamentals   ⁞ engaging your audience   ★ speaking occasions
■ content   ▼ speaking to inform   ✳ resources

even unknowingly, can undermine or destroy whatever **CREDIBILITY** you
have otherwise established with your audience, and it can undercut all the
other good things that you've done on your own.

▲ 57–66

Ethical Decisions about Delivery

Ethical speakers use their verbal and nonverbal delivery skills to share
a meaningful message, not to distract or mislead an audience. A highly
EFFECTIVE DELIVERY that conveys expressiveness, confidence, stage
presence, and immediacy is a powerful thing; it can sometimes persuade
an audience all on its own. But like power in general, skillful delivery can
be misused. If your expressive delivery style springs from a genuine enthusiasm for the subject and an authentic belief in the value of your message
for your audience, then it is ethically appropriate. But when an emotional
performance is used to mask the truth or to present a **FALLACIOUS
ARGUMENT**, it is unethical. Ideally, a speaker's delivery will reflect and reinforce the other ethical decisions they have made about their presentation.

▶ 184–86

◆ 374–80

The Good Audience

Audience members have important ethical responsibilities too. As the third
principle in the NCA ethics credo states, "We strive to understand and
respect other communicators before evaluating and responding to their
messages." So how do you do this?

First and foremost, good audience members are good listeners. They
listen for key ideas and information with open minds. They withhold evaluation until they are sure that they understand what a speaker is saying.
They are also active listeners—they attentively listen to accurately hear,
understand, remember, interpret, evaluate, and respond. They think critically about a speaker's message.

At this point, you may be thinking, "Hey, wait a minute. These are just
good **LISTENING SKILLS**, not ethical responsibilities." But think of it this
way: How can you make fair, well-informed judgments about the speaker
and their message without first listening well? If you don't or won't listen
because you have decided, even before a presentation begins, that you don't
like the message or the speaker, you will have made a consciously unethical

● 30–31

choice. Improving your listening skills is the foundational first step to being an ethical audience member.

Other ethical responsibilities that epitomize a good audience member include the following:[3]

- Ethical audience members allow a speaker to be heard even if they disagree with the speaker's view.
- Ethical audience members provide honest feedback that allows speakers to accurately and appropriately adapt their presentations to audience responses.
- Ethical audience members ask themselves, "Would I want an audience to behave the way I'm behaving if I were the speaker?" As an audience member, you have an ethical responsibility to follow the golden audience rule—that is, to do unto the speaker as you would have an audience do unto you.

Free Speech

Words have power. Speaking can have profound effects. This entire book, and the class you're taking while you read it, rest on the assumption that by applying appropriate communication strategies and improving your speaking skills, you can make a significant impact on the knowledge, attitudes, beliefs, and values of other people.

Of course, like many other powerful tools, speech is just as capable of causing harm as it is of having a positive impact. Words can be hurtful. They can be used to denigrate other people, to espouse offensive ideas, to propose outrageous actions, or even to express contempt and hatred. By now, we hope it's clear that the obligations of an ethical speaker include not using speech in any of these deliberately harmful ways.

But consider this: as recently as the middle of the twentieth century, a large percentage of white Americans would be deeply offended—they would probably even have said *harmed*—by hearing a public speaker assert that interracial marriages between Blacks and whites should *not* be prohibited by law. This view, accepted as it is now, was once considered by many

● getting started   ▶ delivery   ◆ speaking to persuade
▲ fundamentals   ⁝ engaging your audience ★ speaking occasions
■ content   ▼ speaking to inform   ✳ resources

white people to be outrageous, offensive, and harmful—and they actively sought to suppress the speech of people, both Black and white, who made the case for this fundamental civil right. Precisely because they recognized the power of words to change the world, opponents of interracial marriage often did whatever they could to stop civil rights activists from speaking out about it.

All of us have a perfectly understandable human tendency to want to prevent what we regard as harmful or hateful ideas from having an impact. One of the easiest ways to satisfy this urge is to resort to what is sometimes called the "heckler's veto": doing things that cause a speaker to be unable to continue speaking or that prevent the speaker from even having the opportunity to speak. The heckler's veto has been used as a strategic weapon against hateful, inflammatory, and controversial speech on many college campuses in recent years. In the short term, turning away a speaker whose views are offensive or hateful can seem like a victory. But the problem is that once such silencing behaviors become commonplace, whether on a college campus or in the public sphere, they can just as easily be turned against speakers (and ideas) you support as those you oppose.

The First Amendment of the US Constitution protects every American citizen from interference or suppression of their speech by the federal government. The types of speech that are protected under this essential provision of US law are very broad. Even hate speech, for example—the sort of speech that overtly denigrates, insults, or demonizes other people based on their race, ethnicity, gender, or sexual orientation—is legally protected under the First Amendment as long as it isn't a direct "true threat" that causes people to fear imminent physical harm. Of course, there are laws against hate *crimes* because they're based on actions rather than expressions of an opinion.[4]

The legal protection of free speech is such an integral part of American culture that many Americans believe their freedom of speech is absolute—that any time their speech is met with heckling, vocal objections, or some other form of social punishment, their constitutional rights are being violated. This misconception is understandable—and of course our point above about the heckler's veto still stands—but it is nonetheless incorrect.

Although Americans are free to say nearly anything they want to say—even if it is false, highly controversial, or inflammatory—without fear of punishment from their government, there nonetheless may be negative consequences of such speech. If, for example, your statements about someone are false or unjustified, you can be sued for **defamation**—that is, making a false statement that damages a person's reputation. There are two types of defamation: libel (written statements or pictures) and slander (oral or spoken statements).[5]

If you say hateful or inflammatory things about a group or class of people, you may face hostility and harassment from those who choose to be vocal allies of the people you've targeted, as well as sharp criticisms about your character and competence. You may even find your job or career in jeopardy. None of these reactions are, strictly speaking, violations of your constitutionally protected right to free speech.

In the end, the best protection of your right to free speech is to express your opinions respectfully, back up those opinions with legitimate facts and valid reasoning, and provide defensible responses to audience objections. But if reactions to your presentation are extreme, you should honestly reassess the decisions you've made and the rhetorical strategies you've used. If you conclude that you have been truthful, fair, and respectful—in short, that you have exemplified the qualities of an ethical speaker—then you should take comfort in thinking about all the speakers who have come before you (like the civil rights activists mentioned above) whose cause was just and whose ideas eventually prevailed despite attempts to silence them.

As an audience member, you may find it challenging both to defend everyone's right to speak and to productively oppose unethical communication. The sometimes difficult work of understanding, thinking critically about, and responding to other people's **ARGUMENTS** may not be as immediately gratifying as using incendiary language or disruptive tactics to shut them down when they speak in a way that offends you. But it is the more responsible, ethical, and, in the long run, effective strategy.

363–81 ◆

Conclusion

The NCA's Credo for Ethical Communication expresses what should ideally be the guiding values of an ethical speaker in a democratic society. By keeping its principles in mind as you think about your rhetorical situation whenever you speak, you will ensure that you are serving your audience's interests as well as your own. You also have ethical obligations as an audience member—the most fundamental of which is to listen well.

Freedom of speech is an integral part of American life. Precisely because of that, many types of speech—including unethical, untrue, and even hateful speech—are legally protected. But just because speech is free from governmental interference in the United States doesn't mean that unethical speech must be silently tolerated or that it is without consequences. As listeners, we all have the right to meet unethical communication practices with forceful but well-reasoned and respectfully expressed criticisms when they are warranted. The intertwined and sometimes competing principles of communication ethics and freedom of speech make contemporary life complicated and often contentious, but they also give us, in the words of ethics scholar Ronald C. Arnett, "a base from which we can practically pursue truth together in the midst of difficult and uneasy answers in a complex and ideologically diverse human community."[6]

Part 2
Fundamentals

Whenever you speak to a group of people—whether it's an introductory speech to your classmates, a presentation to colleagues about a new policy, a toast at a friend's wedding, or prepared remarks at a town council meeting—you should be aware of three fundamental elements: yourself, as the SPEAKER; your listeners, as the AUDIENCE; and your PURPOSE. The other elements of the rhetorical situation are important, of course, but these three are fundamental—the beating heart of any speaking occasion. The following chapters focus on these elements and will help you make strategic decisions about a presentation before and as you speak.

Fundamentals

2.1 Speaker

When you write something to be read by other people—an essay, a short story, or a report—the words on the page are front and center. But when you speak to an audience, *you*, the speaker, are the focus of attention. Whether you address a handful of people or thousands, your audience will respond to you—your gestures, tone of voice, and personality—as much as they will evaluate the content of your message.

An Effective Speaker's Core Values

Great speakers connect with their audiences in a genuine way. When audience members believe that they're listening to a person whom they trust and with whom they feel a connection, they are much more likely to listen with interest and understanding.

There is no set formula or list of dos and don'ts that will make an audience believe and trust you. It's a lot like making new friends or being a good coworker or team member. Do these things happen in a predictable, step-by-step fashion, as if you're following the instructions in a user's manual? No, of course not. Even so, speakers who succeed in making a genuine connection with audience members are guided by the following core values.

Honest Self-Awareness

To be an effective speaker, you must first have a realistic understanding of who you are: your personality, your interests, your passions, your values, your capabilities (and limitations), and your knowledge. The ancient Greek aphorism "Know thyself!" is an important reminder for every speaker. If you begin with genuine self-knowledge, you will be well on your way to being an authentic speaker—and authenticity is key to winning an audience's trust.

● getting started   ▶ delivery   ◆ speaking to persuade

▲ fundamentals   ⁚⁚ engaging your audience   ★ speaking occasions

▮ content   ▼ speaking to inform   ✳ resources

Armed with a good sense of yourself, you can plan, prepare, and deliver a presentation in ways that reflect who you are. To understand this principle, it's best to consider some negative examples. If you don't care about your **TOPIC**, your presentation may come across as impersonal and insincere. If you're a naturally shy and quiet person, an attempt to perform a more extroverted personality in front of an audience will—unless you have a special talent for acting—probably fall flat or look incredibly awkward. If you don't know much about a topic but still give a talk about it, your audience will resent having their time wasted—especially people who figure out that they know more about the topic than you do. Matching your message to who you are will make you more comfortable as a speaker and will make your audience more comfortable with you.

105–13

A Belief in the Message

Effective speakers genuinely believe they have something worth saying—that their words matter and that they will deliver something of value to their listeners. They want their audience to learn something important, modify their viewpoints in a beneficial way, and/or be inspired to do something meaningful as a result of what they have heard.

A commitment to your audience affects their perception of you. If audience members see your **PURPOSE** as focused on sharing something meaningful with them, your presentation is more likely to have a positive impact. If you appear to be motivated by a private agenda that doesn't address your audience's needs, your listeners won't see you as credible or trustworthy, and your presentation won't be effective.

87–101

An Openness to Feedback

Effective speakers are open to others' responses to their presentations. Those responses can take the form of honest **FEEDBACK** from a trusted friend during preparation and **PRACTICE**, or they can happen during a presentation as an audience shows signs of interest, agreement, and encouragement—or boredom, annoyance, and confusion. Attentive speakers see feedback as an opportunity to understand themselves even better, improve aspects of the presentation they can control, and empathize and meaningfully connect with their audience.

33–34
232–33

● getting started   ▶ delivery   ◆ speaking to persuade

▲ fundamentals   ∴ engaging your audience   ★ speaking occasions

■ content   ◥ speaking to inform   ✳ resources

A Commitment to Ethical Communication

Ethical speakers epitomize truthfulness, fairness, responsibility, and respect for others. They are also committed to **FREEDOM OF SPEECH** and to being fair and open minded about differences and disagreements. Committing to ethical communication isn't just about doing the right thing; it also enhances your credibility. Seen from the opposite point of view, one unethical comment or presentation can diminish your credibility and negatively affect the way an audience sees you in all future encounters.

48–50

These core values provide a solid foundation for everything else you do to develop your speaking skills. They're also an important reminder that even before you start planning a presentation, you should approach the act of speaking with a serious commitment to being a *good* speaker. In the first century CE, the Roman rhetorician Quintilian suggested that the ideal speaker is a *good person speaking well*. This simple, noteworthy phrase claims that a good speaker is both effective and ethical—both good at speaking and good at heart. Before Quintilian, the philosopher Aristotle wrote in his *Rhetoric* about the importance of *ethos*—a Greek word meaning "character"—to a speaker's success. For Aristotle, this word encompasses skill as well as good moral character. Today, communication scholars study the two dimensions of Quintilian's good person speaking well: **ETHICS** and speaker credibility. This chapter primarily focuses on the second concept.

39–51

The Dimensions of Speaker Credibility

Speaker credibility is the extent to which an audience trusts you and believes what you say. Listeners pay more attention to, remember more from, and are more likely to agree with presentations by speakers they perceive as credible.

Note that credibility isn't something you possess. Instead, it is a perception that others have of you. Just because you think that you are credible doesn't mean that people in your audience see you that way. As a speaker, you can try to shape people's perceptions of your credibility. Whether or not members of your audience perceive you as credible, though, is up to them.

Speakers often enter a room with some degree of credibility. Your classmates, coworkers, and friends, for example, may have known you for a while by the time you make a presentation. What you have done and said before that point will have already shaped your credibility. On some occasions, a speaker's credibility may be established or strengthened when someone **INTRODUCES THE SPEAKER**. Other speakers have a good reputation that precedes them, thus establishing their credibility before they speak. Whether or not people know you beforehand, you can't help but influence the audience's sense of your credibility once you begin speaking.

414–20 ★

Four significant dimensions of speaker credibility affect the way audience members perceive you and your effectiveness: *competence, trustworthiness, likability,* and *dynamism.*

Competence

The first dimension of credibility, **competence**, refers to a speaker's perceived expertise and abilities. Competent speakers are seen as well prepared, knowledgeable, and qualified to speak on their topic.

If a speaker is a recognized chef, renowned brain surgeon, celebrated musician, or professional athlete—in short, a person famous for some particular talent or pursuit—an audience is likely to see that speaker as competent as long as they speak about topics within their areas of expertise. Unfortunately, most of us can't rely on fame or renown to demonstrate our competence. In fact, in college courses, we often can't even count on being assigned a topic we know well.

105–13 ■

For those of us whose reputations don't precede us and who don't have the luxury of **CHOOSING A TOPIC** we like or know best, how can we demonstrate to our audience that we are qualified to speak? Use the strategies that follow to demonstrate your competence.

Research Your Subject To demonstrate your competence, you should be knowledgeable about your topic. Research is how you acquire that knowledge. Doing research can be a serious and intense process of reading, writing, and thinking, but it doesn't always need to be. Sometimes it can be as simple as considering what you already know about a subject and what you can learn from people in your life. It's not realistic to know everything about a topic, nor will your audience expect you to, but you should know enough to assure your audience that you have done your homework.

Wise presenters start their research as soon as they know they are scheduled to speak. If you cram your research and planning into the day immediately before a presentation, especially if you are speaking on a topic that isn't familiar, you won't be adequately prepared. As a result, it's possible that your audience may decide you are not credible.

Plan for Questions Perceptions of your competence are often determined by how well you answer audience questions during and at the end of a presentation. Studies suggest that audience evaluations of a speaker are significantly and positively affected by how well the speaker responds to questions and objections.[1] Even if your presentation does not go as well as you planned, an engaging **QUESTION-AND-ANSWER SESSION** can restore an audience's sense of your competence and credibility.

★ 468–78

Use Expert Language If the subject of your talk is new to you, it's not realistic to try to learn everything about it. Instead, focus on a few of the most important concepts and terms that experts in the subject area use frequently. Practice talking about the subject informally with friends or family using this expert language so you'll feel comfortable with the content. When you finally give your presentation, using this language and explaining these concepts in a manner that seems natural and well informed will enhance your perceived competence and credibility. But don't overdo it or your audience will get lost in specialized jargon. As always, think of your audience. Will they know that *starboard* is the right side of a ship when facing forward? Will they know the exact meaning of *microbe*, *meme*, or *meunière*? When in doubt, define the specialized terms you use. Audience members who already know the meaning of these words will feel like experts, and those who don't will have learned a new and useful term.

Share Interesting (Even Surprising) Facts As any good tour guide knows, peppering your talk with a handful of less well known facts can leave an audience impressed with your depth of knowledge, even if you aren't an expert. When audience members think to themselves, "I didn't know that!" you've enhanced your credibility. Consider the following example from a presentation about Christmas:

> Everyone knows what Christmas is, right? It's the annual festival celebrating the birth of Jesus Christ in Bethlehem that is observed as a religious commemoration by billions of Christians around the world. But here are some interesting facts about Christmas you may not know. First, nobody knows when Jesus was born. In fact, for hundreds of years, nobody really cared about the particular date of his birth. December 25 wasn't officially adopted as Jesus's birthday until more than three hundred years after his death! Why December 25? Well, the primary reason was because Christians in the fourth century made it their mission to substitute Christian holidays for pagan celebrations, and one of the most important ones was December 25—the traditional date when pagans celebrated the winter solstice. Did you know that the Christmas tree wasn't popularized until the Victorian era in England? The Victorians celebrated with a Christmas tree and a bunch of other homey traditions we now associate with Christmas in order to replace raucous holiday drinking, which was the norm before the nineteenth century, with family-oriented activities.

Audience members may learn something new about the adopted date of Jesus's birth or about the origins of the familiar tradition of displaying a Christmas tree. Having these sorts of "aha" moments is a pleasurable experience for most listeners and may lead them to see the speaker as knowledgeable and competent.

Highlight Your Experiences You may not be an expert or have deep knowledge of your topic, but perhaps you have some direct experience with it.

253–67 ⋰ Including a personal observation or telling a **STORY** that supports your purpose can enhance the audience's perception of your competence.

Explain How You Learned What You Know If you don't have firsthand experience or cannot claim to be an expert, let the audience know what efforts you made to be well prepared. For example: "After reviewing a dozen textbooks on this subject published during the last five years, I was surprised to learn that none of the authors addressed . . ." or "I spoke, in person, to all five of our county commissioners. They all agree that . . ."

Cite Reputable Sources Our ever-increasing access to information and opinions also increases our exposure to unreliable and biased sources. Think critically about your supporting materials. **EVALUATE YOUR SOURCES** for reliability and accuracy, and use only information and opinions that you are confident will be perceived as valid, up to date, reputable, and relevant by your audience. Also, when making your presentation, **CITE YOUR SOURCES** in plainspoken language; this will also enhance your perceived competence.

120–30

130–32

Practice Your Delivery and Project Confidence If you hesitate as you speak, shuffle through your notes looking for a piece of information, or stumble over terminology, audience members may doubt your competence. Speakers with strong **VOCAL** and **PHYSICAL DELIVERY** are more likely to feel confident and be seen by their audience as highly competent. To most listeners, confidence implies competence. **PRACTICE** your presentation until you are confident in your delivery.

194–209
210–19
220–33

Trustworthiness

As a speaker, are you fair, honest, and reliable? When you present an argument, is your evidence unbiased and your conclusion justified? If your audience's answer to these questions is yes, then they will perceive you to be a trustworthy speaker. An audience's perception of your **trustworthiness**—your perceived honesty, integrity, and good character—is the mirror image of your commitment to being an **ETHICAL SPEAKER**. When you demonstrate ethical choices as a speaker, you are taking the necessary steps to earn your audience's trust. When you don't, listeners won't believe what you say, or they will have doubts about you and your message.

42

And if your listeners don't trust you, it won't matter that you are an international expert, or that you have prepared thoroughly, or that you are a technically skilled speaker. Perceived competence in your subject and obvious oratorical skill won't make up for an impression among your listeners that you are untrustworthy or dishonest.

Employing the following strategies can enhance an audience's perception of your trustworthiness.

Have a Reputation for Reliability People trust people who are reliable. If you are often late for class or your job, or if you fail to meet your obligations to your classmates or coworkers in other ways, they may not trust you as much as you wish when it's your turn to give a presentation. So you should cultivate a reputation for reliability—be on time, follow through on your commitments, and do what you say you're going to do. In situations where your reputation precedes you—in class, in the workplace, in small communities of all sorts—having a reputation for reliability will lead listeners to trust you when you speak.

383–84 ◆

Respect Different Viewpoints Presenting an argument that accurately and fairly summarizes both your own perspective and **OPPOSING VIEWPOINTS** demonstrates that you're not just focused on "winning" but that you have also thought carefully about the issue. By raising both the good and bad about what you are discussing, listeners are likely to appreciate your balanced approach, and you are more likely to be perceived as trustworthy as a result.

Acknowledge Inconvenient Truths When presenting your own perspective on an issue, it's tempting to ignore or downplay facts that may complicate or contradict your message. But if these facts are known to your audience, you can be sure that your listeners will interpret your failure to mention them as a sign that you aren't trustworthy. Trustworthy speakers find ways to make the most common or well-known inconvenient truths part of their presentations rather than attempting to keep them out of the discussion altogether. For example, a Republican speaker might remind colleagues that some of the largest budget deficits have occurred during Republican administrations because, in part, Republicans didn't stay true to the party's core value of fiscal responsibility. Doing this not only has the advantage of keeping your listeners interested (because it is unexpected), but it also shows that you are honest and worthy of their trust.

Likability

Are you someone your listeners would like to know? When you interact with audience members before, during, and after speaking, are you friendly, warm, and empathetic? If so, you are demonstrating the qualities of **likability**. Think about how likability affects your everyday life. If people show you compassion, support, and genuine sympathy when you are grieving or facing a serious problem, or even if they simply do small things to show you that they care about you, don't you feel gratitude and fondness for them? Aren't you inspired to invest more time in your relationships with them, listen to them more attentively, and care about what they say, think, and feel? A similar dynamic applies when audiences perceive a speaker to be likable.

Unfortunately, likability presents challenges for some speakers. For example, if you are a person who is reserved, quiet, and private, you might worry that only extroverts—people who are talkative, assertive, and outgoing—are perceived as likable. But that simply isn't true. Being likable is not the same as being an extrovert. If you are an introvert, you can enhance your likability by other means. You can demonstrate your empathy, kindness, and concern for others in a manner that feels natural to you. Likability is not about changing your personality; it's about being **AUDIENCE CENTERED** in a manner that is true to who you are.

  70–72

For an example of a self-described introvert who is nonetheless a likable and successful speaker, see Notable Speaker: Susan Cain, page 176.

Likability is also often a challenge for female speakers. Think about the women who have been candidates for the US presidency. Many voters did not like them even though they were well qualified and highly competent. Part of the problem is that a woman who is assertive and highly confident (a necessity in competitive political campaigns) violates stereotypical expectations about how women should behave. It is a special challenge for female speakers to come across as both competent and likable. They must communicate warmth, empathy, **EFFECTIVE LISTENING**, **HUMOR**, sociability, and sensitivity to be seen as likable and, at the same time, demonstrate their strength of character and expertise—a tall order for any speaker.

Fortunately, there are a few ways to enhance your likability.

Ask Questions Posing well-chosen questions can be a powerful means of enhancing your likability.[2] When you ask a good question, you communicate to your audience that you are interested in what they know, believe, and care about. **GOOD QUESTIONS** demonstrate respect for the audience and a sincere desire to listen to and adapt to their answers.

Project Friendliness and Openness to Audience Members Some speakers unintentionally allow their **SPEAKING ANXIETY** to overshadow their interactions with listeners. If you give audience members the impression that you are distant or anxious, you may diminish your overall credibility. Instead of worrying about nervousness, smile, interact, and be friendly and approachable with audience members before, during, and after your presentation. You'll find that most listeners reflect that positive energy right back at you.

Be Different—in a Good Way Going against the grain (in an intriguing, nonthreatening way) often makes listeners want to learn more about a speaker. Were you the only one in your high-school class to play the tuba? What was that like? Have you abandoned watching television or using social media? Tell us why, without making us feel attacked for still doing these things. Whatever makes you different from others, consider making that difference a part of your presentation. Doing so increases the chances that your listeners will perceive you as someone they want to know better, which they can do only if they give you their attention.

Tell a Story about Overcoming Adversity Everyone loves to root for the underdog. Telling a personal **STORY** about a serious setback that you've faced—a chronic illness, discrimination, job loss, failure at school, the death of someone close to you—can, if it is appropriate for your message, greatly increase your audience's sympathy for and interest in you. If a story of

30–31
272–75

276–77

15–27

253–67

● getting started
▲ fundamentals
■ content

▶ delivery
∴ engaging your audience
◣ speaking to inform

◆ speaking to persuade
★ speaking occasions
✻ resources

adversity in your own life isn't quite right for the occasion, telling another person's story can both arouse audience sympathy for that person and cause them to see you as more compassionate and likable.

For an example of a speaker who exemplifies most of these principles of likability, see Notable Speaker: Ashton Kutcher, page 156.

Demonstrate Empathy As you engage with your audience, send them signals both through your words and through your nonverbal behavior that show your concerns about their needs. In the stories you tell, show how you understand the characters' feelings and perspectives. All this adds up to an impression that you are comfortable with "perspective taking"—with seeing the world through other people's eyes—and are not merely self-centered or self-serving.

Respect Those Who Disagree Make it clear that despite your differences with another person's perspective on a certain issue, you can be respectful and empathetic. This shows your listeners that you are open to finding **COMMON GROUND**, even as you stake out your own claims—an extremely likable character trait. Barack Obama, after winning his second presidential term in 2012, had this to say about his opponent, Mitt Romney:

▲ 71

> We may have battled fiercely, but it's only because we love this country deeply and we care so strongly about its future. From George to Lenore to their son Mitt, the Romney family has chosen to give back to America through public service and that is the legacy that we honor and applaud tonight. In the weeks ahead, I also look forward to sitting down with Governor Romney to talk about where we can work together to move this country forward.[3]

If you want to be seen as likable in the eyes of your audience, don't fake concern or empathy if you don't feel it yourself. While the above strategies can help shape your audience's opinion of you, they can only do so if they are genuine. If you playact likability, your efforts will probably fail.

Dynamism

275–76

Great speakers are usually dynamic speakers. **Dynamism** is the ability to motivate and **ENGAGE AUDIENCES** with a high level of energy, enthusiasm, vigor, and commitment; arouse listeners' emotions; and inspire them. Put another way, dynamism is the transfer of enthusiasm and passion from you to your audience.

Dynamism often has more to do with how you deliver a presentation than what you say. Planning and practicing your delivery can improve your dynamism in the same way that thorough preparation can help you become a more competent speaker. Here are several ways to demonstrate dynamism:

194–209
210–19

- Be enthusiastic and animated as you speak. Use both your **VOICE** and your **BODY** to communicate excitement.
- Be assertive about what you say, but balance that with a sense of humility and good humor about yourself.

184–85
210–12

- Radiate **CONFIDENCE** and optimism.
- Establish and maintain **EYE CONTACT** with audience members.

Can a speaker overdo dynamism? Of course. In fact, some speakers have too much energy and intensity—so much that they overwhelm and exhaust an audience. A gentle speaker who is competent, trusted, and likable may be more successful than an overly dynamic one. Nevertheless, there is no question that in many rhetorical situations a dynamic speaker can motivate thousands of people.

THE DIMENSIONS OF SPEAKER CREDIBILITY

Competence	Trustworthiness	Likability	Dynamism
• Experienced	• Ethical	• Kind	• Energetic
• Well prepared	• Honest	• Friendly	• Confident
• Qualified	• Fair	• Warm	• Stimulating
• Up to date	• Respectful	• Empathetic	• Bold
• Knowledgeable	• Reliable	• Sociable	• Assertive

⬤ getting started	▷ delivery	◆ speaking to persuade
▲ fundamentals	⁑ engaging your audience	★ speaking occasions
▪ content	▼ speaking to inform	✳ resources

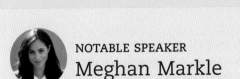

NOTABLE SPEAKER
Meghan Markle

Actress and humanitarian Meghan Markle became a UN Women's Advocate for Women's Political Participation and Leadership in 2015. In this role, Markle has focused on ways to empower women throughout the world to become leaders in their communities. In her speech at the UN Women's Conference in 2015, she encouraged the world community to embrace equality for women.

Search Terms
To locate a video of this presentation online, enter the following key words into a search engine: Meghan Markle UN speech. The video is approximately 9:41 in length.

What to Watch For
[0:00–0:50] At the beginning of her speech, Markle conveys her appreciation for the opportunity to serve in the role of UN Women's Advocate for Women's Political Participation and Leadership. Her nonverbal communication conveys warmth, particularly as she touches her heart to express gratitude for the invitation to speak. She then offers an honest awareness of who she is by telling the audience "I am proud to be a woman and a feminist."

[1:15–4:45] Markle tells a story about seeing a commercial when she was in elementary school that promoted dishwashing soap only to women. She recalls feeling shocked, angry, and hurt when two of her male classmates responded to the commercial by saying that women belong in the kitchen. She uses the story to make a point about what it means to stand up for equality. Markle's use of a personal story highlights her experience and helps establish her competence, trustworthiness, and likability.

(NOTABLE SPEAKER CONTINUED)

[3:35–3:45] To further enhance her likability, Markle smiles frequently and appropriately, uses a sincere tone of voice, and maintains eye contact even though she is using a teleprompter. Despite the appearance of red splotches on her chest and neck, which may indicate she is anxious, Markle continues to engage the audience and show how deeply she cares about the participation of women in their communities and government.

[5:45–6:35] To establish her competence beyond her own personal experience, Markle cites statistics about gender inequality and the slow rise of female parliamentarians around the world. Doing so, she demonstrates that she has researched and thought seriously about the subject matter. By offering a heartfelt and directed "Come on!" in reaction to the statistics and examples, Markle demonstrates her belief that what she is speaking about matters.

EXERCISE

After viewing Markle's speech, reflect on these questions:

1. Which core value(s) of an effective speaker does Markle demonstrate most effectively?

2. Would Markle have seemed less authentic if she hadn't told the story about her fight to get Procter & Gamble to change its marketing slogan?

3. To what extent does Markle's marriage to Prince Harry and their relationship to the royal family affect your reactions to this 2015 speech?

4. How does Markle demonstrate that she cares about this topic? How does Markle demonstrate empathy throughout the speech?

5. Is Markle a dynamic speaker? Why or why not?

6. Before hearing her speak, what was your perception of Markle's credibility regarding women's rights? Did it change after hearing the speech? If so, why?

Conclusion

Effective speakers who make a genuine connection with audience members are guided by several core values and qualities. They have an accurate assessment of who they are, a genuine commitment to share what they think and know with an audience, and a belief that their messages matter. They also have a strong commitment to communicate openly, responsibly, and ethically.

Guided by core values, effective speakers also know that their credibility depends on audience perceptions of their competence, trustworthiness, likability, and dynamism. The strategies and skills described in this chapter can enhance the extent to which audience members believe, trust, like, and appreciate you and your message. With responsible planning and practice, you can shape people's perceptions of your credibility in a way that accurately and positively reflects who you are.

2.2 Audience

A presentation is effective only when you, the speaker, and the people to whom you are speaking (your **audience**) connect in a meaningful way. Your success or failure as a speaker is determined by the quality of that relationship and by the extent to which you and your audience share an understanding of your message.

If members of your audience are better informed about a topic than they were before you spoke, if they are entertained or moved by what you said, if they are persuaded to modify their attitudes, or if they are inspired to reexamine or change an aspect of their lives after listening to you, you can claim success.

In this respect, a presentation to an audience is similar to many other forms of speech communication—including one-on-one conversations and small-group discussions. In your day-to-day life, your ability to communicate with friends, family, coworkers, and acquaintances depends on how well you understand their points of view, how well you adapt to their feedback, and how well you connect with them.

The Central Importance of Your Audience

In some forms of artistic performance—dance, for example—a performer often makes the strongest impression if she delves deeply into herself, enters a trancelike "flow," and puts the audience temporarily out of her mind. But most forms of communication, including presentations to an audience, don't work that way. Speakers must do more than be aware of their audience. They must put the audience at the center of attention in their presentation. This is true at every stage of the speechmaking process—from the moment you decide or are asked to speak, through the various stages of preparation and **PRACTICE**, and even while you deliver the presentation.

228–33 ▶

● getting started	▶ delivery	◆ speaking to persuade
▲ fundamentals	⁂ engaging your audience	★ speaking occasions
■ content	▼ speaking to inform	✳ resources

Audience-centered speakers strive to understand and adapt to audience characteristics and interests, think critically about listeners' points of view, and empathize with listeners' motivations and needs. You can achieve these goals by employing the following three strategies.

Seek Common Ground

Audience-centered speakers look for **common ground**, the values and beliefs they share with their audience. Finding and standing on common ground with your audience builds rapport and establishes trust. When thinking about an audience's likely attitude toward a topic or message, audience-centered speakers look for ways to change negative attitudes into positive ones by identifying and appealing to the things they have in common with their listeners.

Respect Differences

Although they seek common ground, audience-centered speakers avoid making overly broad assumptions about an audience's values, beliefs, and attitudes. They are also alert to and respectful of differences between themselves and the audience, as well as the differences among various audience members. Rather than seeing a **DIVERSE AUDIENCE** as an obstacle to overcome, audience-centered speakers welcome diversity as a chance to learn about, adapt to, and communicate with people different from themselves.

◆ 391–92

Respect for differences is not about avoiding offensive remarks—something you certainly should always do. Instead, it is about ensuring that your presentation is as inclusive as possible. Most audience members will feel that an inclusive presentation is addressed to them and offers them something of value—whether it's the latest information, a new perspective, or the motivation to change their behavior.

Be Mindful of and Responsive to Feedback

The concept of *mindfulness* encapsulates a core principle of audience-centered speaking. Mindful speakers are fully present—aware of where they are, what they're doing, what they are saying, and to whom they are saying it. They are also sensitive to and able to adapt to audience feedback.

When speakers are mindful, they focus on the audience—not on themselves. Audience-centered speakers sincerely believe that what they say (their message) and what they're trying to achieve (their **PURPOSE**) will benefit their listeners. Instead of worrying about how they are being judged, they focus on whether or not they are being understood.

87–101

Audience Analysis

Developing a deeper understanding of your audience requires **audience analysis**—the work you do to understand, respect, and adapt to listeners before and during a presentation. A thoughtful analysis of your audience and their likely responses can help you plan what to say and how to say it in a manner likely to achieve your purpose.

110–11

Audience analysis has practical advantages that help you achieve your purpose. For instance, an understanding of your audience can help you choose, focus, and narrow your **TOPIC**, thus simplifying and shortening your preparation time. It can also help you feel more confident when you finally address your audience because, in a sense, you have become fairly well acquainted with them. Most of us feel a little nervous when we meet new people whose attitudes, values, and beliefs aren't yet known to us, so having some sense of an unfamiliar audience can take the edge off this aspect of **SPEAKING ANXIETY**. Just as in a one-on-one conversation with someone new, knowing what common ground you share with your audience and how you differ can lead to shared understanding.

15–27

Finally, understanding your audience and adapting your presentation to them will significantly increase the likelihood that audience members will be engaged and interested in what you have to say. If they sense that you have planned your presentation with them foremost in your mind and that you are adapting to them as you speak, your audience will much more likely care about and connect with you and your message.

There are, however, rhetorical situations in which you cannot analyze or adapt to every person in an audience. And if you try to please everyone all the time, you'll probably please no one (including yourself) because your message may acquire the consistency of bland pudding. Instead, audience analysis can help you direct your message toward a significant portion of your audience or to key decision makers and people with influence—in other words, to your **target audience**.

Inevitably, some audience members will be spectators to the interactions between you and a target audience. Although these audience members may be less interested or less motivated than your target audience, if you plan and prepare your presentation well, you can successfully connect with a target audience without losing the rest of your listeners.

Regardless of the methods you use to gather information about your listeners (such as conducting a SURVEY), audience analysis should answer several critical questions:

✳ 493–510

- Who are they?
- Why are they here?
- What do they know?
- What are their interests?
- What are their attitudes?
- What are their values?

Who Are They?

When accomplished speakers are required or invited to make a presentation, one of the first questions they ask is "Who will be in the audience?" They are not asking for the names of their listeners. Rather, they are looking for **demographic information** about the audience. Often misunderstood as limited to legalistic categories such as race, age, gender, ethnicity, nationality, religion, and citizen status, demographic information also includes data about occupations, places and types of residence, income, educational levels, political perspectives, organizational affiliations, and social standing, among other things.

Audience analysis begins by researching and gathering information about the characteristics of your audience, interpreting those findings, and selecting appropriate strategies for connecting with that audience. It also requires thinking critically about how audience characteristics may influence the purpose, content, and delivery of your presentation.

Consider the characteristics that bind members of your audience together. Do most of them represent a major demographic group (for example, female or young adult)? Do they share a profession or occupation (for example, accountants, truck drivers, or teachers)? What else do they have in common? Are they all taking the same class? Do most of them have children? Do they own or manage local businesses? Do they work together? Were they alive when an important historical event occurred? Do they all call the same place, town, state, or country "home"?

If, for example, your audience is made up entirely of college students, you can assume that most or all of them believe in the value of education because it requires a considerable investment of money and time—both of which are literally valuable. If you're speaking to a Baptist youth group, it's safe to assume that members of your audience will know more about and have a more favorable attitude toward the Christian Bible than the Hindu Vedas. If most members of your audience were born before 1990, you can be reasonably sure that they have some memory of the terrorist attacks on September 11, 2001. All these are assumptions about your audience that can shape what you say and how you say it.

Of course, people in your audience may share a single demographic characteristic that isn't particularly relevant to the occasion or the topic of your presentation. If you're commemorating an exceptional athlete at an end-of-season banquet for the women's basketball team, is the gender of your audience the most relevant factor? What about the sport that they all play? Or the fact that they are all student athletes? Or that their parents are attending? These other characteristics of your audience may play a bigger role in shaping your presentation than their gender does.

As valuable as demographic information can be, it's important to recognize that every audience is made up of individuals with unique characteristics, motivations, values, and backgrounds. Avoid a "one size fits all" picture of your audience. You may see obvious surface similarities among them—such as their age, race, gender, and even appearance and style of dress—but if you stop there and fail to ask other questions, you will risk

stereotyping your audience, which may lead to mistaken conclusions about their knowledge, attitude, and values.

Why Are They Here?

As much as you may want your audience to be there because they are interested in you and your presentation, this is not always or even usually the case. Discovering answers to the question "Why are they here?" can help you meet your audience where *they* are rather than where *you* are.

Audience members who are interested in your **TOPIC** or who stand to benefit from attending a presentation will be quite different from those who don't know why they are there or who are required to attend. Consider the following reasons for attending a presentation:

108–10

Reason for attending	Example
They are interested in the topic.	Civil War buffs who attend a talk about the 1862 Battle of Pea Ridge
They are interested in the speaker.	Fans of a political candidate, a celebrity, or other well-known public figure
They will be rewarded for attending.	Members of a professional organization who will receive job certification credits
They always attend.	Members of a service club that meets regularly
They are required to attend.	A required class; a mandatory training session

Each reason for attending presents a special challenge for a speaker. For example, a highly interested and well-informed audience demands a knowledgeable, well-prepared, **COMPETENT** speaker. A speaker who appears to know less about the subject than the attendees will bore them; one who appears unprepared will annoy them. On the other hand, an audience that is required or reluctant to attend a presentation may be pleasantly surprised by a **DYNAMIC** speaker who makes a special effort to engage them.

58–61

66

What Do They Know?

Figuring out what audience members know about your topic is an important step in determining what to include in your presentation. Here are some questions to ask about your listeners: Will they understand my vocabulary and specific, topic-related terminology or jargon? Have they heard any of this before? Based on what I now know, how much background material should I cover?

If you answer these questions accurately, your content will match your audience's level of understanding and knowledge. If you haven't thought about these questions, your audience may become confused or bored. On the one hand, if your audience knows very little about your topic, you shouldn't use a specialized vocabulary or shorthand explanations. For example, a student who had worked as a crew member on a cruise ship wouldn't describe his experience to his classmates by using words such as *stern, aft, starboard, port, knots,* and *tenders* without explaining what these specialized terms mean. On the other hand, if he were to make the same presentation to members of a yacht club, they would probably be frustrated and even insulted if he stopped to explain each of those words.

What Are Their Interests?

Answering questions about your audience such as *Who are they?*, *Why are they here?*, and *What do they know?* can also help you gauge your audience's interests. There are two types of audience interests: **self-centered interests** and **topic-centered interests**.

Self-Centered Interests Self-centered interests are focused on personal gain or loss. For example, a political candidate's position on tax increases can result in more or fewer taxes for audience members. A talk by a personnel director can provide information about how to get a more desirable job. A presentation by a classmate about how to change a tire may help every student who drives a car. In all these cases, the listener stands to lose or gain something as a result of the presentation or its outcome.

● getting started   ▶ delivery   ◆ speaking to persuade
▲ fundamentals   ⁙ engaging your audience ★ speaking occasions
■ content   ▼ speaking to inform   ✳ resources

WIIFT ("WIF-it") is a popular acronym used in sales training that stands for the question "What's in it for them?" It's a way of reminding salespeople to focus on customer characteristics, needs, interests, attitudes, and values rather than on WIIFM ("What's in it for me?"). Speakers should also keep WIIFT in mind. Why should this audience listen to me? What do they want? What do I have to offer them? If your audience sees no reason to listen, they won't.

Inexperienced speakers sometimes assume that merely pointing out that something is the case will be enough to help the audience see WIIFT. But it's not. You must show them how your message can lead to a benefit that is important to them. Help them understand what's in it for them, or they won't invest their attention in your message.

Topic-Centered Interests Audience members also have topic-centered interests—subjects they enjoy hearing and learning about. Topic-centered interests can include hobbies, favorite sports or pastimes, or subjects loaded with intrigue and mystery. However, topic-centered interests often tend to be personal. A detailed description of the battle at Gettysburg may captivate Civil War buffs in the audience but not other listeners. A presentation on a new approach to management may intrigue those who enjoy management theory but turn off the hands-on administrators who find such theories restrictive and impractical.

What Are Their Attitudes?

When you think about **audience attitudes**, you are thinking about whether the people in your audience agree or disagree with your position, how strongly they agree or disagree, and what you can do to influence their opinions and/or behavior.

There can be as many opinions in your audience as there are people. Some audience members will already agree with you before you begin to speak. Others will disagree no matter what you say. Some audience members will be neutral or have no opinion. But if you've already thought about other aspects of your audience—who they are, what they know, and what their interests are—you may be able to predict what attitudes many audience members will bring with them to your presentation.

Suppose a speaker wants to persuade an audience that imposing longer jail sentences will deter crime. Consider the following spectrum of audience opinions:

AUDIENCE ATTITUDES: "LONGER JAIL SENTENCES WILL DETER CRIMES."

Strongly agree	Agree	Undecided	Disagree	Strongly disagree
If criminals know they won't be back on the streets in a short period of time, longer jail sentences will deter them and reduce crime.	Because criminals are often released before they have served their sentences, longer jail sentences may help deter and reduce crime.	There are good, strong reasons on both sides of the issue. *or* I don't know or care very much about this issue.	Because longer jail sentences cost more and are unfairly given to poor and minority defendants, these sentences may not be a fair or wise course of action.	Longer jail sentences do not deter or reduce crime; they only create more hardened and dangerous criminals.

Once you determine whether and how many audience members are inclined to agree with you, disagree with you, or have no preconceived attitude about your topic, you may want to start matching **PERSUASIVE SPEAKING** strategies to audience attitudes. But before you do that, keep in mind that even when audience members share the same attitude about an issue, there can be many different reasons for that shared opinion. For example, audience members who oppose longer jail sentences may do so for various reasons. Perhaps they feel that jails are too crowded or lack proper funding. Or they might think rehabilitation is more important than punishment. When analyzing your audience's attitudes, think critically about *why* various audience members may have similar attitudes for different reasons.

382–404 ◆

● getting started   ▶ delivery   ◆ speaking to persuade
▲ fundamentals   ∴ engaging your audience ★ speaking occasions
■ content   ♥ speaking to inform   ✳ resources

What Are Their Values?

Values are the basic standards that guide and motivate our beliefs and actions. When analyzing an audience's values, we consider the ideas and ideals that are fundamental to their lives—the principles that provide the foundation for everything they feel and do.

Universal Values We can safely assume that some values are universal: love, honesty, responsibility, respect, fairness, freedom, and compassion.[1]

An appeal to universal values will be welcomed by most audiences, no matter who they are or where they come from. The challenge is identifying the primary values of audience members that are more likely to affect them directly and to adapt your presentation to appeal to those values—without, of course, sacrificing your own.

Cultural Values Other values are particular to a cultural or organizational context. For example, the Latin phrase *semper fidelis* (always faithful) has long stood for the core value of the US Marine Corps, an expectation that all marines will "remain faithful . . . to Corps and to country, no matter what." Contrast this with the Society of Professional Journalists' Code of Ethics, the first principle of which is "Seek truth and report it." You can probably see how speaking to an audience of marines might be different from speaking to an audience of journalists on the same topic.

For many years, researchers have looked for distinct cultural values that characterize an aspect of a culture that can be described and measured relative to other cultures.[2] One such value that has endured is the degree of individualism or collectivism that is common to most members of a culture. **Individualism-collectivism** describes end points on a continuum from a preference for independence, on one end, to interdependence, on the other. Many people in highly individualistic cultures (the United States, Australia, Great Britain, and Canada, for example) value personal achievement, autonomy, and freedom. People in collectivistic cultures (many Latin American and Asian countries, for example) are more likely to value group identity, group harmony, and collective action. Although these generalizations are still broadly accurate, their degree of importance can vary within cultures.

The impacts on communication are clear. Audience members who value individualism may look for ways that a speaker's message can satisfy their personal needs, and they will be more responsive to speakers with an individualistic and confident speaking style. Those who lean more toward collectivist values will consider the ways that a speaker's messages may benefit their group, community, or nation, and they may be put off by speakers who talk about their own accomplishments and the benefits of competition and personal success.

Thinking critically about your audience's cultural orientation on this scale and being alert to the possibility of other audience members tilting in the opposite direction can help you make smart, audience-centered decisions as you plan your presentation.

Adapting Your Message to Your Audience

Now let's look at how the various elements of audience analysis came together to help a student speaker adjust and refine her plans for a presentation. Kate Sebring, a psychology major, chose the topic "the effects of television and video game violence" for her persuasive presentation assignment in a communication course. Before thinking carefully about her audience, she formulated a preliminary goal: "to warn my audience about the harmful effects of television and video game violence." After speaking with several classmates and analyzing what she knew about her audience, she changed her goal to one that she believed would resonate more effectively with her audience. Here is a short overview of that process:

Topic

The effects of television and video game violence

Preliminary Purpose

To warn my audience about the effects of television and video game violence

Audience Analysis

Who are they? The audience is composed of twenty-five college students, most of whom range in age from eighteen to twenty-five. Five are over twenty-five, two of whom are over forty. About half of them have younger siblings or young cousins; a few are parents of young children.

Why are they here? They are in this class because it is a general education requirement. Some of them will be presenting during the same class period, so they may be more focused on their own presentations rather than on listening to me.

What do they know? They have heard concerns about television and video game violence but may not be aware of the respected studies claiming that children are more likely to become aggressive and antisocial from such exposure.

What are their interests? Most of them are mildly interested; those with children or younger siblings are more interested. Those about to make their own presentation may not listen.

What are their attitudes? Some do not believe that television and video game violence is a major problem. The rest have strong opinions one way or the other: some believe that mediated violence is very harmful; others worry that controlling television and video game content would eliminate entertainment they enjoy.

What are their values? Most class members who are not currently parents say that they plan to raise families someday. A few already are parents. Everyone agrees that children should be protected from things that can harm them.

Revised Purpose

To urge listeners to adopt specific measures that significantly reduce children's exposure to the violent television and video games that can make them more aggressive and antisocial. By sharing vivid examples and recommending preventive actions based on recent validated research studies, I hope to gain their attention and change their attitudes and actions.

Notice the changes that Sebring made in her revised purpose. Rather than discussing the general effects of television and video game violence, she focused on how it makes children more aggressive and antisocial. She also decided to use real, vivid examples to capture and maintain audience attention and strong validated studies to support her claims and recommendations.

Audience analysis and adaptation are not over when you've settled on a strong **PURPOSE STATEMENT** and **CENTRAL IDEA**, have fleshed out that purpose with strategic **KEY POINTS** and relevant **SUPPORTING MATERIAL**, and have practiced how you will **DELIVER** your message. Audience analysis and adaptation never stop. You may discover that you need more and better information about your audience. You may also realize that analyzing and adapting to your audience is just as important when you speak as it is when you are preparing.

95–97 △
137–38 ■
133–36 ■
115–19 ■
181–233 ▶

If you need more help

493–510 ✳
See 9.1, **HOW TO SURVEY AN AUDIENCE**, for more detailed advice about how to gather information about (and adapt to) your audience.

NOTABLE SPEAKER
Zach Wahls

In 2011, the Iowa House Judiciary Committee conducted public hearings about a proposed constitutional amendment to ban gay marriage in the state. Zach Wahls, a nineteen-year-old college student and the son of lesbian parents, spoke against the amendment during a public hearing before the committee. His presentation went viral online and attracted national media attention. It also presented him with opportunities to speak to a variety of groups as well as to author a book called *My Two Moms*. Wahls is now a prominent LGBTQ activist, and in 2018 he won the Democratic primary and was subsequently elected to serve in Iowa's State Senate.

Search Terms
To locate a video of this presentation online, enter the following key words into a search engine: Zach Wahls speaks about family. The video is approximately 3:01 in length.

What to Watch For
[0:00–0:10] In his opening, Wahls seeks common ground with his audience by telling them that he is a sixth-generation Iowan and an engineering student at the University of Iowa. In essence, he is one of them—he comes from the same place that they come from and attends a university that some of them likely attended. After establishing that he is an Iowan, Wahls reveals a unique fact about himself: he was raised by two women.

(NOTABLE SPEAKER CONTINUED)

[0:40–1:09] As a mindful speaker, Wahls doesn't ask for special treatment. He is asking to be understood. He emphasizes the normal, everyday values of his lesbian parents by highlighting things that they and his audience share in common, such as joy about a baby being born (love), spending time with family on vacations (relationships), and standing by your family during difficult times (commitment). Based on these shared values, Wahls argues that his family is like any other family because they don't expect other people to solve their problems. What they do expect is to be treated fairly by their government.

[1:10–1:39] Wahls confronts his topic head-on by posing a question that was asked by his classmates and professors at times in some of his classes: Can gay people even raise kids? In response, he highlights how well he has done as a child of same-sex parents. He mentions his various achievements not to elevate himself but instead to demonstrate the good job that his parents have done raising him. He again seeks to establish common ground by noting that the committee chairman would likely be proud of Wahls if Wahls were his son.

[1:40–1:50] Aware that many in the room have no firsthand knowledge about same-sex parenting, Wahls offers that no one has ever independently recognized that he was raised by a gay couple. Returning to common ground, he points out that neither his family nor the committee members' families "derive [their] sense of worth from being told by the state: 'You're married. Congratulations.'"

[2:02–2:30] Offering a reason why his audience should listen to him, Wahls argues that legislators have an opportunity not to write discrimination into the state's constitution. The benefit for his audience is establishing a precedent whereby all Iowans are treated equally—something that Wahls argues is relevant to everyone in the audience.

[2:50–3:00] The last line of his presentation is a summation of his purpose statement. Here he reminds his audience that the sexual orientation of his parents is not related to the content of his character. This idea echoes a famous line from Martin Luther King Jr.'s most famous speech, "I Have a Dream," thus making clear that the issue of marriage equality is as fundamental and important as the civil rights struggles of the 1960s.

EXERCISE

After viewing Wahls's speech, reflect on these questions:

1. What do you think Wahls did before his presentation to prepare to speak to this particular audience?

2. Do you believe that members of his audience were likely to be persuaded by his argument that his family was no different from their families? Why or why not?

3. What else could Wahls have done, if anything, to establish common ground with his audience?

4. How might Wahls answer the questions: "Why are they here?" and "What does my audience believe about gay marriage and families?"

5. Write a purpose statement for Wahls's presentation.

Conclusion

The presence of a living, breathing audience makes presentation speaking different from most other forms of communication. Audiences make presentations unpredictable, potentially anxiety-producing events. They also make speechmaking one of the most personal, exciting, and empowering forms of communication.

The time and energy you spend learning as much as you can about your audience, analyzing what you've learned about their demographics and viewpoints, and then adapting your presentation to them are at the heart of speechmaking. Your analysis helps you seek common ground, respect differences and diversity, and appropriately adapt to feedback.

Audience-centered speakers know who their audience is, how audience members think, what they value, what they want, and what they need. But a sense of your audience doesn't arise automatically or quickly. Like many other aspects of speech preparation, putting time and effort into the audience analysis and adaptation process before and during your presentation makes all the difference.

● getting started   ▶ delivery   ◆ speaking to persuade
▲ fundamentals   ∴ engaging your audience   ★ speaking occasions
■ content   ▼ speaking to inform   ✳ resources

2.3 Purpose

Have you ever attended a presentation where the speaker didn't seem to know or care why they were speaking? How did you feel after listening for a few minutes? Did you lose interest, drift off, wish you were somewhere else, or leave? Why does this happen? Even when the subject is of some interest to an audience and the speaker's delivery is competent, audience members may become uninterested, confused, and irritated if the presentation lacks a clear *purpose*.

Your **purpose** is the outcome you are seeking as the result of making a presentation. Your purpose answers the question "What do I want my audience to know, think, feel, or do as a result of my presentation?" Purpose is not the same as a topic. Your topic is the subject matter of your presentation. Two presentations on the topic of recycling can be quite different if they have opposite purposes. "I want my audience to support recycling as an important environmental policy" is quite different from "Recycling is costly and ineffective as an environmental policy."

The Importance of Purpose

Why, exactly, is it important to have a clear purpose? Don't some speakers "succeed" without knowing ahead of time what they want to accomplish? No, not really. Or rather, very rarely, and probably only when the speaker is a topic expert or a celebrity whose pointless and rambling message the audience will happily endure. But even in these cases, there is probably an underlying purpose to what they're doing—namely, sharing what they know or think with a group of people who are all interested in seeing a speaker whom they revere or admire.

For the rest of us—99.9 percent of the population—giving a purposeless talk isn't a good idea. Speaking without a purpose can be hazardous to your credibility and jeopardize the outcome of your presentation. If you hope to gain audience attention and interest while speaking and want to achieve something meaningful as a result of what you say, you must have a clear purpose. Here are just a few of the reasons why.

Purpose Is the Measure of Speaking Success

When it comes to measuring your success as a speaker, nothing is more fundamental than determining your purpose. When clearly defined, your purpose is quite literally the standard against which your success as a speaker is measured. Without a clear purpose, you cannot know that you have succeeded, because you won't have established your criteria for success.

Purpose Will Help You Make Good Rhetorical Decisions

Without a clear purpose, you will have difficulty making strategic decisions about key elements of the **RHETORICAL SITUATION**—how to prepare for the occasion, establish your **CREDIBILITY**, adapt to your **AUDIENCE**, determine and organize your **CONTENT**, and **DELIVER** your presentation effectively. But if you have a clear purpose, these decisions will fall into place more easily.

5–10
57–66
80–82
103–79
181–233

Purpose Shows Respect for Your Audience

When speakers do not have a clear purpose, they're not only wasting the opportunity they've been given, they're also wasting their audience's time. Regardless of whether you are speaking in a communication course or in the world beyond the classroom, wasting your audience's time is a serious affront and deeply disrespectful. Conversely, having a distinct purpose, and being able to make that purpose clear to your audience, demonstrates to your listeners that you are an **AUDIENCE-CENTERED SPEAKER**—someone whom they can trust to have their best interests in mind, who genuinely seeks to share something of value with them, and who can clearly communicate a meaningful message.

70–72

Purpose Focuses Your Mind and Can Calm Your Nerves

Having a clear purpose also has practical benefits. If you momentarily forget what you're saying, whether because of noise or other distractions, or simply because you're feeling some symptoms of **SPEAKING ANXIETY**,

15–27

● getting started	▶ delivery	◆ speaking to persuade
▲ fundamentals	⁙ engaging your audience	★ speaking occasions
■ content	◣ speaking to inform	✳ resources

a well-defined purpose can get you back on track. Think of your purpose as something like your presentation's North Star—the point of reference that can navigate you back on course when you momentarily lose your way. For apprehensive speakers especially, a clearly defined purpose can make a world of difference.

Purpose Helps You Make the Best Use of Your Time and Energy

As important as it is to plan and prepare a presentation, it's obvious that there's only so much time available to do so. Having a clear purpose from the start helps you manage your preparation time more effectively, allowing you to limit your **RESEARCH** only to material that will directly support your presentation, **ORGANIZE** your thoughts and plan your presentation in an optimal way, and avoid wasting time producing support material and **PRESENTATION AIDS** that you won't end up needing.

111–12
133–59

282–305

Determining Your Purpose

So how do you determine what you want your audience to know, think, feel, or do as a result of your presentation? To make this determination, start by asking yourself *why* questions like these:

- Why am *I* speaking?
- Why am I speaking *about this topic?*
- Why am I speaking *to this audience?*
- Why am I speaking *in this setting?*
- Why am I speaking *on this occasion?*

To better understand the value of *why* questions to this process, take a look at this exchange between a student and a communication instructor:

STUDENT: I've been asked to give a talk to new students in our department.

INSTRUCTOR: Why?

STUDENT: Why have I been asked, or why do the new students need to hear a talk by a fellow student?

INSTRUCTOR: Both.

STUDENT: Well, I guess they chose me because I've been very involved in the department—between classes and extracurricular activities, I practically live in the department.

INSTRUCTOR: Not to mention that you're a pretty good speaker. But why do new students need to hear you talk? Why not a faculty member?

STUDENT: I know the kinds of questions students have. After all, I'm one of them. New students probably feel more comfortable asking me a question than they would asking a professor.

INSTRUCTOR: What will you talk about?

STUDENT: I sure don't want to talk about the official stuff! They can bore themselves by reading that in the catalog and the department handbook.

INSTRUCTOR: So why are you speaking? What are they going to learn from you that they can't get from the handbook?

STUDENT: I guess it's to give new students the inside scoop—the unwritten rules, the unofficial tips.

INSTRUCTOR: Congratulations! There's your purpose. Can you think of a title that describes both your purpose and your topic?

STUDENT: How about "A Student's Unofficial Guide to Surviving the Communication Department"?

INSTRUCTOR: Good. That's a presentation they'll appreciate.

What question does the instructor keep asking? "Why?" The reason for this is simply that speaking is a means to an end. By first asking yourself why you are speaking, you are focusing on what you want to accomplish in your presentation.

Let's take a moment to acknowledge that your purpose is not the same as the **private goals** you may want to achieve with a presentation. The student speaker who wants to "give new students the inside scoop" in the department survival guide has a clear speaking purpose. However, that

● getting started   ▶ delivery   ◆ speaking to persuade
▲ fundamentals   ⁖ engaging your audience   ★ speaking occasions
■ content   ♣ speaking to inform   ✳ resources

same student may also want to please the faculty members who requested the presentation or use the speaking opportunity as a way to meet new students. These are goals that satisfy personal aspirations and needs the speaker is unlikely to share with anyone.

A presentation should have only one *purpose* but may have several private *goals*. In a communication course, a speaker's private goals frequently relate to academic ambitions: getting a good grade, for example, or securing a future recommendation from your instructor. In a work setting, a presentation is often an opportunity to demonstrate your professionalism, impress your colleagues, and advance your career, but these things are private goals, not your speaking purpose.

You may not need or want to share your private goals. As long as your private goals don't conflict with or undermine your public purpose, there is nothing wrong with using a speaking opportunity to achieve them. There *is* something wrong if pursuing these goals deceives your audience or contradicts your speaking purpose. Making sure your private goals align with your speaking purpose is an essential component of **ETHICAL COMMUNICATION**.

● 39–51

General Speaking Objectives

Before you determine your specific speaking purpose, you should identify the **general objective** of your talk. There are four general speaking objectives:

- To inform
- To persuade
- To entertain
- To inspire

Most of the time, the rhetorical situation will determine your general objective and will help you make appropriate decisions about the content and delivery of your presentation. For example, an **AWARD PRESENTATION** is usually informative and inspiring. A sales presentation is persuasive. And a presentation **INTRODUCING A SPEAKER** can be all four. Knowing your general objective will guide your initial decision making. If your instructor assigns an informative presentation, for example, relying on a

★ 427–32

★ 414–20

series of jokes or emotional pleas won't earn you a decent grade. If your audience expects to be entertained, a detailed statistical analysis or a series of complex arguments will not amuse them.

Speaking to Inform An **informative presentation** seeks to report new information, clarify difficult terminology, explain complex phenomena, or overcome confusion and misunderstanding. Here are some examples:

- *Report new information:* understanding the new campus policy on plagiarism
- *Clarify difficult terms:* the differences between viruses and bacteria
- *Explain complex phenomena:* What is nuclear fusion?
- *Overcome confusion and misunderstanding:* myths about gluten sensitivity

Informative presentations tend to be noncontroversial and concentrate on sharing or explaining information. The main challenge when preparing an informative presentation is to shape your content so it addresses your audience's interests and needs.

If you need more help

307–46 ▼

See Part 6, **SPEAKING TO INFORM**, for detailed strategies that will help you develop and deliver informative presentations.

Speaking to Persuade A **persuasive presentation** strives to change people's attitudes (what they believe, think, or feel) and/or their behavior (what they do). It attempts to change an audience's attitudes, beliefs, and values about an idea, a person, or an object or to persuade listeners to take a particular action or change their behavior. Here are a few examples:

- *Idea:* The Electoral College is an unfair and unrepresentative process for electing a US president.
- *People:* Beyoncé is more talented than Jay-Z.

- *Object:* The Apple iPhone is the best smartphone.
- *Action:* You should become an organ donor.

Advertisers try to persuade customers to buy their products. Political candidates do their best to persuade audiences to elect them. Persuasive presentations occur in courtroom arguments, in religious services, in blood donation drives, around the dinner table, and in daily conversations.

Some persuasive presentations seek to strengthen or weaken an existing attitude; others are designed to change audience attitudes altogether. Some aim to create positive or negative feelings; others attempt to whip an audience into an emotional frenzy. A persuasive presentation can also convince an audience to take action or change a behavior. The main challenge of persuasive speaking is simply this: human beings are generally reluctant to change their minds and behaviors and are slow to do so even when they're open to being persuaded.

If you need more help

See Part 7, **SPEAKING TO PERSUADE**, for detailed strategies that will help you develop and deliver persuasive presentations.

◆ 347–404

Speaking to Entertain As the name implies, an **entertaining presentation** tries to amuse, interest, divert, or "warm up" an audience. Stand-up comedy is a form of entertainment speaking. After-dinner speakers amuse audiences too full to move or absorb serious ideas and complex information. Speakers at a retirement party often "roast" a coworker to the delight of colleagues, friends, and family members.

A successful speech to entertain can ease audience tensions, capture and hold audience attention, defuse opposition, and stimulate action. Listeners remember humorous speakers positively, even when they aren't enthusiastic about a speaker's message.

It requires a lot of work and critical thinking to give a speech of any kind; trying to be entertaining at the same time requires even more work—and a dash of talent too. The main challenge of **HUMOROUS SPEAKING** is to

∴ 272–75

know yourself well enough to decide whether and in what ways you are able to make people laugh and relax. More than almost any other type of presentation, a speech to entertain should be **PRACTICED WITH AN AUDIENCE OF FRIENDS** whom you can trust to be honest about what's working and what's not.

232 ▶

Speaking to Inspire An **inspirational presentation** brings people together, creates social unity, builds goodwill, or arouses audience emotions. Inspirational speaking occurs in special contexts, takes many forms, and can tap a wide range of emotions. Here are just a few examples of types of inspirational presentations and their general purposes:

442–48 ★
449–55 ★
414–20 ★

- **TOASTS**: To invoke joy and/or admiration for a person or persons
- **EULOGIES**: To honor the dead and comfort the grieving
- **INTRODUCING A SPEAKER**: To gain audience interest in and create enthusiasm for a speaker and the speaker's message

427–32 ★
433–41 ★
357–61 ◆

Inspirational speaking also includes commencement addresses, sermons, dedications, and tributes, as well as **PRESENTING AN AWARD** and **ACCEPTING AN AWARD**. The challenge of inspirational speaking is finding ways to **APPEAL TO AUDIENCE EMOTIONS** based on their characteristics, opinions, needs, and values.

Inform, Persuade, Entertain, *and* **Inspire** How do you decide whether you should inform, persuade, entertain, or inspire? Many skilled speakers, regardless of their purpose, will try to do all four of these at once. For example, the primary purpose of a college professor's lecture usually is to *inform*. In order to inform, however, a good teacher also may try to *persuade* students that the information is important and relevant. Such persuasion can motivate students to listen and learn. The professor may also try to *entertain* students so that they will pay closer attention to an informative lecture. Highly skilled professors *inspire* their students to study, learn, and even choose a major or career in the discipline.

Regardless of the type of presentation you have been assigned or have chosen to make, there may be benefits to including components that inform, persuade, entertain, and inspire your listeners.

The Purpose Statement

Once you know why you're speaking and have a grasp of your general objective, you should write a **purpose statement** that, at least preliminarily, specifies the goal of your presentation. A well-written purpose statement is a reality check that ensures you can achieve your goal in a time-limited presentation to a particular audience. "My purpose is to tell my audience all about my job as a phone solicitor" is too general and is probably an impossible goal to achieve in the amount of time you have to speak. "My purpose is to increase audience awareness of two common strategies used by effective phone solicitors to overcome listener objections" is better. In addition to specifying the goal of your presentation in one sentence, an effective purpose statement has three characteristics: it is *specific*, *achievable*, and *relevant*.

Effective Purpose Statements Are Specific

A general, vague, or confusing purpose statement won't help you prepare your presentation. Think of your purpose statement as the description of a destination. Telling a friend "Let's meet in New York City" is too general and vague. "Let's meet at the northwest corner of Fifth Avenue and Forty-Second Street in Manhattan at 5:30 p.m. on Tuesday" is a clear and specific statement that will make sure that both of you end up in the same place at the same time. "Use the government's new food group recommendations as a diet guide for better health" is better than "Learn the benefits of eating well." A specific purpose statement ensures that both you and your audience know where you're going.

Effective Purpose Statements Are Achievable

A purpose statement should establish an achievable goal. Inexperienced speakers often make the mistake of trying to cover too much material or asking too much of their audience. A presentation is a time-limited event, and an audience of less-than-perfect listeners can absorb only a limited amount of information.

Similarly, changing audience attitudes about a firmly held belief can take months rather than minutes. What is the likelihood that a student speaker can convert a class to her religion during a ten-minute talk? What is the likelihood that a speaker can persuade audience members at a rally to donate a hundred dollars to the campaign of a relatively unknown political candidate?

Rather than seeking to convert the whole class to your religion, you may be more successful if you try to dispel some misconceptions about it. Rather than asking for one hundred dollars for a candidate's campaign, ask audience members to take home campaign flyers, to consider signing up as campaign volunteers, or to donate ten dollars. Achieving one small step in your presentation may be much more realistic than attempting a gigantic leap into unknown or hostile territory.

Effective Purpose Statements Are Relevant

Even if your purpose statement is specific and achievable, you may still have difficulty reaching your goal if your topic is irrelevant to your audience's needs or interests. The characteristics of different varieties of tree frogs may fascinate you, but if you can't explain why the topic is relevant and interesting to listeners, you may find yourself talking to a glassy-eyed or annoyed audience. Political candidates usually focus their attention on the issues that matter to a particular audience. Advocating tax breaks for new businesses won't interest a class of kindergartners, for example.

The following table highlights the value of specific, achievable, and relevant purpose statements.

INEFFECTIVE VS. EFFECTIVE PURPOSE STATEMENTS

Ineffective purpose statements	Effective purpose statements
How to maintain your health	Use the government's new food group recommendations in appropriate portions to improve your overall health.
Earthworms are important.	Earthworms aerate soil, fertilize gardens, create compost, and can provide a rich source of food protein.

● getting started   ▶ delivery   ◆ speaking to persuade
▲ fundamentals   ∴ engaging your audience   ★ speaking occasions
■ content   ▼ speaking to inform   ✳ resources

INEFFECTIVE VS. EFFECTIVE PURPOSE STATEMENTS

Ineffective purpose statements	Effective purpose statements
How to take cell phone photographs	Improve the quality of iPhone photographs by following the rule of three, using natural light (not flashes), and sliding the exposure meter.
Abolish the Electoral College because it's unfair and undemocratic.	The Electoral College does not reflect the popular vote: it cancels votes in winner-take-all states; gives more weight to whiter, more rural states; and lets candidates ignore states with fewer elector votes.
Learn the causes, symptoms, treatments, and prevention of depression.	The best treatments for anxiety and depression include antidepressant medications, cognitive behavioral therapy, and/or lifestyle changes.

Having a clear purpose statement is essential, but you shouldn't assume that once you've formulated it, it is set in stone. Occasionally, as you plan and prepare your presentation, you will realize that your purpose statement needs to be rethought. For example, if **AUDIENCE ANALYSIS** shows that your purpose is inappropriate or impossible to achieve for your listeners, you will need to return to the *why* questions above and revise your purpose. Or if, as you research a topic, you discover that there isn't enough valid information to support your purpose statement, you may decide to change it. As with other aspects of the **RHETORICAL SPEECHMAKING PROCESS**, thinking about your purpose requires you to be open to feedback and new information.

▲ 72–80

● 3–14

NOTABLE SPEAKER
Malala Yousafzai

As a fifteen-year old living under Taliban rule in Pakistan, Malala Yousafzai gained international recognition for her work as an education rights activist. Because of her activism, she became the target of a Taliban assassination plot. On October 9, 2012, a gunman shot her in the head, leaving her unconscious and in critical condition. After a lengthy recovery, Yousafzai became an even more engaged activist. She is the recipient of numerous awards, including the International Children's Peace Prize and Pakistan's National Youth Peace Prize. At age seventeen, she became the youngest recipient of the Nobel Peace Prize. At the 2014 Nobel Peace Prize concert to honor her, Yousafzai spoke about her goal to provide an education for every girl in the world.

Search Terms
To locate a video of this presentation online, enter the following key words into a search engine: Malala Nobel Peace Prize concert. The video is approximately 8:37 in length.

What to Watch For
[00:00–02:55] Yousafzai doesn't need to answer all the *why* questions for her audience because the reason is embedded in the occasion and event: She is the recipient of the Nobel Peace Prize. She is speaking to this particular audience because they have gathered to celebrate her as a Nobel laureate by hosting a concert in her honor. She does, however, directly address one question: Why is she speaking *on this topic*? She is speaking about educating girls because she believes that education is a right for all children.

[1:25–1:34] Greeted on stage by an extended, standing ovation, Yousafzai's credibility is already well established. In this speech to inspire, her words and demeanor convey that she genuinely seeks to share something of value with her audience. She connects their desire for peace with her purpose by highlighting their shared vision as peace-loving people.

[2:15–2:25] Yousafzai's purpose is evident early in the speech: "I simply ask that the right to learning should be given to every child. I ask for nothing else." She has left no room for confusion or vagueness about the destination she hopes to reach through her activism.

[4:00–4:45] Yousafzai's goal of giving every child access to education is an inspiring but difficult goal, one that cannot be accomplished in the time-limited event of her speech. What she can accomplish, however, is to motivate her audience to join the collective effort to advocate that every child receive an education. She is direct in her appeal and requests that the audience think about how they can help—how they can become activists as well.

(NOTABLE SPEAKER CONTINUED)

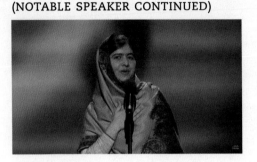

[4:50–6:30] Yousafzai highlights the relevance of her purpose by arguing that caring about the future—something most people do—necessarily means caring about educating children. She pursues her purpose by humbly asking the audience to make the right to education their goal as she has made it hers. By noting that she's only seventeen years old and "not so tall and very small," she appeals to the audience's ability to commit to the objective as well—particularly those who are likely stronger, more powerful, and richer than she is. If, as a teenager, she can consider it her duty to advocate for the education of children, the audience can do the same.

EXERCISE

After viewing Yousafzai's speech, reflect on these questions:

1. How much did you know about Yousafzai's life before viewing her speech? How did your knowledge and feelings affect your reaction to her speech?

2. One of the challenges of inspirational speaking is establishing your credibility as a speaker. How did Yousafzai's credibility influence her ability to inspire this audience?

3. Describe how Yousafzai adapted to the audience's needs as she stirred their emotions.

4. Yousafzai stated her purpose as "I simply ask that the right to learning should be given to every child. I ask for nothing else." In your own words, what is she asking her audience to know, think, feel, or do as a result of her presentation?

5. Although Yousafzai's general objective is to inspire her audience, to what extent and how did she also inform, persuade, and even entertain her audience?

6. Explain why or why not Yousafzai achieved her purpose.

Conclusion

Purpose states your speaking goals and suggests ways to achieve them. It is the measure of success for your presentation, it guides rhetorical decision making, it demonstrates respect for your audience, it can reduce your speaking anxiety, and it makes the best use of your preparation time and energy. Developing a specific, achievable, and relevant purpose statement is not merely an academic exercise; it can help you determine the outcome you seek as well as how to prepare and organize your presentation.

Part 3
Content

Sometimes what you'll talk about—your TOPIC—will be chosen for you, and other times the choice will be yours to make. Once you have a topic, there's much more to think about and plan regarding your content. The chapters that follow help you get a handle on all of this—choosing and refining your topic, RESEARCHING and thinking critically about SUPPORTING MATERIALS, and ORGANIZING your content so that your presentation is clear and compelling for your audience and achieves your purpose.

Content

3.1 Choosing a Topic

"What should I talk about?"

It's an odd question when you think about it. In the world at large, most presenters are required, invited, or decide to speak because they are experts on a subject, passionate about the topic, or recognized leaders or celebrities. Also, their role at a conference, event, or meeting may include making a presentation, a keynote address, or a speech on a specific topic they know or have researched very well. What they should talk about is rarely their first concern.

In a speech course, however, you are not speaking because you are a recognized expert in a specific subject area. Rather, you are speaking to demonstrate your ability to develop and deliver an effective presentation. In this kind of rhetorical situation, choosing a **topic**—the subject of your presentation—can be difficult and seem overwhelming.

Given the varied purposes and large number of potential topics, it's tempting to pick the first topic you think of or one that seems easy to talk about. But if you choose a topic randomly, without giving serious thought to your reasons for selecting it, your presentation will fail to achieve its purpose. Without a clear, achievable, and relevant purpose, there may be no reason for your audience to be interested in or care about your topic. So your choice of topic should begin with critical thinking about the three fundamental elements of the rhetorical speechmaking process: **SPEAKER**, **AUDIENCE**, and **PURPOSE**.

▲ 55–69
▲ 70–86
▲ 87–101

Speaker and Topic

The most important and readily available source for finding a good topic is *you*. You are the first person whose interests, knowledge, and motivation need consideration. If you aren't interested in your topic, your audience won't be either. Think carefully about your *interests*, your *abilities*, your *beliefs*,

---

- ● getting started
- ▲ fundamentals
- ■ content
- ▶ delivery
- ∴ engaging your audience
- ◤ speaking to inform
- ◆ speaking to persuade
- ★ speaking occasions
- ❋ resources

and your *values*. Hiding in plain sight among these is a topic that you'll be able to speak about with commitment and enthusiasm.

Review Your Interests and Abilities

What do you like to do—on the job, in your spare time, with your family or friends? What skills and talents do you have? What have you always wanted to learn more about? What's your favorite topic of conversation?

Most people have something they enjoy doing above and beyond the daily grind—a sport, a hobby, a charitable activity, a political cause, music and other arts, or a subject they like learning about in their spare time. What do you look forward to doing when you've finished schoolwork, when the kids are at school or in bed, when you've left work? Whatever these things may be, they can become the basis for an effective presentation.

How can you get a clear picture of the topics that really interest you? One way is to use leading statements. Here are a few that can help you identify your primary interests:

- I've always wanted to know more about . . .
- If I had an unexpected week off, I would . . .
- I've always been good at . . .
- I've always wanted other people to understand or know more about . . .
- My favorite topic of conversation is . . .
- A lot of people don't know or are surprised to learn that I . . .
- If I didn't have to worry about money at all, I would spend most of my time . . .
- I've always wanted to be able to . . .

Completing these sentences honestly can provide some good leads for promising topics that reflect your interests and abilities.

Draw on Your Beliefs and Values

Your beliefs and values guide how you think about what is right or wrong, good or bad, just or unjust, correct or incorrect. They also trigger emotions and guide actions. Taking an inventory of your beliefs and values when searching for a topic can be just as important as listing your interests.

As with your interests, a good starting point is to use leading statements that help you identify your core beliefs and values. Here are some examples:

- If I could make two new laws, they would be . . .
- I am happiest when . . .
- If I could give away a million dollars, I would . . .
- I am gratified when . . .
- I am shocked when people . . .
- The world would be a better place if . . .
- My proudest moment was when . . .
- I often become upset when I read, hear, or see a news report about . . .
- The greatest lesson I ever learned is . . .

Note that when you complete these leading statements, you may not name a specific belief or value. For instance, if you were to say, "I am gratified when cooking the weekly Sunday meal at the Grace Food Pantry," the activity—cooking—is specific, but the value—helping people in need—is implied. You may very well be happy because you love to cook (in which case, "cooking" should also be added to your list of interests!), but the overall implication of this response is that your satisfaction and happiness are rooted in the act of helping others. You need to ask yourself in each case: What is the belief or value expressed by my answer? Your answers to this and other questions like it can point the way toward your core values.

Another useful exercise is to link the **UNIVERSAL VALUES** you should consider in audience analysis—love, honesty, responsibility, respect, fairness, freedom, and compassion—to an interest or concern of *yours*. Combining a value with an issue can help you find a meaningful topic. As you can see in the first example below, "love" plus "marriage" might generate the idea "the role of love in arranged marriages" for one person. For another person, this combination might suggest "In marriage, love is what you *do*, not just what you *feel*." Either of these (and countless other) statements might be a potentially fruitful presentation topic.

▲ 79

VALUE	+	ISSUE	=	PRESENTATION TOPIC
love	+	marriage	=	*Example:* The role of love in arranged marriages
honesty	+	politics	=	_____
responsibility	+	COVID-19	=	_____
respect	+	religious beliefs	=	_____
fairness	+	taxes	=	_____
freedom	+	gun control	=	_____
compassion	+	refugees	=	_____

Of course, you can pair many other issues with each of these values. For example, in addition to the issue of gun control, the value of freedom can be paired with freedom of speech, the press, religion, or the freedom to marry whom you love.

For an example of a speaker who uses her own beliefs, values, skills, and experiences to choose a topic that also adapts to audience traits, attitudes, and interests, see Notable Speaker: Mileha Soneji, page 323.

Audience and Topic

When choosing a topic, questions about your audience are more difficult to answer than questions about your own interests, expertise, and values. Although your audience can differ in as many ways as there are listeners, effective **AUDIENCE ANALYSIS** can help you identify and adapt a topic to their characteristics and attitudes. For instance, if after thinking carefully about your own interests, you decide that you want to talk about video games, but your audience is a group of retirees, how interested do you think they will be in a presentation about the differences between first-person shooter and role-playing games? Isn't it more likely that this audience—many of whom are grandparents—will be more interested in a presentation that discusses the extent to which an obsession with, or the amount of violence in, video games harms (or doesn't harm) young children?

72–80

● getting started   ▶ delivery   ◆ speaking to persuade
▲ fundamentals   ⁖ engaging your audience   ★ speaking occasions
■ content   ◤ speaking to inform   ✳ resources

Then there are subjects—often called **toxic topics**—that have the potential to turn an audience against you and your message. Only the most skilled speakers know how to approach such topics without turning off their audience. We classify toxic topics into three categories:

1. Topics selected by speakers who are *overzealous*
2. Topics that *overpromise*
3. Topics that *offend* an audience

Overzealous speakers may have the best of intentions, but in their zeal to share their enthusiasm for their topic, they forget to accommodate their audience's characteristics and beliefs. A student with strong religious beliefs will be on safe ground if he speaks about some aspect of his religious life that is especially meaningful to him, but if he tries to convert the audience to his religion by conjuring up fiery visions of the fate that befalls nonbelievers, he will come across as overzealous. Despite their obvious passion for their subject, overzealous speakers rarely persuade anyone. The key to avoiding overzealous speaking is to commit yourself to being an **AUDIENCE-CENTERED SPEAKER**. 70–72

Some topics overpromise—that is, they offer promises that cannot be kept. Would you believe a speaker who claims that you will lose twenty pounds in two weeks without dieting, that you can double your money in a no-risk investment scheme, or that you can grow hair on a bald head with a secret herbal treatment? If you pick a topic that promises something that audience members may regard as too good to be true, be careful how you introduce and develop your content. An audience of **EFFECTIVE LISTENERS** will be highly skeptical if you cannot deliver what you promise. 30–31

Finally, some topics may offend or insult individual members or an entire audience. Talking about a topic that is controversial is fine if you are sensitive to the ways an audience may interpret a potentially offensive message. But choosing a topic that is deliberately hurtful or that singles out a person or group specifically for blame or disdain is almost always a bad idea. Doing so contradicts the values of any **ETHICAL SPEAKER**. To claim that "the terrorist attacks on 9/11 were exactly what America deserved" is a toxic topic. But a presentation about what the attackers believed they 40–41 were doing, based on research you've done into their motives, may be enlightening. If there's any doubt about whether a controversial topic may be perceived by audience members as toxic, you should either refine and narrow the topic, or avoid it altogether.

Be sensitive to your audience's background, attitudes, beliefs, and feelings when you choose a topic. If you are unsure about your choice of topic, ask potential audience members whether your message might be interpreted as overzealous, overpromising, or offensive. If there is even a hint of a yes when they answer, reconsider your topic. But don't be afraid to stand by a topic that reflects your strong interests and deep-seated values if you're confident in your ability to accurately identify and appropriately adapt to audience members' values and feelings.

If you ask yourself questions about who your listeners are, what they value, and what they are interested in—that is, if you take the time to analyze your audience—you will be able to eliminate some topics from consideration, narrow your list of suitable topics, and choose a topic that will have broad appeal.

Scope and Topic

There's an old saying: "Don't bite off more than you can chew." For presentations, the saying should be: "Don't bite off more than your audience can digest." If a topic is too broad, you'll bury your listeners under mounds of information. Ask yourself: "If I have time to tell them only one thing about my topic, what should it be?" Chances are that conveying a single important idea will be enough to achieve a worthy purpose.

Here are a few examples of general topic areas that have been narrowed down into better-defined topics for classroom presentations:

TOO BROAD:	The history of hip-hop
BETTER:	Grandmaster Flash and the development of quick-mix theory, punch phrasing, and scratching in early hip-hop
TOO BROAD:	A review of Greek mythology
BETTER:	The origins of the Greek goddess Aphrodite

| **TOO BROAD:** | The effects of global climate change |
| **BETTER:** | The "death" of the Great Barrier Reef |

| **TOO BROAD:** | Graphic narratives |
| **BETTER:** | The power of graphic novels: *Maus* and *Fun Home* |

Once you've narrowed your topic to a manageable scope, you should be able to further develop and/or refine your **PURPOSE STATEMENT** into a single sentence.

▲ 95–97

Begin Your Research Now

Research is a systematic search or investigation—in books, articles, online sources, interviews, surveys, and/or personal experiences—designed to find useful and appropriate **SUPPORTING MATERIAL** related to your topic. Rather than waiting until you have chosen a topic, refined a purpose statement, determined and organized your key points, and considered how to deliver your presentation, the time to start researching is *now*— that is, as soon as you have some initial thoughts about the rhetorical situation and your topic. In most cases, doing research early will help you sharpen the scope and purpose of a presentation on a particular topic. In some situations, it may even point you toward a better topic.

▪ 115–19

For example, suppose you have been thinking of making a presentation on the best methods for doing homework. As you begin researching, you may find that many educational experts believe that most homework assignments are merely busywork that does not help students learn or improve their skills. You may also discover that, for some students, "studying in a nice quiet place" does not enhance learning. This kind of information might completely shift your topic from a "how to study" presentation to a comparison between "good" and "bad" homework assignments and study habits, or a **PERSUASIVE PRESENTATION** that recommends strict limits on the amount of homework assigned to young children. Starting your research early ensures that you can take advantage of detours like this to make your presentation more focused and interesting. If you wait too long to uncover topic-related ideas and information, you may not have enough time to change course.

◆ 349–50

In some cases, if you have extensive knowledge about your topic, or have thoroughly researched it for some other assignment, doing research may simply be a matter of reviewing what you know about the subject and selecting and **ORGANIZING** the information you need to support your presentation's purpose.

138–48 ▦

Still Stuck? Ask Other People!

If you're still at a loss for a topic, ask other people for advice. Start with friends and family. Because they spend considerable time listening to you talk about many things conversationally, the people closest to you may have an intuitive sense of the subjects that interest you most and about which you can sound **CREDIBLE**. At the very least, they can be a useful sounding board as you consider potential topics.

57–66 ▲

Of course the largest repository of other people's ideas that the world has ever assembled is accessible via the internet. So if all else fails, you can look online. By using the search phrase "speech topics," you will find dozens of sites that list thousands of options. Here are just a few examples:

- Identity theft is a huge problem you can prevent or minimize.
- The federal government should cancel student loan debt.
- Students should learn how to identify fake news.
- Communism and socialism are not the same thing.
- Former felons should have their voting rights restored.
- The federal minimum wage should be $15 per hour.
- Online learning is (or is not) as effective as in-person learning.

If nothing else, speech topic websites may help you find general subject areas that you haven't considered but that may be interesting to you and your audience. But as you explore these sites, be wary of choosing a popular or supposedly "best" topic. Presentations about euthanasia, abortion, and the death penalty, for example, are made so often by so many speakers that—unless you are taking a unique or carefully adapted approach—most audiences will dread hearing more about these topics (and may know more about them than you do).

While it's perfectly acceptable to seek other people's help in choosing your topic, do not take the perilous step of buying or copying a speech written by someone else, whether a friend, a professional, a performer, or an online source. Beyond the ethical problem of **PLAGIARISM**, think about this: someone else's speech isn't going to sound like you, reflect your interests and values, or help you connect with your audience.

44–47

Conclusion

Choose a topic only after you have thought carefully about your interests, abilities, and values; have weighed your audience's needs and expectations against your own; and have confirmed that your sense of purpose is clear. Support that topic with relevant and engaging research findings, and if your research turns up a better approach or topic, change course if you can. Doing all these things in response to the question "What should I talk about?" will transform a merely acceptable presentation into an extraordinary experience for both you and your audience.

3.2 Research and Supporting Material

Many novice speakers believe that once they've identified their purpose and topic, they should simply start writing out what they're going to say and begin designing their visual aids. It's true that if you've given serious thought to your credibility, audience, and purpose, you will already know a great deal about what you want to say. But knowing what you want to say in general is not enough. You also need to think carefully about how you will back up what you say. You need to find relevant, varied, interesting, and valid *supporting material*.

The Importance of Supporting Material

87–101 ▲

Supporting material consists of the ideas, information, and opinions you use in a presentation to advance your **PURPOSE**. Well-chosen supporting material makes a presentation more interesting, more impressive, and more memorable.

Expert speakers are information specialists. They know their subjects well and can share names, dates, statistics, stories, and sayings about their topics. This knowledge enables them to tailor their presentations to suit a variety of audiences, occasions, and purposes.

269–72 ⁘

If you are not an expert on your topic, you will need to do research. Not only can research substantiate your beliefs and opinions, it can uncover supporting material that will **GENERATE AUDIENCE INTEREST**.

Supporting material helps you inform, persuade, entertain, and inspire your audience. It can spice up a speech, demonstrate a principle, or prove a point.

⬤ getting started	▶ delivery	◆ speaking to persuade
▲ fundamentals	⁘ engaging your audience	★ speaking occasions
▪ content	▼ speaking to inform	✳ resources

Types of Supporting Material
Let's look at a few of the most common types of supporting material.

Facts
A **fact** is a verifiable observation, experience, or event known to be true. For example, the statement "*Parasite* won the Academy Award for Best Picture in 2020" is a fact. But the statement "I think *1917* should have won" is not a fact; it's an **opinion**—an evaluation or judgment that is arguable, not settled. Most presentations—regardless of their purpose—include facts.

Facts can be something you know ("It hasn't rained all week") or information you've researched ("The United States pulled out of the UN Human Rights Council in 2018"). Sometimes a little-known or unusual fact can spark audience interest, such as "Testing water in a city's sewage treatment plant can identify the kind and amount of illicit drugs being consumed."

Statistics
Statistics is a type of mathematics concerned with collecting, summarizing, analyzing, and interpreting data. Somewhat confusingly, the numerical data generated by statistical research are *also* called "statistics." Statistics (the numerical data) help you understand the extent of a characteristic or the frequency of an occurrence among a large population. They are also used to analyze and sometimes make predictions about various phenomena—from economic and infection trends to the outcomes of sporting events and elections.

In the following excerpt, a student who worked for the American Diabetes Association demonstrates her familiarity with statistics about diabetes:

> Reports from the Centers for Disease Control and Prevention and the American Diabetes Association estimate that, in 2018, more than 100 million US adults were either diabetic or prediabetic. That's almost half of the adult population. And many of them didn't know they had it. Diabetes is now the sixth-leading cause of death by disease in the United States.

Testimony

Testimony refers to statements or opinions that someone has said or written. Testimony from topic experts can verify and add credibility to your claims.

You can find and use quotations from books, speeches, plays, magazine articles, radio, television, courtrooms, interviews, or various social media and websites. You can quote real people—politicians, scientists, celebrities, experts—who are alive today or from years gone by. Here's an example:

> Great speakers understand the unique challenge of preparing short speeches that are clear, concise, and memorable. As President Woodrow Wilson noted, "If I am to speak for ten minutes, I need a week for preparation; if fifteen minutes, three days; if half an hour, two days; if an hour, I am ready now."

Definitions

A **definition** explains or clarifies the meaning or meanings of a word, phrase, or concept. A definition can be as simple as explaining what *you* mean by a word or as detailed as a dictionary definition. Make sure you define words and phrases that your audience may not know or may misunderstand. In the following excerpt, a speaker uses two very different definitions—one from a music dictionary and the other from a musician's colloquial expression—of the same term to talk about the musical form known as the blues:

> A formal definition of the blues identifies it as a uniquely American musical form . . . characterized by expressive pitch inflections (blue notes), a three-line textual stanza of the form AAB, and a twelve-measure form. Well, that's okay for some, but I like an old bluesman's definition: "The blues ain't nothin' but the facts of life."

Analogies

An **analogy** is a comparison between two different things that highlights some point of similarity. Analogies can identify similarities in things that are somewhat different—for example, "If the traffic plan worked in San Diego, it will work in Seattle." Analogies can also identify similarities in things that are very different: "If a copilot must be qualified to fly a plane, a US vice president should be qualified to govern the country." Analogies

● getting started   ▶ delivery   ◆ speaking to persuade
▲ fundamentals   ⠶ engaging your audience ★ speaking occasions
■ content   ▼ speaking to inform   ✳ resources

are a useful way of **EXPLAINING COMPLEX IDEAS** or relating a new concept to something the audience understands very well.

337

In his opening statement at a US Senate confirmation hearing in 2010, General David Petraeus said:

> Helping to train and equip host nation forces in the midst of an insurgency is akin to building an advanced aircraft while it is in flight, while it is being designed, and while it is being shot at. There is nothing easy about it.[1]

Examples

An **example** uses a specific case or instance to make a larger or abstract idea more concrete. There are examples throughout this book that clarify, emphasize, and reinforce key ideas. Examples can be brief descriptions or detailed stories.

For example, in a presentation about the value of taxpayer-funded scientific research, a student provides a surprising list of everyday items and services that originated in some way from the National Aeronautics and Space Administration: memory foam used to make pillows and mattresses, camera technology in modern cell phones, artificial limbs, enriched baby formula, MRI and CT scans, and solar panels, to name just a few!

Stories

STORIES are accounts of things that have happened or can be imagined to have happened. Audiences remember a good story, even when they can't remember much else about a presentation. Real stories about real people in the real world can arouse attention, create an appropriate mood, and reinforce important ideas. Telling a compelling story is a great way to generate **AUDIENCE INTEREST**.

253–67

268–79

In a public speech about diabetes awareness at the National Press Club in Washington, DC, Nick Jonas, a member of a popular boy band, the Jonas Brothers, tells his own story:

> I was diagnosed with type 1 diabetes in November 2005. My brothers were the first to notice that I'd lost a significant amount of weight, fifteen pounds in three weeks. I was thirsty all the time, and my attitude had changed. My family knew I had to get to a doctor. The normal

range of a blood sugar is between 70 and 120. When we got to the doctor's office, we learned that my blood sugar was over 700. The doctor said that I had type 1 diabetes, but I had no idea what that meant. The first thing I asked was, "Am I going to die?"[2]

Jonas's story is about something that happened to him. Other stories, such as the legend of the young George Washington cutting down a cherry tree and not lying to his father that he did it, are fictional. They may not have happened, but they can nonetheless be effective supporting material that complements your presentation's message and helps you achieve your purpose.

An especially useful type of fictional story for speakers is the hypothetical story. **Hypothetical stories** are not real, but they make a point and have the potential to be very interesting, persuasive, and powerful. While they ask audience members to imagine themselves in an invented situation, hypothetical stories must also be believable. They are particularly useful when you can't find the perfect example or real story to support a key point or when you want the example to be tailored for your audience. When someone offers a hypothetical story, it usually begins with a phrase such as "Suppose you . . ." or "Imagine a situation where . . ." or "Picture this . . ."

Suppose you need the rheumatoid arthritis drug Humira, but—if you're uninsured—you can't afford the $50,000-a-year cost. As a recent letter to the editor published in the *New York Times* points out, for that amount of money, you could fly first class to Paris, stay at the Ritz Hotel, dine at the best restaurants, buy a one-year supply of Humira at local prices in France, fly back home, and finish with enough money to hire a registered nurse to administer the injection every two weeks. Crazy, huh? Perhaps. But what's really crazy is how pharmaceutical companies are making billions of dollars on drugs that people need. And if you're wondering, Humira in France costs 10 percent of what you would pay in the United States.[3]

Presentation Aids

282–305 ⠶

As a form of supporting material, **PRESENTATION AIDS** can reinforce your ideas and information in memorable ways. For example, rather than trying to define or describe the blues, playing a Howlin' Wolf or Muddy Waters recording (an audio aid) can accomplish the same objective—perhaps even

● getting started   ▶ delivery   ◆ speaking to persuade
▲ fundamentals   ⠶ engaging your audience   ★ speaking occasions
■ content   ▼ speaking to inform   ✳ resources

more effectively. A piece of sheet music for a blues song (a visual aid) can show exactly what a three-line stanza and a twelve-measure form look like.

Think about the ways that slides could be used to highlight other types of supporting material. For example, during the COVID-19 pandemic, graphs and maps were used to identify "hot spots" in the United States and across the world. They also showed the relationship between immediate social distancing and fewer COVID-19 infections. The phrase "flatten the curve" became a rallying cry for researchers, doctors, and governments in their search for more rapid testing, preventive strategies, and early treatment.

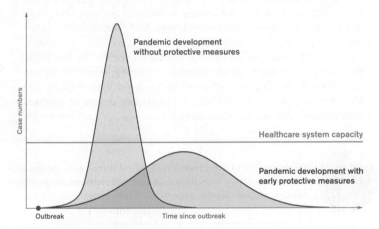

This area graph illustrates why it was important to "flatten the curve" during the early days of the COVID-19 pandemic.

Vary Your Supporting Materials

Effective speakers don't rely on just one type of supporting material. Why? Because using only one type of supporting material can make a presentation seem dull. Most audiences will become bored by an unending list of statistics. They may become frustrated by a speaker who tells story after story, particularly if there's no clear reason for telling the stories. A presentation that is little more than a series of quotations by famous people may convince your audience that you have nothing original to say. Try to use at least three types of supporting material in every presentation. Different types of information will give your presentation life and vitality.

Here's a passage from a speech that uses six different types of supporting material:

Story

Definition

Fact

Testimony

Statistic and Example

Statistic

> The Ku Klux Klan had humble beginnings. Right after the Civil War, six former Confederate soldiers in Pulaski, Tennessee, created a circle of like-minded friends. They chose the name Kuklux, a variation of the Greek word *kuklos*, which means "circle." They added the term *Klan* because they were of Scotch-Irish descent. In 1915, D. W. Griffith's film *The Birth of a Nation*—originally titled *The Clansman*—quoted a line from *A History of the American People* by Woodrow Wilson, who would later become president of the United States. Wilson declared, ". . . at last there has sprung into existence a great Ku Klux Klan, a veritable empire of the South, to protect the Southern country." By the 1920s, the Klan claimed eight million members, including President Warren G. Harding. Today, there are between five thousand and eight thousand Klan members in the United States, split between dozens of different organizations that use the Klan name.[4]

For an example of using several types of supporting material, including a personal story, facts, data, examples, and analogies, see Notable Speaker: Meghan Markle, page 67.

Test Your Supporting Material

On January 22, 2017, the phrase "alternative facts" made the national news when it was used on *Meet the Press*. Kellyanne Conway, a White House representative, defended President Trump's claim that his inauguration audience was larger than Obama's. When the show's host, Chuck Todd, challenged her claim, she said that the White House spokesman "gave alternative facts" about the size of the audience.[5] Here's how Todd responded:

> Wait a minute— Alternative facts? Alternative facts? . . . Look, alternative facts are not facts. They're falsehoods.

Separating facts from falsehoods can be difficult. There was a time when no one knew or paid attention to the potential harms of cigarette smoking. When in the 1940s and 1950s scientists linked it to a worldwide lung cancer epidemic, the tobacco industry falsely claimed that cigarette smoking was not harmful and not linked to cancer. Until the early 1960s, most people believed the "fact" that cigarette smoking was not a health hazard. It took many years for that belief to change into the now universally accepted fact that smoking tobacco is hazardous and has become "the world's deadliest malignancy."[6] Given that supposed facts can be false and real facts can be denied or rejected, everyone—not just speakers—needs to research, analyze, and evaluate the information they believe and use as the basis for their claims.

Speakers use supporting material to enhance their presentations and to demonstrate their depth of knowledge about their topics. However, information that's not accurate and up to date undermines this purpose. Make sure to test the validity of every piece of supporting material before adding it to your presentation. By **valid**, we mean that the ideas, opinions, and information are well founded, justified, and true. Five questions can help you test your information to determine its validity:

1. Is the source identified, credible, and unbiased?
2. Is the source primary or secondary?
3. Is the information recent?
4. Is the information consistent and in context?
5. Is the information from online sources verifiable and valid?

We discuss these five questions on the following pages and then suggest several ways to confirm the validity of the supporting material you use.

Is the Source Identified, Credible, and Unbiased?

The two most important questions to ask when testing the validity of your supporting material are these:

1. Who is the source?
2. Why should I believe this information or statement?

57–66 ▲

No matter where you get your information, you must be able to identify its source and determine whether that source is qualified and **CREDIBLE**. Is the author or speaker a recognized expert, a firsthand observer, a scientist, or a respected journalist? Can you confirm that expertise, experience, or reputation via several sources *other* than the one you're testing? Remember that any source can make *claims* about its (or their) credibility. The key is to confirm these claims independently.

Always note your source as completely as possible, including the date of publication and posting (or revision) and, if applicable, the page number. If you're using an article, what publication does it come from, who wrote it, and when was it published? If you're using a website, ask the same questions. Doing this allows your audience to do their own critical thinking about the credibility of this source.

Additionally, be mindful that you use objective sources of information. A source with a consistent **bias**—a prejudice for or against something—may express claims and opinions so slanted in one direction that they are neither objective nor fair. Biased testimony comes from a person or organization that has a self-centered reason to take a particular position. If the source has a strong opinion or will gain from your agreement, be cautious.

The majority of well-respected sources—regardless of their varied positions on timely issues—will report accurate information. For example, articles in the more conservative *Wall Street Journal* and the more liberal *New York Times* often report the same information and express similar opinions when the facts are undeniable and similar opinions are warranted.

Is the Source Primary or Secondary?

When collecting supporting material for a presentation, make sure you know whether the information comes from a primary or secondary source.

A **primary source** is the document, testimony, or publication in which the data, information, or claim first appears. Examples of primary sources include speeches, scholarly research journals, diaries, clinical reports, and recordings or transcripts of statements and events.

A **secondary source** describes, reports, repeats, or summarizes information from one or more other sources. Examples include a news article that summarizes scientific research, a celebrity magazine or website that relies on rumors and gossip, and a description or analysis of a presentation or event by someone who was not there (or who didn't have a full video recording of the speech or event, which is a primary source).

Look carefully at secondary sources of information to determine, if possible, the primary source. Publications such as small local newspapers, news websites that consolidate reports, and social-trend magazines rarely conduct their own research. As secondary sources, they publish information they have obtained from both primary and other secondary sources. If you rely on secondary sources, ask the following questions:

- Do other secondary sources report similar information?
- If there are differences in evidence and conclusions, is there a valid explanation for those differences?

Lots of speakers, reporters, newscasters, and politicians rely on both pri-mary *and* secondary sources. Your challenge is to think critically about secondary sources to make sure that they correctly report and interpret primary-source data and conclusions.

Is the Information Recent?

Always note the date of the information you want to use. When was the study conducted? When was the article published? In this rapidly chang-ing information age, your supporting material can become old or obsolete very quickly. For example, consider the statistics on COVID-19. Because testing in the United States was unrepresentative of the population for many months in 2020, the confirmed number of cases was lower than the number of people who actually had the disease. Until better testing and reporting were developed, the older statistics were insufficient to measure the epidemic's severity and scope.[7]

For current events or the latest scientific findings, look for the most recent professional journals, news articles, and websites. Current events reported on reliable social media are often way ahead of a newspaper story or journal article. On the other hand, timeliness should not be confused with the validity of supporting material that comes from historical sources. Ancient texts, eyewitness accounts of historical events, and revelations about erroneous scientific findings can be of great value when needed and applicable.

Is the Information Consistent and in Context?

Check to ensure that your supporting material reports information and reaches conclusions that are similar to other information you have on the same subject. For example, if every doctor and medical expert says that penicillin will *not* cure a cold, why believe an internet celebrity or neighbor who recommends it as a treatment? If the evidence from countless scientific studies over many decades clearly shows that cigarette smoking is dangerous, the fact that your grandfather smoked two packs a day and lived to be eighty-five doesn't mean you should ignore the science—just be happy that he was a lucky exception!

In addition to testing information's consistency, make sure you do not take words **out of context**. This occurs if you select isolated statements from a source and distort or contradict the speaker or writer's intended meaning. Politicians often quote their opponents out of context, and film advertisers do the same by quoting the one good thing written about a movie that received terrible reviews.

For example, in May 2018, several news organizations took remarks made by President Trump out of context by suggesting he was referring to *all* undocumented immigrants as "animals." When examined within the context of his presentation, it appears he was referring to members of a violent gang. CNN issued a correction in a tweet: "Trump's remarks . . . were in response to comments about members of MS-13 and other undocumented immigrants who are deported for committing crimes."[8] (The correction itself is complicated by the fact that MS-13 originated in Los Angeles and is not made up of immigrants.)

Some speakers and audience members may use or analyze quotes out of context unknowingly. Sadly, unethical speakers, audience members, and

375–76 ◆

reporters often take testimony out of context in order to **ATTACK A PERSON**, discredit an idea, or gain credibility for something that is not supported by the full context.[9]

Is the Information from Online Sources Verifiable and Valid?

Information from online sources can overwhelm anyone, even people who believe they are skilled at telling the difference between good information and bad. That's because it is both too easy to find information online and

● getting started	▶ delivery	◆ speaking to persuade
▲ fundamentals	⋅⋅ engaging your audience	★ speaking occasions
■ content	♥ speaking to inform	✳ resources

too hard to evaluate everything you find. Add to that the fact that online information, even when it's labeled as an advertisement or is obviously propaganda, can end up persuading or confusing you if you spend too much time with it, even if you started your research with the best intentions of being a **CRITICAL THINKER**. Michael Caulfied, a digital literacy expert at Washington State University, Vancouver, explains, "Even with good intensions, you run the risk of misunderstanding something because [these sites] are way better at propaganda than you are." Referring to white supremacist websites that you might read with the intention of critiquing their ideology, Caulfield says, "You won't get less racist reading [them] critically, but you might be overloaded by information and overwhelmed."[10]

◆ 363–81

Fortunately, there is a respected principle and a set of strategies for evaluating online sources. It is called **lateral reading**—"the practice of doing a quick initial evaluation of a website . . . [but spending] more time reading what others say about the source or related issue." Lateral reading is what professional fact checkers do.[11] Instead of settling for the top result in your online search, you quickly scan the rest of the results for sources that provide similar information but are *not* affiliated with the original source. Then ask: what do other sources say about the initial source and its message? In some cases, you can supplement that search by using sites dedicated to testing the validity of both sources and the information they disseminate. These include sites confirmed as objective and reliable such as FactCheck, FactChecker, PolitiFact, Snopes, and PunditFact. Lateral reading also applies to photographs that may be even more misleading than what you read.

Caulfied took the lateral reading principle further and transformed it into four strategies for initially evaluating the credibility and accuracy of online messages. He calls it **SIFT**, which stands for "Stop, Investigate, Find, and Trace."[12] Here are the steps:

1. *Stop.* Pause and ask yourself: do you recognize the information's source, and do you know anything about the website's message? Regardless of your answer, go to the next step.
2. *Investigate* the source. Where does the information come from? Who wrote it or published it? What is the source's expertise, reputation, and point of view? Is it worth your time to read something

by this source in detail? What have others said about this source? To make sure your investigation is thorough and objective, go to the next step.

3. *Find* trusted coverage. Consider the source's facts and claims. Do other credible sources reach the same conclusions? Do *your* personal viewpoints lead you to trust a particular source even if other highly respected sources criticize its accuracy, truthfulness, and biases? Despite what you now know, make sure you complete the next step and examine the context.

4. *Trace* facts, data, claims, quotes, and media back to their original contexts. Has the information been removed from its original con-text—and thus distorted or purposely misinterpreted its meaning? Can you trace the information back to its original source in order to determine its intended context? Once you know these answers—along with answers to the previous three questions—you can legitimately claim that the supporting materials you finally choose are credible, useful, and valid.

Lateral reading and SIFT help you think critically about the credibility of an online source, the real purpose of its message, and the validity of its claims and supporting material. Once you have determined that a site is worth your time (even if you disagree with it), you can analyze its content more accurately, efficiently, and effectively. SIFT will not solve the problem of online misinformation and dishonesty. It may not tell you whether the information from a particular site is 100 percent true. But it does help you decide whether a source is worth reading and using in a presentation and whether the information is or is not well founded, justified, and true.

Evaluating Statistics

Most of us who are not statisticians are not familiar with the sophisticated research methods that are required to ensure that statistical results are valid. And yet many speakers consider the use of statistical data to be the gold standard for supporting an argument or making a presentation more engaging and persuasive. How many times have you heard the expression "The numbers don't lie"? It's a weird notion when you think about it. So

getting started

▲ fundamentals

■ content

▶ delivery

∴ engaging your audience

◤ speaking to inform

◆ speaking to persuade

★ speaking occasions

✳ resources

weird, in fact, that one of the best books about statistics published in the last hundred years, Darrell Huff's *How to Lie with Statistics*, turned the idea completely on its head. Here's what Huff had to say about the subject (he was speaking about statistics used by writers and interpreted by readers, but it applies equally well to speakers and listeners):

> The secret language of statistics, so appealing in a fact-minded culture, is employed to sensationalize, inflate, confuse, and oversimplify. Statistical methods and statistical terms are necessary in reporting the mass data of social and economic trends, business conditions, "opinion" polls, the census. But without writers who use the words with honesty and understanding and readers who know what they mean, the result can only be . . . nonsense.

Imagine you were told that 100 percent of the physics professors at one college were Black, and 100 percent of the physics professors at a neighboring college were white. What would you think, given only that information? You may well wonder whether some sort of policy of educational segregation was afoot and whether a charge of discrimination could be justified against the latter school. But wait: What if you were then told that there is only one physics professor at each college? Is the claim any less true? No. But is it meaningful? The use of a percentage figure in this case is misleading at best.

Here's a significant (and real-life) example of the effects that flawed statistical methodologies and invalid claims can have. In 1998, Dr. Andrew Wakefield and colleagues published a paper in the British journal *Lancet* that described twelve children with developmental delay—eight had autism. All of these children had intestinal complaints and developed autism within one month of receiving the measles, mumps, and rubella (MMR) vaccine. The study became a key support in the arguments made by "anti-vax" activists against the vaccination recommendations of public health officials. The paper was retracted by the journal more than a decade later, after an independent review determined that Wakefield's data had been misrepresented and that his methodology was deliberately and blatantly flawed. But by then, the anti-vax movement had already become established, and many thousands of misinformed parents had refused to immunize their children.

Among the results of this misuse of statistics is a dangerous resurgence of measles—a disease that had been declared eliminated in 2000.[13]

39–51

Not all misuses of data are a matter of life and death. But it's nonetheless important—in fact it's crucial for all **ETHICAL SPEAKERS**—to test statistics just as rigorously as all the other types of supporting material. When using statistics in a presentation, ask the same questions you would for all types of supporting material: Is the source identified, credible, and unbiased? Do the statistics come from primary or secondary sources? Are the claims recent, consistent with other statistics, and not taken out of context? In addition, you should ask the following three questions:

1. Is the statistical sample adequate?
2. Do the statistics represent a mean or a median?
3. Can you explain how the statistics support your claims?

Is the Statistical Sample Adequate?

Statistics are based on a **sample**, or portion of a population. What makes a sample "adequate"? First, it must be large enough to stand in for the population as a whole. How large is large enough? If the methodology of a study is sophisticated and ethical, researchers may select a relatively small sample to draw conclusions about an entire population. For example, the typical sample size for a Gallup poll (the best-known polling organization in the world) is 1,000 national adults ("national adults" represent all adults age eighteen and older living in United States). For major election predictions, Gallup may survey as many as 15,000 people. These sample sizes are tiny compared to the population that they're meant to represent— in this case, the approximately 209 million adults living in the United States—but because they use a widely respected methodology, Gallup's statistical results are generally seen as valid.[14]

The second important aspect of an adequate sample is that it should be both random and representative. Selecting a random sample is an important means of avoiding **sampling bias**, which happens when some categories of individuals within the overall population are intentionally or inadvertently excluded from the sample. If a sample is large enough and has been chosen randomly, then it should reflect other aspects of the overall population (that you can independently verify). For instance, if a survey's sample is meant to represent all adults in the United States, then that sample should include nearly the same number of women as men and the same percentages of different races and ages in the overall population.

Do the Statistics Represent a Mean or a Median?

Just about everyone is familiar with the concept of an *average*. In statistics, the words *average* and *mean* are used interchangeably. If you add up the heights of all the students in your class and divide by the number of students you measured, you will come up with the average, or mean, height in your class.

The term *median* refers to the figure that is at the midpoint between two extremes. If you create a list or chart of your classmates arranged from the shortest person (five feet two inches) to the tallest person (six feet four inches), and that list has fifteen people on it, you'd look for the person right in the middle of the list—the eighth person. That person's height is not an average of the shortest and tallest; it is not even the most frequent height. Instead, the median value is simply the number (in this case the height) that appears right in the middle of the list.

Failure to appreciate the differences between a mean and median can lead to major misunderstandings. Here's an example: According to US Census Bureau tables, the *median* American household income in 2018 was $63,179. In other words, half of American households made more than that amount, and half made less.[15]

The *mean* American household income in 2019 was much larger—$87,864.[16] Why? Because multimillionaires and billionaires boost the results. To get a better grasp of this concept, let's consider a smaller scale. Imagine eleven people in a room, one of them with a salary of $87 million a year and ten each making $67,000 a year. The mean (average) annual salary of people in the room is the total of all their salaries divided by eleven: $7.97 million. If someone were to tell you that the people in this room make an average of $7.97 million a year, you might assume that they all are extremely wealthy people. But the median annual salary of this group—$67,000—tells a different story. Considering both the mean and median in this scenario together makes clear that there is an unequal distribution of income in the room.

Can You Explain How the Statistics Support Your Claims?

"The numbers speak for themselves"—another common saying. Sure, statistics may "speak," but they definitely don't *explain* themselves. However, you can and should explain them. For example, here's how a speaker explained income inequality:

> The Disney Corporation's chief executive, Bob Iger, made $65.6 million in 2018. Abigail Disney, an heir to the company, complained that the annual compensation was 1,424 times the median salary of a Disney employee—and that it "deepened wealth inequality." Think of it this way: If you made $65.5 million a year and worked a 40-hour week for 52 weeks a year, you'd earn $1.260 million a week. That's $31,650 an hour. The Walt Disney Company responded by saying it had agreed to pay a minimum wage of $15 an hour by 2021. Wow. Fifteen dollars versus $31,650 an hour. If that ain't income inequality, what is?

Document Your Supporting Material

All the supporting material used in a presentation (including information from internet sources and interviews) should be documented. **Documentation** is the practice of citing the sources of your supporting material in a presentation. In-speech documentation enhances your **CREDIBILITY** as a researcher and speaker while informing listeners about the sources and validity of your ideas and information. In most college settings, you are required to include an acknowledgment of the author and the source in your presentation or references.

57–66 ▲

Document Your Sources in Writing

Always be prepared to provide a written list of the references you used to prepare your presentation—just as you would for a written report. In most speaking situations apart from the classroom, you will not be required to provide such a list. Even in those cases, keep a list of your references for

● getting started   ▶ delivery   ◆ speaking to persuade
▲ fundamentals   ∴ engaging your audience   ★ speaking occasions
■ content   ▼ speaking to inform   ✳ resources

your own use. If nothing else, it will remind you of which sources you used in the event that you are challenged about information or asked to repeat or to update your presentation.

Documentation follows one of several accepted formats, such as Modern Language Association (MLA) style or American Psychological Association (APA) style. The documentation sections in their manuals provide models of how to format references, endnotes, and footnotes. If your instructor requires a written list of your references, make sure to ask which documentation format you should use.

Document Your Sources while Speaking

During a presentation, you should document the sources of supporting material out loud. Your spoken citation—sometimes called an **oral footnote**—should include enough information to allow an interested listener to find the original sources. Generally, it's a good idea to provide the name of the person or organization whose work you are using, say a word or two about that person's or group's credentials, and mention the source of the information—for example, "In her 2018 book *The Monarchy of Fear*, philosopher Martha Nussbaum defines *fear* as . . ."

Here are some questions to ask as you prepare an oral citation:

- Who is being quoted or paraphrased?
- What are their credentials?
- From what specific publication *or* source is the information taken?
- What date was the information generated, published, or last updated?

Answers to the above questions can help you decide how to phrase your citation. For example, you may not need to list the credentials of a very famous person, but the date the statement was made or published may be important.

To document electronic sources orally, you could say, "An article on plagiarism in the *Purdue News*, posted online, reports that . . ." You could also display the complete website addresses on a slide (as long as you give listeners enough time to copy it). If you want your audience to have complete citations, prepare a bibliography as a **HANDOUT**.

290–92

44–47

Documentation matters because without it you could fall into the trap of plagiarizing your source material unintentionally. The key to avoiding **PLAGIARISM** is to identify the sources of your information in your presentation. If they're not your original ideas, and most of the words are not yours, you are ethically obligated to tell your audience who wrote or said them and where they came from. This requirement applies equally to material you find on the internet, including photographs, graphics, and PowerPoint slides. Downloading someone else's visual materials and not giving proper credit for it is a form of plagiarism.

Conclusion

Savvy speakers begin collecting supporting material as soon as they know they'll be making a presentation. If they have a general idea about the topic they intend to cover, they begin researching a variety of resources. Good research helps you fill in the blanks where you need material to support your purpose. It also helps you find new ideas to enrich the content of your presentation.

As you search for supporting material, remember that never before in history has there been so much information about so many subjects available to so many people. That's the good news. The bad news is that never before in history has there been so much false, misleading, and biased information about so many subjects available to so many people. Responsible speakers have an ethical obligation to understand the differences between facts and fiction as they choose appropriate supporting material for a presentation. Audience members, too, share that responsibility as they listen to a speaker.

● getting started   ▶ delivery   ◆ speaking to persuade
▲ fundamentals   ∴ engaging your audience   ★ speaking occasions
■ content   ▼ speaking to inform   ✳ resources

3.3 Organizing Content

The **organization** of a presentation is the arrangement of its content into a structured, coherent message. Organization puts the major components of your presentation in an appropriate order and keeps you focused on the development of each idea.

Many speakers underestimate the importance of a well-organized presentation. But as an audience member, you already know how much it matters. You know that a well-organized presentation is easier to listen to and remember than a poorly organized one. You know how difficult it is to understand and remember the message of a speaker who rambles and doesn't connect ideas. In fact, you may never want to hear that speaker again.

Not surprisingly, well-organized speakers are seen as more competent, confident, and persuasive than disorganized speakers. A well-thought-out arrangement of ideas and information helps an audience clearly understand and make informed decisions about a speaker's message, thus making it more likely that the presentation achieves its purpose.

So how do you begin organizing your presentation? By identifying *key points* and your *central idea*.

Identifying Key Points and the Central Idea

Key points are the main ideas or most important issues you want your audience to understand and remember. Inexperienced speakers often feel overwhelmed by what seem to be a mountain of unrelated facts, ideas, opinions, and data that they've assembled during their research. So how do you make sense of it all? How do you select the key points that best support your **PURPOSE**? You begin by looking for patterns or natural groupings of ideas and information. Two methods in particular—*chunking* and *mind mapping*—can help.

▲ 87–101

The Chunking Method

Chunking is the process of separately recording and strategically sorting the ideas and supporting material you've gathered so far. This simple method helps you identify your key points—the basic building blocks of your presentation—and allows you to arrange and rearrange them until you're satisfied with their order.

115–19

Here's how it's done: During the research and planning stage of speech preparation, record each good idea and strong piece of SUPPORTING MATERIAL on a single note card, sticky note, or virtual note. Put only one idea, point, phrase, example, statistic, quotation, or story on each card or note.

Once you have gathered and recorded your ideas and supporting materials on separate notes, you can shuffle them around, spread them out, and look for relationships among them. Looking at your notes in this way, some things will become clearer. You'll notice that some supporting material will back up specific ideas, some ideas will overlap or repeat one another, and some ideas and supporting materials will prove to be unrelated to your topic or purpose.

For each group of notes that belong together, create a unique category label. For instance, if you're preparing a presentation on drinking and driving, you might discover that you've chunked your ideas and supporting materials into three key points:

1. *Stories* about local alcohol-related car accidents
2. *Statistics* about drunk driving in the United States
3. *Proposed changes* to drunk-driving laws

Even if some of your notes don't fit into a distinct category with the others, keep them nearby in a pile of "leftovers." As your presentation develops, some categories might become more important and others less so, and these supposed leftover ideas and supporting materials may end up being relevant again.

Mind Mapping

Another method for identifying key ideas—**mind mapping**—produces a visual representation of potential key points and related supporting materials that clearly link to your topic and purpose.

The most common mind mapping method requires only a piece of paper and a writing tool. There are also dozens of mind mapping software tools available. The mind mapping steps that follow use the paper method.[1]

Record Your Topic, Ideas, and Supporting Material On a single, clean sheet of paper, write your **TOPIC** in the middle of the page and circle it. Everything on your mind map should stem from this word or phrase. Experiment with the ideas that might become candidates for the key points in your presentation. Write down these ideas in the open spaces on the page. Then record the **SUPPORTING MATERIAL** you wish to use near a relevant idea. You may find it necessary to add other ideas that capture the essence of the supporting material. Feel free to be messy. Neatness doesn't count. Initially, there are no bad ideas. What is important is that at the end of this initial step, you should have a one-page conglomeration of topic-related ideas and supporting material that you might include in your presentation.

105–13

115–19

Connect Related Ideas Draw a circle around individual ideas and related supporting material. If two ideas are closely related, let your circles overlap or draw lines between those circles. Eventually, they may be combined into a single key point. Now examine ideas and supporting materials that aren't circled. Are they important? Do they support your purpose? If so, you may need to create a new idea or find more supporting material.

Refine Your Mind Map Critically analyze your mind map. Which ideas seem most significant and necessary as key points? Which ones can be discarded? If they're not important, cross them out. In some cases, you may want to redo your map to organize it further. In a second draft, you can concentrate on making sure that your mind map has adequate and appropriate supporting material for each key point.

The following figure is a mind map created by a student for a presentation about anger. The mind map is a hodgepodge of words, phrases, lists, circles, and arrows. After analyzing what was on her mind map, she identified and circled ideas and supporting materials for each of her key points and put them in a logical order. Given the large amount of interrelated material she found, mind mapping was a useful way to decide how much information she had time to include, identify her key points, and begin the organizational process.

Consider the Rule of Three

You may be tempted to include in your presentation all the key points and supporting material you've identified. Resist that temptation. Even the most attentive listeners in your audience will not remember everything you say. Ask yourself: Which key points are the most essential? Which points will help me achieve my **PURPOSE**? Which ones are most likely to **INTEREST** and **PERSUADE** my audience?

87–101 ▲
268–79 ⁝·
349–50 ◆

Is there an ideal number? Generally, communication experts agree that an effective presentation should offer at least two key points and no more than five. Three key points are often ideal. In fact, audience members frequently expect speakers to make three points in their speeches. These findings are sometimes referred to simply as the **rule of three**. Keep in mind that the rule of three is a guideline, not an absolute, unbreakable rule. It all depends on the rhetorical situation. But in general, keeping the number of key points in your presentation in the two-to-five range will ensure that your audience remains interested in and able to remember what you say.

The Central Idea

Whether you use chunking, mind mapping, or some other method to sort, organize, and think critically about the various ideas and supporting material you've assembled, you will eventually have a handle on your key ideas that reflect or modify your purpose statement. Now it's time to write out your *central idea*.

Your **PURPOSE STATEMENT** identifies the goal of your presentation— what you want your audience to know, think, believe, or do. Your **central idea** (sometimes called the **thesis statement**) summarizes your overall message and key points in one sentence. It describes specifically what you intend to say.

▲ 95–97

> **PURPOSE:**   To spread awareness of the ways that earthworms aerate soil, fertilize gardens, create compost, and can provide a rich source of food protein
>
> **CENTRAL IDEA:** You may know that people who fish or tend gardens appreciate earthworms, but you may not know how they can enhance composting and provide a protein-rich meal.

Compare the above purposes statement to the central idea. Which one would you rather say to an audience? When you've finished your presentation, audience members should be able to remember and rephrase your central idea in their own words.

Writing down your central idea is a useful test to determine if you have, in fact, captured the core meaning of your message. If you find that it takes more than one sentence to state your central idea, you may be trying to do too much with your presentation, or you may not have a clear purpose or discrete set of key points. The following two examples illustrate how topic area, purpose, and central idea are different but closely related to one another.

> **TOPIC AREA:**   Refugee families
>
> **PURPOSE:**   To increase donations to the church's refugee assistance program
>
> **CENTRAL IDEA:** Because the church's refugee families' program has been a blessing for all of us—the families, our church, and you—please continue to make financial contributions to our ministry.

TOPIC AREA:	Muzak
PURPOSE:	To make the audience more aware of the purpose and power of Muzak
CENTRAL IDEA:	The next time you hear Muzak playing, you will remember how pervasive it is, how it originated, and how it tries to lift your spirits and productivity.

A strong central idea connects your purpose to your key points (and connects your key points to one another) in a succinct and memorable way. Once you have drafted a central idea that captures what you want to say in your presentation, you can turn to the details of organization. But keep in mind that your initial central idea is not set in stone. As you organize your content, **DOCUMENT** your research, or revise your presentation in response to changes in the rhetorical situation, you may find that you will need to modify and improve your central idea.

130–32

Patterns of Organization

In most cases, the nature of your topic, your purpose, and your key points will dictate the overall organization of your presentation. If you are sharing a recipe, for example, there is a clear set of consecutive steps. If you are looking at a historical event, you can begin at the beginning and work your way forward to the finish. In other cases, the best arrangement won't be immediately apparent to you. Fortunately, there are several commonly used **organizational patterns** that can help you find an appropriate arrangement for your presentation. The following isn't a complete list of possible organizational patterns, but it does give a taste of the different ways that key points can be arranged and presented.

Arrange by Categories

Categorical arrangement divides a large topic into smaller categories within that topic. For example, you could divide the topic of alcoholism into its symptoms and treatments, or you could devote your entire presentation to describing several treatments. Here's an example of categorical arrangement that focuses on the Shaker religion:

● getting started ▶ delivery ◆ speaking to persuade
▲ fundamentals ⁖ engaging your audience ★ speaking occasions
■ content ▼ speaking to inform ✳ resources

TOPIC AREA:	The Shakers
PURPOSE:	To appreciate the legacy of the Shaker religion in the United States
CENTRAL IDEA:	The Shaker religion is a unique American religious group with distinctive beliefs about Christian life and inventiveness as a productive community.
KEY POINTS:	A. Origin of the Shaker religion
	B. Core beliefs about the perfect Christian life
	1. Communal living
	2. Celibacy
	3. Confession of sins
	C. Shaker inventions
	1. Agriculture
	2. Architecture and furniture
	3. Tools

Here's an example of categorical arrangement that emerged from the mind map on page 136. Instead of including everything, it narrows its focus to why anger can be counterproductive:[2]

TOPIC AREA:	Common myths about anger
PURPOSE:	To explain why anger can harm relationships
CENTRAL IDEA:	Three myths about anger focus on an erroneous assumption, inappropriate expression, and a misattributed cause.
KEY POINTS:	A. Myth: Anger and aggression are natural human instincts.
	B. Myth: Forcefully expressing your anger is a healthy response.
	C. Myth: Anger is caused by the action of other people.

Sequence in Time

Some topics lend themselves to **time arrangement**, a series of steps or points in time. Sharing recipes, assembly instructions, and technical procedures often require a time arrangement, as do presentations about historical events. You also can use a time arrangement for a past-present-future pattern or for a before-after pattern. Here's an example of time arrangement:

TOPIC AREA: Conducting effective meetings

PURPOSE: To explain how to use meeting time effectively and efficiently

CENTRAL IDEA: Well-run meetings have a definite purposeful beginning, a well-organized middle, and useful ending.

KEY POINTS: A. Convening the meeting

B. Following the prepared agenda

C. Ending the meeting

Position in Space

If your information can be placed in different locations, you may want to use a **space arrangement** as an organizational pattern. A proposed highway system is hard to describe unless you can show where it will go and what it will displace. Here's another example:

TOPIC AREA: Brain structure

PURPOSE: To explain how different sections of the brain are responsible for different functions

CENTRAL IDEA: A guided tour of the brain begins in the hindbrain, moves through the midbrain, and ends in the forebrain, with side trips through the right and left hemispheres.

KEY POINTS: A. The hindbrain

B. The midbrain

C. The forebrain

D. The right and left hemispheres

Present Problems and Solutions

Problem-solution arrangement describes a harmful or difficult situation (the problem) and offers a plan to solve the problem (the solution). This

● getting started   ▶ delivery   ◆ speaking to persuade
▲ fundamentals   ⁎ engaging your audience   ★ speaking occasions
■ content   ◣ speaking to inform   ✳ resources

pattern can be applied to both **INFORMATIVE** and **PERSUASIVE** presentations. When speaking to inform, you may describe a problem that is
relatively simple and not controversial (a squeaking door, for example) and
then describe how to solve it (lubricate the hinges). In a persuasive presentation, you describe a significant problem that is complex, possibly controversial, and not easily solved. Then you advocate a particular action or
actions to minimize or solve the problem (for example, advocating a publicity campaign to enact tougher laws to reduce the problem of drunk driving).
Here is one example of a problem-solution arrangement in an informative
speech:

307–46

347–404

TOPIC AREA: Sitting, inactivity, and health

PURPOSE: To recommend methods for reducing the aches and
pains of sitting too long

CENTRAL IDEA: Sitting for long periods of time can cause serious health
problems, but standing up and moving around on a
regular schedule can offset the harms.

KEY POINTS: A. Extended sitting can be harmful to physical health.
(Heart disease and cancer both increase with num-
ber of hours per day spent sitting.)

B. A sedentary lifestyle increases the risk of certain
mental health problems, such as depression and
dementia.

C. A regular schedule of simple physical activities (for
example, standing up, walking, doing chores) significantly reduces health risks.

Show Causes and Effects

A **cause-and-effect arrangement** either presents a cause and its resulting
effect (cause-to-effect) or describes the effect that results from a specific
cause (effect-to-cause).

In a *cause-to-effect arrangement*, you might claim that eating red meat
causes disease and depression, that lower taxes result in more business
investment and personal savings, or that large classes, poor discipline, and

low teacher salaries explain the decline in educational achievement. In the following cause-to-effect arrangement, the speaker claims that excessive television watching harms children in many ways:[3]

TOPIC AREA: Children and television

PURPOSE: To describe how watching too much television causes harmful effects in children

CENTRAL IDEA: Television harms children and their families because it steals time that could be spent on more important activities.

KEY POINTS:
A. Television has a negative effect on children's physical fitness.

B. Television has a negative effect on children's school achievement.

C. Television is a hidden competitor for more important activities.

D. Television watching may become a serious addiction.

In an *effect-to-cause arrangement*, you describe a situation or behavior, create curiosity in your audience about its cause or causes, and then explain why the situation or behavior exists. For example, you might start by pointing out to your audience that in the last decade, the population of fish in a nearby lake has declined by 50 percent. Why did this happened? You might identify an increase in harmful chemicals in the lake water and a similar increase in the number of camps and homes built on the waterfront during that same time.

In the following effect-to-cause arrangement, the speaker identifies some of the causes of obesity:

TOPIC AREA: Obesity

PURPOSE: To understand why so many Americans are obese

CENTRAL IDEA: Understanding five reasons why people are obese is the first step in combating its harmful effects.

KEY POINTS:
A. Effect: Obesity is a serious medical problem in the United States.

● getting started   ▶ delivery   ◆ speaking to persuade
▲ fundamentals   ⁘ engaging your audience ★ speaking occasions
■ content   ◣ speaking to inform   ✳ resources

B. Causes:

    1. Hidden dangers in processed and fast foods

    2. Lack of exercise

    3. Psychological factors: anxiety, low self-esteem, excessive use of alcohol and tobacco

    4. Family influence, habits, and lifestyle

    5. Genetics

Arrange Scientifically

Scientists present claims by using the **scientific method arrangement**. When sharing the results of a scientific study or explaining the development of a theory—either your own or the work of a scientist—consider using an organizational pattern that follows the steps prescribed by journals that publish scientific research. Usually there are five basic sections in a scientific research report:

1. Explain the research question and why it is important.
2. Review previous research on the topic in question.
3. Describe the scientific methods used to study the research question.
4. Analyze and present the research results.
5. Discuss the implications of the research.[4]

The following example outlines a speech explaining the results of a study on the relationship between presentation anxiety and the preparation process:

TOPIC AREA: Presentation anxiety and the preparation process

PURPOSE: To explain why anxious speakers should study and master the process of preparing an effective presentation

CENTRAL IDEA: Learning effective preparation skills can reduce your level of speech anxiety and improve the quality of your presentation.

KEY POINTS: A. Research question: What is the relationship between speaker anxiety and preparation skills?

    B. Review previous research

C. Describe the research method

D. Present the research results

E. Discuss the implications of the research: Learning effective preparation skills can reduce presentation anxiety.

Tell Stories and Give Examples

117 ■

Sometimes a series of memorable **STORIES OR EXAMPLES** are so compelling and interesting that they can easily become the backbone of a speech. For example:

TOPIC AREA:	Leaders and adversity
PURPOSE:	To convince listeners that disabilities are not a barrier to success
CENTRAL IDEA:	Many noteworthy leaders have lived exceptional lives with disabilities.
KEY POINTS:	A. Franklin D. Roosevelt, president of the United States, paralyzed by polio
	B. Jan Scruggs, wounded soldier and founder of the Vietnam Veterans Memorial Fund
	C. Helen Keller, deaf and blind author, lecturer, and disability advocate

Compare and Contrast

A **comparison-contrast arrangement** shows your audience how individual things are similar to or different from each other. There are two basic ways to do this: *block* and *point-by-point* comparisons.[5] If you use the block method, you describe the relevant information about one item and then compare it to the relevant information about another item. For example:

TOPIC AREA:	America's big cities
PURPOSE:	To show that each of America's big cities is an excellent place to live, depending on your values

CENTRAL IDEA: Choosing to live in New York, Los Angeles, or Chicago depends on understanding the advantages and disadvantages of each one.

KEY POINTS:
A. New York: Advantages and disadvantages of the Big Apple

B. Los Angeles: Advantages and disadvantages of the City of Angels

C. Chicago: Advantages and disadvantages of the Windy City

Alternatively, when you do a point-by-point comparison, you focus on specific points of comparison between the things you are comparing. The following example compares medium-size family sedans, based on four points of comparison: performance, comfort, fuel economy, and reliability:

TOPIC AREA: Family sedans

PURPOSE: To recommend a way of evaluating medium-size cars

CENTRAL IDEA: Comparing performance, comfort, fuel economy, and reliability can help you select and purchase a new mid-size car for your family.

KEY POINTS:
A. Performance

B. Comfort

C. Fuel economy

D. Reliability

A different type of the comparison-contrast arrangement is called a *figurative analogy*. An **ANALOGY** compares something unfamiliar with something more familiar, showing how two unrelated items have certain common characteristics. Betting on the winner of a horse race is obviously not the same thing as predicting a student's success in college, yet the former provides a good analogy for thinking about the latter, as in this example:

116–17

TOPIC AREA: Student success in college

PURPOSE: To identify the multiple factors that affect student success in college

CENTRAL IDEA: Predicting student success is like picking the winning horse at the racetrack and must include considerations of a student's high school record, teachers, advisers, parents' education, and the college environment.

KEY POINTS:
A. High school grades and test scores = Track record

B. Parents' education = Horse's breeding record

C. Teacher and adviser = Trainer and jockey

D. College environment = Track conditions, length of race, and so on

Use Memory Aids

Journalists use the five Ws—who, what, where, when, and why—to remind them of the key questions they should answer in a news story. First-aid instructors teach the ABCs of first aid: open the airway, check for breathing, and check for circulation. Speakers, too, can use easily remembered letters, words, or phrases to organize their speech, or in combination with any of the other organizational patterns we've been discussing, to help their audience follow along and, later, to remember their key points. Here's an example:

TOPIC AREA: Organizing a presentation

PURPOSE: To provide an effective method for developing the key points of a presentation

CENTRAL IDEA: The four Rs represent a series of critical thinking steps—review, reduce, regroup, refine—for generating a presentation's key point.

KEY POINTS:
A. Review

B. Reduce

C. Regroup

D. Refine

Other Organizational Patterns

The previous patterns are not the only way to organize the key points of a presentation. Rather, they represent some of the most frequently used formats. There are additional patterns for various professions and special

getting started   ▶ delivery   ◆ speaking to persuade

▲ fundamentals   ⁙ engaging your audience   ★ speaking occasions

■ content   ▼ speaking to inform   ✳ resources

occasions, and several organizational patterns best suited for **PERSUASIVE SPEAKING**, such as problem-cause-solution, comparative advantages, refuting and objections, and persuasive stories, as well as what's known as **MONROE'S MOTIVATED SEQUENCE**.

◆ 393–99

◆ 397–99

Depending on the rhetorical situation, audience characteristics, your credibility and purpose, and the topic area, you may be able to adapt a common pattern or invent one of your own. Creative thinking can produce original patterns. For example, in some cases, you can transform your key points into commonly asked questions rather than statements. Think about how an audience might react to the following questions about the death penalty, as opposed to having the key points presented to them as statements:

- Does the death penalty *deter* people from committing murder?
- What *costs* more—life in prison or the legal process leading to execution?
- Do victims' families have a right to *revenge* and emotional closure?

Using common questions as key points is one way of addressing your audience directly with a series of thought-provoking issues.

A creative organizational pattern can also enhance your **CREDIBILITY** and boost your **AUDIENCE'S INTEREST**. For example, a creative presentation by Patricia Phillips, a customer-service expert, used excerpts from popular songs—"(I Can't Get No) Satisfaction" by the Rolling Stones, "Help!" by the Beatles, "Respect" by Aretha Franklin, "Don't Be Cruel" by Elvis Presley, and "Hit the Road Jack" by Ray Charles—to begin each major section of her training seminar. These well-known songs provided an upbeat and creative way to move into each new section of the customer-service seminar.

▲ 57–66

⁘ 268–79

Sequencing Key Points

Some of the organizational arrangements described above (for example, time arrangement and scientific method arrangement) more or less dictate the order of your key points. Others don't. The following general considerations can help you decide which key points should go first, next, and last.

Strength and Familiarity

If one of your points is not as strong as the others or is less familiar to your audience, place it in the middle position. For example, how would you order the key points within the stories and examples organizational pattern in a presentation on leadership and physical disabilities that focuses on President Franklin Roosevelt, Jan Scruggs, and Helen Keller? Whereas most US audiences would be familiar with the first and third person, they probably wouldn't recognize Jan Scruggs, a disabled Vietnam veteran who founded the Washington Vietnam Veterans Memorial Fund. Put the least familiar story in the middle of the presentation in order to start and end with better-known examples.

Audience

72–80 Whether you "put your best foot forward" by leading with your strongest point or "save the best for last" will depend in part on what your purpose is and what you learn during AUDIENCE ANALYSIS. If your audience of colleagues at work comes to your presentation wanting information about current sales figures, make sure that you satisfy that need early on in your presentation. An audience motivated to hear something very particular from you shouldn't be made to wait for it. Other points can come later. On the other hand, if an audience is not very interested in your topic or simply not knowledgeable about it, don't begin with your most technical, detailed point. You may be better off beginning with a point that explains *why* understanding the topic is important and then build up to your strongest point at the end. At any rate, it's always a good idea to consider your
76–77
75 audience's NEEDS and MOTIVATIONS when deciding on the order of your key points.

Logistics

The logistics of a speaking situation can sometimes affect the order of key points. If you're one of a series of presenters, for example, there is a chance that you will end up with less time to speak than was originally scheduled. In that case, you should organize your presentation so that the most important key points come first. That way, if you have to shorten your presentation at the last minute, your audience will still have heard the main
302–4 thing you came to say. If the facility is not conducive to using PRESENTATION AIDS, you may have to change the order of your key points or even delete one that is highly dependent on a set of graphs.

● getting started	▶ delivery	◆ speaking to persuade
▲ fundamentals	∴ engaging your audience	★ speaking occasions
■ content	▼ speaking to inform	✷ resources

Connecting Key Points

Connectives link one part of a presentation to another, clarify how one idea relates to another, and identify how supporting material bolsters a key point. Without connectives, a well-organized presentation can sound choppy and awkward. Connectives provide the "glue" that attaches major parts of a presentation to one another. They help your audience follow, understand, and remember your message.

There are four kinds of connective phrases: *internal previews*, *internal summaries*, *transitional phrases*, and *signposts*.

Internal Previews

In the introduction of a presentation, an **internal preview** reveals or suggests your key points to the audience. It tells them what you are going to cover and in what order. In the body of a speech, an internal preview describes how you are going to approach a key point. Here's how one student internally previewed his presentation on weight loss:

> How do researchers and doctors explain obesity? Some offer genetic explanations while others identify psychological ones. Either or both factors can be responsible for our never-ending battle with the bathroom scale. Let's begin by looking at . . .

Internal Summaries

Whereas an internal preview begins a section, an **internal summary** ends a section and helps to reinforce important ideas. Internal summaries also give you an opportunity to pause in a presentation and repeat critical ideas or pieces of information. Here's an internal summary section on the genetic factors that influence overeating:

> So remember, before spending hundreds of dollars on diet books and exercise equipment, make sure that your weight problem is not influenced by your hormone levels, your metabolism, or the amount of glucose in your bloodstream.

Transitions

The most common connectives are **transitions**—words, numbers, brief phrases, or sentences that help you lead your audience from one key point or section to another. They are bridges that help you get from one idea to the next. Transitions can be quite simple and consist of little more than a word or phrase. They can also be one or two complete sentences that help you move from one major section of a presentation to another. Some common transitions are highlighted in the following examples:

- Yet it's important to remember . . .
- In addition to metabolism, there is . . .
- On the other hand, some people believe . . .
- Another reason why he should be elected is . . .
- Finally, a responsible parent should . . .

Transitions can also function as mini-previews and mini-summaries that link the conclusion of one section to the beginning of another. For example: "Once you've eliminated these four genetic explanations for weight gain, it's time to consider several psychological factors."

Relying only on the transitions above won't add interest or variety to a presentation. A presenter who says little more than "in addition," "next," and "finally" will sound tedious. Savvy speakers use a variety of transitional phrases and strategies to avoid repetition and to suit the particular needs of each moment in their presentation. Here are some examples:

- *Bridge words* alert listeners that you are moving on to a new thought. Examples include "furthermore," "meanwhile," "however," "in addition," "consequently," and "finally."
- *Trigger transitions* use the same word or phrase twice to connect one topic to another. For example: "That wraps up our *examination of* genetic *factors*. Now we can begin an *examination of* psychological *factors*."
- *Questions* shift the audience's attention from one point to another. For example: "Now that we've examined how genetic factors influence weight gain, you may be wondering, 'But what about the psychological factors?'"
- *Flashbacks* link a previous point to a new one. For example: "Do you remember when I talked about the research on obese mice a few minutes ago? Another kind of research looks at genetics in a different way."

⬤ getting started   ▶ delivery   ◆ speaking to persuade
▲ fundamentals   ⸫ engaging your audience   ★ speaking occasions
◼ content   ▽ speaking to inform ✳ resources

- *Delivery transitions* use **MOVEMENT**, **GESTURES**, or **VISUAL AIDS** to signal a transition from one thing to another. Examples include the "on one hand" and "on the other hand" gestures, moving one's body from one place to another in the room while describing a transition, or shifting from talking to using a visual aid.[6]

▶ 217
▶ 213–15
•• 302–4

Signposts

A final and important type of connective is the signpost. Just as most travelers like to know where they are, where they've been, how they got there, and where they're going, audiences appreciate a speaker who uses connectives for similar reasons. **Signposts** are short, often numerical references that, like highway signs, tell or remind your listeners where you are and how far you have to go. A signpost can be as simple as "Let's begin by looking at your family's history of weight gain" or saying you will describe four physiological causes of weight gain and then beginning each explanation with a number—first, second, third, and fourth—as in: "Fourth and finally, make sure your glucose level has been tested and is within normal levels." Making explicit how many points you will cover not only offers a preview for your audience but also lets them know when you have made your last point and are about to **CONCLUDE YOUR PRESENTATION**.

■ 169–75

For an example of a speaker who identifies, repeats, and rephrases three key points throughout a presentation, see Notable Speaker: David Epstein, page 342.

Constructing Your Presentation

Once you've identified your topic, purpose, central idea, key points, and supporting material, and once you've thought critically about the best organizing pattern and order for everything, you have the pieces you need to construct an effective, well-organized presentation. The two methods that follow—*outlining* and something we call the *speech framer*—can help you take the last major organizational step: building a complete blueprint or substantial structure for your presentation.

Outlining

Just about everyone knows what an outline is. **Outlining** organizes ideas in a specific order and uses formatting conventions (indenting, numbering, and so on) to indicate the relative importance of, and the relationships among, those ideas. Thomas Leech, a communication consultant and executive speech coach, observes this about outlines:

> Presenters sometimes say that they don't outline because it will constrain their thought process and take away their natural flow. Yet a speech must be constrained. It must be tightly packaged, with all the extraneous ideas and materials excluded. An audience deserves and will insist upon a concisely organized message that achieves its goals in the least possible time.[7]

A well-developed outline of a presentation can provide a logical framework in which to position every component of a presentation. As you move through the speechmaking process, three types of outlines—the *preliminary outline*, *full-sentence outline*, and *speaking outline*—can help you effectively organize the content during different phases of the preparation process.

Preliminary Outline A **preliminary outline** helps you develop and arrange your key points and supporting material into a sketch of your presentation. It lets you try out different ways of organizing your content into a coherent message.

Full-Sentence Outline Some speakers (and students required to do so by their instructors) take the outlining process much further. They expand their preliminary outline into a **full-sentence outline**—a comprehensive overview of your presentation. Most speakers outside the classroom don't create full-sentence outlines.

Speaking Notes Outline In the context of speechmaking, there is a third type of outline—the **speaking notes outline**—that guides you through your presentation as you speak. Whereas preliminary and full-sentence outlines can help you organize your presentation, the speaking outline is your presentation's GPS—a guide that you can use to keep you on course during the presentation itself. In addition to making sure you move through the key points and supporting material in order, it can include **DELIVERY CUES** and let you see exactly where you are in a presentation and where you need to go.

▶ 227–28

If you need more help

See 9.2, HOW TO OUTLINE A PRESENTATION, for more detailed guidance about how to create effective preliminary outlines, full-sentence outlines, and speaking notes outlines.

✳ 511–24

The Speech Framer

Some speakers don't like outlining because its rules and format can constrain their thought process and the natural flow of ideas. An effective alternative to outlining (and the method that the authors of this book prefer) is the **speech framer**, a visual framework that identifies a place for every component of a presentation.[8] The speech framer also

- Makes it easier to modify, add, and delete content on a single page
- Encourages experimentation, originality, and creativity
- Is easily transformed into a complete outline, if necessary
- Serves as efficient and flexible speaking notes

Here's what the general structure of the speech framer looks like:

Introduction

Central idea

Key points 1.   2.   3.

           Connect to 2.   Connect to 3.

(Continued)

Support
_____

Support
_____

Support
_____

Conclusion

_____

If you use the space in the speech framer efficiently, you should be able to fit all your presentation's most important content—including all your key points and supporting materials—on a single page. The speech framer provides an at-a-glance assessment of your presentation's organization, which is helpful both as you're building your presentation and as you're giving it. Although the empty grid above shows three key points, you can simply add extra columns to the frame if needed. Similarly, if you have more (or fewer) supporting materials for each key point, you can add (or delete) rows.

The following example shows how a student used the speech framer to organize a presentation on the dangers of sleep deprivation. By using the single-page frame as her speaking notes, she could practice comfortably in an extemporaneous speaking style and see her entire presentation laid out before her as she spoke.

- getting started
- fundamentals
- content
- ▶ delivery
- •• engaging your audience
- ▼ speaking to inform
- ◆ speaking to persuade
- ★ speaking occasions
- ✳ resources

THE SPEECH FRAMER: ASLEEP AT THE WHEEL

Introduction: Story about my best friend's death in a car accident

Central idea: "Fall-asleep crashes" count for 100,000 car accidents and more than 1,500 deaths every year. Everyone knows about the dangers of drunk driving, but few of us know about the dangers of sleep deprivation—and what to do about it.

Key points	1. Why we need sleep Connective: What happens when you don't get enough sleep?	2. Sleep deprivation affects your health, well-being, and safety. Connective: So how can you ease your tired body and mind?	3. Three steps can help you get a good night's sleep.
Support	Would you drive home from class drunk? 14 hours without sleep is akin to 0.1 blood alcohol level.	Lack of sleep affects your attitude and mood (cite quotation from sleep study).	Decide how much sleep is right for you: • Keep a sleep log. • Most people need 8 or more hours a night.
Support	Circadian clock controls sleep and also regulates hormones, heart rate, body temperature, and so on.	Lack of sleep affects your health. Most studies recommend a seventh and eighth hour of sleep.	Create a comfy sleep environment. • Don't sleep on a full or empty stomach. • Avoid fluids and eliminate alcohol and caffeine before sleep.
Support	Things that rob our sleep: • 24-hour stores • Internet • Television	Symptoms: • Crave naps or doze off? • Hit snooze button a lot? • Hard to solve problems? • Feel groggy, lethargic?	Don't take your troubles to bed. • Can't sleep? Get up. • Play soothing music. • Read a book, but not on an electronic device.

Conclusion: Recognizing that you may be sleep deprived is the first step. The hardest thing to do is to alter your habits. Retraining yourself to follow a normal sleep pattern isn't going to happen overnight. But once you discover that a few extra hours of sleep will help you feel more rested, relaxed, and revitalized, giving up that extra hour on the internet or watching TV will have been worth it. There so much in life to enjoy. Sleep longer, live longer.

NOTABLE SPEAKER
Ashton Kutcher

After being discovered by a talent agent in college, Ashton Kutcher began his career as a model. He transitioned into acting when he landed the part of Kelso on the television sitcom *That '70s Show*. Perhaps his most significant role as a dramatic actor came in 2012 when he was cast as Steve Jobs in the biopic *Jobs*. His work outside the industry includes cofounding Thorn, an organization devoted to stopping human trafficking and the sexual exploitation of children.

In 2013, Kutcher was the recipient of MTV's Ultimate Choice Award at the annual Teen Choice Awards ceremony. The awards honor various achievements in fashion, television, film, and music, among other areas, and are voted on by viewers aged thirteen and over. Kutcher was thirty-five when he received the award.

Search Terms
To locate a video of this presentation online, enter the following key words into a search engine: Ashton Kutcher Teen Choice Awards. The video is approximately 4:41 in length.

What to Watch For
[0:26–1:40] Using a comfortable conversational style, Kutcher demonstrates that he has analyzed his audience, purpose, and content in order to make strategic choices about what to say and how to say it. He uses lessons he has learned in life to inspire his audience to work hard, be kind, and build a life (his purpose). His focus on life lessons is appropriate for a young audience who could benefit from his experiences.

[1:00–1:45] As he begins to lay out his purpose, Kutcher says he'll share some "insider secrets" with his audience about how to build a career in Hollywood. Then he says something that surprises his listeners (we can tell because they quiet down considerably after he says it): "I feel like a fraud. My name is actually not even Ashton. Ashton is my middle name. My first name's Chris." By doing this, he captures his audience's attention and signals that his purpose will connect who he was as Chris to who he is now as Ashton. "There were some really amazing things that I learned as Chris," he says, and he wants to share these things with his audience. This important and unexpected pivot provides a direct transition to the first of three key points Kutcher will make in the remainder of his acceptance speech.

[1:45–2:00] He organizes his presentation into three distinct key points. "The first thing is about opportunity," he says, "the second thing is about being sexy, and the third thing is about living life." The simplicity and clarity of the organization improves his audience's ability to retain his central idea and key points, as well as the most relevant examples he uses to support his claims.

[2:48–3:32] Using a categorical arrangement pattern, Kutcher makes three key points (the rule of three). His second point about being sexy draws screams and cheers from the teenage audience. In an unexpected turn, he confides that being sexy has nothing to do with what they look like but everything to do with being smart, kind, and generous. The audience cheers louder as he encourages them not to buy into messages that make them feel "less than" based on how they look.

(NOTABLE SPEAKER CONTINUED)

[3:32–3:40] To reinforce his second main point, Kutcher uses an internal summary to repeat those ideas. He summarizes: "Be smart. Be thoughtful. Be generous." As he moves on to his next point, Kutcher uses a signpost to remind the audience where he is in the presentation. In this instance, he uses a numerical reference at the outset of the point: "The third thing . . ." His third point is tied to his most recent accomplishment—making the film about Steve Jobs. This point reinforces the connections between lessons he learned as Chris and where he is now as Ashton.

EXERCISE

After viewing Kutcher's speech, reflect on these questions:

1. Would you have chosen the same order as he did for his key points? Why or why not?

2. What are some characteristics of the occasion and audience that Kutcher probably considered as he was deciding what key points to select?

3. Did you find it easy to remember Kutcher's key points after his presentation? Why or why not?

4. What was his central idea? To what extent did his key points reflect that central idea?

5. Describe a creative organizational pattern Kutcher could have used to organize his key points.

6. How well did Kutcher anticipate and adapt his message and delivery to an audience of screaming fans?

Conclusion

Clear and coherent organization may not be the sexiest or most exciting aspect of your presentation, but it is among the most important things your presentation needs in order to be effective. A coherent organizational structure helps you develop compelling and relevant key points that support your central idea in a way that enhances your audience's understanding and interest. A presentation that is organized badly—no matter how skillfully you deliver it—will be much less likely to succeed.

Think of it this way: A speech without structure is like a human body without a skeleton. It won't stand up. Spineless, like a jellyfish. Having structure won't make the speech a great one, but lacking structure will surely kill all the inspired thoughts—because listeners are too busy trying to find out where they are to pay attention.[9]

3.4 Introductions and Conclusions

In June 2012, Susan Cain, author of *Quiet: The Power of Introverts in a World That Can't Stop Talking*, delivered a TED talk about the talents and abilities introverts bring to our homes, classrooms, and workplaces. Here's how she began her talk:

> When I was nine years old, I went off to summer camp for the first time. And my mother packed me a suitcase full of books, which to me seemed like a perfectly natural thing to do. Because in my family, reading was the primary group activity. And this might sound antisocial to you, but for us it was really just a different way of being social. You have the animal warmth of your family sitting right next to you, but you are also free to go roaming around the adventure-land inside your own mind. And I had this idea that camp was going to be just like this, but better. I had a vision of ten girls sitting in a cabin cozily reading books in their matching nightgowns.
>
> Camp was more like a keg party without any alcohol. And on the very first day, our counselor gathered us all together and she taught us a cheer that she said we would be doing every day for the rest of the summer to instill camp spirit. And it went like this: "R-O-W-D-I-E, that's the way we spell ROWDIE! ROWDIE, ROWDIE, let's get ROWDIE!"
>
> Yeah. So I couldn't figure out for the life of me, why we were supposed to be so rowdy, or why we had to spell this word incorrectly.[1]

Cain's talk has been viewed more than twenty-two million times since 2012; it is among the most popular talks on the TED website. How is it that an introduction about reading books at camp could be interesting enough to make millions of people want to listen to her? (For more information about Susan Cain's TED talk, see the Notable Speaker feature at the end of this chapter.)

getting started   ▶ delivery   ◆ speaking to persuade

▲ fundamentals   ∴ engaging your audience   ★ speaking occasions

■ content   ▼ speaking to inform   ✳ resources

Before you answer, consider the next example from a student's presentation. Without the benefit of being a well-known speaker, she also captures our interest.

> On June 23 at 7:43 p.m., a smoldering car was found twisted around a tree. Two dead bodies. One adult. One baby. Why did this happen? Was it drunk driving? No. Adverse road conditions? No. A defect in the car? No. Something else took the life of my best friend and her baby brother. Something quite simple, quite common, and deadly: she fell asleep at the wheel.
>
> "Fall-asleep car crashes" account for one hundred thousand accidents and fifteen hundred deaths every year. And unlike the problem of drunk driving, which is so difficult to solve, the problem of driving while drowsy can be significantly reduced once you know more about it and how to prevent it.

Both of these introductions—Susan Cain's and this student's—show the power of a strong opening.

The Goals of an Introduction

"You never get a second chance to make a first impression"—so the saying goes. Think about your own snap judgments about people and things within the first few seconds or minutes of experiencing them. If your first impression of a date isn't positive, you're likely to write that person off as a potential romantic partner. If the first few minutes of a TV show bore you, you may switch to something else. Likewise, if the beginning of your speech isn't interesting, you may lose your audience. Although they may not walk out on you, they might tune you out, misunderstand you, forget you, or, even worse, remember you as a poor speaker. On the other hand, a good beginning can create a positive, lasting impression and can pave the way for a presentation that achieves its purpose. Psychologists describe the power of first impressions as the *primacy effect*. The **primacy effect** is a tendency to recall the first items you see or hear in sequenced information. The primacy effect suggests that audience members are more likely to remember the beginning of a presentation because that's when their attention is at its peak.

Your introduction creates a critical relationship among three elements in your presentation: *you*, your *audience*, and your *message*. The beginning of a presentation introduces you and your topic to the audience; it also introduces your audience to you. Your introduction gives the audience time to adjust, settle in, block out distractions, and focus their attention. At the same time, it gives you a chance to get a feel for the audience, calm yourself down, and make any last-minute adjustments to what you want to say and how you want to say it.

There are five main goals of any introduction.

Focus Audience Attention and Interest

268–79 • 115–19 ■ 184 ▶

Your introduction should gain **AUDIENCE ATTENTION** through your use of compelling **SUPPORTING MATERIALS**, **EXPRESSIVE SPEAKING**, and active involvement of audience members.

Connect to Your Audience

72–80 ▲

You should link your message to the **AUDIENCE'S CHARACTERISTICS**, attitudes, needs, and interests. Give audience members a good reason to listen to you by explaining how your presentation will benefit them.

Put You in Your Presentation

57–66 ▲

Your introduction should link your expertise, experiences, and personality to your purpose and topic. The audience perceptions of you, the **SPEAKER**—what they think about your competence, trustworthiness, likability, and dynamism—can be just as important as what they think about your message.

Set the Mood

239–45 • 220–25 ▶

Make sure that your **WORDS**, **DELIVERY STYLE**, and choice of supporting materials are appropriate for the mood of your message. The mood and emotions you express in your introduction can be positive and upbeat, respectful and sober, playful and amusing, or urgent and serious. It all depends on your **PURPOSE**.

87–101 ▲

● getting started   ▶ delivery   ◆ speaking to persuade

▲ fundamentals   • engaging your audience   ★ speaking occasions

■ content   ▼ speaking to inform   ✳ resources

Preview the Message

In most speaking situations, you should give your audience a sneak preview of the content of your message. State your **CENTRAL IDEA**, if appropriate, and briefly list the **KEY POINTS** you will cover. In some situations— a **PERSUASIVE PRESENTATION**, for example, or when **PRESENTING AN AWARD**—you may not want to reveal your central idea or key points at the beginning of a presentation.

■ 137–38
■ 133–36
◆ 386–87
★ 427–32

You may not always be able to achieve all five goals. Just remember this: the single most important goal of any introduction is simply to *focus audience attention and interest*. In order for your audience to learn from or agree with your message, they have to listen to it first!

Ways to Begin

There are almost as many ways to begin a presentation as there are speakers, topics, and types of audiences. Following are some effective ways to begin a presentation that work separately or in combination with one another.

Use an Interesting Statistic or Example

If you anticipate a problem gaining and maintaining your audience's attention, an unusual, dramatic, or unexpected **STATISTIC** or **EXAMPLE** can help focus their eyes, ears, and minds on you and your message. Here's an example:

■ 115
■ 117

> How much money do you make? How much do you plan to make in the future? Too bad you're not Mark Hurd, CEO of Oracle. According to the *Wall Street Journal*, his reported annual compensation (including salary, bonuses, acquisition awards, and deferred pension) in 2019 was $108 million. It almost makes you feel sorry for Tim Cook, CEO of Apple, whose annual compensation was a mere $16 million—$307,000 a week. Even if he worked on weekends, his daily compensation was only $44,000 a day. "Poor" Tim!

Quote Someone

Rather than trying to write the perfect beginning yourself, you may find that someone else has already done it for you. As you research your topic, you may uncover a dramatic statement or eloquent phrase that is an ideal beginning for your presentation. A well-chosen quotation can overcome audience doubts, especially when the quotation is from someone who is highly respected or an expert source of information.

131–32 When quoting someone, make sure you identify the writer or speaker with an **ORAL FOOTNOTE**. In some cases, you need to state only the name of the person you are quoting. In other cases, you may need to provide more information about the person, circumstances, or publication.

Consider this example, in which a speaker quotes Warren Buffett:

> Warren Buffett is the fourth-richest person in the world. His net worth is more than $70 billion. When asked about the skill that was most important in improving his success, his answer is public speaking. Yet, as a young man, he was frozen with fear of speaking. How bad was it? Here's how he tells it: "I would throw up. In fact, I arranged my life so that I never had to get up in front of anybody." He went on to say that, in his opinion, "you can improve your monetary value by 50 percent just by learning . . . public speaking." Let's take a closer look at why he is so adamant about the value of this skill and why you should heed his advice.

Depending on the length of the quotation and how well you've practiced the opening, you may be able to quote someone without looking at your notes. Otherwise, you can refer to your notes as a way of showing that you want to quote your source accurately.

Tell a Story

253–67 Some speakers begin presentations with **STORIES** about their personal hardships or triumphs. Others share stories they've read about or heard from others. The following example comes from a student presentation:

> When I was fifteen, I was operated on to remove the deadliest form of skin cancer, a melanoma carcinoma. My doctors injected ten shots of steroids into each scar every three weeks to stop the scars from spreading. I now know that it wasn't worth a couple of summers of being tan to go through all that pain and suffering. Take steps now to protect yourself from the harmful effects of the sun.

Stories do not have to be personal or tragic. They can come from history, literature, TV programs, and films. Think of the lessons to be learned from the Harry Potter books and films, from television characters, and from the biographies or autobiographies of great women and men.

getting started   ▶ delivery   ◆ speaking to persuade

▲ fundamentals   engaging your audience   ★ speaking occasions

■ content   ▼ speaking to inform   ✳ resources

Ask a Question

Asking a question or group of questions can attract your audience's attention and interest because it encourages them to think about the possible answers. Although a few listeners may be able to answer the questions you pose, many more will think to themselves, "I have no idea!" and will be intrigued to hear more from you. Here is an example from a student presentation:

> What is the basis for the 2018 international ranking of China, Iran, Saudi Arabia, Vietnam, Iraq, Egypt, and the United States? Something to do with oil or weapons development? No. Statista, an international provider of data, reports that these seven countries lead the world in the number of annual executions. Now ponder these questions: Why is the United States the only highly developed, democratic nation on the list? And why—given that many states and other countries have abolished the death penalty—is the United States still on the list?

Establish a Personal Link

Use your introduction to link your background and experiences to those of your audience. Even though you may not know or may be quite different from the members of your audience, your experiences may be similar. When Margaret Muller, a middle-school student with Down syndrome, made a presentation to seventh- and eighth-grade classes, here's how she began:

> Today I'd like to tell you about Down syndrome. My purpose for talking about this is to be able to say, "Yes, I have Down syndrome. Sometimes I have to work harder to learn things, but in many ways I am just like everyone else." I would like to tell people that having Down syndrome does not keep me from doing things I need to do or want to do. I just have to work harder.[2]

Refer to an Event, Place, or Occasion

An obvious way to begin a presentation is to refer to the place where you are speaking or the occasion for the gathering. Your audience's memories and feelings about a specific place or occasion can conjure up the emotions needed to capture their attention and interest.

When Martin Luther King Jr. made his famous "I Have a Dream" speech on the steps of the Lincoln Memorial, his first few words echoed Abraham Lincoln's Gettysburg Address ("Four score and seven years ago"). Here's how he began: "Five score years ago, a great American, in whose symbolic shadow we stand, signed the Emancipation Proclamation."

Important events that occur shortly before a presentation or in the recent past can connect you with some of what your audience knows, thinks, and feels about an issue, as with this example:

> Dr. Larry Nassar, a physician who worked with the US Olympic Gymnastics Team, was accused of more than 250 sexual assaults against minors. In January 2019, he was sentenced to 40 to 175 years in jail for criminal sexual conduct—adding to a previous child pornography conviction of 60 years. Sadly, there are many sexual predators disguised as healers, teachers, soldiers, and business executives who have never been prosecuted or jailed.

Address Audience Needs

In a crisis situation, a speaker may need to address the problem immediately. If budget cuts will require salary reductions, audience members will want the details. They won't want to hear a humorous story, a clever question, or an unusual statistic. When your listeners' jobs or futures are threatened, don't take up their time with a clever beginning. In fact, such introductions may even make the audience angry and damage your credibility. Get right to the point. Here's an example:

> As you know, the state has reduced our operating budget by $2.7 million. It is important that you know this: All of you will have a job here next year—and the year after. There will be no layoffs. Instead there will be cutbacks in non-personnel budget lines, downsizing of programs, and, possibly, short furloughs.

137–38
133–36

This speaker went directly to the **CENTRAL IDEA** and previewed the **KEY POINTS** of her speech. After explaining that no one would be fired, she then explained how the budget cutbacks, downsizing, and short furloughs would be implemented.

Mix the Methods

Many speakers combine introductory methods to begin their presentations. For instance, this speaker offers a personal experience, statistics, and vivid examples as she begins her speech about funding medical research on Lou Gehrig's disease (ALS) among veterans:

● getting started ▶ delivery ◆ speaking to persuade
▲ fundamentals ∴ engaging your audience ★ speaking occasions
■ content ▼ speaking to inform ✳ resources

My grandfather died from ALS. He used to stumble a lot and had difficulty pronouncing words. It's a horrible disease. You can't walk or
talk. You choke on food, you can't swallow. You often suffocate to
death. Here is what's odd. Four of his friends also suffered from ALS.
Given that only about six thousand people get diagnosed with the
disease each year, what are the odds that five people who all knew
one another get the same diagnosis? What did they have in common?
One thing—they all served in the Army. In fact, serving in the military
makes you 60 percent more likely to get this horrifying disease. But no
one knows why. Today I want to speak about . . .

Tips for Starting Strong

As important as introductions are, many inexperienced speakers don't
prepare them with the care they deserve, thus setting themselves up to
make fundamental errors at the very beginning of their presentations. The
following tips will help you start strong by avoiding the most common
introductory errors.

Plan the Beginning at the End

Simply put, don't plan the introduction to your presentation before you've
developed the body of the speech. There are many decisions to make when
developing a presentation; how to begin should not be the first. Because a
strong introduction can help you achieve your purpose, it should
ADAPT TO YOUR AUDIENCE and closely relate to your message. You have to
know what you will say before you can preview your **KEY POINTS**.

80–82
133–36

Don't Apologize

Wouldn't it be strange if an actor came out on the stage before a play to
tell the audience that he hadn't memorized his lines very well and that
he'd had a lot of trouble singing the first song in the second act? Why, then,
do speakers apologize for their presentations before they give them? Too
often, speakers begin with apologies or excuses: "I don't speak very often, so
please excuse my nervousness"; "I wish I'd had a few more days to prepare
for this presentation, but I just found out on Tuesday that I had to make it."

Comments like these do not accomplish very much and in fact can
adversely impact your **CREDIBILITY**. If your message is meaningful and
well delivered, your excuses may only confuse your audience. If it's awful

57–66

(or you just think it is), let the audience draw their own conclusions. Your introduction should not make excuses or apologize for your level of preparation or the quality of your **DELIVERY**.

184–86 ▶

Avoid "My Speech Is About . . ."

Beginning statements such as "I'm going to talk about . . ." or "My topic is . . ." may be true, but they're unlikely to help you gain the audience's attention or interest. Even though "My speech is about . . ." may introduce your topic, it will not necessarily make that important connection between you and your audience.

Nevertheless, like many rules, there are exceptions. "I'm going to talk about how I was surrounded by killer sharks and survived" would probably make the most jaded audience listen. "My talk will be about the budget crisis and how it will affect your jobs" will likewise hold audience attention and interest. Middle-schooler Margaret Muller's introduction (see p. 165) may appear to violate the rule too, but by putting herself in the presentation right from the start, she openly and confidently addresses the one thing her classmates already knew about her—that she has Down syndrome—and, as a result, appropriately establishes a connection with her audience.

Don't Overpromise

95–97 ▲

Speakers who have no trouble creating a specific and relevant **PURPOSE** may become so committed to it that they set unachievable goals for a short or single presentation. Their introductions promise more than they can deliver. Our advice is simple. Never say: "By the end of this speech you will . . . be a different person," ". . . know the foolproof secret for becoming fabulously rich," ". . . get all A's," ". . . be irresistible to the opposite sex," ". . . never smoke another cigarette," or some other impossible outcome. You can aspire to make a meaningful impact with your presentation, but don't be disappointed if your audience's reaction doesn't match your aspirations.

Avoid Most Jokes

Many public speaking books recommend beginning a presentation with a joke. As much as we enjoy a good laugh, we rarely endorse this strategy.

● getting started ▶ delivery ◆ speaking to persuade
▲ fundamentals ⁘ engaging your audience ★ speaking occasions
■ content ▼ speaking to inform ✳ resources

Just because you know a good joke doesn't mean you should share it when you begin a presentation. The audience may remember the joke but forget your message. Introductory jokes are great when they perfectly match the purpose, topic, and audience. If they don't match, save them for your friends.

The biggest reason to avoid using jokes in an introduction is that you can ruin your chance of making a good first impression. What if no one laughs? Even worse, what if audience members are offended? Avoiding jokes doesn't mean avoiding **HUMOR** in an introduction—an amusing example, a strange statistic, a funny story, or a great line from a comedian can work wonderfully. For example, Susan Cain (the speaker quoted at the beginning of this chapter) demonstrates how a personal, humorous story can harmonize with and support her message. Effective speakers know that carefully chosen, relevant humor can gain audience attention and provide a hint about the mood and direction of a talk.

272–75

Keep It Short

Generally, we recommend that your introduction take up no more than 10 percent of your speaking time. If it takes more time than that, your audience may lose patience. There are, of course, exceptions to the 10 percent guideline. For instance, Susan Cain's introduction is more than 10 percent of her speaking time, but it doesn't make the introduction feel burdensome to the audience. In order for her to provide a foundation for the central idea, she needed the time to tell the story in the manner that she told it. If you are facing a distrustful or hostile audience, you may need more time to establish your credibility, generate a more hospitable mood, and reduce audience concerns about your message. In most cases, however, 10 percent of a presentation is ample time for achieving the goals of an introduction.

The Goals of a Conclusion

Have you ever been disappointed by the ending of a book or a movie? Have you ever had a bad dessert ruin a decent meal? Have you ever squirmed in your seat when a speaker went on and on with a long, rambling conclusion? What you say and do during the last few seconds of your presentation can determine whether and how well you achieve your purpose.

Psychologists describe the power of last impressions as the *recency effect*. The **recency effect** is the tendency to recall the last items you see or hear in sequenced information. Because it isn't followed by any additional information to crowd it out of listeners' short-term memory, the conclusion of a presentation is likely to stay in audiences' minds long after the speech is over. A strong conclusion ensures that your audience will remember you and your message. In short, the goodbye matters as much as the hello.

Like your introduction, your conclusion should establish a relationship among three elements: *you*, your *message*, and your *audience*. It should accomplish the following goals.

Signal That You Are Concluding

As obvious as it may seem, your audience will appreciate knowing that you are wrapping up your presentation. If you signal that you are concluding your presentation, audience members are prompted to assess your message and to think about their own interpretations and judgments about what you've said.

Summarize Your Message

Repeat the one thing you want your audience to remember at the end of your presentation. Don't use the conclusion to add new ideas or to insert something that you left out. Use the conclusion to reinforce your **CENTRAL IDEA** and **KEY POINTS**.

137–38
133–36

Be Brief

The announced ending of your presentation should not be longer than 10 percent of your speech. Whereas introductions may require some time to gain audience attention and enhance speaker credibility, conclusions should be short and sweet in most rhetorical situations. As one old saying goes, "Be clear. Be brief. Be seated."

● getting started	▶ delivery	◆ speaking to persuade
▲ fundamentals	⁖ engaging your audience	★ speaking occasions
■ content	▼ speaking to inform	✳ resources

Ways to End

There are almost as many ways to end a presentation as there are ways to begin one. Several methods can help you create a strong, lasting impression on listeners that connects you, your message, and your audience.

If you have difficulty deciding how to end your presentation, consider using the **bookending method**—that is, ending the same way you began. If you began your presentation with a quotation, end with the same or a similar quotation. If you began with a story, refer back to that story. If you began by referring to an event or incident, ask your audience to recall it. For example:

> Remember the story I told you about two-year-old Joey, who had a hole in his throat so he could breathe, a tube jutting out of his stomach so he could be fed? For Joey, an accidental poisoning was an excruciatingly painful and horrifying experience. For Joey's parents, it was a time of fear, panic, and helplessness. Thus, it is a time to be prepared for and, even better, a time to prevent.

As is the case with introductions, each of the following concluding methods can be used separately or combined with others.

Summarize

A concluding summary reinforces your **CENTRAL IDEA** and **KEY POINTS**. Good summaries are clear, logical, and brief. And if you pay careful attention to the **LANGUAGE** and **SUPPORTING MATERIAL** you select for your summary, your conclusion can also be memorable.

137–38
133–36
237–52
115–19

The conclusion of this student's presentation on sleep deprivation sums up her major ideas clearly without labeling each key point with numbers or reciting them word for word:

> Recognizing that you may be sleep deprived is the first step. The hardest thing to do is to alter your habits. Retraining yourself to follow a normal sleep pattern isn't going to happen overnight. But once you discover that a few extra hours of sleep will help you feel more rested, relaxed, and revitalized, giving up that extra hour on the internet or watching TV will have been worth it. There is so much in life to enjoy. Sleep longer, live longer.

Quote Someone

A memorable quotation can give your speech a dramatic and effective ending.

A few hours after the fatal *Challenger* disaster on January 28, 1986, President Ronald Reagan addressed the nation from the Oval Office. The shuttle broke apart only a few seconds into the flight, killing all seven crew members, one of whom was a civilian schoolteacher. Reagan ends his conclusion with a line from "High Flight," a sonnet written by John Gillespie Magee, a pilot with the Royal Canadian Air Force in World War II who died at the age of nineteen during a training flight.

> The crew of the space shuttle *Challenger* honored us by the manner in which they lived their lives. We will never forget them, nor the last time we saw them, this morning, as they prepared for their journey and waved goodbye and "slipped the surly bonds of earth" to "touch the face of God."[3]

Tell a Story

253–67 ⁙

Ending with a good **STORY** can be as effective as beginning with one. It can help audience members visualize the desired outcome of your presentation. A well-told story can also help an audience remember the main idea of your presentation. A public speech by Marge Anderson, chief executive of the Mille Lacs Band of Ojibwe Indians, uses a story to conclude:

> I'd like to end with one of my favorite stories. It's a funny little story about Indians and non-Indians, but its message is serious. You can see something differently if you are willing to learn from those around you. Years ago, white settlers came to this area and built the first European-style homes. When Indian People walked by these homes and saw [windows], they looked through them to see what the strangers inside were doing. The settlers were shocked, but it made sense when you think about it: windows are made to be looked through from both sides. Since then, my People have spent many years looking at the world through your window. I hope today I've given you a reason to look at it through ours.[4]

Share Your Personal Feelings

Putting yourself into the ending of a presentation by disclosing how you feel can touch the emotions of your audience and leave them with a strong

● getting started	▶ delivery	◆ speaking to persuade
▲ fundamentals	⁙ engaging your audience	★ speaking occasions
■ content	▼ speaking to inform	✳ resources

memory of you, the **SPEAKER**. Earlier in this chapter, you read the introduction to Margaret Muller's speech on Down syndrome to seventh and eighth graders. Here is how Margaret concluded:

55–69

> I am not sad about the fact that I have Down syndrome. It is just part of me. I have a great brother (most of the time), and parents who love me a lot. I have wonderful friends who enjoy hanging out and having fun with me. I have teachers who help me keep on learning new things. I am glad to be a student at Lincoln Middle School, because it is a great school and almost everyone is really nice. Down syndrome has not stopped me from having a worthwhile life.[5]

Use Poetic Language

USING LANGUAGE in a way that inspires and resonates is one of the best ways to ensure that your conclusion is memorable. If Martin Luther King Jr. had said "Things will improve" near the end of his famous "I've Been to the Mountaintop" speech, his words would not have had the impact that his use of the lyrics from the "Battle Hymn of the Republic" did: "I'm not worried about anything . . . . 'Mine eyes have seen the glory of the coming of the Lord.'" Poetic words can make your conclusion sing.

237–52

You don't have to be a poet or a famously eloquent politician to conclude your presentation poetically. This student ends his presentation about respecting older people by changing the ending—"and old authors to read"—of Francis Bacon's short but poetic phrase:

> Old wood best to burn, old wine to drink, old friends to trust, and old people to love.

Call for Action

A challenging but effective way to end a presentation is to **CALL FOR ACTION**. Use a call for action when you want your audience to do more than merely listen—when you want them to *do* something.

398

Here is how Dr. Robert M. Franklin, president of Morehouse College, ended remarks delivered to a town hall meeting of students on his campus:

> Morehouse is your house. You must take responsibility for its excellence . . . .
> If you want to be part of something rare and noble, something that the world has not often seen—a community of educated, ethical, disciplined

Black men more powerful than a standing army—then you've come to the right place . . . . Up you mighty men of Morehouse, you aristocrats of spirit, you can accomplish what you will![6]

Mix the Methods

As with introductions, many speakers rely on more than one way to conclude a presentation. Note how this student speaker uses statistics and a personal story to end a speech on alcoholism:

As you now know, about one in eight adults—that's 12.7 percent of the American population—abuse alcohol or are alcoholics. Few, if any, of these people planned on becoming alcoholics. And many, like my sister, were well informed about the disease before falling victim. I've told you her story and alerted you to the role of denial in the hope that someday, if that doubt ever creeps into your mind and you find yourself asking whether you might have an alcohol problem, you'll remember my speech and take a harder, more objective look at that question. It didn't save my sister's life. But it could save yours.

Tips for Ending Effectively

Taking time to create a well-planned, well-delivered conclusion may be the last thing you want to worry about as you near the end of the preparation process. But because we know that last impressions linger—that the last thing you say can be just as important as the first—you should at least make sure that your conclusion achieves the following three objectives.

Make Sure the Ending Matches the Rest

Sometimes we tell students, "Don't go for fireworks without a reason to celebrate." In other words, don't tack on an irrelevant or inappropriate ending. If you have given a serious speech about the need for better childcare, don't end with a tasteless joke about naughty children. If you have explained how to operate a new and complicated machine, you probably shouldn't conclude with flowery poetry. Match the mood and method of your ending to the mood and style of your presentation.

● getting started   ▶ delivery   ◆ speaking to persuade

▲ fundamentals   ⁙ engaging your audience   ★ speaking occasions

■ content   ◤ speaking to inform   ✳ resources

Have Realistic Expectations

What if you issue a call for action and no one in your audience acts? Don't expect more from your audience than is reasonable. Only an inexperienced speaker would expect everyone in an audience to sign an organ donation card following a presentation on eye banks. Most audiences will not act when called on unless the request is carefully worded, reasonable, and possible. Don't conclude by demanding something from your audience unless you are reasonably sure that you can get it.

End When You Say You Will End

How do you react when you hear a speaker say, "And in conclusion . . . ," and then she takes ten minutes to finish speaking? The announced ending of a presentation—signaled by phrases such as "In conclusion" or "Let me close by"—should be used only when the ending of your speech is very near. Never go beyond a minute after saying a phrase like this. When you say you are going to end, *end*.

Write Your Introduction and Conclusion

Unless you are very familiar with your audience and your topic, we recommend that you write out your introduction and conclusion word for word with the expectation that you will change and improve the wording several times—even as you speak.

Because the beginning and ending of a presentation matter so much, every word counts. However, instead of reading from a **MANUSCRIPT**, practice your introduction and conclusion so often that you won't need detailed notes (unless you're including a long quotation or complicated set of statistics). Because you will probably be most nervous at the beginning of your speech, knowing your introduction very well will help you mask and minimize any **SPEAKING ANXIETY** you may be feeling. As you close, make sure you can deliver a well-crafted conclusion that allows you to focus on your audience and "clinch" your message. We are not recommending that you memorize and recite your introduction and conclusion. Rather, make sure you can begin and end your presentation with only a few notes and plenty of eye contact with your audience.

222–23

15–27

NOTABLE SPEAKER
Susan Cain

After practicing corporate law for seven years, Susan Cain left her successful career behind to pursue her childhood passion for reading and writing. This passion led her to research and think critically about the general cultural preference for extroverts in the United States. As the self-described "Chief Revolutionary" of an organization she has called the Quiet Revolution, Cain has authored two best-selling books and led hundreds of workshops about the often-overlooked power of introverts in everyday life. She took to the TED stage in 2012 to address the challenges faced by introverts living in a world favoring extroverts—a topic that she had written about in her book *Quiet: The Power of Introverts in a World That Can't Stop Talking.* The talk has been viewed more than twenty-two million times and was featured by the curators of the TED website on their homepage. In 2014, she was named one of the world's top fifty leadership and management experts by *Inc.* magazine.

Search Terms
To locate a video of this presentation online, enter the following key words into a search engine: Susan Cain introverts. The video is approximately 19:04 in length.

What to Watch For
[0:00–1:19] Cain focuses her audience's attention and interest by beginning her talk with a compelling story about her time away at summer camp as a young girl. She adds a visual component by holding a suitcase in her hand as she talks about how her mother packed her a suitcase full of books to take to camp. She continues to draw the audience into her personal experience by sharing the "ROWDIE" cheer with them. This brings a touch of humor to the story and lightens the mood before she expresses the more serious point behind the story.

[1:34–2:06] Cain connects with her audience by contrasting her desire to read books while at camp with
her counselor's desire that she should work hard to
be outgoing. In doing so, she highlights experiences
that some audience members will recognize at some
level. An emotional tone in the message emerges as
she moves the suitcase behind her to demonstrate
hiding away a passion so that she could fit in with the
other girls. She then tells the audience that she could
have shared fifty similar stories with them—each one
highlighting a time that she was told that she should
try to pass as more of an extrovert. In essence, she
is asking the audience to connect with her human
experience of not fitting in.

[2:31–4:02] She notes that a third to half of the population at large are introverts, which is one of every two
or three people each of the audience members know—
partners, children, and colleagues. From this foundation, she states her central idea: "When it comes to
creativity and to leadership, we need introverts doing
what they do best." In order to achieve this goal, she
advocates a better balance between extroverts and
introverts. This balance can be achieved if people accept
and appreciate introverts' work-style preferences, such
as more autonomy and less group work.

[13:21–15:54] As Cain prepares to end her talk, she
returns to the suitcase. She pulls out several books from
it and tells the audience that these books were written
by some of her grandfather's favorite authors. Referencing the suitcase serves as a bookend to the beginning of the talk. The suitcase becomes a focal point
of how books have affected her and how she wants
her message to affect her audience. One of the lasting
ideas she wants her listeners to embrace is the value of
having time alone to think and to reflect. She reinforces
her central idea by underscoring her belief that we are
on the cusp of a cultural shift in how we understand
and accommodate the unique skills of introverts.

(NOTABLE SPEAKER CONTINUED)

[16:21–18:32] She ends the speech with a very clear call for action. She asks the audience to stop the "madness of constant group work," to unplug and get inside their own heads more, and to take a good look at what's inside their own "suitcase" and why they put it there. This last call to action is another clear reminder of how the suitcase serves as a centerpiece of making her message memorable.

EXERCISE

After viewing Cain's speech, reflect on these questions:

1. Explain whether or not Cain effectively and appropriately incorporated herself into the introduction, body, and conclusion of her presentation.

2. Cain's introductory story is two-and-a-half-minutes long—that's about 25 percent of her speech. What did such a long introduction achieve?

3. Explain the role of the suitcase in her talk. Did it help her or distract you?

4. How successfully does Cain's speech demonstrate the primacy/recency principle?

5. How does the delivery of her very last line—"So I wish you the best of all possible journeys and the courage to [in a quiet voice] speak softly"—help reiterate her central idea?

Conclusion

You don't have to be a social scientist or psychologist to know this truth: the first and last impressions you make on someone are important and long lasting. That's why you want to look and sound good at the start of a date, a job interview, or an important meeting. It's also why you want to leave a favorable impression when the date, interview, or meeting is about to end.

The same commonsense behaviors apply to the introductions and conclusions of presentations. A good first and last impression helps you achieve your purpose while enhancing your credibility as a speaker. However, introductions and conclusions are not the same. Their goals differ, as can the methods you use to achieve those goals.

Well-crafted and skillfully delivered introductions gain audience attention and interest, without which listeners may not wait for or listen to your conclusion. The introduction is your best opportunity for connecting with your audience, demonstrating your competence and credibility, setting the appropriate mood, and previewing your message.

A well-crafted and skillfully delivered conclusion is the finale of a presentation. It lets the audience know you're about to sum it up, make a final appeal, and/or create a memorable moment. At the same time, it's a good general rule to "Be clear. Be brief. Be seated."

Part 4
Delivery

Whenever we speak to an audience, whether in person or through an audiovisual medium, our voice and our body play an important role in shaping our audience's impressions. The following chapters focus on the various ways you can improve your **VOCAL DELIVERY** and **PHYSICAL DELIVERY** skills so that your audience is as impressed by the way you speak and present yourself as they are by your words and ideas.

Delivery

4.1 The Importance of Delivery

As much as you may want audience members to appreciate your message and believe *what* you say, they often judge you and your presentation based on *how* you say it.

When you make a presentation, as in life generally, first impressions matter. Audience members begin evaluating you the moment they see you—the way you are dressed, whether you have interacted with audience members before a presentation, how you walk to the front of a room, or what you do while sitting on a stage waiting to speak. Before you say your first word, you have made an impression.

Similarly, once you begin speaking, your **delivery**—the way you use your voice and body in a presentation—will significantly affect how audience members interpret and evaluate the meaning of your message. If you haven't thought about and effectively practiced your delivery, you may leave your audience unimpressed and unmoved by what you say.

You, the **SPEAKER**, are the most important factor in an audience's perception of a presentation. When you speak, audience members will often mirror your attitudes as they perceive them. Here are some examples:

▲ 55–69

- If you seem unenthusiastic, your audience may feel that way too.
- If you appear **NERVOUS**, your audience may be concerned or uneasy.

● 15–27

- If you constantly fidget, audience members may interpret your movements as a lack of self-control and, as a result, may question your **CREDIBILITY**.

▲ 57–66

- If you sound or look disorganized, unprepared, or uninterested as you speak, your audience may become confused and lose interest.

● getting started	▶ delivery	◆ speaking to persuade
▲ fundamentals	⁝ engaging your audience	★ speaking occasions
■ content	▼ speaking to inform	✳ resources

In short, if you neglect to prepare and practice your delivery, you might as well send your audience the text of your presentation and not show up. Effective delivery is the heart and soul of successful speaking.

The Qualities of Effective Delivery

Effective delivery has multiple components: a clear speaking voice at an appropriate volume, rate, and pitch; appropriate eye contact, gestures, and posture; and meaningful facial expressions that complement what you're saying. In addition to mastering specific delivery skills, effective speakers combine and calibrate them to create a unique and flexible delivery style that adapts to each RHETORICAL SITUATION. Your delivery when giving a EULOGY at a funeral, for example, will be very different from your delivery when you are making a TOAST at a wedding reception.

5–10 ●
449–55 ★
442–48 ★

Effective speakers make strategic decisions about delivery based on the nature of the occasion and the characteristics of their audience, as well as the purpose, content, and organization of their presentation. Developing an adaptive delivery style requires an understanding of four significant and interrelated qualities that transcend individual delivery skills: *expressiveness*, *confidence*, *stage presence*, and *immediacy*.

Expressiveness

Expressiveness—the vitality, variety, and authenticity of your delivery— has a strong impact on audience attention and interest. Expressiveness is more than enthusiasm. It's more than the sound of your voice, how you look, or how much you've practiced. It is an extension of who you are and what you care about.

If you care about your message and are sincerely interested in sharing your ideas with others, you are well on the way to being expressive. Speakers who know a lot and care a lot about their topics and their audiences are usually more expressive than presenters who don't know much about their subject or who don't particularly care.

Confidence

Confident speakers are very convincing. They are self-assured and believe they have the ability to do something well. For example, researchers claim

---

● getting started   ▶ delivery   ◆ speaking to persuade
▲ fundamentals   ∴ engaging your audience   ★ speaking occasions
■ content   ◤ speaking to inform   ✳ resources

that jury members are more likely to believe the testimony of confident eyewitnesses than the testimony of hesitant witnesses—even though confident witnesses are no more accurate when describing an event than are hesitant witnesses.[1]

There is a strong relationship between whether speakers look and sound confident and whether audience members believe they are **COMPETENT**. Unfortunately, some speakers with great ideas do not appear confident, which may lead audience members to ignore or reject their ideas. Other speakers with ordinary or even awful ideas may appear self-assured, and as a result, audiences may accept and applaud their message. Revelations about the deceitful behavior of politicians, corporate executives, and celebrities who look and sound confident add an ethical component to this quality. Bullies and tyrants are often confident but should not be trusted or admired.

58–61

So how do you project a sense of confidence that benefits you and your audience? You do it by believing in your message and learning how to develop and deliver presentations with skill. Confidence is more likely to emerge when you adequately prepare and **PRACTICE** your presentation. It can also emerge as you develop a rapport with your audience.

228–33

As with expressiveness, communicating too much confidence can hurt your credibility and the success of your presentation. If you seem too sure of yourself and appear too authoritative, audience members may be suspicious or offended by your arrogance and question your motives. Communicating confidence is not the same as bragging. Unwarranted confidence can backfire.

Stage Presence

Stage presence is the ability of great actors, dancers, musicians, and even athletes to captivate, connect with, and command an audience's full attention based on their talent, **DYNAMISM**, attractiveness, and charm.[2] It is about "owning" the stage. This characterization also applies to great speakers.

66

Many people point to the late Steve Jobs, the genius inventor and entrepreneur (who in real life wasn't the most likable guy), as exemplifying stage presence. In addition to the clear and persuasive words he used to describe and sell Apple products, his delivery style made his presentations exceptional and memorable. He dressed differently than most speakers (mock black turtleneck, faded blue jeans, gray sneakers, and round rimless glasses specially designed for him), walked to the stage while maintaining eye contact with his audience, rarely or never glanced at his notes because he was thoroughly prepared and well rehearsed, used expansive gestures and an open posture, lovingly held up products, appeared both relaxed and energized at the same time, and personified expressiveness as he moved around the stage.[3]

Immediacy

In communication studies, the term **immediacy** describes behaviors "that simultaneously communicate warmth, involvement, psychological close-ness, availability for communication, and positive affect."[4] Although immediacy behaviors include both verbal (words) and nonverbal (vocal and physical) delivery, nonverbal immediacy is more powerful. Speakers who demonstrate immediacy—direct eye contact, smiling, expressive tone of voice, and physical closeness with audience members—are more likely to achieve their purpose. When skillful presenters act in an immediate manner, audience members like them and, as a result, are more willing to listen to and remember what those speakers have to say. A speaker's immediacy has a significant effect on **AUDIENCE ENGAGEMENT**, motivation, and recall.

275–76

Achieving nonverbal immediacy combines many aspects of vocal and physical delivery. The key is consistency among all your behaviors. If, for example, your facial expressions and tone of voice communicate one emotion, but your words communicate another message, the inconsistency can undermine your credibility and reduce immediacy.

Researchers have identified several characteristics of nonverbal immediacy.[5] Here are some examples:

- Close proximity to audience members
- Smiling
- Warm and expressive voice
- Direct face-to-face body orientation
- Direct and frequent eye contact
- Relaxed body posture

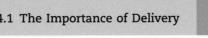
The Components of Good Delivery

You may not reach the performance heights of a celebrated speaker, famous actor, popular musician, impassioned preacher, or charismatic leader. But by mastering effective delivery skills, you can communicate expressiveness, confidence, stage presence, and immediacy in a variety of rhetorical situations. With practice, your delivery can increase the impact and memorability of your message and enhance your credibility.

Interestingly, there *are* exceptional speakers who demonstrate the value and impact of expressiveness, confidence, stage presence, and immediacy without having a perfect voice, animated body movements, or even presentation aids. Their message is so important that effective delivery requires little more than clarity and conviction. Based on what listeners at the time reported, there was nothing remarkable about Abraham Lincoln's *delivery* of the Gettysburg Address, but no one doubts the significance and impact of that speech.

For an example of a speaker who had her audience in tears even though her delivery lacked significant gestures, facial expressions, props, or vocal variety, see Notable Speaker: Malala Yousafzai, page 98.

At this point, you may be asking: So what can I do to improve my delivery? There must be more than waking up and saying, "I'm going to be more expressive, confident, and have stage presence." Of course there is. Every speaking situation requires skillful control and coordination of *vocal delivery* and *physical delivery* made as natural as possible through productive *practice*.

- **VOCAL DELIVERY** is the strategic use of breath control, volume, projection, articulation, pronunciation, rate, pitch, inflection, and fluency.   194–209
- **PHYSICAL DELIVERY** is the strategic use of eye contact, facial expressions, gestures, movement, and appearance.   210–19
- **PRACTICE** uses regular, repeated, and strategic rehearsals that focus on improving delivery skills and developing expressiveness, confidence, stage presence, and immediacy.   220–33

The three chapters that follow will address in detail each component of effective delivery.

Ethics and Delivery

There is also an overriding component of good delivery: ethics. Some unethical speakers enlist impressive and dynamic delivery skills to disguise their beliefs, attitudes, and behaviors for the purpose of misleading or deceiving an audience by "selling" listeners a message that may not be in their best interests. The outcomes of their presentations are more likely to harm rather than help audience members. If you try to fake expressiveness or immediacy with the intention of deceiving audience members or selling them on a message that you don't believe or that isn't in your audience's best interests, you have crossed the line between **ETHICAL AND UNETHICAL COMMUNICATION**.

39–51

Unskilled listeners are often wooed by a speaker's exceptional delivery and appearance. Responsible audience members use **EVALUATIVE LISTENING** and critical thinking to determine whether a speaker's delivery is masking ulterior motives and false information.

31

Remember Quintilian's description of the ideal speaker as *a good person speaking well*. Good speakers behave ethically as they choose strategies that gain and maintain audience attention with skilled and authentic delivery, and with a purpose that benefits the audience.

- getting started
- ▲ fundamentals
- ■ content
- ▶ delivery
- ⁜ engaging your audience
- ▼ speaking to inform
- ◆ speaking to persuade
- ★ speaking occasions
- ✳ resources

NOTABLE SPEAKER
Yassmin Abdel-Magied

An Australian immigrant born in Sudan who now lives in London, Yassmin Abdel-Magied is a writer, broadcaster, and social advocate. After working as a mechanical engineer for nearly a decade, Abdel-Magied became a full-time author and speaker. Her TED talk, "What Does My Headscarf Mean to You?" has been viewed more than two million times and was selected as one of TED's top ten ideas in 2015. During the talk, Abdel-Magied challenges perceptions of race and religion in a creative and thought-provoking manner. She points the audience toward meaningful ways that they can combat unconscious bias and serve as a mentor to people with different life experiences from their own. In 2018, Abdel-Magied received the Young Voltaire Award for free speech.

Search Terms
To locate a video of this presentation online, enter the following key words into a search engine: Yassmin TED talk. The video is approximately 14:01 in length.

What to Watch For
[0:00–0:14] We know that first impressions matter and can be the most important factor in determining audience opinions about a speaker. As a Muslim woman speaking to a predominantly non-Muslim audience, Abdel-Magied made a series of strategic decisions based on her analysis of audience characteristics and attitudes. She knows that, even before she utters her first word, the audience is evaluating her based on how she looks. She begins by asking the audience what they think when they see someone like her. The question introduces the role that unconscious bias plays in limiting opportunities for people who are different.

(NOTABLE SPEAKER CONTINUED)

[0:44–1:19] Abdel-Magied demonstrates expressiveness, confidence, stage presence, and immediacy. Her voice, facial expressions, eye contact, and physical movements express warmth for the audience and the importance of the topic. The vitality, variety, and authenticity of her delivery is rooted in her desire to help the audience understand the meaning and consequence of unconscious bias as something that "we"—both her audience and Abdel-Magied herself—need to overcome.

[1:52–2:32] Throughout the presentation, Abdel-Magied's facial expressions—including a communicative ironic smile—convey how she feels. When reassuring the audience that she doesn't believe that "there's a secret sexist or racist or ageist lurking within" them, her facial gestures are a bit playful. Moments later, she uses a more serious facial expression as she talks about how bias is not an accusation but something that we need to identify in ourselves.

[2:50–4:05] Abdel-Magied projects a sense of confidence in her message throughout the presentation. Because she thoughtfully developed the message beforehand, she can present it here clearly and coherently, backed up by strong supporting material. She offers illustrations that clearly required adequate preparation in order to present them effectively. In one case, she discusses the lack of female musicians in orchestras and an experiment that was conducted to unearth the unconscious bias about men being better musicians than women.

[6:00–7:28] About midway through the speech, Abdel-Magied wonders aloud whether the audience members think they have a good read on her. With a photo of an oil rig behind her, she asks them if they would believe that she runs one of them. "Can you imagine me walking in and being like, 'Hey boys, this is what's up—this is how it's done'?" Her stage presence—her ability to capture and keep the audience's attention—is solidified as she removes her abaya (the full-length outer garment worn by some Muslim women) to reveal the orange jumpsuit she wears on oil rigs. She tops off the wardrobe change by placing a hard hat on her head. By presenting herself in her work uniform, Abdel-Magied dramatically (and suddenly) alters her audience's impression of her.

[8:55–10:45] Abdel-Magied's vocal delivery also plays an important role in her speech. At the beginning of this segment, she slows down her rate and lowers her volume to signal a change in tone and direction. A slower rate emphasizes the importance of the message that follows, which is a description of ways that the audience can help combat unconscious bias.

Abdel-Magied also moves back and forth between standardized speech and the colloquial language of Australia. Consider how she speaks a mix of language styles: "If I see a Muslim chick who's got a bit of attitude, I'm like, 'What's up? We can hang out.'" And, "Because ladies and gentlemen, the world is not just. People are not born with equal opportunity."

(NOTABLE SPEAKER CONTINUED)

[10:45–12:30] Although Abdel-Magied is confident throughout her talk, she does not act so confident that her message seems too polished to be believable. For example, while she maintains fairly consistent fluency, there are times when it appears that her breathing is a bit rapid, causing her to trail off at the end of a sentence or to pause in order to fill her lungs with air. When she removes her orange oil rig uniform, Abdel-Magied struggles to get her feet out of the pant legs. Although it is a bit awkward to stand there with the uniform down around her ankles, she carries on as if saying: I don't have time to worry about this. My message is more important.

[13:40–13:45] Despite having a remote in her hand during most of her speech, Abdel-Magied's gestures are a natural outgrowth of what she feels about the topic and what she has to say about it. Her gestures do not feel forced or fake but instead are an effective complement to the rest of her delivery. During the last line of the speech, she uses a wave-like gesture moving from one arm to the other to show that sometimes people are not who and what you think they are. And then, finally, she extricates herself from the pant legs.

EXERCISE

After viewing Abdel-Magied's speech, reflect on these questions:

1. What strategies did Abdel-Magied use to manage the audience's first impression of her before she spoke her first word? What, if any, alternative strategies would have worked as well?

2. To what extent did the combination of Abdel-Magied's vocal and physical delivery skills increase the impact and memorability of her message?

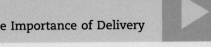

3. How do you think Abdel-Magied used practice sessions to improve her delivery skills? More specifically, what might she have done during these sessions to develop her expressiveness, confidence, stage presence, and immediacy?

4. How does Abdel-Magied's speech represent the importance of delivery as described in the chapter? Provide some specific examples (other than the ones provided above).

5. In what ways, if any, could Abdel-Magied have improved the content and delivery of her presentation?

Conclusion

Effective vocal and physical delivery is expressive and confident. It conveys stage presence and immediacy, a factor that draws in audience members and commands their attention. The quality of your delivery can connect you and your message to your audience in a positive and productive relationship. Expressiveness, confidence, stage presence, and immediacy do not appear out of thin air; they are built on the foundation of competent and practiced vocal and physical delivery skills and, perhaps most important, on a commitment to ethical communication.

4.2 Vocal Delivery

Vocal delivery is how you use and integrate effective breath control, volume, rate, pitch, inflection, fluency, articulation, and pronunciation when you speak. The sound of your voice strongly influences how audiences react to you and your message. People who hear "rough, weak, strained or breathy voices tend to label the speakers as negative, weak, passive, or tense." People with clear, expressive voices "are seen as successful, sexy, sociable, and smart."[1]

If you don't like the sound of your voice and wish you could change it, you're not alone. The reality is that very few speakers are born with beautiful voices. Developing a more effective speaking voice requires time, effort, and practice—just as it does when you are learning any skill.

Think of your voice as the instrument you use to produce sounds. Much like a musical instrument, the structure or anatomy of your vocal instrument dictates the kind of sound you produce. Fortunately, there are several ways to improve the quality of your voice.

Breathing for Speech

All the vocal sounds in the English language are made by exhaling air from your lungs. If you doubt this fact, try talking while breathing in! The key to effective breathing for speech is to control your outgoing breath. Effective breath control improves the sound of your voice in several ways:

- *Projection:* Effective breath control enables you to project a strong voice across a large and crowded room.
- *Duration:* Effective breath control lets you say more with a single breath.

- *Authority:* Effective breath control enables you to speak with a richer and more resonant, powerful, and persuasive voice.
- *Quality:* Effective breath control enhances the overall appeal of your voice and reduces the likelihood of vocal problems such as harshness or breathiness.

The first step in learning to breathe for speech is to note the differences between the shallow, unconscious breathing you do all the time and the deeper breathing—sometimes called abdominal or diaphragmatic breathing—that produces a strong, sustained vocal quality. Whether teaching speakers, actors, or singers, voice coaches always begin their training with something like the following exercise to learn abdominal breathing. Although you may find the exercise strange and your progress slow, your reward will be a stronger and more controllable voice.

1. Lie flat on your back on a flat, comfortable surface. Support the back of your knees with a pillow.
2. Place a moderately heavy hardbound book on the top part of your abdomen, right below your rib cage. The lower edge of the book should cover your navel.
3. Relax and breathe through your mouth. The book should move up when you breathe in and sink down when you breathe out.
4. Place one of your hands on the upper part of your chest as if you're reciting the Pledge of Allegiance. As you inhale and exhale, this area should barely move in and out.
5. Remove the book and replace it with your other hand. Your abdomen should be moving up when you breathe in and sinking down when you breathe out.
6. Once you're comfortable with step 5, try doing the same kind of breathing while sitting up or standing.

Once you've learned how abdominal breathing feels, you can begin to add sounds. For example, try saying *ahh* with each exhalation. Then hold the *ahh* for five seconds. Now try counting out loud from one to five, holding the sound of each number for at least a full second.

When you're breathing correctly for speech, your voice will be clear, expressive, and more controlled. With practice, you will develop muscle memory for harnessing your breath effectively.

Components of Vocal Quality

There are entire books and programs of study devoted to improving the quality of your voice. In this chapter, we have combined dozens of individual vocal qualities into five major components that are essential for effective presentation speaking: *volume, projection, rate, pitch,* and *fluency.* If you focus on improving these five components, you'll be well on your way to speaking in an **EXPRESSIVE** and **CONFIDENT** voice that enhances your **STAGE PRESENCE** and **IMMEDIACY** with your audience.

184
184–85
185–86
186

The five components of vocal delivery combine to create the unique sound of your voice. They do not work in isolation. A loud or soft voice won't communicate the meaning of your message if your pitch doesn't vary or you lack fluency. But when they're combined with skill, these five components convey more than a clear sound—they add meaning to your message and evoke emotions. For example, speaking at a moderate volume that incorporates changes in pitch and tempo is associated with pleasantness, vitality, and happiness. Whereas a loud voice is associated with fear or anger, a soft voice may connote boredom, sadness, or uncertainty.[2] A warm and sincere voice that expresses a variety of emotions appropriately can enhance immediacy.

Volume

If your audience can't hear you, you won't achieve your purpose. The loudness, otherwise known as **volume**, of your voice determines whether or not your audience will hear what you have to say. Here are some ways to ensure that your volume is appropriate for various rhetorical situations.

Evaluate and Adjust Your Volume One of the best ways to make sure that everyone in your audience can hear you is to **PRACTICE YOUR PRESENTATION** out loud, rehearsing the volume you intend to use in front of your audience. As you practice, make sure that you are breathing correctly for speech and are standing up straight with good posture to ensure that your airway is open.

228–33

getting started ▶ delivery ◆ speaking to persuade
▲ fundamentals ∴ engaging your audience ★ speaking occasions
■ content ◣ speaking to inform ✳ resources

In addition to practicing on your own, ask someone to listen to your practice session—someone you trust to give you honest **FEEDBACK**. If possible, practice in a room about the same size as the one where you will be speaking. Ask your listener to sit in a far corner and report your volume level. If you are not loud enough, increase your volume until your friend is satisfied. If no one is around to help you, place a recording device at the back of a room and experiment with different volumes until the voice you hear in the recording is clear and strong.

33–34

Speakers are rarely too loud. More often, they are not loud enough. Sometimes, after soft-spoken students finish a presentation in one of our classes, we ask them to repeat the first ten seconds of their presentation in a louder voice. After these students respond with some hesitancy and a slightly louder beginning, we ask for a louder one. And after that, we ask for an even louder one. In bewilderment, students often say, "But I'm shouting!" We then ask the class for a verdict and the answer is always the same: "You're not shouting; your volume is just right. That's how you should always speak." A quiet person is comfortable using a soft voice. For that person, what seems like a shout may be the perfect volume for a presentation. You can do the same activity on your own or with a friend who will tell when your volume is "just right" for your particular rhetorical situation.

Sometimes speakers can't be heard for a very simple reason: they barely open their mouths. If you don't open your mouth wide enough when speaking, your voice won't carry or reach your audience because the sounds you make can't escape your mouth. Here's a technique to understand this phenomenon: Try saying the tongue twister "Peter Piper picked a peck of pickled peppers" in three ways:

1. Say it as if your lips are almost glued together and your jaw is all but wired shut.
2. Say it with normal movement of your lips and jaw, as you would in a personal conversation.
3. Say it with more lip and jaw movement. Open your mouth almost as wide as you can.[3]

When you say this tongue twister in these ways, can you tell the difference? It's really quite simple: your voice will sound stronger and louder with an open mouth.

Vary Your Volume Listening to someone who speaks at the same volume throughout a presentation is tedious. In conversations, we unconsciously raise and lower our volume based on a word or phrase's importance and emotional mood. Varying your volume during a presentation makes it more pleasing and interesting to your listeners, and even more important, doing so helps you emphasize some things more than others. For instance, you may vary your volume within a sentence in order to stress an important word: "This is the *only* vaccine that works for shingles."

In addition to varying your voice to emphasize important words, ideas, and information, you should also adjust your volume to suit a room's **acoustics**—the properties or qualities of a room that determine how sound is transmitted in it. The shape of the room, the amount of noise-absorbing materials, the height of the ceiling, and the number of people in the audience can make it easier or more difficult to be heard by all listeners. If you are regularly in the room where you'll be speaking, you already know the room's acoustics. If it is an unfamiliar room, pay attention to the feedback you get from your audience as you begin to speak.

Master the Microphone In some rhetorical situations, you may be offered or expected to use a microphone. Don't say "No thanks" until you've considered the audience, the acoustics, and the advantages of amplification. Audience members with hearing disabilities and/or who rely on hearing devices will comprehend more if you speak into a microphone. In a crowded or large space, amplification makes it possible for everyone to hear, listen, and understand. When you're presenting in a **MEDIATED SETTING** (using Zoom, for example), check how you sound. If you have access to one, try a separate microphone. Even an inexpensive USB microphone will make you sound much more professional than your computer's built-in mic.

479–89 ★

A second reason for using a microphone is that no matter the size of an audience or room, a microphone can help you convey subtle emotions and highlight important ideas. Speakers who know how to use a microphone can move from a gentle whisper to a powerful roar with ease.

Unfortunately, microphones also present unique challenges. When speakers don't know how to use a microphone, the sound of their voice can be distorted, the letter "p" can make an annoying popping sound, and speakers may fumble with the equipment. To deliver your presentation

● getting started	▶ delivery	◆ speaking to persuade
▲ fundamentals	⁂ engaging your audience	★ speaking occasions
■ content	◤ speaking to inform	✳ resources

effectively with a microphone, you should speak more slowly, articulate more clearly, and make sure the system can accommodate changes in your volume. If you speak too loudly, you may sound as though you are shouting (for real this time!)—and your audience will probably grimace in response to your artificially amplified volume. If you speak too softly or don't speak directly into the sensitive part of a microphone, it may not pick up everything you say. Audiences generally forgive a few lost words, but they will be less forgiving when you use a microphone because they expect to hear you very clearly.

If possible, test the microphone before the audience is in the room. Ask someone to sit at the back of the room and monitor your amplified voice. Can you speak at an audible and understandable volume without the microphone? If you can and want a more personal connection with your audience, you may not need a microphone. But if you do decide to use one, here are some strategies to keep in mind:

- Determine whether the microphone is sophisticated enough to capture your voice from several angles and distances or whether you need to keep it close to your mouth.
- If you are using a stationary microphone, put five to ten inches between the microphone and your mouth. If you are using a handheld microphone, hold it *below* your mouth at chin level.
- If a microphone is clipped to your clothing or is an inconspicuous headset microphone, test it thoroughly before your presentation. These kinds of microphones can produce distracting noises and may be difficult to readjust.
- Focus on your audience, not on the microphone. Don't tap it, lean over it, or keep readjusting it as a test.
- Keep in mind that a microphone will do more than amplify your voice; it will also amplify other sounds—coughing, shuffling papers, and tapping a pen or pointer.
- Stand up straight when using a microphone. Don't hunch over it or bend your head down while speaking.
- To be more forceful, speak farther away from the microphone and project your voice. This technique minimizes distortions and will make your presentation sound more powerful.

- Most important of all, speak the same way you would *without* a microphone. If you have a good microphone and don't put it too close or too far away from your mouth, the dynamic characteristics and power of your voice will be fully projected.

Projection

The verb *to project* means "to extend, throw, or shoot something outward using a controlled force to reach a specific target." For speakers, **projection** describes a controlled vocal energy that gives clearness and power to your voice. To reach every audience member, even those farthest from you, you need to project your voice. Projection requires concentration, strong breath control, and a desire to communicate with your listeners. A projected voice is beamed to listeners. It does not just reach them; it penetrates them.[4] So, how do you project?

One simple technique can instantly improve your projection during a presentation: look directly at the people in the back row and deliberately think about making them hear you. The mere act of looking at and consciously thinking about these listeners will cause you to project your voice more effectively. What you will notice when you do this is that your volume alone won't do the trick.

Improving Your Projection Here's an exercise to help you improve the projection of your voice. Ask someone to sit at the back of the room or auditorium where you will be speaking. Then read a nonsense sentence in a loud and clear voice. Ask your listener to repeat the sentence back to you to test whether or not they heard you accurately. After a few tries, you will discover that merely speaking more loudly won't necessarily help your listener understand what you're saying. In addition to volume, you need to pronounce the consonants and vowels in the words more clearly and forcefully. Try to project your reading of the following sentences to someone sitting far away:

- Samuel Hornsbee threw a turkey at the dragon's striped Chevrolet.
- Twenty-seven squirrels sang chants for the Christmas-in-May ball.

Using nonsense sentences ensures that your listener cannot anticipate the correct words. When asked to write down or repeat what you have said, your listener won't be able to guess a logical ending to your sentence. But if you project with both force *and* clarity, your audience will be able to hear, understand, and even be amused by what you've said.

Later in this chapter, we examine how two other important factors, clear *articulation* and correct *pronunciation*, contribute to how well your words reach everyone in the audience.

Rate

Your speaking **rate** is the number of words you say per minute (wpm). Just as there are different driving speed limits for different roads and traffic conditions, speech rates vary for different situations. Generally, a speaking rate less than 125 wpm is too slow, 125–145 wpm is acceptable, 145–180 wpm is better, and 180 wpm or more exceeds the speed limit. However, don't carve these numbers in stone. Your natural speaking style, your presentation topic's urgency, complexity, and mood, your language, and your audience's interest, concern, and listening ability should all affect your rate.

So what speaking rate should you use? Some researchers claim that speakers who talk fast, clearly, and energetically are seen as smarter, more credible, and more persuasive while slow speakers are seen as dull, less intelligent, and uninspiring.[5] Is this true? As is often the case, it depends on who you are and how you adapt your presentation to the rhetorical situation.

If you want to be **PERSUASIVE**, fast talk is often more effective. Fast talkers can seem more persuasive because the audience doesn't have time to think critically or question the speaker's **CLAIMS**. Or if listeners expend significant effort to follow an argument, they become more invested in the argument.

◆ 349–50

◆ 352–54

On the other hand, if you want to make a personal connection with your audience and ensure they understand your message, slower may be better. Slow talkers can be more persuasive because there is plenty of time for listeners to comprehend and agree with a message shared by a seemingly conscientious, **AUDIENCE-CENTERED SPEAKER**.[6]

▲ 70–72

In general, it's a good idea to use a slower speaking rate when your audience's listening ability and concerns demand it—for instance, when speaking to older audiences or listeners who are not fluent in English, when giving your listeners step-by-step instructions, or when making an important point or explaining a difficult concept. Think about the ways that respected medical experts explained the nature, consequences, and treatments of COVID-19 on television. They spoke slowly and clearly when

333–46 ⬛

defining terms, **EXPLAINING COMPLEX IDEAS**, and recommending applicable responses.

Some nervous speakers and "motormouths" speed through their presentations, stumble over words, and rarely look at audience members. Not only does this behavior harm your credibility, audience members may misinterpret your message or give up trying. The obvious solution is to slow down. Here are some guidelines for finding an appropriate and effective rate:

- *Monitor you speaking rate.* Time yourself when you practice. If you're much above 160 wpm most of the time, keep reminding yourself to slow down.
- *Practice in front of friends, and record it.* Let listeners interrupt and say, "What? I have no idea what you just said. Say it again—but slower."
- *Repeat yourself when saying something very important.* Give your audience time to catch up.

There is, however, another rate feature as important as speaking fast or slow. It answers the question: How well and often do you pause? Your overall rate will change depending on the number and length of pauses you use within or between sentences and sections of a presentation.

A pause is a meaningful period of silence. Effective speakers use breath control and vary the frequency and length of their pauses so that their presentation isn't choppy and monotonous. For example, Martin Luther King Jr.'s "I Have a Dream" speech—which many people consider the most exceptional address of the twentieth century—opened at approximately 90 wpm but ended at 150 wpm and was punctuated by many dramatic and effective pauses along the way.[7]

In Hamlet's famous line, "To be, or not to be, that is the question," the obvious pauses are after the commas. But should both pauses be the same

---

● getting started   ▶ delivery   ◆ speaking to persuade
▲ fundamentals   ∴ engaging your audience   ★ speaking occasions
■ content   ⬛ speaking to inform   ✳ resources

length? Most actors make the second pause longer. Try it yourself—first with equal pauses after each comma, then with a pause twice as long after the second comma. Do you hear the difference? Does that difference influence your interpretation of the sentence's meaning? Now consider John F. Kennedy's "Ask not what your country can do for you—ask what you can do for your country." The enduring power of these words depends, in large part, on Kennedy's pause before the second half of the sentence. Without appropriate pauses, the meaning of your words may be difficult to understand and lose their impact. Speakers who use pauses appropriately are seen as more effective than those who are perfectly fluent but without pauses. Those who pause too much are seen as unsure and inarticulate.[8]

Here's the bottom line: Speak at a rate that feels right for you and appropriate for your audience, purpose, content, and delivery. And make good use of pauses to vary your rate and give your message dramatic power. Think of it this way. There's too fast, too slow, and just right. It's your job to figure out what's just right for the you, your audience, your purpose, your content, your delivery, and the occasion.

Pitch

Just like the notes on a musical scale, **pitch** refers to how high or low your voice sounds. Anatomy determines pitch. Most men speak at a lower pitch than women do. Most adults speak at a lower pitch than children do.

Americans seem to prefer low-pitched voices. They think men and women with deeper voices sound more authoritative and effective. To compensate for a high natural voice, some speakers push their voices down into a lower range of notes. However, overdoing this limits the voice's expressiveness, can make it sound harsh, and damages the voice by putting a strain on the vocal folds, also known as vocal cords.

Optimum Pitch Instead of obsessing about how to lower your voice's pitch in pursuit of a questionable cultural ideal, you should determine *your* **optimum pitch**, the natural pitch at which you speak most easily and expressively. Unstrained, expressive speaking will always be better received by an audience than an artificially low pitch that sounds strained or harsh. Speaking at your optimum pitch offers the following advantages:

- Your voice will be stronger and less likely to fade at the end of sentences.
- Your voice will not tire easily.
- You won't sound harsh, hoarse, breathy, or squeaky.
- You will have "room to move" above and below the pitch, an absolute must for an expressive and energetic voice.

To find your optimum pitch, try the "sing *sol-la-ti*" method. This exercise requires the ability to sing a musical scale. Sing the lowest note you can sing. Then sing up the scale—*do, re, mi, fa, sol, la, ti, do.* Next, go back to your lowest note and sing up the scale again, this time stopping at *sol.* Can you easily sing an octave (eight notes) above *sol?* Try *la* and then *ti.* If you have to strain a little to reach the octave above *la* or *ti,* go back to *sol.* Your best pitch is probably between the fifth (*sol*) and seventh (*ti*) note above your lowest note. Test your *sol, la,* and *ti* notes to see if you can increase your volume with minimal effort and strain. Then sing an octave higher than that note. The sound should be clear and unstrained. If you can't or don't know how to sing up a scale or reach for a higher octave, ask someone who plays a musical instrument (the piano is usually the best) to demonstrate the pitch of each note. Many college students find the *la* note to be their average optimum pitch.[9]

Finding this pitch doesn't mean you should speak at only that one note. Instead, think of this pitch as "neutral," and use it as your baseline for increasing the expressiveness of your voice. Now try to say a familiar nursery rhyme or the Pledge of Allegiance quickly at your optimum pitch. Can you produce the sound easily? Do you feel any strain? Is the sound higher or lower than the pitch at which you usually speak? If it is higher than your normal pitch, try raising your overall pitch when you speak.

Inflection When we refer to the changing pitch within a syllable, word, or group of words, we're talking about **inflection**. Inflection makes speech expressive. Without inflection, you have what most people call a **monotone voice**, which occurs when there is very little change in the pitch of sounds within words or the pitch of words within phrases and sentences.

● getting started   ▶ delivery   ◆ speaking to persuade
▲ fundamentals   ∴ engaging your audience   ★ speaking occasions
■ content   ▼ speaking to inform   ✳ resources

Inflection helps you emphasize important and meaningful words or phrases. Inflection may not seem very important since the resulting change in pitch can be a fraction of a note. Yet, like the effects of any strong spice in a recipe, a small rise or drop in inflection can change the entire meaning of a sentence or the quality of your voice. Consider the following examples:

- *I* was born in New Jersey. (You, on the other hand, were born in Maryland.)
- I *was* born in New Jersey. (No doubt about it!)
- I was *born* in New Jersey. (So I know my way around.)
- I was born in *New Jersey*. (Not in New York.)

Changing the inflection of the words in this short sentence can produce four different meanings. Inflection is a key ingredient in making your voice more interesting, exciting, emotional, and empathetic.

For an example of a speaker whose inflection in pitch makes his vocal delivery expressive and interesting, see Notable Speaker: Ron Finley, page 400.

Fluency

Fluency is the ability to speak smoothly without tripping over words or pausing at an awkward moment. As with so many other aspects of effective speaking, practice is the key to greater fluency. The more you practice your presentation, the more fluent you become. Even Barack Obama, an often eloquent and inspiring speaker, began his career as a less fluent presenter. As a young attorney, his speaking style was unimpressive and filled with too many "uhs" and "ers." By listening to other speakers and figuring out what made them effective, he learned and practiced how to speak fluently.[10]

Lurking in the background of many presentations is a common fluency problem: **filler phrases**, a general term given to all the verbal interruptions, blunders, restarted sentences, and repeated words that fill space while we search for the next meaningful part of the sentence we're speaking. Filler phrases are quite common in our everyday speech, making up more than 5 percent of the words we use every day.[11]

The most common filler phrases are "um" and "uh." In fact, words similar to "uh" are universal speech fillers in every language on earth, and they seem to become part of our vocabulary before age three.[12] Even though they are clearly fillers, there is nothing wrong with using an occasional "um" or "uh" in otherwise fluent speech. When used sparingly, "uh" and "um" can play a meaningful role in a presentation, signaling a significant word, phrase, or idea is about to be said. "Uh" usually appears more often before a short pause; "um," before a longer pause. Thus, an "um" is signaling a more important thought.[13] In most presentations, it is perfectly okay to use a few of these short filler phrases—not five or six per sentence. Eloquent speakers use them too, but their "ums" go unnoticed because they are fluent and confident.

Occasional filler phrases are perfectly acceptable, but you want to avoid excessive use. Too many filler phrases, *you know*, *like uh*, *okay*, break up, *um*, your fluency and, *uh*, can drive your audience, *right*, *like*, crazy.

To determine if you overuse filler phrases, record one of your practice sessions or an actual presentation and listen for them. Count them. The result can be embarrassing, but it can also motivate you to use them less often. To break an excessive filler phrase habit, you need to slow down and listen to yourself as you practice. At first, you will be less fluent, stopping at almost every phrase, correcting yourself. But you will soon recover your fluency and become a better speaker.

Vocal Clarity and Correctness

A strong, well-paced, optimally pitched voice that is also fluent and expressive may not be enough to ensure the successful delivery of a presentation. The clarity of the words you speak and the way you pronounce those words will also influence your audience's impressions of your vocal delivery.

Articulation

Articulation (or *diction*) is how clearly you make the sounds in the words of a language. Poor articulation is often described as "sloppy speech" or just plain mumbling. If friends ask, "What?" after you've said something in conversation, they are rarely asking you to speak louder; they are asking you to articulate.

Certain sounds account for most articulation problems. The most common culprits are combined words, "ing" endings, and final consonants. For instance, when read aloud by a speaker who isn't articulating properly, "First, I'm going to tell you what's the matter with saying and reading this sentence" might sound like "Firs, 'm gonna telya watsumata wi' sayin and readin thisenens." Many of us combine words—"what's the matter" becomes "watsumata"; "going to" becomes "gonna." Some of us shorten the "ing" sound to an "in" sound: "sayin" instead of "saying." And others leave off final consonants, such as the "t" in "first."

The final consonants that get left off most often are the ones that pop out of your mouth in a micro-explosion. Because these consonants—p, b, t, d, k, g—cannot be hummed like an "m" or hissed like an "s," it's easy to lose them at the end of a word. Although you can hear the difference between "Rome" and "rose," poor articulation can make it difficult to hear the difference between "rack" and "rag," "hit" and "hid," or "tap" and "tab," to give a few examples. Make a note of words ending with these consonants and practice articulating the final sounds correctly and audibly. And, without overdoing it, try to enunciate each word as you speak. It will force you to have better articulation.

For an example of a speaker whose vocal delivery is clear and fluent, see Notable Speaker: Monica Lewinsky, page 24.

Pronunciation

Pronunciation refers to whether you say a word correctly—whether you put all the correct sounds in the correct order with the correct stress. It can be embarrassing to mispronounce a common word. Once one of us heard a speaker give a presentation on the importance of pronunciation, but she undermined her effectiveness by referring to "*pronounciation*" throughout her presentation!

Finding a word's correct pronunciation is not difficult; if you're unsure, look it up in a dictionary. Online dictionaries can be especially helpful because they often give you an audio example of a person saying the word correctly. If you know someone who knows how to pronounce a word (for example, your roommate is a biology major and you are planning to use several biology terms), ask them for help. Speakers who don't take the time to check the pronunciation of words they're unsure about may find themselves embarrassed in front of an audience.

Accents

People from non-English-speaking countries often ask, "How can I get rid of my accent?" The honest answer is that in most cases, you can't. The better answer is this: Why do you want to? An accent generally doesn't hinder your ability to communicate. Sometimes an accent adds charm and interest to your presentation.

An **accent** is a way of speaking shaped by a combination of geography, social class, education, ethnicity, and first language. Everyone has an accent. There is no such thing as perfect, neutral, or unaccented English—or any other language.

In fact, what is commonly called **Standard American English** is nothing more than another accent. Granted, it is the dominant accent spoken by major newscasters and actors as well as many national politicians or corporate officers. In general, people who speak Standard American English are judged as more intelligent, competent, and successful, even when the judges themselves speak in a different American accent. Terms like *southern drawl* or *midwestern twang* send a clear signal about the negative status often attached to ways of speaking that deviate from Standard American English.[14] Does that mean you should only speak Standard American English when you give presentations in school and at work? No, not at all. As in all other ways, understanding the rhetorical situation and **KNOWING YOUR AUDIENCE** is the key to achieving your purpose.

Sometimes speakers change their accent and speaking style when speaking to different audiences. This ability—called **code-switching**—

72–80

● getting started   ▶ delivery   ◆ speaking to persuade
▲ fundamentals   ⁖ engaging your audience ★ speaking occasions
■ content   ▼ speaking to inform   ✳ resources

describes how we modify our verbal and nonverbal communication in different contexts. Code-switching enables a southerner to speak Standard American English in the North, Midwest, and West and then revert to more of a southern accent when speaking at home. Many middle-class African Americans speak both Black English and Standard American English, switching between the two when appropriate.[15] They have learned to code-switch when the audience expects, welcomes, or is more likely to understand a different style.

As with many other aspects of the speechmaking process, how you adjust (or don't adjust) your accent depends on the particulars of each rhetorical situation.

Conclusion

Everyone who speaks has a unique voice. It's how you can recognize a good friend on the phone or a recording of a favorite singer. The same is true of speakers. For example, the voices of presidents Biden, Trump, Obama, Bush, and Clinton are easily recognized and clearly distinct. Keep in mind that your voice is one of a kind. Don't try to sound like someone else or try to develop a "perfect" voice. Instead, work to improve the quality of the voice you have so that it works for you.

An effective, expressive voice is the skilled combination of breath control, volume, projection, articulation, pronunciation, rate, pitch, inflection, and fluency. You can't will your voice to improve. It requires time, effort, and practice to develop a natural-sounding voice that easily adjusts to your message and your audience in a variety of rhetorical situations.

4.3 Physical Delivery

A successful presentation depends on more than the words you use and the quality of your voice. Your **physical delivery**—the way you walk to the front of a room and look at your audience, your facial expressions, and the way you stand, move, and gesture—also has a significant impact on the success of your presentation. Your physical delivery tells an audience a great deal about who you are and how much you care about reaching them.

In this chapter, we identify five components of physical delivery: *eye contact*, *facial expressions*, *gestures*, *posture* and *movement*, and *appearance*. If you focus on improving these five components, you'll be well on your way to communicating expressiveness, confidence, stage presence, and immediacy in your physical delivery.

Eye Contact

Establishing and maintaining visual links with individual members of your audience—otherwise known as **eye contact**—is one of the most important and sometimes difficult physical delivery skills. When used effectively, eye contact initiates and controls communication, enhances **SPEAKER CREDIBILITY**, and provides speakers with a means of assessing listener **FEEDBACK**. Generally, the more eye contact you have with your audience, the better.

57–66
33–34

When you establish eye contact with your audience, you indicate that you are ready to begin speaking and that they should get ready to listen. Lack of eye contact communicates a message too: it says you don't care to connect with your audience. Whatever your reason, even if it's an understandable one, if you don't look at your audience, they have very little incentive to look at *you*.

Questionable folk wisdom about where to look while speaking to an audience is quite common. For example, you may have been told to look over and between the heads of the people in your audience, to find a spot on the back wall and look at it throughout your presentation, or to move your gaze up and down or across every row or look at groups of people in every section of the room. Each of these suggestions is bad advice. They simply don't work. In fact, they can make you look ridiculous. If you fix your eyes on a clock at the back of a room, you'll look like a zombie or a sleepwalker. If you look up and down every aisle, it will seem as though you're robotically taking attendance. There's really no secret to eye contact. Just look at individual people in your audience—eye to eye.

Of course, for every piece of general advice, there are exceptions. The value of eye contact is not universal. For example, in many Asian and some Caribbean cultures, meeting another person's eyes directly can be perceived as rude or aggressive. When asked a question, Canadians are more likely to look up; Japanese are more likely to look down when answering. Even in cultures where eye contact is appreciated, some autistic speakers may not make eye contact with the audience, and some autistic audience members may not return the gaze of a speaker.[1]

Most speakers in the United States try to maintain direct eye contact with members of their audience because in general American audiences perceive such speakers as strong and effective. Effective speakers learn to adjust to their **AUDIENCE** and to the **RHETORICAL SITUATION**, to sense when eye contact is appropriate while avoiding gazing directly at audience members who appear uncomfortable.

80–82
5–10

Here are some additional guidelines for gaining and maintaining effective eye contact with an audience:

225–28
222–23

- Even when using a set of **PRESENTATION NOTES** or a **MANUSCRIPT**, try to look at your audience as much as you can—at least 75 percent of your speaking time. If you are a reserved person, that percentage may be lower. But no matter what, try to focus your eyes and attention on your listeners.
- Establish eye contact and connect with as many individual listeners as you can, but don't jump rapidly from one person to another.
- Look at individual audience members the same way you would talk to and look at people familiar to you.
- Move your gaze around the room, settle on someone, and establish eye contact. Then move on to another person. Don't be surprised if

some listeners avoid shared eye contact. It can be uncomfortable for some people.

- Look at audience members seated farthest away or off to one side as often as you look at those in the center and near you.

479–89 ★

- When delivering **MEDIATED PRESENTATIONS** (such as Zoom speeches), you face a potential problem with eye contact. Assuming your camera is at the top of your computer screen, when you look at images of your listeners, it will appear that you're looking down and not at them. Try this: Attach a sticky note ("Look here!") or a picture of someone right above the camera to remind you where to look.

Facial Expressions

Regardless of why, where, when, and to whom you are speaking, listeners look at your face. Your **facial expressions** reflect your attitudes and emotional states, provide nonverbal feedback, and, next to the words you speak, are a primary source of information about you and your message.[2] Despite the enormous significance of facial expressions, they can be difficult to control. Some people show little expression—they have a blank "poker face" most of the time. Other people are "like an open book"—you have little doubt about how they feel. It's very difficult to transform a poker face into an open book—and vice versa.

Unless your topic is very solemn or serious, a smile is a great way to start a presentation. A smile shows your listeners that you are comfortable and eager to share your ideas and information. Looking at a smiling speaker can also make audience members feel happy and positive, and they are more likely to smile at you in response.

If you don't feel comfortable smiling, don't force it—most listeners are likely to know if your smile is false.[3] In the end, the best advice is to let your face do what comes naturally. If you communicate your message sincerely and focus on your listeners, your facial expression will be appropriate and effective. As you become more physically confident while speaking, you'll become more comfortable smiling too.

Try to manage your emotional displays while you speak. For example, if someone asks you a question, you want to look confident as you answer. But when the answer to a question is clearly obvious to you and the audience, don't frown or roll your eyes. Your facial expression should make the questioner feel just as respected as other questioners.

During many presentations, there are points when you want to look thoughtful, sad, or happy. If you nod while talking, listeners will probably nod as well—and that can lead to them agreeing with the point you are making.

Gestures

A **gesture** is a body movement that conveys or reinforces a thought, an intention, or an emotion. Most gestures are made with your hands and arms, but the shrug of a shoulder, bending of a knee, and tapping of a foot are gestures too. Gestures can clarify and support your language, help you relieve **NERVOUS TENSION**, arouse **AUDIENCE ATTENTION**, and function as a **PRESENTATION AID**.

15–27
268–79
293

We can't tell you how to gesture because you already know how to do it. You gesture every day—when you speak to friends, family members, coworkers, and even perfect strangers. "Yes," you may say, "but surely that's not the same kind of gesture you need for a presentation?" Of course it is. Too often, we've seen naturally graceful and energetic people become as stiff and straight as a stick when they speak in front of a group. Why? They become so worried about how they look and how to gesture that they stop doing what comes naturally. Sometimes we'll ask a student speaker who seems self-conscious or stiff a few easy questions at the end of a presentation, such as "Could you tell me more about this?" or "How did you first become interested in that?" In the blink of an eye, the speaker starts gesturing, moving naturally, and showing a lot of expression. The speaker has stopped thinking about how they look in order to answer a question.

Hand Gestures

"What should I do with my hands?" is a common question. Our answer is deceptively simple: Do what you normally do with your hands. If you gesture a lot, keep doing what comes naturally. If you rarely gesture, don't try to invent new and unnatural hand movements.

Effective gestures are a natural outgrowth of what you feel and what you have to say. Rather than thinking about your hands, focus on your audience and your message. In all likelihood, your gestures will join forces with your emotions in a spontaneous mixture of verbal and nonverbal communication.

If you still worry about your gestures or want to gesture more often, there are a variety of techniques that liberate your hands during a presentation. Begin by linking your gestures to a specific word, concept, or object. For example, introduce the number of key points in your presentation by holding up the correct number of fingers. Then lift one finger for the first point, two fingers for the second, and so on. If you are **DESCRIBING AN OBJECT**, you can use your hands to trace its shape or size in the air. If you are telling a **STORY** in which someone scratches his head, points in a direction, or reaches into his pocket, you can do the same. If you're talking about alternatives, illustrate them first on one hand and then on the other. But remember, if none of these gestures come naturally or improve with practice, avoid them.

320–21 ▛

253–67 ⁖

Improving Your Gestures

Unless you have a lot of speaking or acting experience, it's very difficult to plan your gestures. In fact, it's downright dangerous because most pre-planned gestures look artificial and awkward. When speakers try to preplan their gestures in the same way they would plan a dance step, the results can be ineffective and even comical.

Almost any natural gesture is acceptable if it is timely and appropriate. Clasping your hands in front of or behind your body is okay if it isn't the only way you position your hands. If your gestures fall into a pattern, your physical delivery can become distracting.

205–6 ▷

One way to improve your gestures is to avoid **fidgets**—the small, repetitive movements that act like a physical **FILLER PHRASE**. Constantly pushing up on your eyeglasses, repeatedly tapping a lectern with a pencil, jingling change or keys in your pocket nonstop, unconsciously playing with a necklace or tie, swaying back and forth, repeatedly hiking up your pants and tucking in your shirt, pulling on a favorite earlobe or lock of hair, and playing around with a pointer are fidgets. Not only can fidgets annoy audience members, many of whom will focus on the fidget rather than on your

---

● getting started   ▷ delivery   ◆ speaking to persuade
▲ fundamentals   ⁖ engaging your audience   ★ speaking occasions
■ content   ▛ speaking to inform   ✳ resources

message, they can also reduce an audience's perception of your **CREDIBILITY**. 57–66
One of the easiest ways to stop fidgeting is to record a video of your practice
session and then watch it. Once you see how often you jingle change or sway
back and forth, you'll never want to inflict your fidgets on an audience again.

Adapting Gestures to Cultural Differences

People all over the world "talk" with their hands. The meanings of gestures,
however, may be very different in different cultures and contexts—both
domestic and international. While professors in the United States may
put their hands in their pockets or hold them behind their back during
a lecture without students thinking twice about these gestures, we know
from a colleague who taught at Bangkok University in Thailand that these
gestures make some Thai listeners uncomfortable because they violate a
cultural norm of keeping one's hands visible when communicating.[4]

Most of our hand gestures are culturally determined, and some can
even have different meanings within the same cultural context. One of
the best examples is a gesture where you touch the tips of your thumb
to index finger to form a circle with the three remaining fingers held up.
In the United States, this gesture has traditionally meant that everything
is okay. Not so anymore. Some extremist groups use the okay gesture to
identify and connect with people who agree with their ideology and
to recruit internet trolls.[5] The same gesture can mean a sign for a sex
act in some South American countries and a sexual insult in several
European countries on the Mediterranean. To the French, however, the
sign may indicate that someone is a "zero," and in Japan it is used to
symbolize money.[6]

Clearly, the okay gesture is no longer just okay. This is true with many
gestures. Bottom line: if you are talking to a diverse audience or speaking
to people in another culture, check the appropriateness of gestures before
speaking.

Posture and Movement

Posture and *movement* involve how you stand, sit, and change your position
when speaking. Taken together, they can either enhance or detract from
your presentation. Effective speakers use their bodies to take charge of a

presentation and do so in a way appropriate for each rhetorical situation. They know how to convey physical confidence and move with comfort and conviction.

Posture

184–85
185–86
57–66
194–96

Your **posture**—the way you hold your body—communicates. A comfortable posture can radiate CONFIDENCE and STAGE PRESENCE. If you are stooped and unsure on your feet, you will communicate apprehension or lack of interest. Not only does good posture add to your CREDIBILITY, but it also aids proper BREATHING FOR SPEECH and gives you a strong stance from which to gesture.

Speakers who look comfortable and confident standing in front of an audience use an **open posture**. Their shoulders are relaxed; their arms are not crossed or touching their bodies. One way to describe the open position is to imagine you are about to hug someone. Or you can turn the palms of your hands up and opened as though you're saying, "I have nothing to hide." An open posture puts nothing between you and your audience—it makes you appear accepting and confident, and it opens you up to others rather than protecting or concealing yourself. This posture also opens your airways and helps you PROJECT YOUR VOICE without straining.

200–201

In some cases, you may be able to choose whether you sit or stand. If sitting is an option, for instance at a table, should you choose it? There are good reasons why we say no. First and foremost is this: you are your own best VISUAL AID. Why hide that advantage behind a table? Standing up is a way of taking charge and capturing audience attention. As a practical matter, it's easier to see your audience and maintain eye contact if you stand, and it's easier to gesture if you have your full body's length to use. It's also easier to breathe for speech if you stand.

293

Even in situations where other speakers are sitting—for instance, in panel discussions—we recommend you find a way to stand up (if it's appropriate and doesn't break any rules), even if only for a portion of your presentation. Get up and use a flip chart or move to the head of a conference table. By standing when everyone else is sitting, you become the focus of attention. And that's exactly what you want to be during a presentation.

● getting started   ▶ delivery   ◆ speaking to persuade
▲ fundamentals   ∴ engaging your audience   ★ speaking occasions
■ content   ▼ speaking to inform   ✳ resources

There is an exception to the idea of standing when you are presenting. In many **MEDIATED PRESENTATIONS**, sitting may be a better idea. You'll be closer to the camera, and you'll seem more relaxed. Zoom presentations are often more personal and conversational than traditional public speeches.

★ 479–89

For an example of a speaker who maintains a strong and open posture throughout a complex presentation, see Notable Speaker: David Epstein, page 342.

Movement

Effective speakers move comfortably and purposefully as they speak. Movements that are natural and meaningful attract attention, channel nervous energy, and emphasize a point. Lack of movement or, worse, aimless or repetitive movement can distract audience attention and dampen interest. There's almost nothing more boring than something that never moves and nothing more distracting than something that moves about erratically.[7]

Speakers often use movement to get them closer to the audience so that they can achieve **IMMEDIACY**. They move around the room, occasionally walking toward the audience, rather than lingering in a corner or against the wall when speaking. Even though a lectern may provide a convenient place to put your notes, you may want to come out from behind the lectern and speak at its side. In this way, you can be close to your notes *and* get closer to the audience. Getting close to your audience is what it's all about when delivering a presentation.

▷ 186

Appearance

A speaker's **appearance** can affect the success or failure of a presentation. Audiences see you before they hear you. And what they see will make a strong first impression. Obviously, you cannot change physical characteristics such as your height, basic body shape, or facial structure—these are the result of genetics. Fortunately, you do not have to look like a movie star or wear the clothes of a supermodel to make a favorable impression on your audience.

"What should I wear when I make a presentation?" Our first answer is always this: dress to create a positive impression. How do you know whether an outfit will create a good impression? By being aware of and responsive to the components of the **RHETORICAL SITUATION**. What you wear should be appropriate for the **OCCASION** and meet audience expectations. The last thing you want is an audience distracted or annoyed by what you're wearing. In one of our classes, a student delivered an emotional presentation about child abuse while wearing a T-shirt with a large yellow happy face on the front. How could she have ignored or been oblivious to the message on her T-shirt? Effective speakers devote significant attention to what they wear and to the impression their appearance makes on the audience.

5–10

405–89

In addition to wearing clothing that is appropriate for the rhetorical situation, make sure you are *comfortable* in what you're wearing. If your shoes hurt, you won't move naturally, and you'll be preoccupied with the pain. An outfit that looks and feels good while you're standing in front of a store's three-way mirror may be constricting and unattractive when you are sitting on a stage or standing at a lectern. If you perspire a great deal, wear cool fabrics and colors that mask wet stains. Presentations are stressful enough, so don't wear things that add another source of discomfort.

Do you need to break the bank on a wardrobe to make a positive impression? No. Your clothes don't have to be expensive, and they don't have to make a fashion statement. Again, the speaking occasion and your audience's expectations should guide you. The common saying "When in Rome, do as the Romans do" is a handy reminder that you can't go wrong if you dress in a manner that harmonizes with the outfits worn by key members of your audience. If you know in advance that everyone will be wearing cowboy boots, exercise outfits, or fishing clothes, use your best judgment and consider joining them or wearing something that complements what they're wearing.

At the same time, and especially if you have a strong sense of style, don't abandon a signature piece of clothing or accessory just to fit in. Some of our most distinguished colleagues wouldn't look right without these unique items: Sam would not be Sam without his bow tie. Judy would look

● getting started   ▶ delivery   ◆ speaking to persuade
▲ fundamentals   ∴ engaging your audience   ★ speaking occasions
■ content   ▼ speaking to inform   ✴ resources

unusual in anything but bright colors and high heels. Ellen needs her dark eyeglass frames to fully be Ellen. Being yourself means finding clothes and colors that fit *your* style and *your* body.

Although it's perfectly fine to have a signature style, make sure that nothing on your body is so noticeable that it creates a distraction. A bad hair day, an offensive tie, or poorly chosen accessories can devalue your credibility and cheapen your message. If your hair falls in your face and requires rearranging throughout your presentation, your audience will be both distracted and probably annoyed, so find a way to keep it up and away from your face. If you've brought things with you that might become fidgets during your presentation—a pen, coins, keys, or even a handbag—set them aside, away from where you'll be speaking.

In short, your presentation should be the center of your audience's attention. If something about your appearance might distract your listeners, fix it or leave it behind. Looking professional does not mean you must copy the latest look in a fashion magazine. Find an appropriate and comfortable outfit that will also enhance your credibility and strengthen your message.

Conclusion

Your body is uniquely yours. If it's short or tall, big or small, it won't change for a presentation—you are who you are. But what *can* change is how comfortable you feel in your own skin as you speak.

The key is to become comfortable with all five components of physical delivery: eye contact, facial expressions, gestures, posture and movement, and appearance. Eye contact should be directed to individual members of your audience for most of your presentation. Your facial expressions should match the meaning of your message. Your gestures should emphasize important ideas and do so naturally. Your posture and movement should project confidence and conviction that lend support to you purpose. Your appearance should genuinely reflect who you are and be appropriate for the occasion. Physical delivery skills are a significant determinant of your ability to achieve expressiveness, confidence, stage presence, and immediacy.

4.4 Practicing Your Delivery

You now understand that your delivery has a significant impact on how an audience evaluates you and your message. And you've learned how you can improve particular aspects of your vocal and physical delivery. But to make your various delivery skills come together in a meaningful way, you must think about and *practice* your delivery holistically—not just in bits and pieces. A quick run-through of your presentation the night before you're scheduled to deliver it isn't practice. What's needed instead—if you want to achieve expressiveness, confidence, stage presence, and immediacy—is an effective practice plan. The first step is choosing an appropriate *form of delivery*.

Forms of Delivery

There are four basic types of delivery: *impromptu*, *extemporaneous*, *manuscript*, and *memorized* delivery. A presentation may be delivered in one form or in a combination of forms. The following describes the four forms of delivery, with their advantages and disadvantages, and provides examples of each one.

Impromptu Delivery

Impromptu delivery occurs when a presentation is delivered with little or no preparation or practice.

Advantages
These are some advantages of impromptu delivery:

- Uses a natural and conversational speaking style
- Maximizes EYE CONTACT
- Allows freedom of MOVEMENT
- Can easily adjust to audience FEEDBACK

210–12
215–17
33–34

- getting started
- fundamentals
- content
- delivery
- engaging your audience
- speaking to inform
- speaking to persuade
- speaking occasions
- resources

- Demonstrates speaker's knowledge and skill
- Can exceed audience expectations

Disadvantages

These are some disadvantages of impromptu delivery:

- Limited time to make decisions about occasion, speaker, audience, purpose, content, and delivery
- May be awkward and ineffective
- Difficult to gauge speaking time
- Limited or no **SUPPORTING MATERIAL**

115–19

Examples

Some examples of impromptu delivery include:

- Answering a question from the audience that requires more than a simple answer
- Sharing ideas and opinions without advance notice

If you need more help

See 8.1, **IMPROMPTU SPEECHES**, for more detailed advice about impromptu delivery.

★ 407–13

Extemporaneous Delivery

Extemporaneous delivery uses notes as a guide through a well-prepared presentation.

Advantages

These are some advantages of extemporaneous delivery:

- More preparation time than impromptu speaking
- Seems spontaneous but is well prepared
- Allows time to think critically about the **RHETORICAL SITUATION**: occasion, speaker, audience, purpose, content, and delivery

5–10

72–82 ▲
- Easier to **ANALYZE AND ADAPT TO THE AUDIENCE** and feedback
- Allows more eye contact and audience interaction than manuscript speaking
- Response from audiences generally positive
137–38 ■
- Can include concise language for **CENTRAL IDEA** and **KEY POINTS**
133–36 ■
- Can become the most powerful form of delivery—with practice

Disadvantages
These are some disadvantages of extemporaneous delivery:

15–27 ●
- Likelihood of **SPEAKING ANXIETY** about content not covered by notes
205–6 ▶
- Reliance on notes hampering **FLUENCY** and physical delivery
239–45 ∴
- Difficult to choose appropriate words and **SPEAKING STYLES**
- Difficult to estimate speaking time

Examples
Some examples of extemporaneous delivery include:

- Classroom presentation
- Lecture
- Business briefing
- Courtroom argument
- Oral report
- Informal talk

Manuscript Delivery
Manuscript delivery involves reading a well-prepared speech aloud, word for word.

Advantages
These are some advantages of manuscript delivery:

239–45 ∴
- Allows careful attention to all the basic principles of effective speaking
- Allows speaker to carefully select and use appropriate **SPEAKING STYLES**
- Can ease speaking anxiety
- Allows speaker to stay within the time limit

● getting started   ▶ delivery   ◆ speaking to persuade

▲ fundamentals   ∴ engaging your audience   ★ speaking occasions

■ content   ▼ speaking to inform   ✳ resources

- Allows for rehearsal of the same presentation every time
- Ensures accurate reporting of content

Disadvantages

These are some disadvantages of manuscript delivery:

- Possibility of dull delivery
- Difficult to maintain sufficient eye contact
- Limits gestures and movement
- Can constrain some into a formal speaking style
- Difficult to modify content and adapt to the audience and situation while speaking
- Can be disastrous if the manuscript is lost

Examples

Some examples of manuscript delivery include:

- Important public speech or formal address
- **EULOGY**
- Media statement and testimony

★ 449–55

Memorized Delivery

Memorized delivery involves speaking entirely—or almost entirely—from memory.

Advantages

These are some advantages of memorized delivery:

- Shares the preparation advantages of manuscript speaking
- Shares the delivery advantages of impromptu speaking
- Maximizes eye contact and freedom of movement
- Opportunity to craft language and vary language styles

Disadvantages

These are some disadvantages of memorized delivery:

- Requires extensive time to memorize
- Can be disastrous if memory fails

- Can sound stilted and insincere
- Difficult to modify or adapt to the audience or situation
- Can lack a sense of spontaneity unless expertly delivered

Examples

Some examples of memorized delivery include:

442–48 ★

- **TOAST**
- Reciting selections from famous or eloquent literature or speeches
- Speech contest

5–10 ●

So, which form is the best? The answer is that there isn't one best form. Rather, it depends on what works for the occasion, speaker, audience, purpose, and content—in short, it depends on the **RHETORICAL SITUATION**. Extemporaneous delivery is the most common form, especially in speaking courses, but it is not appropriate in every rhetorical situation. In some cases, the best strategy is to mix and match delivery forms in a single presentation.

An impromptu speaker may recite a memorized statistic or a rehearsed argument in much the same way a politician responds to anticipated questions from voters and the press. An extemporaneous speaker may read a lengthy quotation or a series of statistics and then deliver a memorized ending. A speaker reading from a manuscript may stop and tell an impromptu story or deliver memorized sections that benefit from direct eye contact with the audience. A speaker may pause in a memorized presentation to repeat a key phrase or reexplain an idea. Your decision about which delivery forms to use is important, and in non-classroom settings and occasions, it's usually yours to make.

There is, however, a unique type of delivery that may *appear* to be impromptu, extemporaneous, or memorized, but is not. Most news anchors and many professional speakers use teleprompters. For live speaking events, teleprompters look like clear glass panels placed on either side of the speaker. The technician who controls them moves the script in tandem with the speaker and pauses if they go off script. Several Notable Speakers featured in this book use such teleprompters. They are using manuscripts the audience cannot see.[1]

● getting started	▶ delivery	◆ speaking to persuade
▲ fundamentals	⁘ engaging your audience	★ speaking occasions
■ content	👜 speaking to inform	✳ resources

If you are free to choose a method of delivery, how do you make that decision? By experimenting with your options (and different combinations thereof) as you prepare and practice your presentation. This will help you determine which form is appropriate and most natural to you as a speaker and thus has the best chance of achieving your purpose in a particular rhetorical situation.

Using Notes Effectively

Regardless of the delivery form you select, be prepared to use notes. The look and scope of your notes will vary depending on the form of delivery you use. For impromptu delivery, you may have little more than six words written on a scrap of paper. In an extemporaneous presentation, you may use note cards or an **OUTLINE** to guide you through your talk. A manuscript or memorized presentation requires a carefully prepared, word-for-word script that may include graphic cues to remind you when to pause, when to cue up a slide, and when to emphasize a particular word or phrase. Even though you do not use notes while delivering a memorized presentation, you should have your manuscript nearby in case you need it.

152–53

Many excellent speakers feel naked without their notes. Even though they are familiar with their material and have delivered the same message over and over, they still feel incomplete without a set of notes in hand. Great Britain's eloquent prime minister during World War II, Winston Churchill, was one such speaker. When asked why he always had notes for his speeches, even though he rarely used them, he replied, "I carry fire insurance, but I don't expect my house to burn down." For Churchill and for most effective speakers, notes are a kind of safety net—there if you need them, even when you don't.

Although the length and content of your notes will differ in every rhetorical situation, there are general guidelines for using them effectively and efficiently. One overriding guideline rises above the rest: Establish and maintain as much **EYE CONTACT** as you can with your audience. Don't bury your head in your notes or manuscript. Make sure your notes are printed or written in type large enough to be seen clearly at arm's length.

210–12

Even if you want to read a full quotation accurately or share critical data, you can practice these sections well enough to look at your audience as you glance at your notes. Create and use the note cards, outline, or manuscript as you speak in every practice session.

Note Cards and Outlines

Extemporaneous speakers often use note cards to record key points and the details of some supporting material. Think of each card as a visual aid poster or PowerPoint slide. They should contain just enough information to trigger an idea or supply a vital piece of supporting material and its source. Put key words, rather than complete sentences, on *only one* side of each card. Don't overload the card with detailed information or use small print. To stay organized or rearrange key points at the last minute, number each card.

133–36 ▨
115–19 ▨
130–32 ▨
If you prefer or are required to use an outline, it can range from 8½" × 11" versions of your note cards to a comprehensive, full-sentence outline in which your **KEY POINTS**, **SUPPORTING MATERIAL**, and **SOURCES** are written out word for word.

If you need more help

511–24 ✳
See 9.2, **HOW TO OUTLINE A PRESENTATION**, for more detailed guidance about how to create effective preliminary outlines, speaking notes outlines, and full-sentence outlines.

Manuscripts

If you decide to write major portions or the entirety of your presentation in manuscript form, make sure your manuscript works with you rather than against you. Double-space each manuscript page and use a large font size. Print only on the top two-thirds of the page to avoid having to bend your head to see the bottom of each page and lose eye contact with your audience or constrict your windpipe. Set wide margins so you have space on the page to add any last-minute changes. Number each page and don't staple the pages together.

⬤ getting started   ▶ delivery   ◆ speaking to persuade
▲ fundamentals   ⁞ engaging your audience   ★ speaking occasions
▨ content   ▼ speaking to inform   ✳ resources

If you are using a lectern, place your manuscript on the left side of the lectern and slide the pages to the right when it's time to go on to the next page. And don't let your manuscript hang over the front of the lectern. Some speakers put their manuscript in a three-ring notebook that they can set on a lectern or hold in one hand, turn pages with the other hand, and still be able to gesture. If you don't have a lectern or don't want to use one, it may be difficult to hold several pages of a manuscript as you speak. Here, too, a three-ring notebook may help you keep your manuscript under control.

Marking Up Your Notes

Many speakers mark up their speaking notes and manuscripts to help them with delivery, filling their pages with graphic cues as well as last-minute changes. Marking up your note cards, outline, or manuscript provides additional "punctuation," telling you which words or phrases to emphasize as well as when to pause, gesture, or move. The figure below shows a few of the cues we've seen on manuscripts.

/	Short pause
//	Medium pause
///	Long pause
<	Speak louder
>	Speak softer
∧	Speak faster
∨	Speak slower
★	Key point or important sentence follows
◉	Make eye contact with audience
☺	Smile
☐❶	Slide 1
☐❷	Slide 2

In addition to using these or other symbols, you can <u>underline</u>, use **bold**, or even use ALL CAPS for words you want to emphasize. Some speakers use a bright highlighter to make important words and phrases stand out.

Practicing Your Presentation

The best advice we can give anyone striving to become a more effective speaker is this: *practice, practice, practice*. If you spend time and energy practicing your presentation, you have less reason to be nervous. Many excellent, even celebrated, speakers attribute their success to practice. Although it takes valuable time, the payoff is a confident and seemingly effortless presentation.

Practice is essential to the rhetorical speechmaking process, no matter how little time you have available to devote to it. Practice tells you whether there are words you have trouble pronouncing or sentences that are too long to say in one breath. It can help you discover (when there's still time to do something about it) that what you thought was a ten-minute talk takes fifteen minutes to deliver. You don't want to discover that audience members sitting farther back than the fifth row can't hear you because your speaking voice isn't clear or loud enough. Every one of these incidents can undermine your CREDIBILITY. Dedicated practice can prevent such surprises.

57–66 ▲

Practice is especially important when your speech involves the use of PRESENTATION AIDS, which require you to be aware of not only what you're saying but also what you're showing. It's not a question of whether you should practice; rather, it's deciding which aspects of your performance need the *most* practice. Practicing is the only way to make sure you sound and look good during a presentation.

302–4 ⁛

When we extol the virtues of practice, our students often ask an understandable question: How can I practice if I'm speaking extemporaneously? Won't my presentation be different each time? It's true that, by their very nature, extemporaneous presentations are slightly different each time you practice and deliver them. Unlike an actor who memorizes a script or a gymnast who practices an exact routine over and over again, extemporaneous speakers must learn to practice without a manuscript.

As you practice an extemporaneous presentation, you will notice that you say slightly different things each time, but your note cards or speaking outline still guide you through the presentation on more or less the same path, with the same **KEY POINTS**.

133–36

The more you practice, the better you will recall word-for-word sections from your practice sessions. When you practice, you're linking the words you're speaking with your delivery, and by doing that, you create something like a "muscle memory" for the presentation—a familiarity with your material that feels natural and unforced, much like the feeling you have when you finally achieve mastery of a physical skill such as riding a bike or throwing a ball. The more you practice extemporaneous presentations, the more comfortable and skilled you will be with this delivery form.

Regardless of the delivery form, your most productive practice sessions will be those when you deliver your presentation just as you would when speaking to an audience. If you will be standing for the presentation, stand in your practice sessions. Speak loudly enough to be heard by all listeners, rehearsing the vocal and physical delivery you intend to use. Practice your presentation with your notes just as you intend to use them during your presentation. If you will be using visuals, display them as you practice. Bringing all the elements of your presentation's delivery together in practice sessions will help you either confirm that you have a handle on how all the parts fit together or make clear that you need better ways to express your ideas.

Practice can take many forms. It can be as simple as closing your door and rehearsing your presentation in private or as complex as a series of full onstage, videotaped dress rehearsals. Depending on how much time you have, the length and importance of your presentation, and your familiarity with your material, there are several different ways to practice.

Practice in Private

Initially, practice is a solo activity. You may go over your presentation as you drive your car, while you shower, behind a closed door in your home or office, or all by yourself in the room where you will be speaking.

194–209 ▶
210–19 ▶

Regardless of where you practice, you should try to practice your **VOCAL** and **PHYSICAL DELIVERY**.

If you'll be standing during your presentation (and you should!), then stand when you practice. Speak at the volume, rate, and pitch with the inflections you intend to use. Listen to your articulation, pronunciation, and fluency.

Glance at your notes only occasionally, use direct and frequent eye contact with an imagined audience, and practice facial expressions, gestures, posture and movement the same way you intend to use them in your presentation. And think about your appearance—how you will look and what you will wear. At first, you may feel a bit strange while talking to yourself. It may help to remember that musicians rehearse alone, athletes exercise alone, and actors recite their lines alone. Speakers, too, must learn how to practice alone.

Some speakers like to practice in front of a full-length mirror, and more than a few public speaking books recommend this practice technique. We do not share the general enthusiasm for this method. In fact, we discourage it. Try it, and you will see why. When you start talking to a mirror, you'll notice your face, your hair, your clothes, and your eyes. You will notice your mouth moving, your hands gesturing, and your posture. Staring at yourself in a mirror as you are giving your presentation may cause you to criticize your performance *even as it is happening*. This is likely to distract you from focusing on the audience, purpose, and content.

Practice by Recording Yourself

If you practice in private, it's difficult, if not impossible, to concentrate on delivering your presentation *and* evaluating it at the same time. That's why we don't recommend the mirror method. But without a mirror, how can you know whether you are speaking clearly, maintaining enough eye contact, avoiding filler words and fidgets, moving and gesturing appropriately, and in general improving your presentation? The answer lies in technology. Recording your practice session with your phone, camera, or computer can tell you a lot about what you are saying, how you sound, and what you look like as you are presenting.

● getting started   ▶ delivery   ◆ speaking to persuade
▲ fundamentals   ⁘ engaging your audience   ★ speaking occasions
■ content   ◣ speaking to inform   ✹ resources

One of the first things you will notice if you listen to the audio part of a recording is that your voice doesn't sound the way you thought it would. But remember, you hear your voice from inside your head; your audience hears it projected across a room. The outside sound will be different. As you listen to yourself, listen as an audience member would. Do you understand what is being said—the ideas and information as well as individual words and phrases? Was your rate of speaking appropriate? Was your voice expressive? Did you finish within your allotted time without seeming rushed?

If your recording is a video, you can also assess how you look. Watching a video of practice sessions can tell you how to polish and improve your presentation. When watching the recording, be aware that in all probability, you won't like what you see. At first, you may be distracted by the way your hair looks, the way you gesture, or aspects of your physical appearance you dislike. It helps to begin by first watching it alone and then with a friend. Because it can be difficult to watch yourself objectively, an honest friend's opinions may help erase some of your concerns and calm your nerves. Once you've gotten past these initial feelings of discomfort, apply the same **AUDIENCE-CENTERED** thinking to your physical delivery as you did to your vocal delivery. Are your movements, gestures, and expressions natural and open? Are you prone to particular fidgets? Are you looking at your (imagined) audience in a manner that seems appropriate and immediate?

▲ 70–72

Revise as You Practice

As you practice your presentation, you may find it necessary to make several revisions. For example, you may realize that the way you're telling a **STORY** isn't connecting to your purpose, key points, or overall message. As a result, you may revise the story or delete it. You may need to write several drafts of your notes before you settle on the one that is most helpful to you. The first draft of your speaking notes is unlikely to be your final draft.

253–67

Consider the circumstances in which your message or delivery may need to change as you speak. What if an expected audience member about whom you intend to tell a story isn't there? What if you have technical problems with visual aids? Will you be able to speak without them, if necessary? What if you have to shorten the presentation? What if a major news story breaks right before you speak? Plan and practice how you would adjust your content and delivery in response to situations such as these.

Practice in Front of Others

After you have practiced alone, recorded your practice sessions, and made adjustments based on what you've heard and seen in those recordings, try to practice your presentation in front of several different people. Your listeners don't need to be trained public speakers to say, "I couldn't hear you," "You didn't look at me during the last section," or "I'm not sure what you were trying to prove with those statistics." Equally important, because we often are our own harshest critics, practicing in front of friendly listeners can reassure you and give you an extra dose of confidence. Their reaction can help you put the finishing touches on a well-prepared and well-delivered presentation.

Practice Session Guidelines

Generally, it's a good idea to practice your entire presentation several different times rather than devoting one long session to the process. In addition, you should schedule five-to-ten-minute sessions where you practice portions of your speech, concentrating on your introduction, a single key point, or your conclusion. If you rehearse your entire presentation every time you practice, you'll become tired, bored, and frustrated, particularly when some sections go well and others need more practice.

Schedule at least three complete run-through sessions but nowhere near ten. The reason for the upper limit is that too much practice can make you sound *canned*, a term used to describe speakers who have practiced their presentation so often or who have given the same presentation so many times that they no longer sound spontaneous and natural. Rather than prescribe the number of practice sessions, we offer this advice: Keep practicing until you feel satisfied. Then practice with the goal of improving the fine points of your presentation. Then stop.

● getting started	▶ delivery	◆ speaking to persuade
▲ fundamentals	∴ engaging your audience	★ speaking occasions
■ content	▼ speaking to inform	✳ resources

As you prepare to practice a presentation, ask yourself some questions that may help you develop a practice plan:

- Where do you envision yourself practicing the most? Will you make sure those spaces are available when you need them?
- What days and times work best for you to practice your presentations? How often will you rehearse your presentation? Will you make sure to practice short sections as well as the entire speech?
- What challenges do you anticipate with speaking extemporaneously or using a manuscript? How might you handle them? To what extent will practice help you decrease or augment details in the note cards or speaking outline you will use?

If you need more help

See 5.4, **PRESENTATION AIDS**, for advice on how to ensure that visual and other presentation aids complement your delivery.

282–305

Conclusion

Before you begin practicing a presentation, you have two important questions to answer: What forms of delivery will I use—impromptu, extemporaneous, manuscript, and/or memorized? And depending on that decision, you should ask: What is the best format for speaking notes—none, index cards, an outline, or a manuscript? These decisions will determine how you should prepare and practice your presentation.

The surest way to be confident and poised while speaking to an audience is to be well prepared and well rehearsed. Effective speakers practice every aspect of their presentation—not just the sound of their voice and the words in their message. They practice walking to the front of a room with confidence. They practice their presentation as though an audience is present. This kind of practice allows you to integrate and sharpen physical delivery skills that generate expressiveness, confidence, stage presence, and immediacy when it's time for the real thing.

Engaging Your
Audience

Part 5

Engaging Your Audience

"How can I be more interesting?"

It's a question we often hear from students in communication courses. What they're asking has less to do with their personalities when they're alone with friends and family, and everything to do with their public speaking persona. They want to know: how can I win and maintain my audience's attention throughout my presentation? How can I make my speech more engaging, worthwhile, and memorable? This section offers some answers to these questions. By using expressive and vivid LANGUAGE, tapping the power of STORIES, encouraging AUDIENCE PARTICIPATION, and designing and sharing interesting and relevant PRESENTATION AIDS, you can capture and keep your audience's interest from start to finish.

Engaging Your Audience

5.1 Using Language

The great American writer Mark Twain once declared, "The difference between the almost right word and the right word is really a large matter— 'tis the difference between the lightning bug and the lightning." Well-chosen words lie at the heart of memorable presentations. The right words teach, influence, motivate, and delight listeners. As the most fundamental building block of any presentation, language is the best place to start a discussion of how to successfully engage an audience. The words you choose matter.

Defining Language

Every one of the five thousand to six thousand **languages** spoken on this planet is a system of interrelated words and grammatical rules used to express thoughts and construct messages that can be understood by other people. Without words, you cannot create and share complex stories, follow and give meticulous directions, or express and explain a full range of emotions.

Denotative and Connotative Language

Most words have several meanings. Dictionaries specialize in one type of meaning: denotation. Your personal thoughts and emotional reactions to a word produce a second type of meaning: connotation.

Denotation refers to the objective, literal meaning or meanings of a word. Speakers should make sure they understand the proper usage of every word in their presentation. Consider the word *turkey*. It's a bird we eat at Thanksgiving, a country spanning Europe and Asia, three consecutive strikes in bowling, and a Broadway play that's a failure.

Connotation refers to the feelings that words arouse in a person who reads, hears, or speaks them.[1] Connotation is more likely than denotation to influence the way an audience responds to words. For example, *turkey* can mean a delicious, mouthwatering dish at Thanksgiving, but to a vegetarian it can mean a disgusting slab of dead flesh.

How would you describe an *overweight* person: *fat, heavy, prosperous, plump, chubby, gross,* or *obese?* If you choose a word with a negative connotation, such as *gross,* your listeners may be offended. *Prosperous* is less offensive but has connotations of its own.

Abstract and Concrete Language

An **abstract word** refers to an idea or concept that cannot be observed or touched. Words such as *love, patriotism,* and *transportation* may not have the same meaning for everyone. A **concrete word** refers to a specific thing that can be perceived by our senses. Words such as *diamond engagement ring, American flag,* and *ten-speed bicycle* have a much narrower range of possible meanings.

87–101 ▲

Effective speakers choose words that help them achieve their **PURPOSE**. Concrete words are less likely to be misunderstood. Although abstract words can rally people around a shared value or goal, they can also lead to confusion. For example, audience members may support more *border security.* Without a concrete definition of this phrase, however, some listeners may think it means building a wall while others may think it means increased surveillance at legal ports of entry.

Active and Passive Voice

In grammatical terms, *voice* refers to whether the subject of a sentence performs or receives the action of the verb. If the subject performs the action, you are using an **active voice.** For example, "The student read the *Iliad*" is active. If the subject receives the action, you are using a **passive voice.** "The *Iliad* was read by the student" is passive.

Look at the differences in these sentences:

ACTIVE VOICE: Sign this petition.

PASSIVE VOICE: The petition should be signed by all of you.

An active voice keeps your presentation moving. A passive voice takes the focus away from the subject of your sentence. Because an active voice requires fewer words, it also keeps your sentences short and direct. Here's an example: In July 2020, infectious disease physician Anthony Fauci was asked about White House efforts to discredit him and his advice about responding to the COVID-19 pandemic. He said, "It's a bit bizarre. The divisiveness that's going on. We've got to own this, reset this, and say, 'OK, let's stop this nonsense. We've got to do better.' . . . I just want to do my job . . . and I'm going to keep doing it."[2]

Speaking Styles

Champion athletes have unique styles of play. Renowned opera singers have recognizable vocal qualities. Authors have distinctive ways of expressing themselves. The same is true of speakers.

Speaking style refers to how you use vocabulary, sentence structure and length, grammar, and **STYLISTIC DEVICES** to convey a message.[3] Your personal speaking style can add a distinctive flavor, emotion, and clarity to your presentation. Would anyone confuse the speaking styles of President Obama, President Trump, and President Biden? Probably not.

245–49

There are four **CORE** speaking styles: clear, oral, rhetorical, and eloquent. You must decide which is best suited to you, your **PURPOSE**, your **AUDIENCE**, and the **SPEAKING OCCASION**.

87–101
70–86
405–89

The Clear Style

In highly effective presentations, clarity always comes first. If your speaking style isn't clear, your audience may not understand your message and may question your **CREDIBILITY**. The **clear style** uses

57–66

- Short, simple, common words
- Direct language
- Concrete words
- Active voice

In times of crisis, the clear style can evoke calmness and resolve. President George W. Bush's televised address to the nation on the day of the 9/11 attacks exemplifies a clear style:

This is a day when all Americans from every walk of life unite in our resolve for justice and peace. America has stood down enemies before, and we will do so this time. None of us will ever forget this day, yet we go forward to defend freedom and all that is good and just in our world.

Using short, simple, and common words does not mean using the same words over and over again. Simplicity is not the same as repetition. For example, what's another word for *problem*? *Difficulty, challenge, hurdle, snag, obstacle, puzzle, trouble.* You sound more competent if you can describe something with a variety of words. (Notice, too, the different connotations of *problem* and *puzzle*.) Add details when appropriate. Which sounds more credible: "The project will be done in a few months" or "The project will be done in nine weeks"? Precision builds trust in the speaker's **COMPETENCE**.

58–61 ▲

The Oral Style

There is often a big difference between the words we use for written documents and the ones we use in presentations. The **oral style** uses

- Short, familiar, conversational words
- Short, simple sentences
- Contractions
- Personal language

The oral style sounds more like the way you talk than the way you write. Instead of writing *elucidate*, you might say *explain*. Rather than write, "He returned from the point of his departure," you could say, "He came back." With contractions, you can say something simple, like "We won't let him." Without contractions, you might write, "We will not allow him to do this."

The oral style also uses personal language freely and frequently. Pronouns such as *I, me,* and *my* make you responsible for your message and can enhance your **CREDIBILITY**. Pronouns such as *we, us,* and *ours* intensify the connection between you and the audience. "We shall overcome" has significantly more power than "You shall overcome" or "I shall overcome."

57–66 ▲

When preparing and **PRACTICING** a presentation using the oral style, reconsider complex words or sentences. Simplicity almost always beats formality. The following introduction to a student's informative presentation on CliffsNotes uses the oral style:

> Eight o'clock Wednesday night. I have an English exam bright and early tomorrow morning. It's on Homer's *Iliad*. And I haven't read page one. I skip tonight's beer drinking and try to read. Eight forty-five. I'm only on page 12. Only 482 more to go. Nine thirty, it hits me. Like a rock. I'm not going to make it.

His short words and sentences, personal pronouns, contractions, and casual expressions paint a vivid picture of an unprepared and somewhat desperate student who is facing a major exam.

228–33

The Rhetorical Style

A speaker who wants to **PERSUADE**, motivate, and/or impress an audience should incorporate features of the rhetorical style. Drawing on elements from the clear and oral styles, the **rhetorical style** also uses

349–50

- Intense language
- Vivid language
- Powerful words

A former student began a persuasive presentation with a story. Her use of the rhetorical style created an unforgettable image. Read the following introduction out loud, paying careful attention to her language:

> Picture two-year-old Joey. A hole in his throat so he can breathe. A tube jutting out of his stomach where a surgeon implanted a new esophagus. It all began when Joey found an open can of drain cleaner and swallowed some of its contents. However, this is not going to be a speech about poisoning and how to prevent it, because Joey's tragedy was not caused by the drain cleaner. It occurred because Joey's mother followed an old set of first-aid instructions. She gave him vinegar. But instead of neutralizing the poison, the vinegar set off a chemical reaction that generated heat and turned Joey's tiny digestive tract into an inferno of excruciating pain.

Language intensity refers to the degree to which your language deviates from dull, neutral terms. Instead of using a word like *nice*, try *delightful* or *enchanting*. A *vile* meal sounds much worse than a *bad* one. "An inferno of excruciating pain" is much more intense than *very painful*.

Be cautious, though, because language intensity can backfire. Speakers who are consistently too intense may jeopardize their credibility. Effective speakers *vary* their language intensity. On an important issue or **KEY POINT**, they're more intense. Then they take a breath by using more neutral language so that the audience will be ready for the next big idea.

133–36

Vivid language elicits strong, memorable images in the minds of listeners. Whereas language intensity refers to the degree to which your words deviate from a bland baseline, vivid language refers to the level of detail you describe. Compare "The glass broke" with "The delicate champagne flute fell with an expensive-sounding crash, shattering into pieces of sharp confetti across the marble floor." Which do you think is more vivid?[4] Again, be careful: you can easily overdo vividness.

Powerful words express your confidence, certainty, and commitment to your purpose, whereas **powerless words** are weak and unconvincing. Avoid the following types of words, which characterize powerless speech:[5]

352–54

- *Hesitations and fillers.* "Uh," "um," "well," and "you know" are phrases that reduce the force of a speaker's **CLAIMS** and convey a lack of **FLUENCY**.

205–6
184–85

- *Qualifiers and hedges.* Words such as "sort of," "maybe," "kind of," and "I guess" communicate a lack of **CONFIDENCE**.

- *Tag questions.* When speakers "tag" a statement with a question, as in "She is responsible for the problem, *don't you think?*" it suggests they're uncertain about what they're saying.

- *Disclaimers.* Statements such as "I'm not an expert, but . . ." and "I'm in the minority, but . . ." imply that the audience should understand or make allowances for the speaker's lack of competence. Make your point without excuses.

- *Feeble intensifiers.* When speakers use feeble intensifiers such as "very," "really," "actually," "awfully," "pretty," or "so" to modify a word, they may rob the phrase of its power.

Powerful words are direct, concrete, and expressive. Sunsets are more than *nice*; they can be *beautiful*, *glorious*, or a *glimpse of heaven*. In an emergency, you wouldn't *say* "fire"—you would *shout* it!

Here is governor of New York Andrew Cuomo speaking about President Trump's responses to the COVID-19 pandemic in New York in September 2020:[6]

> I believe the President is fundamentally a bully which I've said too many times and I've known him very well for a very long period of time. It doesn't work in New York because you can't bully New Yorkers. We just don't get bullied. We don't respond well to it. . . . This nation has not been attacked by an enemy who has killed more and ravaged more than COVID since World War II, and the president and commander-in-chief has been an abysmal failure in the war against COVID. That's the facts.

Each of your language choices should maximize their effect on the audience. When you're trying to make an important point, say what you mean and mean what you say. As long as you don't go overboard with flowery or abstract words, the richness of your vocabulary can **INSPIRE** your listeners and boost your **CREDIBILITY**.

▲ 94
▲ 57–66

The Eloquent Style

Great novelists, poets, and playwrights have the remarkable ability to capture profound ideas and emotions with words. So do eloquent speakers. The **eloquent style** combines artistry and persuasion in ways that make thoughts and feelings clear, inspiring, and memorable. It seeks to motivate and electrify audiences.

Think of the eloquent style as the peak of a mountain built on clear, oral, and rhetorical speaking styles. Phrases such as Abraham Lincoln's "government of the people, by the people, for the people shall not perish from the earth" are inspiring and memorable because Lincoln spent considerable time and effort searching for the best words to communicate his thoughts and feelings. Eloquence does not mean relying on long, fancy words. It uses a subtle, plain style that projects power. In Winston Churchill's first speech as prime minister to the United Kingdom's

Parliament in 1940, he said, "I have nothing to offer but blood, toil, tears and sweat." When President Ronald Reagan spoke in Berlin, he demanded, "Mr. Gorbachev, tear down this wall."

In *Eloquence in an Electronic Age*, Kathleen Jamieson notes that in today's busy and mediated world, eloquent speakers comfortably disclose their personal feelings and skillfully share stories.[7] They use personal pronouns and an oral style to call on their own past and strong beliefs to inspire an audience. The following excerpt from Barack Obama's "A More Perfect Union" speech, made during his 2008 campaign for president, provides an excellent example:

> I am the son of a black man from Kenya and a white woman from Kansas. I was raised with the help of a white grandfather who survived a Depression to serve in Patton's Army during World War II and a white grandmother who worked on a bomber assembly line at Fort Leavenworth while he was overseas. I've gone to some of the best schools in America and lived in one of the world's poorest nations. I am married to a black American who carries within her the blood of slaves and slaveowners—an inheritance we pass on to our two precious daughters. I have brothers, sisters, nieces, nephews, uncles and cousins, of every race and every hue, scattered across three continents, and for as long as I live, I will never forget that in no other country on Earth is my story even possible.[8]

Use All Four CORE Speaking Styles

The CORE speaking styles are not separate and distinct; all four are often heard in a single presentation. Keep in mind that there is a natural progression from clarity to eloquence. Also, the language style(s) you choose will depend on the **OCCASION** as well as the **PURPOSE**, **AUDIENCE**, **CONTENT** of your message, and the way you **DELIVER** your presentation. Skillful use of all four speaking styles will enhance your credibility as an effective and ethical speaker.

The figure below illustrates how the CORE speaking styles build on one another. The clear style is concise and direct. The oral style builds on this

405–89
87–101
70–86
103–79
181–233

● getting started   ▶ delivery   ◆ speaking to persuade
▲ fundamentals   ⁘ engaging your audience   ★ speaking occasions
■ content   ▼ speaking to inform   ✳ resources

foundation and makes the message more personal. From there, speakers who use a rhetorical style add vivid and effective language. The eloquent style enlists clear, oral, and rhetorical language, to which it adds memorable words and phrases, effective storytelling, and personal revelations.

THE FOUR CORE SPEAKING STYLES

The Eloquent Style	E
The Rhetorical Style	R
The Oral Style	O
The Clear Style	C

Stylistic Devices

Stylistic devices—also called figures of speech, rhetorical devices, and language tropes—include a variety of word strategies that can make your message more effective, engaging, and memorable. If chosen wisely, they can enrich all four CORE speaking styles.

There are hundreds of figures of speech. Here we focus on a select group of stylistic devices that are effective and applicable to many speaking occasions:

- Repetition
- Alliteration
- Metaphors, similes, and analogies
- Lists of three
- Avoidance of clichés

Repetition

Long before ancient people developed reading and writing, they listened to speakers. Oral poetry and storytelling in early societies used repetition to help people remember cultural and religious information. Because listeners cannot go back and immediately rehear what you've said, **repetition** helps reinforce ideas by highlighting important words and phrases.

Winston Churchill's war address, made over the radio as the British people faced the threat of German bombings during World War II, demonstrates the power of repetition: "We shall fight on the beaches, we shall fight on the landing grounds, we shall fight in the fields and in the streets, we shall fight in the hills; we shall never surrender."[9] Dr. Martin Luther King Jr. said "I have a dream" eight times in his famous 1963 speech in Washington, DC. He used the phrase "let freedom ring" ten times.

You don't have to be a world leader to use repetition effectively. Naomi Wadler was eleven years old when she spoke at the 2018 March for Our Lives rally in Washington, DC, led by survivors of the shooting at Stoneman Douglas High School in Parkland, Florida. She used the phrase "I am here today to represent" repeatedly and then varied it with "I am here today to acknowledge and represent":

> I am here today to represent Courtlin Arrington. I am here today to represent Hadiya Pendleton. I am here today to represent Taiyania Thompson, who at just 16 was shot dead in her home here in Washington, DC. I am here today to acknowledge and represent the African-American girls whose stories don't make the front page of every national newspaper. Whose stories don't lead on the evening news.[10]

Alliteration

Alliteration is a form of repetition where speakers use a series of words (or words placed closely together) that begin with the same sound. Although subtle, it is often found in memorable speeches. One of the most quoted phrases from President Bush's 2003 State of the Union address is this: "The dictator of Iraq is not disarming. To the contrary, he is deceiving."[11] President Bill Clinton used the same technique during his acceptance address at the 1992 Democratic Convention: "Somewhere at this very moment a child is being born in America. Let it be our cause to give that child a happy home, a healthy family, and a hopeful future."[12]

Alliteration captures audience attention because it makes language easier to remember—even when it's brief. But don't get carried away. The result may sound like a tongue twister—she sells sea shells by the seashore—rather than an effective and memorable phrase.

Metaphors, Similes, and Analogies

A **metaphor** compares two things or ideas without using connective words such as *like* and *as*. Shakespeare's famous line "All the world's a stage" is a classic metaphor. The world is not a theatrical stage, but we do play and act many parts during a lifetime. Metaphors leave it to the audience to get the point for themselves.[13]

Metaphors are so deeply embedded in our language that we often use them without realizing it. For instance, you've probably tried something new by "getting your feet wet" or held a "dead end" job. Some of our common metaphors borrow the names of body parts: *teeth* of a comb, *mouth* of a river, *foot* of a mountain, *tongue* of a shoe, *eye* of a needle or storm, and *head* of a corporation.[14] Politicians know that effective metaphors can distill complex ideas into simple phrases, such as President Trump's promise to "drain the swamp."

Metaphors are potent tools. Some of the best ones appeal to sensory experiences—what audience members see, hear, feel, smell, or taste. Here are some sources of common metaphors:[15]

- *Up/bright and down/dark. Up* is usually linked to happiness, health, life, and virtue, whereas *down* characterizes sadness, sickness, death, and low status. Martin Luther King Jr. referred to the "sunlit path of racial justice" (an up image) as compared with the "dark and desolate valley of segregation" (a down image).
- *Natural phenomena.* Metaphors often use natural phenomena and weather to describe serious consequences. We talk about being overwhelmed by "a flood" of requests or being "swamped" by work. We describe armed forces as moving and attacking with "lightning speed."

When linguists point to metaphors as the most prevalent and powerful stylistic device, they often include *similes* and *analogies*. Like metaphors, **similes** make a direct comparison between two things or ideas, but they usually use the words *like* or *as* to link the two items, as in boxing champion Muhammad Ali's famous quotation "Float like a butterfly, sting like a bee."

319–32 ▼
336–39 ▼

Analogies expand similes and metaphors in order to **REPORT NEW INFORMATION** and **DESCRIBE SCIENTIFIC PHENOMENA**. For example, you can describe electricity as water flowing through pipes, the heart as a pump, and the liver as a filter.[16]

Analogies can also be expressed as similes and metaphors. Consider the following analogy: "Just as orchestra conductors must grasp the entire musical score while inspiring great performances from individual players, effective leaders must understand the big picture while motivating team members to perform at their full potential." Here, the same idea is expressed as a simile: "Effective leaders are like great orchestra conductors—they know the score and inspire great performances." And now as a metaphor: "Great leaders conduct an orchestra of talented team members who learn their individual parts to play the same tune."

72–80 ▲

As you practice your presentation, be on the lookout for **mixed metaphors**, where mismatched comparisons are combined in an illogical and often laughable statement, as in this example: "What we are dealing with is the rubber meeting the road, and instead of biting the bullet on these issues, we just want to punt."[17] Also keep in mind your **AUDIENCE ANALYSIS**. Every culture has different metaphors, similes, and analogies. If you say, "He hit a home run at the meeting!" folks in the United States and baseball fans everywhere will understand that this is a compliment, but everyone else might not have a clue what you mean.

Lists of Three

136 ▦
133–36 ▦

Recall the **RULE OF THREE**. Audience members often expect speakers to have three **KEY POINTS**. The pattern is so common that some people will even prepare to applaud as they hear the third item in a series. The same is true of words and phrases.

Below is an excerpt from First Lady Michelle Obama's September 11, 2010, commemorative speech at the Flight 93 National Memorial site in Shanksville, Pennsylvania. Rather than highlighting three words in one sentence, she uses groups of three to highlight phrases and sentences.

● getting started   ▶ delivery   ◆ speaking to persuade
▲ fundamentals   ⁖ engaging your audience   ★ speaking occasions
▦ content   ▼ speaking to inform   ✳ resources

I come [here today] as an American, filled with a sense of awe at the heroism of my fellow citizens. I come as a wife, a daughter, and a sister, heartbroken at the loss so many of you have endured. And I come as a mother, thinking about what my daughters, and what all of our sons and daughters can learn from the forty men and women whose memories we honor today.[18]

Avoidance of Clichés

A **cliché** ("klee-SHAY") is a trite or tired expression that has lost its originality or force through overuse. Here are some examples:

- Crystal clear
- Better late than never
- Hit the nail on the head

Clichés lack force because they are predictable rather than original. So how do you know if you're using a cliché? Try this simple test: Say the beginning of the following sentences and see if you or others can guess the last word. If you can, it may be a cliché.

BEGINNING OF SENTENCE	END OF SENTENCE
He's as blind as a	bat.
It's selling like	hotcakes.

A critical look at these and other clichés reveals another weakness: they often make no sense. When is the last time hotcakes sold well? And although bats may not see well with their eyes, their radar system is far more powerful than our sense of sight.

Sometimes clever speakers will use a cliché to make a point. You could use the cliché "as blind as a bat" to begin a presentation about the misunderstandings we have about bats or the marvels of modern radar. Even better, convert the cliché into something more interesting and original. Here's an example of how a student speaker took the cliché "butterflies in my stomach" and transformed it into something fresh and memorable about her nervousness: "If the feeling in my stomach is caused by butterflies, there must be a horde of them, with horseshoes on."[19]

Language and Your Audience

72–80

Effective speakers match their words to their listeners. Take your **AUDIENCE'S CHARACTERISTICS** into account as you select key words for your presentation.

In 1989, the scholar Dr. Henry Louis Gates Jr. delivered a speech at the *New York Times* President's Forum on Literacy.[20] What assumptions did Gates make about his audience by including the following quotation?

> In the resonant words of W. E. B. Du Bois: "I sit with Shakespeare, and he winces not. Across the color line, I move arm in arm with Balzac and Dumas, where smiling men and welcoming women glide in gilded halls. . . . I summon Aristotle and Aurelius and what soul I will, and they come all graciously with no scorn or condescension."

Gates assumed that his audience was college educated and had read or would recognize the quotation from Du Bois's 1903 book *The Souls of Black Folk*. He also assumed that they understood Du Bois's references to Shakespeare, Balzac, Dumas, Aristotle, and Aurelius. These assumptions were fine for his audience, but had he been addressing a group of sixth graders, many in attendance would not have understood him.

At the beginning of the same presentation, Gates used a simpler style that made other assumptions about his audience:

> I grew up in a little town on the eastern panhandle of West Virginia, called Piedmont, population two thousand, supposedly (we could never find the other one thousand people). I started school in 1957, two years after the *Brown v. Board* decision, and in that year, 1957, my father bought a full set of the *World Book* encyclopedia.

Even though his words are not complex and the story folksy, Gates assumed his audience knew the importance of the Supreme Court's *Brown v. Board of Education* decision. His mixing of styles—clear and oral at the start of his speech, more rhetorical and eloquent in the middle—demonstrates another fact about audiences: variety keeps them interested.

Avoid Gender Bias

For many years, the pronoun *he* was used to refer to an unspecified individual. Older textbooks used sentences such as "Every speaker should pay attention to his words." Interestingly, *he* was also used to refer to a student, scholar, or a professional, whereas *she* was used to refer to a nurse, school teacher, or secretary. Certainly you can say, "Martha couldn't find her wallet" or "Walter couldn't find his wallet" when the gender is correctly identified for the subject of the sentence. Fortunately, there are several ways to avoid gender bias and confusion in the use of pronouns:

- Use gender-neutral terms for jobs and professions. For example, the word *actor* has replaced *actress* for women in theater and film. The word *waiter* and *server* apply to both genders.

- Use plural pronouns. Instead of saying, "Every speaker should pay attention to his choice of words," substitute "All speakers should pay attention to *their* choice of words."

- Avoid using a pronoun entirely. In some cases, you can rephrase a sentence and remove the pronoun altogether, as in "Good speakers pay careful attention to language."

- Use the pronoun *they/their* when it is the subject's preferred gender pronoun or when you're referring to someone whose gender is unknown or not relevant to the matter at hand, as in "A good speaker pays special attention to their choice of words."

Avoid Cultural Bias in Your Language

Audience members who do not speak English as their first language may have difficulty understanding you—as you would have trouble if you were listening to someone speak in a language that is not your native tongue. If your audience includes nonnative speakers of English, consider the following strategies:

- Use language that is clear and simple.
- Use complete sentences on **PRESENTATION AIDS**.

282–305

- Use a more formal speaking style, and address individuals by their formal titles.
- Avoid clichés and common expressions that they may not grasp.

It's also important to use the preferred designations for racial or ethnic identities. For example, *Black* and *African American* are accepted terms today. Remember that the term *America* includes both North, Central, and South America. And avoid stereotyping people based on their place of origin.

Avoid Exclusionary Language

Exclusionary language reinforces stereotypes, belittles people, or excludes them from understanding a particular group's message. Exclusionary language widens the social gap by separating the world into *us* and *them*. You don't have to be excessively politically correct— for example, using *vertically challenged* for *short*—but you should avoid language that might alienate people. Try not to mention age, health and abilities, sexual orientation, or race and ethnicity unless these characteristics are relevant to your presentation.

Conclusion

Using language effectively is just as important in class or work presentations as it is in noteworthy public speeches. If you're not sure that you are using language that will gain and maintain your audience's attention, record a practice session and listen to it carefully. If your message is clear, oral, rhetorical, and eloquent when appropriate, your language will increase your presentation's effectiveness. If your message seems difficult to grasp and gets bogged down, the problem may be that you have not paid enough attention to the use of concete words, active voice, appropriate speaking style, and audience-adapted language choices. Speak the way you talk, and use stylistic devices that make your message more understandable, interesting, inspiring, and memorable.

Although language has the power to personalize, enliven, and enrich your message, it's important that your words match the characteristics of your audience. Avoid language that has a gender or cultural bias as well as exclusionary language that reinforces stereotypes or prevents audience members from understanding your message. Chosen wisely and well, the words you use in conjunction with the four CORE speaking styles will help you achieve your purpose.

5.2 Telling Stories

Once upon a time—before humans could read or write—stories were one of the only ways to share memorable experiences and lessons about life. Still today, well-told stories capture our attention and have a huge impact on our lives.

Steve Jobs, cofounder of Apple, told the following story during his commencement address at Stanford University in 2005:

> About a year ago I was diagnosed with cancer. I had a scan at 7:30 in the morning, and it clearly showed a tumor on my pancreas. I didn't even know what a pancreas was. The doctors told me this was almost certainly a type of cancer that is incurable, and that I should expect to live no longer than three to six months. My doctor advised me to go home and get my affairs in order, which is doctor's code for prepare to die.[1]

Jobs could have simply said, "I was diagnosed with terminal cancer." But the story he tells does so much more than communicate a medical diagnosis. You can see yourself in his condition. You can imagine the anxiety he felt, the sense of hopelessness. As the speech continues, Jobs talks about the lessons he learned—the value of doing what you want, the importance of family, and the wisdom of using your limited time wisely.

As you may know, Jobs lived for another six years after giving this speech. It still inspires today.

The Power of Stories

All humans tell stories, whether depicted in prehistoric cave paintings, written in novels, recounted to children, depicted in film and video, or shared on social media. Ancient peoples passed down stories that commemorated famous people and events, explained natural and supernatural phenomena, and chronicled great adventures. We still do this with our families, friends, and coworkers and when we make effective presentations.

Stories describe experiences in a way that triggers listeners to imagine and/or believe them as real.[2] Stories help listeners engage with speakers and their messages. They can be short or long, comic or tragic, personal or anonymous. The clergy use parables—stories with a lesson or moral—to apply religious teachings to everyday life. Parents read fables, fairy tales, and folktales to children to demonstrate that "slow and steady wins the race" ("The Tortoise and the Hare") or that "appearances can be deceiving" ("Little Red Riding Hood"). Companies offer stories about how their new products were discovered:

> University of Oregon track coach Bill Bowerman was obsessed with inventing a better running shoe. In 1971, his wife served them breakfast waffles made on an old waffle iron—a 1936 wedding gift. He stared at the waffle and realized that by turning it upside down—where the waffle part would come in contact with the track—he'd have a self-adjusting shoe that would work on different kinds of surfaces. The rest is history. Nike's Waffle Trainer debuted in 1974. And the original, now rust-coated and broken-in-the-process waffle iron is on display at Nike's World Headquarters near Portland, Oregon.[3]

57–66 ▲
Stories enhance your **CREDIBLITY** when you tell them well and draw meaningful lessons from then. Storytelling can also reduce your
15–27 ●
SPEAKING ANXIETY. Why? Because stories are relatively easy to remember, particularly when they're drawn from personal experiences. Even a short
133–36 ■
anecdote about something that amazed you, embarrassed you, or made
352–54 ◆
you stop and think can clarify a **KEY POINT**, support a **CLAIM**, or provide
160–79 ■
an **INTRODUCTION AND CONCLUSION** to your presentation. The stories you
87–101 ▲
tell can and should reinforce your **PURPOSE**.

Finding Stories

Stories are everywhere—from children's books to holy scriptures. Good speakers keep their eyes and ears open for the ones that can be used in presentations. When you encounter a useful story in a newspaper, magazine, book, movie, or online, save it for later. When someone tells you a story that dramatizes a concept you'll be discussing, write it down. But the best stories are often your own.

● getting started   ▶ delivery   ◆ speaking to persuade
▲ fundamentals   ⁂ engaging your audience   ★ speaking occasions
■ content   ◤ speaking to inform   ✳ resources

Student speakers often worry that they don't know any stories or that they're not good at telling them. But everyone can tell a story when it's the right one. So where should you look for the right story?

You

You are a living, breathing collection of stories. The following table offers eleven suggestions for priming your personal story pump:[4]

Your name	What's the story of your name? Were you named for someone? If so, what was their story? Does your name have a special meaning in your own or another language? Does it reflect your ethnic background? Have you changed your name? Why?
Your past	Start by filling in the following blanks: *When I was in _____, I _____.* For example, *When I was in kindergarten, I used to play tricks on my best friend.* What happened? Why do you remember it so vividly? What did you learn that may benefit an audience?
Your family's roots	Where does your family come from? How far back can you trace your lineage? Are there unique customs in your family? What's your family's ethnic background? Is there someone famous, funny, notorious, or eccentric in your family?
Your special places	Is there a special place in your life? Perhaps a vacant lot where you played with childhood friends? A venue where your family holds reunions? A view from a beloved mountaintop? The place you were married?
Your mentors	Who has helped guide you through life's challenges? Your parents, a teacher, a coach, a relative, a best friend, a mentor? What did they do for you? What advice did they share? Can their counsel benefit others?
Your successes	What have you done that makes you proud? Have you earned an award, helped people in need, done the right thing in a crisis, or survived a tragedy? How can your story of success help other people?

(Continued)

Your failures	What have you learned from a particular failure? How did failing make you feel? How did you overcome it? What did you do to make sure it wouldn't happen again? How can your story help other people?
Your values	What are your deep-seated values? Do you value fairness, honesty, tradition, equality, and/or justice? Do you value your family and friends, your country, your environment, or profession? There's probably a story about why you strongly value what you believe and do.
Your pivotal moments	When did you know you were an adult? What did you learn from being laid off from a job? When did you first truly understand love?
Your pet peeves	What bothers you a lot? Bad customer service, a grade you didn't deserve, name-calling? Why? What happened?
Your special knowledge	Do you know how _____ was discovered? Do you know why the town of _____ was founded? Do you know that _____ happened here one hundred years ago today?

For an example of using a personal story as an introduction to an informative presentation, see Notable Speaker: Susan Cain, page 176.

Your Audience

76–80 ▲

If you have spent sufficient time analyzing your audience, you should be able to find stories related to their **INTERESTS, BELIEFS, AND VALUES**. If your audience is deeply religious, you may share a story about a friend who gave up their worldly goods to work on a mission. If your audience loves sports, you may share a story about your own triumphs and defeats as an athlete. If your audience is culturally diverse, you may share a story about how you, a friend, or colleagues succeeded in bridging such differences.

● getting started   ▶ delivery   ◆ speaking to persuade
▲ fundamentals   ∴ engaging your audience   ★ speaking occasions
■ content   ▼ speaking to inform   ✳ resources

Other People

All of us know people with fascinating backgrounds and experiences. Think of someone you could interview whose story might illuminate the subject of your presentation. It could be a combat war veteran who heroically saved a friend; a parent or grandparent who, against all odds, immigrated to the United States and created a successful business; or a professional musician, writer, actor, or athlete who overcame adversity to achieve their goals. Remember one thing: if you're going to tell someone else's story, never use it to embarrass or divulge private information, and make sure to get their permission before you tell it.

The Occasion

When and where will you be speaking? Does the venue have a fascinating history? How will the situation and setting affect your delivery? What's happening in the news or in the neighborhood? Was someone famous born on the day you're speaking? If Mother's Day is coming up, could you talk about something your mother said or did that is relevant to why you are speaking? What happened the first (or previous) time you attended this event or spoke in a similar situation or setting? The key is finding something you've done, witnessed, known, or believed that is relevant to the **SPEAKING OCCASION**.

★ 405–89

Storytelling Strategies

Most of us are good storytellers in everyday conversations. We can easily recount something that happened to us or something we witnessed. Telling a story in a presentation, however, is not the same as describing your day. A story told in a presentation must be carefully developed and delivered. The following strategies will help guide you through this process:

- *Use a simple story line.* Long stories with complex themes are hard to follow and difficult to tell. If you can't summarize your story in fewer than twenty-five words, don't tell it.

- *Limit the number of characters.* Unless you're an accomplished actor, limit the number of characters in your story. Good storytellers distinguish their characters by modifying their **VOCAL DELIVERY** and

▶ 194–209

210–19

PHYSICAL DELIVERY. Using a combination of distinctive volumes, rates, pitches, tones, and body movements can be tough for a novice speaker, so it's best to look for stories with no more than three characters.

57–66
72–80

- *Connect with your listeners.* Your audience will pay more attention if they can connect emotionally with the setting, characters, and plot of your story. To maintain your **CREDIBILITY**, make sure your story is appropriate based on **AUDIENCE ANALYSIS**.

- *Make a point.* Imagine you concluded your story with "And so what this means for you is . . ." The best stories, however, aren't as explicit as that. Instead, the message is usually obvious by the end. Whatever the point you're trying to make, it must be clear and connect with your **PURPOSE**.

87–101

- *Tell it efficiently.* According to Shakespeare, "Brevity is the soul of wit." Try to tell your story in less than two minutes, not by speaking quickly but by **USING LANGUAGE** and storytelling skills efficiently.

237–52

- *Create tension.* Effective stories create uncertainty about what will happen next. Will Beauty kiss the Beast? Will Wonder Woman help win the war? Will Dorothy get back to Kansas? Will you get the job after flubbing a question at the interview?

64–65

- *Make it personal.* The best **STORIES** are often about you, the speaker. Talking about how you handled a difficult situation can, if well told, be far more interesting than a story about some historical figure who faced the same thing.

- *Exaggerate effectively.* Think about the ways you might alter your delivery when reading to a child. Exaggeration can make a story more vivid. The tone of your **VOICE**, the sweep of your **GESTURES**, and your **FACIAL EXPRESSIONS** add a layer of meaning and emphasis to your message.

196–206
213–15
212–13
136

- *Remember the rule of three.* Stories make frequent use of the **RULE OF THREE**: Abraham, Isaac, and Jacob; Papa Bear, Mama Bear, and Baby Bear; three little pigs; the Scarecrow, Tin Man, and Cowardly Lion;

● getting started   ▶ delivery   ◆ speaking to persuade
▲ fundamentals   ∴ engaging your audience   ★ speaking occasions
■ content   ◥ speaking to inform   ✳ resources

Violet, Klaus, and Sunny Baudelaire. Think of the many times a folktale character is given three wishes, three guesses, or three tries to overcome adversity. Good storytellers know there is magic in the rule of three.

- *Practice for sense and rhythm.* Storytelling improves with **PRACTICE**. 228–33 Once you can tell a story without notes, practice telling it to someone else—a friend, neighbor, or family member. Tell the story twice. The first time, ask them whether the story makes sense. The second time, ask whether the story flows from event to event and has a rhythm 201–3 of its own. A well-told story has meaningful pauses and appropriate 203–5 variations in **RATE**, **PITCH**, and **VOLUME**. 196–200

Shaping Stories

Good stories, no matter how short or simple, share similar elements. The beginning introduces a situation where someone has to overcome an obstacle or solve a problem. The middle explains what the characters did or didn't do to resolve the situation. And the end shows the resolution and, in some cases, offers a meaningful lesson.

The following **story-building chart** provides a template that poses questions and recommends strategies to help you make sure all the right pieces of your story are in the right place:[5]

STORY-BUILDING CHART: TEMPLATE

Title

- *Questions:* What is the title of your story? Does the title capture the essence, mood, or spirit of the story?
- *Suggestion:* Although you don't have to share the title of a story with your audience, it can help you focus on the **PURPOSE** of your presentation. 87–101 A title such as "The Big Bad Man in the Back of the Building" suggests a very different story from one titled "The Happy Haven behind Our House."

(Continued)

NOTABLE SPEAKER
Rita Pierson

In 1972, Dr. Rita Pierson followed in the footsteps of her grandparents and parents to become an educator. For more than forty years, Pierson spent her professional life being a champion for students, teaching elementary school and junior high school as well as special education. She led numerous professional development workshops on a variety of topics focused on underresourced learners and early intervention strategies. Pierson was also an antipoverty advocate and served her community in various capacities, always working to help those in need. In May 2013, at a TED Talks Education event, Pierson called on educators to be champions for their students. Her inspirational talk has been viewed more than ten million times. Her family announced her sudden death in June 2013—just weeks after her TED talk aired on PBS.

Search Terms
To locate a video of this presentation online, enter the following key words into a search engine: Rita Pierson. The video is approximately 7:49 in length.

What to Watch For
[0:00–1:30] Pierson begins her talk by saying "I have spent my entire life either at the schoolhouse, on the way to the schoolhouse, or talking about what happens in the schoolhouse." Not only does this statement build her credibility, it describes the source of the stories she'll use to achieve her purpose. Note her use of "we" statements as a way to involve her audience: "And we know why kids drop out. We know why kids don't learn." The "we" statements also convey her unspoken message: "I'm talking to you! So listen up!"

[1:30–5:57] Pierson uses one- to two-minute stories both to organize her talk and to provide supporting material. All but the final story about her mother include dialogue. She also uses humor to capture and hold the audience's attention. In some cases, it is a simple statement, such as "Tell a kid you're sorry; they'll be in shock." In other cases, she uses self-effacing humor to show the audience that she is an ordinary, fallible human being—to show that even education experts get it wrong sometimes.

[6:12–7:35] Throughout the presentation, Pierson's delivery personifies the talents of a skilled storyteller. She is expressive, confident, immediate, and a model of stage presence. She maintains consistent and direct eye contact while smiling at appropriate moments. Her body movements are fluid and natural, helping establish her credibility and making her appear confident and relaxed. She effectively varies her volume, rate, pitch, and inflection to emphasize different parts of her message. When she tells the story of teaching a difficult class, her tone changes, her volume drops a bit, and she slows down her rate of speaking. In the opening and ending of her talk, her delivery communicates the urgency and seriousness of her message.

[7:14–7:43] Although she continues to share both amusing and consequential stories about students, she wraps up her speech by returning to the need for strong relationships between teachers and students. She calls out to her audience: "Every student deserves a champion, an adult who will never give up on them." She then skillfully uses short, urgent questions and answers to conclude because she knows that her audience is now with her. "Is this job tough? You betcha. Oh God, you betcha. But it is not impossible. We can do this. We're educators. We're born to make a difference."

EXERCISE

After viewing Pierson's speech, reflect on these questions:

1. What is the purpose of Pierson's presentation? How did she make this purpose relevant to her audience?

2. What strategies and supporting material did Pierson use to gain the attention of and engage her audience?

3. What other strategies could Pierson have used to involve the audience in her presentation?

4. Explain whether or not you believe that Pierson's sense of humor supported her purpose. How did it strengthen or diminish her credibility?

5. Describe how Pierson's delivery (expressiveness, confidence, state presence, and immediacy) affected audience interest, motivation, and recall.

6. In what ways, if any, could Pierson have improved the content and delivery of her presentation?

STORY-BUILDING CHART: TEMPLATE

Background information

- *Questions:* Where and when does the story take place? What is going on? Did anything important happen before the story begins?
- *Suggestion:* Use **CONCRETE WORDS** and **VIVID LANGUAGE** to set the time, place, and occasion of the story.

238
242

Character development

- *Questions:* Who is in the story? What are their backgrounds and relationships to one another? What do they look and sound like? How do you want the audience to feel about them?
- *Suggestion:* Bring the characters to life with vivid descriptions and adapt your **VOCAL DELIVERY** and **PHYSICAL DELIVERY** to make each character distinct from one another.

194–209
210–19

Action or conflict

- *Questions:* What is happening? What obstacles or challenges did the characters face? What did they see, hear, feel, smell, or taste? How did they react to what's happening?
- *Suggestion:* Let the action build as you tell this part of the story.

● getting started	▶ delivery	◆ speaking to persuade
▲ fundamentals	⁖ engaging your audience	★ speaking occasions
■ content	▼ speaking to inform	✳ resources

STORY-BUILDING CHART: TEMPLATE

High point (climax or punch line)

- *Questions:* What is the culminating event or moment of greatest intensity? What is the turning point in the action? When does the tension that's been building reach its peak? What sentence makes the story funny?
- *Suggestion:* All action should lead to a discovery, decision, or outcome. Show the audience how the character has grown or has responded to a situation or problem. If you don't include a climax or punch line, the story won't make sense—so make sure it has one!

Conclusion and resolution

- *Questions:* How is the situation resolved? How do the important characters respond to the climax?
- *Suggestion:* The conclusion pulls the strands of the story together. Make sure you don't leave the audience wondering about the fate of a character. In some cases, a story doesn't need a conclusion—the climax or punch line may conclude it for you.

Central point

- *Questions:* Is there a lesson to be learned from the story? How does it relate to the rest of your presentation?
- *Suggestion:* Like the title, make sure the central point of your story supports the **PURPOSE** of your presentation. You don't need to state the central point. Just make sure you know what it is and that the story reflects its message.

▲ 87–101

The following example uses "The Three Little Pigs" as a model. Although this children's story is longer than one you might use in a presentation, it demonstrates the universal structure of most good stories.

STORY-BUILDING CHART: EXAMPLE

Title: The Three Little Pigs

Background information: Once upon a time, three little pigs set off to seek their fortune.

(Continued)

STORY-BUILDING CHART: EXAMPLE

Character development: Each little pig built a home. One was made of straw, one was made of sticks, and one was made of bricks.

Action or conflict: Soon a wolf came along. He blew down the house made of straw, so the first pig ran to the house of sticks. The wolf blew down the house of sticks, so both pigs ran to the house of bricks. Then the wolf went to the house of bricks and said, "Little pig, little pig, let me come in." All three pigs responded: "Not by the hair of my chinny chin chin." So the wolf huffed and puffed but couldn't blow the house in.

High point (climax): The wolf was very angry. "I'm going to climb down your chimney and eat all of you up," he declared, laughing, "including your chinny chin chins." The pigs heard the wolf on the roof and hung a pot of water over a blazing fire. When the wolf jumped down the chimney, he landed in the pot of boiling water. The pigs quickly put the cover on it, boiled up the wolf, and ate him for dinner.

Conclusion and resolution: And the three pigs lived happily ever after.

Central point: The time and energy you use to prepare for trouble will help you survive and flourish.

Why Stories Work

The best stories have two essential qualities: *probability* and *fidelity*.[6] Good stories also follow accepted storytelling principles that sustain the meaning and value of *story truths*. Understanding these principles can help you make stories work for you in a presentation.

Story Probability

Story probability describes the formal features of a story, such as the consistency of characters and their actions, and asks, "Would this really happen?" It refers to whether or not a story follows its own internal logic. Would it, for example, seem right if Harry Potter double-crossed his best friends and teachers (unless, of course, he was under a diabolical spell)?

When assessing a story's probability, ask the following questions:

● getting started   ▶ delivery   ◆ speaking to persuade
▲ fundamentals   ∴ engaging your audience   ★ speaking occasions
■ content   ♥ speaking to inform   ✴ resources

- Does the story make sense? Can I follow what's happening? Do I believe the plot?
- Do the characters behave in a consistent manner? Do I wonder, "Why did they do that?" or "How could they do that given everything else they've said and done?"

If you find yourself saying, "That just couldn't happen," you are questioning the story's probability.

Story Fidelity

Story fidelity focuses on the story's connection to the audience and asks, "Is the story faithful to what they already know?"

When assessing a story's fidelity, ask the following questions:

- Do the events in the story seem believable?
- Does the story reflect the storyteller's values, beliefs, and experiences? What about the **BELIEFS, VALUES**, and experiences of the audience?   77–80
- Does the story omit or distort any key facts or events?
- Does the story use logical **ARGUMENTS** and patterns of reasoning when appropriate?   363–81
- Does the story create the impact that the storyteller wants?

Story Truths

Good stories aren't always true stories. Both "The Three Bears" and "Cinderella" are charming works of fiction—as are many stories depicted in plays, films, and television shows. They are not *true* in the sense of depicting real events, but all good stories—fact or fiction—contain *truths*. **Story truths** refer to accepted principles that underlie the meaning and values in a story.

Peter Guber, producer of such films as *Rain Man*, *Batman*, and *The Color Purple*, describes the four truths of storytelling.[7] In the following table, we've modified them so that they apply to a variety of **RHETORICAL SITUATIONS**:   5–10

FOUR TRUTHS OF STORYTELLING

55–69 ▲ 57–66 ▲	**Truth to SPEAKER**	When you speak truthfully and share your genuine feelings in a story, you enhance your **CREDIBILITY**. When relevant, storytellers reveal their beliefs and values openly and honestly. Even if the story is fictional, a good storyteller conveys the anger, embarrassment, sadness, fear, or joy experienced by their characters.
70–86 ▲ 72–80 ▲	**Truth to AUDIENCE**	**AUDIENCE ANALYSIS** should guide your storytelling. When you arouse audience expectations, make sure you meet them. If you promise a thrilling story, you have to follow through. If you use humor, your audience should laugh. Use personal pronouns such as *we*, *you*, and *I* to invite the audience to share the experience and feelings you describe.
87–101 ▲	**Truth to PURPOSE**	Be true to your purpose! What is your overall objective? Does the story express the values you believe in and want others to adopt as their own? When a story is true to your purpose, you can invest more energy and emotion into telling it—and you'll be more successful at reaching your audience.
405–89 ★	**Truth to OCCASION**	As with any good presentation, a good story is never told the same way twice. If your time is limited, you'll have to shorten your story. If the occasion is somber, you may tell a different story entirely. If the setting calls for a louder voice, arrange the room so you are closer to your listeners, or practice so you can project.

In 2018, Oprah Winfrey accepted the Cecil B. DeMille Award for lifetime achievement at the Golden Globe Awards ceremony. She began with a story. Can you identify the ways that Winfrey achieved each of the four story truths?

> In 1964, I was a little girl sitting on the linoleum floor of my mother's house in Milwaukee watching Anne Bancroft present the Oscar for best actor at the 36th Academy Awards. She opened the envelope and said five words that literally made history: "The winner is Sidney Poitier." Up to the stage came the most elegant man I had ever seen. I remember his tie was white, and of course his skin was black, and I had never seen a black man being celebrated like that. I tried many,

---

● getting started   ▶ delivery   ◆ speaking to persuade

▲ fundamentals   ∴ engaging your audience   ★ speaking occasions

■ content   ▼ speaking to inform   ✻ resources

many times to explain what a moment like that means to a little girl, a kid watching from the cheap seats as my mom came through the door bone tired from cleaning other people's houses. But all I can do is quote the explanation in Sidney's performance in *Lilies of the Field*: "Amen, amen, amen, amen."[8]

Conclusion

You don't have to publish a novel or produce a film script to be a good storyteller. Stories are everywhere. You can begin by looking for them close to home. Is there a story about your name, your location, or your family? About a special place or mentor, a success or failure?

Good stories are more than spur-of-the-moment recollections or retellings of classic tales. The beginning introduces a challenging situation faced by the characters. The middle explains what the characters did or didn't do to resolve the situation. The end describes how they overcame the challenge, and in some cases, offers a meaningful lesson. The best stories are meticulously crafted, truthful, and strategically adapted to all elements of the rhetorical situation.

5.3 Generating Interest

When communication students and professional speakers rated the importance of twenty-four speaking skills—such as organizing a presentation, using your voice effectively, and reducing stage fright—one skill topped the rest: keeping your audience interested.[1] Generating and maintaining audience interest is a significant and thought-provoking challenge for all speakers. Novice speakers often *assume* they're not interesting. They can't imagine why an audience would want to listen to them. They have heard boring speeches and fear theirs will be doomed to the same fate. Rarely is either assumption true. In many rhetorical situations, audience members are eager to hear you and your message.

29–30 Still, you may need to overcome an audience's lack of interest or their own **POOR LISTENING** skills. Fortunately, there are steps you can take to get your listeners interested in and excited about your message. In the preceding chapter, we discussed one of the most effective ways:
253–67 **STORYTELLING**. There are, however, several other useful methods.

Limit the Length of Your Presentation

Some of the most famous speeches in history were quite brief. Abraham Lincoln's Gettysburg Address was only about three minutes long. In the 1970s, the US Navy tried to determine how long people can listen to and retain information. The answer: eighteen minutes.[2] That's about the length of a riveting bedtime story, President John F. Kennedy's famous inaugural speech, and the time limit for most TED talks.[3] A similar number applies to virtual learning on a medium such as Zoom. Students' attention tends to fade after watching between fifteen and twenty minutes of video.[4]

5–10 Many presenters are limited to less than eighteen minutes to speak. A speech given for a class presentation or a public hearing would be much shorter. Depending on the **RHETORICAL SITUATION**, it might be wise to

● getting started   ▶ delivery   ◆ speaking to persuade
▲ fundamentals   ∴ engaging your audience   ★ speaking occasions
■ content   ▼ speaking to inform   ✳ resources

prepare two versions of your presentation: one that matches the assigned speaking time and one that is half of that. For example, if you've prepared a twenty-minute presentation for a particular occasion, know how you would quickly cut it by ten minutes or more if needed. You may be surprised to find that, in some cases, the shorter version is stronger because it focuses the essence of the message you want your audience to understand and remember. Here are a few questions that can help you trim and revise your presentation:[5]

- Will audience members be able to reach the conclusion you want without your help? If so, don't burden them with irrelevant information, explanations, or visuals.
- Do you have too many examples or stories, potentially distracting listeners from your message? If yes, drop some of them.
- Have you said the same thing in too many different ways? Pick your most striking example, fact, or argument, and get rid of the rest.
- Is the audience already inclined to believe what you're saying? If so, don't spend a lot of time establishing COMMON GROUND.
- Does the audience definitely need to know this? If not, delete or shorten any CLAIMS or pieces of SUPPORTING MATERIAL that aren't relevant to your PURPOSE.

71
352–54
115–19
87–101

Keep in mind that it can be difficult to gauge how long your presentation will be when SPEAKING FROM NOTES. So PRACTICE what you intend to say out loud, particularly while your presentation is still in the early stages of development. Assess the exact timing of each section during final rehearsals. You may discover that some sections are too long and vague while others are wonderfully brief and clear.

225–28
228–33

Use Multiple Forms of Supporting Material and Language Styles

You are more likely to generate audience interest if you use multiple forms of SUPPORTING MATERIAL. For instance, after citing a startling statistic, share a dramatic example or tell a compelling, relevant story. Use

115–19

245–49
133–36
334–36

well-designed presentation aids or provide clear handouts to visually rein-force your message. **STYLISTIC DEVICES**, such as repetition and metaphors, can help you emphasize or clarify a **KEY POINT** or **CONCEPT**.

Enliven Your Content

Have you ever been half listening to someone speak when suddenly you hear something that sparks your attention? Here are some ways you can get your audience to sit up and listen.

Counterintuitive Notions

If you say something that contradicts audience expectations, their interest may be aroused. For example: you quote a Republican who argues for strong gun control, a nutritionist who claims that eating fat is a good thing, or a dentist who says that tooth brushing is not necessary.

Here is an example in a speech by Jacinda Ardern, prime minister of New Zealand (who, by the way, was a communication major in college). At the memorial for the people killed at two Christchurch mosques by an Australian man in 2019, Ardern spoke:

> We gather here, 14 days on from our darkest of hours. In the days that have followed the terrorist attacks on the 15th of March, we have often found ourselves without words.
>
> What words adequately express the pain and suffering of 50 men, women and children lost, and so many injured? What words capture the anguish of our Muslim community being the target of hatred and violence? What words express the grief of a city that has already known so much pain?
>
> I thought there were none. And then I came here and was met with this simple greeting. As-salaam Alaikum. Peace be upon you.
>
> These were simple words, repeated by community leaders who wit-nessed the loss of their friends and loved ones. Simple words, whispered by the injured from their hospital beds. Simple words, spoken by the bereaved and everyone I met who has been affected by this attack.
>
> As-salaam Alaikum. Peace be upon you.[6]

Repeating "As-salaam Alaikum" and its translation "Peace be upon you" was probably not what the audience expected. Doing this showed respect for the religion of the victims.

● getting started ▶ delivery ◆ speaking to persuade
▲ fundamentals ⁖ engaging your audience ★ speaking occasions
■ content ▼ speaking to inform ✳ resources

Relevancy

If your audience sees no reason to listen to you, they won't. Why should they listen to or care about your topic if it's not relevant to their interests, wants, and needs? Ask **WIIFT**: "What's in it for them?" It's all about audience analysis and adaptation.

▲ 77

   Here's an example: Surveys report that almost half of drivers age thirty-six and older can change a tire while on the side of a road. Only 27 percent of eighteen- to twenty-year-old drivers can do the same. If you are speaking to a group of college students about the importance of mastering this skill, you could make it more relevant by asking, "How many of you regularly drive a car? What would you do if you were driving to an important event and you had a flat tire?"

Consequential Information

Give your audience an important reason to listen to you. For example, an instructor in a chemistry classroom notices that the students aren't paying attention. In an urgent, loud voice, she tells the class to be careful when mixing two specific chemicals. "This is an important warning. If you do this incorrectly, you're going to get seriously burned. Now let's review how to do this experiment safely."

Novelty

Most audience members enter the setting of a presentation without noticing much about it. Everything is familiar. There are seats, perhaps a lectern and some projection equipment. Then one day they walk into the same room and see something totally unexpected. An image of a train wreck displayed on the screen or the speaker standing silently onstage, dressed as a tennis player. What is different is interesting.

For an example of challenging audience beliefs and expectations by using clothing, slides, and stories to gain attention, interest, and curiosity, see Notable Speaker: Yassmin Abdel-Magied, page 189.

Emotions

In most presentations, audience members do not witness a full display of a speaker's emotions. If, however, a speaker pauses, chokes up, and a tear drops from one eye, the room may grow still. Everyone is paying attention.

87–101 ▲
70–86 ▲

57–66 ▲
357–61 ◆

We are not suggesting you cry while speaking. But if you care about your **PURPOSE** and **AUDIENCE** and you show your feelings honestly—whether it's fear, sadness, joy, anticipation, anger, surprise, or disgust—audience members are more likely to listen, remember your message, and grant you high **CREDIBILITY**. Showing your own feelings is one way to **APPEAL TO YOUR AUDIENCE'S EMOTIONS**.

Vivid Descriptions

Vivid descriptions make presentations more interesting. For example, in President Barack Obama's 2020 eulogy for John Lewis, he extolled the bravery of a civil rights leader who in 1965, at the age of twenty-five, led six hundred protesters over the Edmund Pettus Bridge in Selma, Alabama, on a day that has come to be known as Bloody Sunday:

> And we know what happened to the marchers that day. Their bones were cracked by billy clubs. Their eyes and lungs choked with tear gas. They knelt to pray, which made their heads easier targets. And John was struck in the skull. And he thought he was going to die, surrounded by the sight of young Americans gagging and bleeding and trampled.[7]

Use Humor

Injecting humor into a presentation can capture and hold audience attention and help listeners remember you and your presentation. Humor can defuse anger, ease tension, and stimulate action. Audience members tend to remember humorous speakers positively, even when they are not enthusiastic about the speaker's message or topic. Humor also encourages listeners to have a good time while listening.

The best humorous speakers know which type of humor to use in a particular situation in front of a particular audience. Some audiences respond well to one-liners, puns, funny stories, and goofy props. Others love

● getting started   ▷ delivery   ◆ speaking to persuade
▲ fundamentals   ⁑ engaging your audience   ★ speaking occasions
■ content   ◤ speaking to inform   ✳ resources

funny quotations, cartoons, wacky definitions, silly headlines, misspelled signs, and funny song lyrics.

Explaining how to be humorous is something like explaining how to ice skate. You can read about ice skating, you can watch video of Olympic skaters, but nothing will replace putting on a pair of skates and getting on the ice. The same is true about using humor in your presentations. You can read about it and borrow funny lines from books and comedians, but nothing replaces trying it—repeatedly—in front of real audiences. A few funny lines here and there is all you need to get started.

Deciding Whether to Use Humor

Before using humor, first consider its advantages and disadvantages. Although humor can capture **AUDIENCE ATTENTION**, it can also distract from your message. Humor can enhance your **CREDIBILITY**, but it can have the opposite effect if it's inappropriate or offensive. The more thorough your **AUDIENCE ANALYSIS**, the easier it is to decide whether humor might heighten or hinder your ability to establish a positive connection with your listeners.

268–79
57–66

72–80

Ask yourself the following questions: Am I a funny storyteller? Do people laugh at my jokes? Can I summon up a humorous comeback when someone challenges my opinion? If not, you may want to avoid using humor until you learn to do it well. Now try this: Where would you place yourself on a scale from 1 (not funny) to 10 (hilarious)? If you'd give yourself a score of 5 or below, you may not want to use humor as a strategy for generating audience interest.

Self-Effacing Humor

In most cases, you are your own best source of humor. **Self-effacing humor**—your ability to direct humor at yourself—lowers the barrier between you and your audience by showing them you are an ordinary, fallible human being. You also don't have to worry about offending anyone if you are the butt of the joke. You could poke fun at your job, family, experiences, or failures.

Former president Ronald Reagan was well known for using this kind of humor. For example, to defuse criticism about him being, at that point in time, the oldest president in US history, he said:

There was a very prominent Democrat who reportedly told a large group, "Don't worry. I've seen Ronald Reagan, and he looks like a million." He was talking about my age.[8]

Self-effacing humor can also occur spontaneously. If something strange happens while you are speaking, enjoy the experience with your audience. If you make a mistake—forgetting something, dropping a visual aid, using the wrong slide—don't let your self-consciousness get in the way. Instead, smile and brush it off with a self-effacing comment. A sense of humor helps when there are equipment glitches, too. For example, a noted educational consultant recently gave a Zoom presentation called "Tips for Teaching Online" to a group of teachers. After introducing himself to his listeners, he paused to adjust the volume on his microphone and began talking. His listeners chuckled. One of the teachers said, "You're muted!" Quickly, he turned the sound back on, smiled sheepishly, and said, "In the immortal words of George Bernard Shaw, 'Those who can—do. Those who can't—teach!'" Everyone laughed.

63–65 ▲

58–61 ▲

Although a little self-effacing humor can enhance your **LIKABILITY**, it should be used sparingly. Otherwise, you may diminish the audience's impression of your **COMPETENCE** and weaken the power of your message.

Inappropriate Humor

There are some sorts of humor that an audience will not and should not forgive. **Offensive humor** tops the list because it insults your audience and seriously damages your credibility. Imagine, for example, an elected official at a legislative luncheon beginning his discussion of newly proposed legislation with an embarrassing joke about a very old wealthy man who marries a very young sexy woman. Some listeners may laugh, but many in the audience would not be amused.

Use what you've learned from your audience analysis to make sure your humor won't offend anyone. This is not about political correctness but about common courtesy and respecting audience sensibilities. In general, it's safe to apply the following guidelines for nearly any rhetorical situation:

● getting started
▲ fundamentals
■ content

▶ delivery
⁂ engaging your audience
◤ speaking to inform

◆ speaking to persuade
★ speaking occasions
✳ resources

- Avoid insulting, explicit, or profane language.
- Don't tease anyone in your audience (unless the occasion is a roast).
- Steer clear of jokes about ethnicity, race, religion, gender identity, sex, politics, or other sensitive issues.
- Stay focused on your **PURPOSE**. Don't mistake your presentation for a stand-up routine.

87–101

Another type of inappropriate humor is **irrelevant humor**, which wastes the audience's time and makes you appear poorly prepared. If the joke doesn't have a meaningful connection to you and your message, don't use it, even if you think it's funny.

Be Energetic and Expressive

One aspect of delivery that has a particularly strong impact on audience interest is **EXPRESSIVENESS**—the vitality, variety, and sincerity you put into your presentation.

184

An expressive voice and appropriate body movements can ensure that the audience hears you, sees you, and understands your message. Vary your **RATE**, **PITCH**, and **VOLUME** to enhance your vocal inflection, emphasize important words and phrases, and communicate warmth, involvement, and confidence. Establish and maintain direct **EYE CONTACT**, which tells audience members, "I'm talking to you!"

201–3
203–5
196–200
210–12

Strive to establish **IMMEDIACY** with your audience in order to gain and maintain their attention and interest while enhancing your **CREDIBILITY**. Verbal and nonverbal immediacy is associated with physical closeness, a sense of humor, inclusive personal pronouns ("us" and "we"), and openness to the opinions of your audience.

186
57–66

Three days after the collapse of the World Trade Center in September 2001, President George W. Bush gave a short speech at Ground Zero. He spoke from atop a pile of rubble, with his arm around a firefighter. Someone in the crowd said he couldn't hear the president, so Bush grabbed a bullhorn and responded, "I can hear you. The rest of the world hears you! And the people—and the people who knocked these buildings down will hear all of us soon."[9] Without question, his immediacy with the exhausted rescuers and the millions of television viewers transformed what was a good speech into a famously memorable one.

Employ Audience Participation

One of the best ways to generate audience interest is to get the audience involved early and often. Audiences pay more attention if they know that at some point they may be asked to participate. Although there are rhetorical situations where audience involvement is impossible or discouraged, many presentations offer opportunities for well-planned participation.

Ask Questions

One of the easiest ways to involve audience members is to ask for their reactions to what you've said. Even if audience members do little more than nod their heads in response, they will have become part of a transaction with the speaker.

72–80 ▲

479–89 ★

One special type of audience question, the poll, combines involving listeners and doing a quick form of **AUDIENCE ANALYSIS**. Pose a question and ask for a show of hands if you are in the room with your audience. If you are **SPEAKING ONLINE** using a mediated technology like Teams or Zoom, conduct a poll. For example, ask:

- How many of you know someone who . . . ?
- How many of you have visited . . . ?
- Have any of you heard of . . . ?
- Do we have anyone here who was born or raised in . . . ?

The responses will tell you something about your listeners while also letting audience members know whether they share common experiences, opinions, or beliefs.

At a Virginia Press Association's minority job fair, Marvin Leon Lake, public editor of the *Virginian-Pilot*, began his presentation by announcing he was going to tell a true story. He then spoke about a young journalism student who, at a previous job fair, had volunteered to be interviewed by a panel of strangers in front of an audience. The student went on to become a successful journalist. When he finished, Lake asked the audience: "What is the moral of this story?" One student raised her hand and said, "When given an opportunity—even in the face of public scrutiny—do it!" Another audience member said, "If you stand out in a crowd, you will be noticed." A third listener suggested you should always be prepared, both physically and mentally, to accept a challenge. Lake said all the answers were correct.

Lake engaged his audience by telling a relevant story and then involving them in a discussion about what it meant. The students attending the job fair had a lot to remember, but at the top of their lists were Lake, his story, his question, and his presentation's important lesson about being prepared to meet a challenge.

You can also be creative in the way you poll your audience. For example, a speaker on Zoom was talking about travel safety during the COVID-19 pandemic and asked her audience to briefly turn off their video if they felt uncomfortable about travel. Many screens went from live video to an image of initials. The effect was immediate: Everyone saw that a lot of people were worried.

Encourage Interaction

Asking listeners to interact with one another can enhance interest, recall, and learning. At the start of your presentation, you can ask audience members to introduce themselves to the people sitting around them if they are unacquainted. Depending on the **PURPOSE** of your message, you could add something beyond a handshake. For example, in a talk about child care, you could request that the audience share the number, ages, and genders of their children with one another. If you're talking to young college students, ask them to identify where they live, their majors, the high schools they attended, or their career aspirations.

▲ 87–101

One of the real advantages of Zoom, WebEx, and other mediated technologies is the opportunity to use breakout rooms in **ONLINE PRESENTATIONS**. To effectively use them, you might:

★ 479–89

- Ask one person in each breakout room to be the organizer. That person should take notes about what audience members say and then describe their discussion to the larger group.
- Suggest specific topics that you want audience members to discuss or activities you want them to perform while in the breakout room.
- Assign a time limit. A brief interaction is far better than dead air.

Involve Their Senses

315–16 ▼

Try to **EMPLOY SENSORY IMAGES** in your presentation, and not just those that involve sight and sound. For example, if you are speaking about a certain kind of cloth, ask your audience to feel it. This involves touch *and* reinforces your content. If your presentation is about a favorite food, encourage your audience to taste or smell it. This lets them interact directly with the subject of your presentation. Ask them follow-up questions to reinforce this connection. Is your product softer, sturdier, or more effective than one your audience is familiar with? Does your chocolate chip cookie recipe produce a chewier, sweeter, and thicker cookie than another recipe?

Conduct an Activity

Both simple games and complex training exercises can involve audience members with your presentation and with one another. Most large bookstores have shelves filled with manuals that describe these kinds of activities. They range from brainstorming a name for a new product to suggesting solutions to hypothetical or real problems. Interrupting your presentation with a group exercise gives the audience and you a break, during which they can interact in different but meaningful ways.

Ask for Volunteers

328–31 ▼

Volunteers can help you **DEMONSTRATE** how to perform a skill or how to use a piece of equipment. They can engage in role-playing exercises. You might even persuade someone to wear funny hats or sing songs—if those activities are relevant to your presentation. Of course, make sure your volunteers aren't going to be embarrassed, and if possible, find a way to reward

● getting started　　▶ delivery　　◆ speaking to persuade
▲ fundamentals　　⋰ engaging your audience　　★ speaking occasions
■ content　　▼ speaking to inform　　✳ resources

them afterward—with a small prize or special thanks. Once audience members see that volunteering is risk-free, they may be more willing to participate.

Conclusion

There is no reason that a well-prepared, audience-centered should be dull or boring. If you're concerned that your audience will be uninterested or indifferent to your presentation, there are many speaking strategies you can use to generate and maintain interest, boost your credibility, and improve listener recall. Shortening your presentation, using various types of supporting material, enlivening your content, and making your delivery more expressive will help.

Even if an audience is prepared and eager to listen, you can further boost their attention and interest by using humor, where appropriate, and by interacting with your audience. Ask them questions, conduct a structured activity, engage their senses, and encourage peer interaction. If you choose strategies that take into account all six elements of the rhetorical situation, it will be difficult for audience members to deny you their attention and interest.

NOTABLE SPEAKER
Joe Smith

Joe Smith is a semiretired lawyer and environmentalist in Oregon. He took to the TED stage in 2012 to teach people about one of his personal passions: reducing paper waste by using paper towels properly. His talk has been viewed more than three million times and has received coverage in a wide array of online publications. It even inspired one viewer, Cecelia Warner, to launch a website, Shake & Fold, to spread the word. In addition to his environmental advocacy work, Smith has served in a variety of roles in Oregon politics including as a district attorney and executive assistant to the speaker of the Oregon House of Representatives.

Search Terms

To locate a video of this presentation online, enter the following key words into a search engine: Joe Smith TED talk. The video is approximately 4:31 in length.

What to Watch For

[0:00–0:40] Prior to taking the stage, Smith could safely assume that he knew more and cared more about paper towel use than his audience. By using a variety of inventive strategies to generate and maintain audience interest, he creates an engaging and memorable presentation. Although he fumbles his first line, Smith nevertheless grabs the attention of his audience by explaining why his message should matter to them: 571,230,000 pounds of paper could be saved annually if each person reduced their paper towel usage by just one paper towel a day.

[0:41–1:12] Smith uses several methods to overcome audience disinterest and information overload: limiting the length and complexity of his presentation, repeating important phrases and behaviors, and demonstrating expressive delivery and immediacy. Two other strategies—using humor and audience participation—make his talk more memorable, all but ensuring that listeners will heed his advice.

[1:13–4:13] Smith increases his listener's interest by assigning half the audience to say "shake" and the other half to say "fold" at his direction. He also gives the audience an easy way to remember to shake their hands twelve times after washing by associating the number with the twelve apostles, twelve months, and twelve zodiac signs. Finally, by repeating the method with each of the different types of paper towels he displayed at the beginning of his talk, he makes it more likely that the audience will remember his waste-reducing method after the presentation is finished.

EXERCISE

After viewing Smith's speech, reflect on these questions:

1. In addition to the aforementioned, what other techniques did Smith use to gain and maintain audience interest?

2. How did you feel when Smith botched his first line? Did it affect your overall reaction to him and his talk? Why or why not?

3. How did the setting, his demonstration techniques, and presentation aids affect your level of interest?

4. How credible was Joe Smith? To what extent was he knowledgeable, trustworthy, likable, and stimulating?

5. At one point, Smith mentioned that the shake and fold approach works because of a phenomenon known as interstitial suspension. Should he have stopped to explain what the phrase means? Did it matter that he didn't stop? Why or why not?

6. In what ways, if any, could Smith have improved the content and/or delivery of his presentation?

5.4 Presentation Aids

Since the advent of presentation software like PowerPoint, Prezi, and Keynote, many audience members expect speakers to display slides of images and text during their presentations. And why not? It's become easy—even fun—to create memorable audiovisual slide shows. But **presentation aids**—the supplementary audio, visual, and hands-on resources available for presenting and highlighting key ideas and supporting material in a presentation—are not limited to what you can project on a screen. From simple notes on a whiteboard to elaborate audiovisual productions, from homemade cookies to samples of perfume, appropriate presentation aids engage your audience's senses in a way that boosts their interest, enhances message comprehension, and stimulates critical thinking.

The Benefits of Presentation Aids

Presentation aids are common and expected in many rhetorical situations. Used poorly, presentation aids can be a distraction, but used wisely and well, they offer many benefits. They can

- Attract and hold audience attention
- Enhance clarity and comprehension
- Set an appropriate mood
- Convey meaning better than words can for image- and sound-based topics
- Save you and your audience time, particularly when trying to explain **COMPLEX IDEAS** or a set of **STATISTICS**

333–46 ▼
115 ■
70–72 ▲

AUDIENCE-CENTERED SPEAKERS figure out what their listeners need to know, understand, and remember *before* creating presentation aids. They ask themselves, "Where would presentation aids help me achieve my

87–101

PURPOSE?" Only after answering that question do they decide what types of aids would be useful. In some cases, they may decide that presentation aids aren't even necessary.

No matter how appropriate or powerful they are, presentation aids should not be what defines your presentation. Imagine you misplace your presentation aids, or the technology you depend on to display them breaks down. Would you still be able to communicate your message? If the answer is no, or even if you're not sure, you are probably relying too much on your aids. Your aids are there to support you, not to take your place. No matter what kind you use, keep one basic principle in mind: *Presentation aids are only aids; they are not your presentation.*

Before you embark on the task of creating presentation aids, review the following questions to make sure you have considered other effective options:

Will your presentation aids gain and maintain audience attention?	*or*	Will telling a story, describing a significant, relevant event, sharing dramatic examples and data, or asking the audience questions achieve the same goal?
Will your presentation aids clarify and reinforce your ideas?	*or*	Will adding examples, analogies, and up-to-date evidence make your presentation more comprehensive and consequential?
Will your presentation aids enhance your audience's comprehension?	*or*	Will a more rigorous audience analysis help adapt your message and delivery without using any or as many presentation aids to enrich audience comprehension?

Types of Presentation Aids

Once you decide that presentation aids would indeed enhance your presentation's effectiveness, the next task is deciding which type or types of aids you should use. Here we examine the various types of presentation aids in terms of what they do and how you can use them strategically to reinforce key points and achieve your purpose.

Pie Charts, Graphs, and Tables

Some of the most common presentation aids are used to answer the question "How much?" These include pie charts and graphs.

Pie charts show proportions in relation to a whole—for example, the percentages of students at a four-year school who are freshmen, sophomores, juniors, and seniors. Generally, the wedges in a pie chart should be arranged in a progression from small to large or large to small in a clockwise direction. If, however, the pie chart depicts age groups, begin with the youngest category and end with the oldest, regardless of wedge size. Gene Zelazny, a visual communication expert, explains that "because a circle gives such a clear impression of being a total, a pie chart is ideally suited for the one—and only—purpose it serves: showing the size of each part as a percentage of some whole."[1]

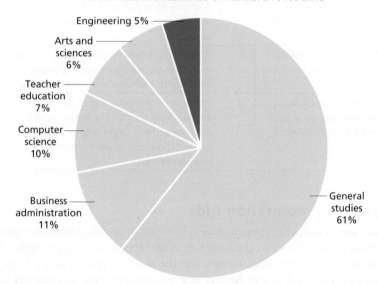

**THE ENGINEERING PROGRAM HAS
THE SMALLEST PERCENTAGE OF TRANSFER STUDENTS**

Engineering 5%

Arts and sciences 6%

Teacher education 7%

Computer science 10%

Business administration 11%

General studies 61%

A pie chart should be easy to comprehend at a glance.

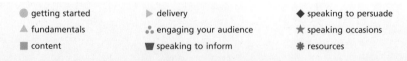

● getting started　　▶ delivery　　◆ speaking to persuade

▲ fundamentals　　∴ engaging your audience　　★ speaking occasions

■ content　　▼ speaking to inform　　✳ resources

Pie charts work best when they are simple in design, clearly labeled, have no more than six pieces, and show the percentage relationship between parts and the whole. Using more than six wedges makes a chart difficult to read. If you need more than six, select the most important components and group the remainders into an "others" category. To add emphasis, use the most contrasting colors or intense shading pattern for each slice of the pie chart, or insert a thick white line between wedges to make sure that they are clearly separated. Resist the urge to render a pie chart in 3D—doing so distorts the size of the wedges, making it difficult for our brains to interpret the data.[2]

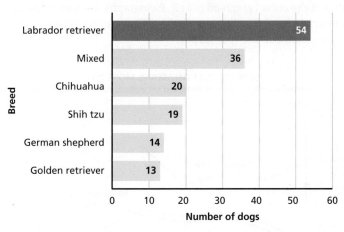

LABRADOR RETRIEVERS ARE THE MOST POPULAR BREED IN TOWN

Use a contrasting color to highlight important data on a bar graph.

Graphs also show how much, but they are primarily used to compare data and show patterns. For example, a graph can show how the stock market has gone up or down during a single day or over a period of months and years. Graphs can illustrate trends that show increases or decreases. Graphs represent countable things, like the number of different responses

493–510 ✳

to a **SURVEY** question, the number of cars sold in a three-month period, the number of men and women in a particular occupation, or the trend in daily COVID-19 infections over time. There are four basic types of graphs: bar graphs, line graphs, area graphs, and pictographs (also called pictograms).

When using a **bar graph**, make sure the space *between* bars is smaller than the width of the bars, and, if needed, use a contrasting color or shading to emphasize the most important item on the graph. **Line graphs** are better than bar graphs when tracking small changes. They can also be used to compare changes over the same period of time for more than one group. **Area graphs** fill in the space below the points in a line graph with a color and are used to depict individual and competing trends (see, for example, the "flatten the curve" graph on p. 119). **Pictographs** use a series of repeated icons or symbols to visualize simple data. They can be more dramatic and interesting than bar and line graphs.

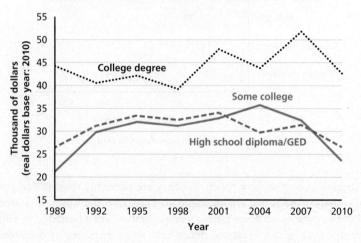

MORE EDUCATION MEANS MORE INCOME:
Median wages over time based on education level, ages 22–29

A line graph can compare multiple chains of data over time.

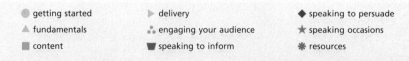

● getting started   ▶ delivery   ◆ speaking to persuade

▲ fundamentals   ⁘ engaging your audience   ★ speaking occasions

■ content   ◤ speaking to inform   ✳ resources

MEN MAKE MORE MONEY THAN WOMEN DOING THE SAME JOB[3]

This pictograph uses coins to visualize the gender pay gap.

Tables take many forms. Some summarize and compare data or information, such as lists of ideas or key phrases, into rows and columns. They depict goals, functions, types, formats, recommendations, and guidelines. Items listed on a text chart may be numbered, bulleted, or simply set apart on separate lines. But, as Margaret Rabb, author of *The Presentation Design Book*, notes: "When graphs aren't specific enough and verbal descriptions are too cumbersome, tables offer elegant solutions for showing exact numeric values."[4] Fortunately, your word processing software includes ready-to-use templates for making attractive tables that come in various colors and designs. Various kinds of tables appear throughout this book, including two later in this chapter (see pp. 294 and 302).

Diagrams and Models

Diagrams, such as flow charts and organizational charts, show how things work on a two-dimension page or slide. They can depict a process—the steps in assembling a piece of furniture, baking a cake, or even delivering a presentation. Diagrams can chart time lines, provide floor plans, and even "explode" a physical object so you can see the inside of, say, an engine, a heart, or a flower. Architects, engineers, and builders would fail to effectively communicate their ideas without their multiple drawings, floor plans, and project designs. And so would a speaker trying to explain a process or complex structure without diagrams.

There are many types of diagramming software available online, with hundreds of templates, that can help you arrange information and data on organizational charts, flowcharts, mind maps, and process diagrams. Your word processing software probably has a pull-down menu of diagram templates depicting pyramids, processes, cycles, hierarchies, matrixes, and plain old lists. All you have to do is fill in the blanks.

Models are usually three-dimensional representations of an object on a smaller scale than the original. They can range from small physical models

THE ANATOMY OF A FLOWER

Stigma

Pollen Tube

Stamen — Filament
Anther

Pistil

Style

Petal

Sepal

Ovule

Ovary

Receptacle

Pedicel

Diagrams can be used to show the inside of something in two dimensions.

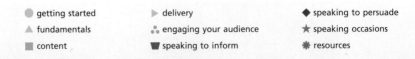

● getting started   ▶ delivery   ◆ speaking to persuade
▲ fundamentals   ⁂ engaging your audience   ★ speaking occasions
■ content   ▼ speaking to inform   ✳ resources

of historic cars to a larger see-through model of a car engine in which all of the major parts are visible and working. A model can be a miniature stage set or a new community development project that fills a room. Doctors often use models to show a patient the parts of a heart or the bones in a foot. Much like diagrams, models can be simple or elaborate, made at home or purchased, held in your hand or shown on a screen.

Photographs and Illustrations

Photographs and illustrations depict an action or skill, enliven interest in a message, direct audience attention, and evoke emotions. They are especially good at quickly gaining your audience's understanding when describing something visually unique or complex: consider how difficult it would be to describe basic ballet movements such as the arabesque, jeté, and pirouette without a photograph or illustration. They are also often very powerful means of evoking an audience's emotions. Words such as *beautiful, dramatic, funny, heartbreaking, terrifying,* and *awesome* will better register in an audience member's mind when reinforced by an appropriate photograph or illustration. They can also depict abstract ideas. For example, Albert Einstein's face has become a symbol for genius, and the Statue of Liberty is a symbol of freedom and liberty.[5]

Photos and illustrations can also tell (or help tell) a **STORY**. For instance, if you want to illustrate the destruction of rain forests in South America, you can use a series of aerial photos showing how the forest has shrunk in the last few years. If you want to show how smartphones have become a worldwide phenomenon, you could show a montage of people from around the world using an iPhone.

253–67

Cartoons are a type of illustration that comments on, pokes fun at, or ridicules a real situation or issue in a clever, succinct way. When thoughtfully used (and appropriate for the audience and the rhetorical situation), cartoons can both amuse and entertain your audience and help them understand a point almost immediately. But like any type of humor, you need to be alert to the ways that a cartoon might backfire. First and foremost, you should be very careful that it will not offend anyone or be in poor taste. And second, you should make sure it's a good match for your purpose and your key points. It shouldn't be too complex or rely on insider knowledge—you should be sure that your audience will get the point and understand the humor quickly.

THE PUBLIC SPEAKING PROCESS

Cartoons poke fun at real situations.

Maps

Maps show where; they "translate data into spatial patterns."[6] They also help explain the scale of a place or phenomenon. In presentations, maps can locate and direct an audience's attention to a troubled traffic intersection or a complex battle scene. Maps can also link statistical data to population characteristics.

You can find plenty of maps online that will help illustrate a point you want to make. Consider how hurricane forecasts display a tracker cone over a map of the locations that may be affected at different points in time, or how maps of the United States identified COVID-19 "hot spots" during the pandemic. Whereas a complex line graph could show the same data, maps provided an instant snapshot of the disease's spread across the nation.

Handouts

Handouts can help listeners comprehend the meaning of your message. Generally, it's a good idea to use handouts if your presentation contains a lot of technical information or if you don't want your audience to take many notes. Handouts also help audiences follow the presentation's organization and flow and/or provide additional information about the topic the speaker

getting started   delivery   speaking to persuade
fundamentals   engaging your audience   speaking occasions
content   speaking to inform   resources

THE NORTHWEST HAS THE HIGHEST CONCENTRATION OF PEOPLE WITH SOME COLLEGE EDUCATION, BUT NO DEGREE

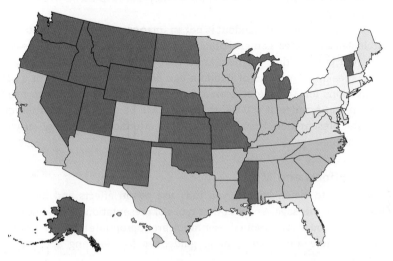

Percentage of 25- to 64-year-olds with some college education, but no degree

20%   22%   24%   26%

A map can help you show the spatial patterns of data.

may not cover. The most common presentation handouts are ones that show the slides you will use with space for listeners to take notes. You can also provide a list of key points or a collection of important data.

The problem with handouts is that many speakers don't know what to put on them or when to hand them out. Do *not* distribute a text of your speech. Why should your listeners sit through a recitation of the presentation if it's clear they could read it on their own?

The nature and content of your handout should determine at what point you share it with audience members. If you want audience members to have copies of your handout before you speak, place them on each seat in the room, distribute them at the door as they enter, or place a stack on a table near the entrance of the room so they can help themselves before taking a seat.

When, however, the handout is not an integral part of the presentation but instead provides content that your audience may want to consult after your presentation, let them know that you will pass it out when you finish speaking. This kind of handout can be a list of references or a set of directions for a recipe or a procedure members of the audience need to learn and practice. If you tell them they will be given this information after the presentation, they can focus their attention and energy on you and your message.

Sound Effects and Music

In addition to visual images, you may use sound effects and music to support your message. As with other types of presentation aids, make sure any sounds and music in your presentation are appropriate for the rhetorical situation. Here are a few general guidelines for selecting appropriate sounds:[7]

- Make sure the sounds match your message. For example, you might use music clips when describing a singer, choir, or instrumental performance; the sound of a jet taking off if you are addressing airport noise pollution; or the sound of a human heart if talking about cardiovascular health.

- Recorded expert testimony or excerpts from a taped speech can enliven a presentation. Instead of quoting someone, you can share a good sound clip from a speech to highlight and reinforce your message.

- Avoid trite sound effects. The drum rolls, chimes, and cash register sounds that come with presentation software can be corny, amateurish, and annoying, particularly when you're discussing a serious topic.

- Keep each sound clip brief. Ten seconds is usually enough time. Anything longer will interrupt the flow of your presentation.

Video Clips and Animation

If you want to use video clips and animation in your presentation, there are several guidelines worth remembering. First and foremost, make them brief. Audience members are not there to watch a movie; they are there to watch and listen to you. Second, make sure that the image quality of the video is good enough to be shown. Poor resolution or awkward angles can distract audience members and lead them to question your skills and standards. Finally, show only videos that are relevant to your purpose. A cute cat video might be fun to share with your friends, but you'll almost never need one in a presentation.

Others

There are many other types of presentation aids—objects, costumes, physical demonstrations, and audience activities. Regardless of the form or type, the key to selecting effective presentation aids is making sure that they are relevant to your topic and purpose and have the potential to gain attention, save time, and clarify or reinforce the content of your message.

There is, however, one type of presentation aid that is more important than all the others previously mentioned: *you*. Your **APPEARANCE**, your **VOICE**, your nonverbal behavior, and your **PHYSICAL DELIVERY** can affect audience interest and attitude as much as or more than a graph or photograph. When you are demonstrating a medical procedure, sign language, a yoga pose, or even the qualities of a good speaker, *you* are the most important presentation aid.

▶ 217–19

▶ 194–209

▶ 210–19

Matching Presentation Aids to Your Purpose

No matter how good your presentation aids look or sound, they may fall short if they don't match and support the content of your presentation. Some presentations are almost impossible to give without presentation aids. Try making an **INFORMATIVE PRESENTATION** about American Sign Language without demonstrating a few signs, or try explaining the differences between major and minor musical keys without an audio example of some kind.

▼ 307–46

87–101 ▲

Choosing the right presentation aids relies on matching the aids you choose to your **PURPOSE**, as shown in the following table:

Purpose	Presentation aids
To explain the parts of an internal combustion engine	• A drawing of an engine • Physical pieces of an engine • Animated cartoon of an operating engine
To compare rap music and talking blues	• Audio excerpts of each musical form • Live performance • Table comparing distinct musical characteristics
To demonstrate how to separate egg whites from egg yolks	• Live demonstration • Still photos on slides • Audience participation
To learn the causes and treatment of sickle cell anemia	• Table listing symptoms • Diagram or illustration of a sickle cell anemia blood cell • Family tree diagram tracing inheritance of the disease
To identify the perils of climate change in the United States	• Graph of trends since 1950 • Map of recent weather disasters in the United States • Handout listing validated research studies and essays

Applying Ethical Standards to Presentation Aids

40–41 ●

When preparing presentation aids, apply **ETHICAL STANDARDS** to how you select, prepare, and use them. If you want to alter an image or use a portion of an audio or video recording as a presentation aid, make sure that it accurately represents what is depicted in the original context of that image, audio clip, or video. Similarly, when depicting data in a graph, pie chart, or other form, make sure that you're not doing so in a way that deliberately misleads your audience. For example, the scale in the first bar graph on the next page starts at $200,000 instead of $0, exaggerating the change in house prices between 2000 and 2015. The second bar graph presents the same information accurately.

● getting started	▶ delivery	◆ speaking to persuade
▲ fundamentals	∴ engaging your audience	★ speaking occasions
■ content	▼ speaking to inform	✳ resources

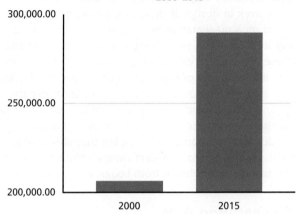

This bar graph would mislead an audience to think there was a much bigger change in average housing prices between 2000 and 2015.

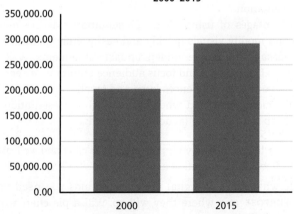

This bar graph accurately presents the data described in the headline.

As is the case in all presentations, you have an ethical and legal responsibility to acknowledge the source of presentation aids that are someone else's work or design. If there's an image, graph, map, or even a quote displayed on a presentation aid that is not your original work, you must identify its source. The same is true for art, video, and audio that is available online. If you grab a video clip from a film, TV show, or YouTube, or if you copy an audio excerpt of music or a speech, you must acknowledge the source. In some cases, you will also be required to pay the creator a fee to use their work. Fortunately, students may use copyrighted material without requiring permission or paying a fee to the rightsholder under a set of "fair use" rules for educational purposes, but they still must identify and acknowledge the source. Ethical speakers always include source attributions on slides that use materials drawn from books, articles, and websites.

Digital Presentation Aids

Digital presentation aids are created, viewed, and/or heard, distributed, modified, and preserved on electronic devices using software such as

115–19 ■

PowerPoint, Prezi, and Keynote. Used effectively, they display **SUPPORTING MATERIAL** when the audience expects or needs it most. They usually incorporate text, color, pictures, and/or audio to help you achieve the purpose of your presentation.

The advantages of using digital presentation aids are myriad. You can make and modify visuals quickly and easily. Bullet points can reduce complex messages to simple, understandable statements. Well-designed images and text can attract and focus audience attention, are easy to present, and can be seen by audiences large and small.[8]

When deciding how and when to use digital presentation aids, it's helpful to keep the following guidelines in mind:

138–48 ■

- Make sure the content of your presentation is clear and well **ORGANIZED** before choosing presentation aids.

87–101 ▲

- Decide what types of digital presentation aids you need to support your **PURPOSE** and where they will go. Will a pie chart work better than a table? Does a diagram tell a story better than a photograph?

● getting started	▶ delivery	◆ speaking to persuade
▲ fundamentals	⁎ engaging your audience	★ speaking occasions
■ content	▼ speaking to inform	✳ resources

- Assess the number and sequence of your presentation aids. Are they in the best order? Are there too many or too few to support your message?

- Plan for verbal **TRANSITIONS** between one presentation aid and another, as well as from text to presentation aid and back to text. Allocate your speaking time accordingly.

149–51

- If a digital presentation aid—no matter how beautiful, clever, or tragic—does not support your **CENTRAL IDEA** and/or **KEY POINTS**, cut it.

137–38
133–36

Basic Strategies for Creating Digital Presentation Aids

Even with the best intentions, equipment, and cutting-edge software, slides will fail to have an impact if they are unattractive, distracting, or difficult to follow. Regardless of the types of supporting materials or media you choose, you should apply these three critical strategies for creating digital presentation aids:

1. Headline your visuals.
2. Preview and highlight.
3. Build sequentially.

Headline Your Visuals A **headline** is an engaging title that communicates a visual's message or point of view. Headlines are conclusions, not topics, that capture and focus audience attention. Suppose you are speaking about how women often are paid less than men for the same job. "Differences between Males and Females" is a vague and ineffective headline; "Men Make More Money than Women Doing the Same Job" is specific and much stronger.

A good headline reduces the risk that audience members will misunderstand your message. Visual designer Gene Zelazny uses the pie chart on the next page to show the usefulness of a headline. What is the significance of this pie chart? Without a headline, most viewers would probably focus on the West, assuming that the main point of the chart is to illustrate that the West accounts for almost half of profits. But perhaps the purpose of the chart was instead to highlight that the North generates the smallest profits.

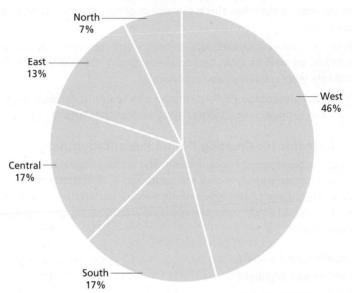

SHARE OF PROFITS, BY REGION

North
7%

East
13%

West
46%

Central
17%

South
17%

Which region are we supposed to notice in this pie chart? Without an effective headline, your visual aid will distract and confuse your audience.

Putting a title on your visuals reinforces your message and ensures that your audience focuses on the aspect of the data you want to emphasize.[9]

Preview and Highlight Your slides don't need to include every fact, statistic, and quotation from your talk. Instead, your visuals should preview what you will say and highlight the most important facts and features of your presentation. Your audience needs to see only what clarifies or enhances your message.

Some speakers display an outline near the beginning of a slide presentation and then show it again at transition points during the presentation. An outline gives a visual preview of your message. It is your presentation's table of contents. When an outline first appears, it telegraphs the structure of your presentation and helps audience members understand and remember your message. When it appears again, it highlights important points and the relevance of supporting materials. Depending on how sophisticated your equipment is, you can incorporate a marker or change in color that moves down the outline as the presentation progresses.

Build Sequentially Use what is called *progressive disclosure* to reveal each concept on a slide individually so listeners do not get ahead of you. This will focus their attention on you rather than the words or images on the screen. Progressive disclosure is useful when you want to build a chart or table by adding sections to it in sequence. By building your visuals sequentially, you can raise audience anticipation, focus on the point you are talking about without visual distractions, and in some cases, save a punch line or conclusion until the end.

Visual Design Principles for Digital Presentation Aids

Although there are thick handbooks and entire courses for learning and applying visual design principles to digital presentation aids, a few of these principles stand out as established guidelines for creating purposeful, effective, and memorable digital presentation aids. When designing digital slides, you should

- Create a consistent look
- Exercise restraint
- Choose readable type
- Select suitable colors and templates

Create a Consistent Look Regardless of your message, make sure your digital aids have a uniform appearance throughout your presentation. Create a master design for your presentation to ensure consistency, and no matter what sort of visual element you present within that design, make sure that it looks appropriate and complements that overall look and feel. Every presentation using slides should have its own signature style.

Exercise Restraint Presentation software has made it possible for speakers to use a dazzling array of graphics, fonts, colors, and other visual elements, as well as sound effects. At first, it's tempting to use them all. Resist that temptation. A fireworks background can overpower your message. An under-the-sea template can drown your words. More often than not, a simple slide or image is more effective and memorable than a complex one. The following recommendations apply to almost all types of presentation aids, but they are particularly important when creating a presentation supported by slides:

- Slides are meant to be visual, so replace words with graphics, images, and diagrams when you can. If you can easily explain something with words alone, why use a slide?

- Instead of complete sentences, use key words or phrases to arouse audience curiosity and highlight important information.

- Limit the number of bullet points on a slide. There are plenty of bullet point rules—4 × 4, 5 × 5, 6 × 6, and 7 × 7—which offer guidelines for restricting the amount of text you're asking the audience to read. For example, the 6 × 6 rule recommends that no more than six lines of text appear on a slide (excluding the headline) with no more than six words per line. Although these rules have good intentions and you may want to keep them in mind as a general guide, designer Robin Williams suggests a more important rule: "You're much better off putting the right number of lines and words on slides based on the needs of your speech." This is how, she adds, you will "make every word count."[10]

- Make only one key point on each slide, and make sure the headline states that point.

- Limit the number of slides. Fifty slides do not necessarily convey information better than ten carefully curated slides.

Choose Readable Type As a general rule, don't use more than two different typefaces on a slide. Avoid ornate and other difficult-to-read type. Instead, opt for more legible typefaces, such as Helvetica, Verdana, Arial, and Times New Roman. You should also avoid using all uppercase letters. Not only do they take more space, but also the text will take more time to read than text set with appropriate capitalization, and audiences may interpret it as

getting started   ▶ delivery   ◆ speaking to persuade
fundamentals   engaging your audience   ★ speaking occasions
content   speaking to inform   ✳ resources

shouting rather than as emphasizing an important word or point. Bold or italics can highlight your text, but you should use them sparingly; if overused, they are visually distracting to your audience.

Some designers recommend specific type sizes for slide presentations: 44-point type for titles, 32-point type for subtitles, and 28-point type for text. In general, we recommend a minimum type size of 24 points. When in doubt, use bigger type sizes. Here's a tip: Print out your slides on 8½" × 11" paper, then set each page on the floor. Stand up straight and look down at the page. If you can read every word clearly, the type size is probably large enough.

Select Suitable Colors and Templates Choose text colors that ensure the words on your slides are legible and engaging. If you use a light background, use dark text, and vice versa. Also consider whether the color scheme is appropriate for the rhetorical situation and your purpose. If you're in doubt about color, stick to proven color schemes. Most presentation software recommends sets of colors that effectively contrast with each other, such

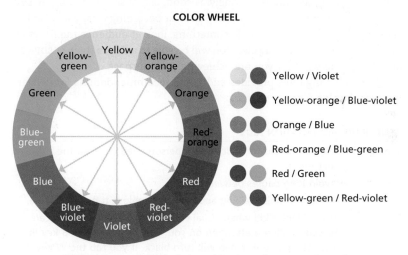

A color wheel can help you find a variety of complementary color options.

as blue and orange or yellow and violet. Try to avoid red and green because some people have a type of color blindness that makes these two colors indistinguishable. Even for those without red-green color blindness, this combination is difficult to read because the colors do not contrast effectively.

Unless you work for an organization that requires the use of a corporate style guide and template, you can find numerous templates on your own computer or on easily accessible software. In most cases, simple templates work the best.

Delivering Presentation Aids

After planning and preparing your presentation aids, make sure you know how to integrate them smoothly and professionally into your delivery. Two delivery techniques that apply to all presentations are particularly important when using presentation aids. First, speak **EXTEMPORANEOUSLY**, or at least try to sound as though you speak that way. Unless the presentation is highly technical, use notes sparingly. Second, establish and maintain **EYE CONTACT**. Rather than reading from a slide or becoming totally involved in showing the audience how to do something, look at audience members as much as you can. If nothing else, you will be able to analyze their **FEEDBACK** and determine whether you are achieving your purpose.

221–22

210–12

33–34

The following table provides additional recommendations for delivering presentation aids:

DELIVERING PRESENTATION AIDS

Timing	• Display the aid for as long as a person needs to read the text twice.
	• Avoid long pauses between aids.
	• When you finish talking about an aid, remove it or put it aside.
	• Use a blank slide when visual content isn't needed so you can refocus audience attention on *you*. (Tip: If you hit the B key in PowerPoint, your screen will turn black. If you tap the W key, your screen will turn white. To get back to your slides, simply hit the letter again.)

● getting started ▶ delivery ◆ speaking to persuade
▲ fundamentals ⋰ engaging your audience ★ speaking occasions
■ content ▼ speaking to inform ✳ resources

DELIVERING PRESENTATION AIDS

Focusing	• Establish rapport with your audience before you start using your aids.
	• For most **SPEAKING OCCASIONS**, it is better not to show the visual aid until after you've started speaking.
	• Don't turn your back to the audience or focus your attention on the aid.
	• Number each of your slides. If you need to go back or skip ahead because of time or because someone asks a question, your listeners can easily find where you are.
	• When using Zoom, Teams, or another mediated technology, remember what the audience will see. You may be in a little box in the upper corner, and your slide might take up the rest of the screen.
Pointing	• Avoid laser pointers. Their beam is small and can be difficult to hold steady.
	• If necessary, rest your hand or a rigid pointer gently on a flip chart, board, or screen.
	• Put the pointer down when you are finished with it. Don't wave it around.
	• Touch, turn, talk: touch the aid, turn toward the audience, talk.
	• In many mediated technologies, you can use your computer's cursor as a pointer.
Show and tell	• Explain what is relevant and important about the aid.
	• Show and tell at the same time. Give verbal cues as you handle and highlight features of an object or point to a slide component.
	• In most cases, don't read aloud all the written words on a visual to your audience. (Sometimes, though, you may want to read an important phrase to reinforce its importance.)
	• If possible, use a remote to change slides.

★ 405–89

▶ 228–33

PRACTICE using your presentation aids as often and as rigorously as you would for any other presentation. Talking and handling a visual aid of any kind is, in fact, doing two things at once. Speaking well and keeping your eye on a screen, your hands on an object, or your writing on a flip chart or board requires focus and reliance on strong, competent delivery skills. Even though you've added presentation aids to your speech, you still need to demonstrate **EXPRESSIVENESS, CONFIDENCE, STAGE PRESENCE, AND IMMEDIACY**.

184–86 ▶

Four of the Notable Speaker features in this book demonstrate how to use presentation aids effectively. The examples range from slide shows with high production value to others that do their job more simply. Some presentations are filled with visual aids while others don't need as many and/or create an appropriate time to introduce them. What these examples have in common is that all four speakers made sure that their presentation aids were appropriate for the rhetorical situation.

David Epstein's presentation explains, with significant help from his slide show, why contemporary athletes may seem faster, better, and stronger than their historic counterparts (see p. 342). He uses sophisticated imagery, powerful photographs, a consistent design format (both in color and in black and white), and effective audio effects to explain the facts, statistics, and stories in the content of his talk. He transforms small facts (the size of gymnasts, the freestyle world record, the speed of one-hundred-meter runners) into clear and captivating graphics.

Yassmin Abdel-Magied's presentation challenges her audience to look beyond their initial and unconscious biases in order to become more thoughtful when dealing with people who are "different" (see p. 189). Although the content of her talk on its own is strong and well delivered, she uses simple slides and changes her attire to make her message more compelling. Abdel-Magied becomes her own presentation aid. When she removes her abaya to reveal the orange jumpsuit she wears on an oil rig, she dramatically alters her audience's initial impression of her.

● getting started   ▶ delivery   ◆ speaking to persuade
▲ fundamentals   ∴ engaging your audience   ★ speaking occasions
■ content   ◥ speaking to inform   ✳ resources

Joe Smith's four-and-a-half-minute talk is a demonstration that primarily relies on two obvious presentation aids: a bowl of water and a variety of single paper towels (see p. 280). There are, however, other presentation aids that are not as obvious. His appearance and speaking style communicate friendliness and likability. Behind him are twinkling theater lights and green scenery, which put him in a supportive environment. The audience's "shake-fold" participation is effective as an auditory presentation aid and as a way of engaging his listeners.

Ron Finley uses projections to strengthen his arguments, appeal to audience emotions, justify his proposed solution, and enhance his credibility (see p. 400). He begins, "I live in South Central. This is South Central," and shows three slides: (1) liquor store, (2) fast food, (3) vacant lots. He then repeats the same slides, showing that the newly named South Los Angeles still looks the same. His varied projections support his claims with statistics, quotations, and photographic comparisons.

Conclusion

If you decide to use presentation aids, always remember the one abiding principle: presentation aids are only aids; they are *not* your presentation. At the same time, strategically chosen, well-crafted presentation aids can grab audience attention, raise their interest, and help in comprehension. They can also generate an appropriate mood that matches your purpose and even conveys your message as well as or better than words. Presentation aids are also efficient, saving you and your audience time and energy.

Keep in mind that using presentation aids will increase the time you need to practice, as well as the length of your presentation. Just as you should practice your vocal and physical delivery, you should work on the timing and handling of your aids. They must be well rehearsed so you can share them as part of your message. And remember: in the end, *you* may be the presentation aid best remembered by the audience.

Part 6
Speaking to Inform

Informative presentations come in many different forms: a corporate briefing, a convention presentation, a campus tour, a how-to video, an oral report, or a college lecture, to name a few. Over the course of your life, informative speaking will be the most common type of presentation speaking you will be asked to do. The chapters that follow provide helpful guidance about how you can gain and maintain your audience's attention when REPORTING NEW INFORMATION and EXPLAINING COMPLEX IDEAS.

Speaking to Inform

6.1 Understanding Informative Speaking

Informative speaking is the most common type of presentation. Businesses use informative presentations to orient new employees, present status reports, and explain new policies. Colleges use informative presentations to advise new students and report to boards of trustees. Instructors make informative presentations in lectures, whether in person or online.

An informative presentation is efficient and effective when it gains and maintains audience attention, is well organized and well rehearsed, uses a variety of supporting material, is delivered expressively and confidently, and encourages audience involvement. So what, then, is an informative presentation?

What Is an Informative Presentation?

Informative presentations provide new information, explain complex concepts and processes, and/or clarify and correct misunderstood information. They do so by instructing, defining, enlightening, describing, reminding, and demonstrating. You will prepare and deliver many informative presentations throughout your life, so learning how to do them well will give you a competitive edge. Consider the following examples that identify the **OCCASION**, **AUDIENCE**, and **TOPIC** of four different informative presentations:

★ 405–89
▲ 70–86
■ 105–13

- A college student orally summarizes the purpose, methodology, and results of a research project to their instructor and peers in a science class.

● getting started   ▶ delivery   ◆ speaking to persuade

▲ fundamentals   ∴ engaging your audience   ★ speaking occasions

■ content   ▼ speaking to inform   ✳ resources

- A charge nurse explains the policies and procedures for tracking patient medications to a group of newly hired nursing assistants.
- An experienced landscaper talks at a homeowners' association meeting about the various native plants that grow best in the local climate.
- The assistant vice president of a bank gives a tour to a group of elementary-school children.

As you can see, informative presentations address a wide range of topics. But regardless of whether you're speaking to third graders in a classroom or CEOs attending a seminar, effective informative presentations help audience members understand and remember something of value.

349–50 ◆ At first, it may be difficult to determine where an informative presentation ends and a **PERSUASIVE PRESENTATION** begins. Most informative presentations contain an element of persuasion. Explaining the scientific causes of climate change might convince an audience that we need stricter laws regulating air pollution. Demonstrating the proper way to change a tire could persuade listeners not to call the nearest garage because the task may not be as difficult as they once thought. Conversely, persuasive presentations have informative content. If you are trying to persuade people to eat healthier food, you will need to include factual information. There is, however, a clear dividing line between informative and persuasive presen-87–101 ▲tations: your **PURPOSE**. When you ask listeners to change their opinions or behavior, your speech becomes persuasive.

Informative Speaking Guidelines

235–305 ⸫ Informative presentations often require a concerted effort to **GAIN AND MAINTAIN AUDIENCE ATTENTION**. In a communication class, students can choose exciting topics, but most informative speakers don't have this advantage. Imagine the challenge facing presenters with the following assignments:

- Compare the features of the health insurance policies offered by a company to new employees.

● getting started ▶ delivery ◆ speaking to persuade
▲ fundamentals ⸫ engaging your audience ★ speaking occasions
■ content ▼ speaking to inform ✳ resources

- Explain how to analyze statistical methods used in social psychology research.
- Overcome factual misunderstandings about the need for and safety of routine vaccines.

Given the pervasiveness of informative presentations, you've certainly encountered them in a variety of contexts. You probably have vivid and long-lasting memories of some of them and absolutely no recollection of others. What made the memorable speeches exceptional? In order to build an impressive informative presentation, you should

- Include a value step
- Avoid information overload
- Employ sensory images

Include a Value Step

Just because *you* love bluegrass music, photography, or bicycling doesn't mean listeners will share your enthusiasm. In most informative presentations, you *know* more and *care* more about your topic than your audience does. But if there's a good reason for you to make a presentation, there should be a good reason for your audience to listen. Don't rely on the audience to figure it out, though. Tell them by including a value step.

A **value step** explains why your message should matter to your audience and how it can affect their well-being and success. Incorporating a value step in the **INTRODUCTION** of your informative presentation gives them a reason to look forward to what comes next. Though not necessary for every **SPEAKING OCCASION**, the inclusion of a value step at the beginning of a presentation can motivate a disinterested audience to listen. You might refer to the setting or the reason your audience is assembled. You could mention how a recent event has affected them in the past or will affect them in the future. Or you could involve them by asking questions or telling a **STORY** about people who are like them. Note how the following speaker uses a value step to motivate her audience to listen to a presentation about new rules in a staff evaluation plan, a potentially dull topic:

161–69

405–89

253–67

Last year one of your coworkers was denied a promotion. She was well qualified—better than most applicants. She received the highest recommendations. But she wasn't promoted. She didn't get her well-deserved raise. Why? Because she didn't read the new rules in the staff evaluation plan and missed the revised deadlines. When it was time to give out promotions, her application wasn't in the pool of candidates. Today I'll point you to key sections of that plan so that this doesn't happen to you.

72–80 ▲

The best way to begin your search for a value step is through **AUDIENCE ANALYSIS**. Effective speakers ask themselves, "How will audience members benefit from listening to this presentation?" In other words, "What's in it

77 ▲

for them?," or **WIIFT**. Make a list of the ways the information you plan to present will be useful to your listeners. Ask yourself whether your presentation provides any of these benefits:

- *Social benefits.* Will you describe strategies and skills for interacting with others more effectively in order to develop strong relationships, become more popular, resolve interpersonal problems, or even throw a great party?

- *Communal benefits.* Will your presentation serve your community, colleagues, friends, and family in a way that will improve the quality of life, work, or play?

- *Physical benefits.* Will you offer advice about improving the audience's physical health, tips on treating common ailments, or expert recommendations on diet and exercise?

- *Psychological benefits.* Will you explain common and interesting psychological topics, such as the causes and treatment of stress, depression, and anxiety, or will you provide descriptions of interesting—even seemingly bizarre—psychological disabilities? Will your presentation help audience members feel better about themselves?

- *Intellectual benefits.* Will you help your audience learn difficult concepts or explain intriguing and novel discoveries in science? Will you demonstrate the value of intellectual curiosity and creativity?

- *Economic benefits.* Will you show your audience how to make or save money? Will you explain or clarify monetary and economic concepts? Does your presentation offer advice about employment opportunities?
- *Professional benefits.* Will you demonstrate ways that audience members can succeed at and prosper in a career field or profession? Will you provide expert instruction on mastering professional strategies and skills?

This list is not comprehensive, nor is it meant to prevent you from choosing more than one benefit. For example, an informative presentation on designing **DIGITAL PRESENTATION AIDS** could have social, communal, and professional benefits for your audience.

296–302

Note how the following two examples identify several reasons why audience members may be motivated to listen to and remember what you say about the selected topic area:

TOPIC:	Combating fire ants
POSSIBLE VALUE STEPS:	Prevents painful, dangerous stings (physical)
	Preserves gardens (economic)
	Protects pets and local wildlife (communal)

TOPIC:	Reading music
POSSIBLE VALUE STEPS:	Helps you become a better musician or more appreciative audience member (professional and psychological)
	Helps you understand the complexity of musical compositions (intellectual)
	Helps you talk about music with other music lovers (social)

By offering value steps early in your presentation and employing a variety of methods to **ENGAGE YOUR AUDIENCE** throughout, you can turn a simple informative talk into a thought-provoking and memorable presentation.

235–305

Avoid Information Overload

Take a moment to think about the following saying: knowledge is power. If that's true, then why does access to more information make so many people feel powerless? **Information overload** describes the stress that occurs when you try to process, understand, and remember everything you hear and see. It helps explain why some of us feel overwhelmed by the quantity of information we receive, even if the information itself is clear and nonthreatening. Information overload makes it difficult to sort what's useful from what's useless and to distinguish **VALID** and invalid data and opinions.

120–30 ■

As much as you may want to share everything you know about a subject, remember that information overload is a major reason why audiences stop listening. *Less* information can mean *more* comprehension. If you carefully choose and edit the information you share, listeners are more likely to remember your message. Regardless of whether you deliver a fifty-minute lecture or a three-minute briefing, be courageous—offer your audience less so they will remember and get more out of your presentation. How do you do this? **NARROW THE SCOPE OF YOUR PURPOSE AND TOPIC**.

110–11 ■
95–97 ▲

Make sure your **PURPOSE STATEMENT** is specific, achievable, and relevant. A tightly focused purpose statement can help you avoid the mistake of trying to cover too much material or asking too much of your audience. Consider the following exchange between a speaker and a listener:

LISTENER: I heard your presentation on the new employee evaluation plan.

SPEAKER: What do you remember about what I said?

LISTENER: Well, you went through the plan page by page, explaining how the new provisions would apply.

SPEAKER: What was one of the new provisions?

LISTENER: Well . . . there was something about new forms to be filed with human resources, I think. I don't know—I'll look it up when I have to use it.

Exactly. The listener will look it up. The speaker's purpose—explaining the whole plan—was much too ambitious for a single presentation. Audience members are intelligent, but they won't remember everything you say.

● getting started   ▶ delivery   ◆ speaking to persuade
▲ fundamentals   ⁙ engaging your audience   ★ speaking occasions
■ content   ▰ speaking to inform   ✳ resources

How could this speaker simplify her presentation? First, she should make sure that all employees already have a copy of the evaluation plan. She could then choose the essential elements to focus on during the presentation, knowing that the audience could **ASK QUESTIONS** or look up the information later if necessary. She might explain the differences between the new and old plans, or she could display the new forms employees must submit, along with their respective deadlines.

★ 468–78

Perhaps the easiest way to avoid information overload is to remember two phrases: "Keep it simple, speaker" (KISS) and the **RULE OF THREE**. Ask yourself if everything you plan to say is vital. If not, throw it out. Concentrate on no more than three important details, not ten. As tempting as it may be to tell a funny but irrelevant story or include a beautiful but distracting presentation aid, don't do it. Keep asking yourself whether your **KEY POINTS** and **SUPPORTING MATERIAL** directly support and advance a specific, achievable, and relevant purpose. KISS!

■ 136

■ 133–36
■ 115–19

Employ Sensory Images

What does the topic "ice hockey" make you think of? Fights, penalty boxes, screaming fans, chaos on ice, and body checks? Could one presentation incorporate all these images? What does "goalkeepers' protective equipment" bring to mind? Perhaps you see a person bundled to near immobility or a menacing-looking face mask. A topic like "herbal medicines" can conjure up a witch's brew of ingredients. "Chamomile," on the other hand, is easier to imagine—a strongly scented herb with tiny yellow blossoms.

Effective speakers make informative presentations more interesting and memorable by **USING LANGUAGE** that evokes a sensory experience based on sight, sound, taste, smell, and/or touch. When one of our students chose garlic as the subject of her informative presentation, she worried that there wouldn't be enough to say. But after completing some initial research, she was overwhelmed with information, so she narrowed her topic to garlic's powerful odor and ways to get rid of it. Even a talk on something as uninspiring as a new employee evaluation plan could benefit from a visual image such as a sample evaluation form with a deadline stamped across it.

⁘ 237–52

Looking for sensory images takes some creative thinking. If you want to give instructions on how to bake delicious chocolate chip cookies, for example, you could begin by thinking about how to apply each of the five senses to your topic:

- *Sight:* A thick brown cookie with visible chips
- *Sound:* A cookie that doesn't snap when it's broken
- *Taste:* A sweet cookie dough mixed with strong chocolate
- *Smell:* A cookie with a mouth-watering smell during and after baking
- *Touch:* A soft and chewy cookie

An informative presentation could focus on how to make sure cookies are thick with visible chips that are moist and chewy. Or you could emphasize the different tastes of different chocolates. No matter your topic—whether it's buying a new car, demonstrating how soap cleans, or explaining the Confederate loss in the Battle of Gettysburg—consider using sensory images to create a vivid and memorable informative presentation. You might be surprised by what you come up with.

Two Types of Informative Presentations

87–101
138–48

72–80

Many speakers believe that effective informative presentations require only a clear **PURPOSE**, interesting information, and a logical **ORGANIZATIONAL PATTERN**. Certainly, these elements are essential. Even so, informative speaking also requires a sound strategy that matches your informative purpose and content to **AUDIENCE CHARACTERISTICS**, interests, attitudes, and needs. In other words, you must look for, carefully analyze, and then choose the most appropriate methods for achieving your informative purpose in a particular rhetorical situation.

In her **theory of informative communication**, communication scholar Katherine Rowan explains how to make strategic decisions about the content and structure of an informative presentation. Her two-part theory focuses on the differences between informative presentations that report new information and those that explain complex ideas.[1]

When you **report new information**, your purpose is to create or increase audience awareness about an object, person, event, or procedure. Much like

● getting started   ▶ delivery   ◆ speaking to persuade
▲ fundamentals   ∴ engaging your audience   ★ speaking occasions
■ content   ◤ speaking to inform   ✳ resources

news reporting, you are creating awareness by presenting accurate, interesting, and up-to-date information about a topic. Informative presentations that report new information answer "What did I learn?" or "What do I know now that I didn't before the speech?"

When you **explain complex ideas**, your purpose is to enhance or deepen audience understanding about a difficult term, a complex phenomenon, or a frequently misunderstood idea or concept. Good explanatory presentations address questions such as "How?," "Why?," or "What does that mean?"[2]

TYPES OF INFORMATIVE PRESENTATIONS

For example, telling a group of new ten-speed bicycle owners how to shift gears more efficiently and effectively reports new information. Describing how the gears are constructed or why bicycles stay upright when a rider pedals requires a speaker to explain a complex idea. A presentation describing the origins of the Rosh Hashanah holiday to a non-Jewish audience is an example of reporting new information. But a talk clarifying for an audience *why* Rosh Hashanah is considered a high holy day is an example of explaining a complex set of ideas. The following table provides additional examples of these two types of informative goals:

REPORTING NEW INFORMATION AND EXPLAINING COMPLEX IDEAS

Goal: To report new information	Goal: To explain complex ideas
• A recipe for chocolate cake	• The principles of baking
• Directions to the nearest airport	• The architectural requirements of modern airports
• A report about a city council meeting	• An in-depth analysis of a proposed bill
• Baseball trivia	• Detailed analysis of last year's World Series
• A short biography of Charles Darwin	• A description of natural selection

Effective informative speakers understand when they need to report new information and when they need to explain more complicated or misunderstood concepts and processes. Not surprisingly, different types of informative messages have different purposes and require different communication strategies. In the next two chapters, we'll examine Rowan's strategies and advice for developing each type of informative presentation.

Conclusion

Of all the types of presentations, you'll make informative presentations more often than any other. Not surprisingly, the foundational elements of the rhetorical situation—occasion, speaker, audience, purpose, content, and delivery—are essential for every informative speech. First and foremost, effective informative speakers must know *why* they are speaking. They focus on their purpose as they research, prepare, and deliver their presentation.

Three important guidelines can improve the quality of your informative presentation and merit a positive response from your audience. Put a value step near the beginning of your presentation that identifies the ways that listeners can benefit from your talk. Then minimize information overload and use sensory images.

As you think critically about the purpose of your informative presentation, make sure you know whether you will be reporting new information or explaining a complex idea. That determination will help you select effective informative strategies, strong supporting material, an appropriate organizational pattern, and, if needed, presentation aids to ensure that your presentation is as effective and engaging as possible.

● getting started	▶ delivery	◆ speaking to persuade
▲ fundamentals	⁝ engaging your audience	★ speaking occasions
■ content	▼ speaking to inform	✳ resources

6.2 Reporting New Information

Reporting new information is what journalists do when they answer the questions *who, what, where, when, why,* and *how*. They write about *who* is doing what to *whom*, as well as *where* and *when* an event occurred. They also report *how* or *why* something happened without explaining complex or difficult-to-understand details. New information is shared through newspapers, magazines, television networks, social media, and books.

Presentations that report new information have a similar focus. Speakers try to increase audience awareness about a topic by reporting accurate and up-to-date facts. They also report new information when giving instructions or demonstrating how to perform a task. At first, this kind of informative presentation may seem easy to prepare and deliver. Yet depending on the rhetorical situation—occasion, speaker, audience, purpose, content, and delivery—reporting new information can be as difficult as any other type of presentation.

You face two major challenges when reporting new information. First, if your information is *very* new, an audience may have trouble grasping your key points. Second, they may need a reason to listen, learn, and remember. Fortunately, we can turn to Katherine Rowan's **THEORY OF INFORMATORY AND EXPLANATORY COMMUNICATION**, in which she recommends four strategies for sharing new information with an audience:[1]

■ 316–18

1. *Include a value step in the introduction.* Tell audience members why this new information is important and beneficial to them.

2. *Use a clear organizational pattern.* Provide an organizational structure that helps audience members understand and remember what you say.

3. *Use multiple types of supporting material.* Use facts, statistics, testimonies, definitions, analogies, description, examples, and/or stories.

4. *Relate the information to audience interests and needs throughout the presentation.* If audience members see no reason to learn the information, they are likely to stop listening.

152–53
87–101
137–38
311–13
138–48
133–36

Presentations reporting new information differ from one another based on the choices you make when applying these four strategies. Two speakers can give very different informative presentations about the same subject, depending on the value step, how the content is organized, the types of supporting material used, and the prior knowledge and needs of the audience. To get a better understanding of this process, let's examine how to develop a presentation that reports new information about *objects*, *people*, *events*, and/or *procedures*. Notice how each **OUTLINE**—regardless of the topic area—includes a **PURPOSE**, **CENTRAL IDEA**, **VALUE STEP**, **ORGANIZATIONAL PATTERN**, and related **KEY POINTS**.

Informing Audiences about Objects

315–16

Students in communication classes often choose objects as the topic area of their informative presentations because a tangible thing can be described, perceived by one or more of our **FIVE SENSES**, and even brought to class. Informing about objects, however, can be challenging because an object is not by itself a purpose statement or central idea. The following is a short list of objects:

- Valuable coins
- Fire ants
- Features of a safe, reliable bicycle
- Kudzu

Valuable coins and kudzu may spark your interest, but neither is enough to generate an informative presentation on its own. Although an object

● getting started   ▶ delivery   ◆ speaking to persuade
▲ fundamentals   ∴ engaging your audience   ★ speaking occasions
■ content   ▼ speaking to inform   ✳ resources

may seem to speak for itself, you should broaden your focus based on your
PURPOSE and **AUDIENCE ANALYSIS**. Consider the following sample outline:

▲ 87–101
▲ 72–80

TOPIC AREA:	Fire ants
PURPOSE:	To familiarize audience members with the external anatomy of a fire ant
CENTRAL IDEA:	A tour of the fire ant's external anatomy will help you understand why these ants are so invasive and hard to exterminate.
VALUE STEP:	In addition to inflicting painful, sometimes deadly stings, fire ants can eat up your garden, damage your home, and harm your pets and local wildlife.
ORGANIZATION:	**SPACE ARRANGEMENT**—a visual tour of the fire ant's external anatomy
KEY POINTS:	A. Integument (exoskeleton)
	B. Head and its components
	C. Thorax
	D. Abdomen

■ 140

The above outline could produce an effective informative presentation, but
it isn't the only way to report new information about fire ants. If you had
a different purpose—for example, familiarizing audience members with
various methods for exterminating fire ants—you would need a different
central idea, value step, organization, and set of key points.

Informing Audiences about People

Reporting new information about people is similar in many ways to giving
presentations about objects. Like an object, people are tangible—in this
case, flesh-and-blood personalities. You can focus on a historical or literary figure, a famous living individual, or someone you know. Regardless of
whom you select, describe that person's life and accomplishments to tap
audience interests and emotions, making sure that your purpose, central

idea, value step, organizational pattern, and key points are a good match.
If the person is well known, look for new, intriguing information to keep
your audience engaged. Consider how presentations about the following
ten people would differ from one another:

Thomas Edison	W. E. B. Du Bois
Bob Dylan	Amanda Gorman
Catherine the Great	A Holocaust survivor or rescuer
Mustafa Kemal Atatürk	A famous novelist or biographer
Gypsy Rose Lee	A noteworthy relative or friend

The following outline includes a value step and key points that make
the topic of early female blues singers relevant and interesting to audience
members:

TOPIC AREA: Early female blues singers

PURPOSE: To demonstrate how three female blues singers of the
1920s have influenced popular musicians in later eras

CENTRAL IDEA: In the 1920s, Sippie Wallace, Bessie Smith, and Gertrude
"Ma" Rainey paved the way for other female blues
singers.

VALUE STEP: If you call yourself an honest-to-goodness blues and
rock-and-roll fan, you should know more about the
major contributions made by early female blues singers.

ORGANIZATION: STORIES AND EXAMPLES ARRANGEMENT—brief, interesting biographies of each blues singer supported with
audio examples

KEY POINTS: A. Sippie Wallace

B. Bessie Smith

C. Gertrude "Ma" Rainey

● getting started   ▶ delivery   ◆ speaking to persuade
▲ fundamentals   ∴ engaging your audience ★ speaking occasions
■ content   ▼ speaking to inform   ✳ resources

NOTABLE SPEAKER
Mileha Soneji

From an early age, Mileha Soneji thought about how products might be re-designed to better suit the needs of the people using them. This led her to complete a bachelor's degree in product design and to pursue graduate studies in strategic product design. In 2015, she delivered a public speech about her uncle's experience with Parkinson's disease and her efforts to use human-centered design to improve his quality of life. The spill-proof cup she invented for him is available to the public and has been featured on National Public Radio and the *Huffington Post*. In her current position as a senior user-experience researcher, Soneji focuses on using market analysis and user needs to guide product design.

Search Terms
To locate a video of this presentation online, enter the following key words into a search engine: simple hacks for life with Parkinson's. The video is approximately 6:57 in length.

What to Watch For
Soneji uses the categorical organizational pattern to touch on four key points: (1) defining Parkinson's disease and its effects on thousands of people and families, (2) creating a spill-proof cup, (3) making walking easier and more comfortable on flat surfaces, and (4) making "a smarter world" with simple solutions. She also uses several informative speaking strategies for reporting new information. In addition to a clear organizational pattern, she uses her own family as a backdrop to emphasize why her message is important and beneficial to all families.

[0:04–2:02] Soneji begins her presentation by telling a story about a favorite uncle who would play with the kids at family get-togethers. When he was diagnosed with Parkinson's disease, he went from being an energetic person to hiding from people because of his tremors. Using her uncle's story as a backdrop, she explains what Parkinson's is and notes that sixty thousand people are diagnosed with the disease each year. She introduces her central idea: creative thinking can solve simple problems, which leads to a better quality of life for many Parkinson's patients and their families, and audience members.

(NOTABLE SPEAKER CONTINUED)

[2:03–2:49] Soneji describes her quest to make everyday tasks easier for her uncle with Parkinson's disease by designing a no-spill cup. She displays the cup and illustrates how she solved the problem of liquid spilling out during a tremor with a diagram that explains why it works. The cup, she says, is not just for Parkinson's patients. The cup could also "be used by you, me, any clumsy person"—something the audience can value and use in other contexts.

[2:50–5:49] Soneji describes her second challenge: understanding why her uncle could descend and climb a staircase with ease but not walk on a flat surface. She shows a video of her uncle easily walking down steps. She follows with another photo and video of the "staircase illusion" floor, which tricks her uncle's brain into seeing a flat surface as a staircase. The audience responds with enthusiastic applause as they watch her uncle walking across the floor with the same relative ease he displayed on the stairs. She asks the audience to see how the staircase illusion can be used in homes and hospitals to help patients feel comfortable and "much more welcome."

[5:50–6:44] Her final key point emphasizes her central idea in a clear oral style: smart solutions can be simple and effective. She tells her audience to not be afraid of complex problems: "Break them, boil them down into much smaller problems, and then find simple solutions for them." Her conclusion gives audience members a reason to remember her presentation: "Imagine what we all could do if we all came up with simple solutions." Her concluding line is "Let's make a smarter world, but with simplicity." This summary reinforces her central idea in a warm and sincere speaking style.

EXERCISE

After viewing Soneji's speech, reflect on these questions:

1. What informative strategies for reporting new information does Soneji use most effectively to help her audience listen, learn, remember, and value her presentation?

2. How would Soneji's presentation have been different if she had not used videos of her uncle?

3. Does Soneji use a value step in her presentation? If so, explain whether or not you think she did so effectively.

4. Identify the purpose of Soneji's presentation. Did she achieve her purpose? Why or why not?

5. How does Soneji's credibility influence the audience's willingness to listen to her presentation?

6. In what ways, if any, could Soneji have improved the content and/or delivery of her presentation?

Informing Audiences about Events

As you do with objects and people, you can report new information about historical or current events. History professors often center their lectures on important moments from the past. Politicians often speak to commemorate an event, such as the opening of a new museum. Business executives may review the company's founding to trace its evolving mission.

An event can be a single incident, such as an athlete winning an Olympic gold medal or the dedication of a new high school. An event can also be a series of incidents, a holiday, or milestones that became historic, such as the race to the moon, Kwanzaa, or the founding of Facebook. Regardless of the event's date, size, or significance, the purpose of your presentation determines how you will talk about it.

The following example outlines a way of reporting new information to a non-Indian audience in an informative presentation about Diwali, an important holiday in India:

TOPIC AREA: Diwali

PURPOSE: To familiarize audience members with facts about a significant holiday in India

CENTRAL IDEA:	Most Hindus, Jains, Buddhists, and Sikhs in India observe Diwali as a family-centered national festival that celebrates universal values.
VALUE STEP:	Learning more about one of India's major national holidays can help you understand that country's rich culture, its focus on family values, and how those fundamental factors affect US-Indian relations.

138–39

ORGANIZATION:	CATEGORICAL ARRANGEMENT—the features of an unfamiliar holiday supported with visual images
KEY POINTS:	A. Origins of Diwali
	B. Meaning of Diwali
	C. The five days of Diwali

An event does not have to be famous, historical, or significant to a large number of people. What matters is that the event is important for a specific group of people in a specific time and place. The following example is much smaller in scope than the celebration of Diwali:

TOPIC AREA:	Our company's fiftieth anniversary
PURPOSE:	To preview the events scheduled for the company's upcoming anniversary
CENTRAL IDEA:	The events for our fiftieth anniversary will have something for everyone.
VALUE STEP:	Making our fiftieth anniversary celebration a success will bring more attention and—as a result—more business and profits for the company and benefits for employees.

138–39

ORGANIZATION:	CATEGORICAL ARRANGEMENT—three main events
KEY POINTS:	A. Dedication of the new office annex
	B. Concert open to the public at the city's amphitheater
	C. Speech by a nationally recognized industry expert

Informing Audiences about Procedures

A procedure is a method or series of actions for doing something, usually in a specific order or manner. You can describe how to throw a curve ball, adjust a digital camera to maximize clarity and color, make a paper airplane, bake bread, ride a unicycle, play a bagpipe, or do CPR. In many rhetorical situations, audience members will not be able to throw a curve ball or play a bagpipe when you've finished, but they will better understand how it's done.

Informing an audience about a procedure focuses on *how* to do something rather than *why*. Changing a tire, assuming a basic yoga pose, and sewing on a button may not be difficult, but there are accepted steps for doing each of them well.

Many athletic coaches, physicians, and business trainers share a seemingly simple method for teaching a procedure, the **tell-show-do** technique:

1. *Tell:* Verbally describe how to do a procedure, sometimes with presentation aids.

2. *Show:* Physically demonstrate how to do a procedure with accompanying verbal instructions, sometimes with presentation aids.

3. *Do:* Require audience members to do the procedure on their own with supervision.

Depending on the rhetorical situation, you may use one or more of these three approaches to achieve your purpose. For example, if you want to increase audience awareness about the viola, you *tell* listeners how it is played and how it differs from other string instruments. Then, if appropriate, you can *show* them by playing a short piece of music so they can hear what it sounds like. Or you could do the reverse (show-tell), first playing the viola and then sharing facts about its history, characteristics, and techniques. However, unless you are training a group of viola players, you would and should not let them *do* it because they would probably produce a horrible, screechy sound and might even damage your instrument.

Tell: Describe the Procedure

Every informative presentation about a procedure requires telling. Regardless of the topic, you may start by identifying the key steps of the process in their correct order. For example, anyone who has tried to cook a perfect hard-boiled egg knows that following the right procedure makes the difference between a perfect, uncracked hard-boiled egg and a mess of white albumen floating around in a pot of hot water.

TOPIC AREA: Cooking hard-boiled eggs

PURPOSE: To teach listeners how to make foolproof hard-boiled eggs

CENTRAL IDEA: There are four steps to cooking perfect hard-boiled eggs.

VALUE STEP: Rather than wasting or throwing away cracked eggs, the proper procedure will make sure your hard-boiled egg is perfect.

ORGANIZATION: **TIME ARRANGEMENT**—step-by-step instructions

KEY POINTS:
    A. Place eggs in cold water and bring to a boil.
    B. Remove from the heat.
    C. Let stand for twenty minutes.
    D. Rinse in cold water.

139–40

Describing how to make foolproof hard-boiled eggs does not require a physical demonstration. It's a fairly simple procedure that can be described and, if needed, illustrated with a visual aid that shows each step in the process.

Show: Demonstrate the Procedure

Telling audience members about a procedure may not cover—or even need to cover—every step in a process. *Showing* them how to do something requires a display of the details. This common type of presentation is called a demonstration speech. In a **demonstration speech**, your goal is to teach the audience how to do a procedure by physically presenting a series of essential steps with verbal instruction. In some cases, you may use

235–305

PRESENTATION AIDS to show how it's done as you speak. Many people turn to YouTube when learning how to do something—all these videos are demonstration speeches.

Demonstration speeches have two interdependent components: verbal instructions and a physical performance. Regardless of whether you are showing audience members how to use a new GPS system or how to do a half-cobra yoga pose, you would accompany your demonstration with descriptions of how each step leads to a desired outcome.

When preparing a demonstration, use the following organizational framework:[2]

- *Purpose.* What is the goal—to understand how the procedure is done or to actually do it? Is the goal achievable? What methods will you use to achieve it?

- *Prerequisites.* What knowledge, skills, and materials do you need to make the presentation? What does the audience already know, and how can you build on that knowledge?

- *Action.* What steps or actions are needed to demonstrate the procedure?

- *Cautions and warnings.* What should you avoid, what can go wrong, and how can you fix it or solve a problem during the presentation?

What follows is the outline for a demonstration speech that teaches audience members how to sew on a button. The steps are clear, chronological, and doable by most people. Notice how the presentation addresses the aforementioned questions about preparing a demonstration speech.

TOPIC AREA:	Sewing on a button
PURPOSE:	To teach classmates the correct method for sewing on a button
CENTRAL IDEA:	By following each step carefully and correctly, you can sew on a button that will stay put.
VALUE STEP:	Because everyone has loose buttons or buttons that fall off, you should know how to sew on a button correctly

and not embarrass yourself by having to ask or pay someone else to do it.

139–40

ORGANIZATION: **TIME ARRANGEMENT**—prerequisites, actions, cautions

KEY POINTS: A. Materials

B. Step-by-step procedure

C. Common mistakes

Because demonstrations combine verbal instructions and a physical presentation, speakers face several challenges. The following guidelines can help you demonstrate a procedure:

311–13

- *Start with why.* Share your purpose and a **VALUE STEP**. State exactly what you want your audience to learn as well as why and how this knowledge can benefit them.

221–22

- *Speak without notes.* Unless the demonstration is highly technical, try to speak **EXTEMPORANEOUSLY**.

276–77

- *Encourage questions.* Encourage audience members to **ASK QUESTIONS** during and/or after the demonstration.

As with all kinds of presentations, it's helpful to learn from successful demonstrations. Observe YouTube videos, infomercials, cooking programs, and athletic coaching to understand what works and what doesn't. For example, notice how the host of a cooking show often has all the ingredients and tools ready and available. In some cases, an interim procedure, such as peeling onions or separating egg whites from their yolks, is completed in advance. Ask yourself: What does my audience need to see and hear *now*, and what can I physically prepare ahead of time?

For an example of informing an audience about a procedure using *tell* **and** *show*, **see Notable Speaker: Joe Smith, page 280.**

● getting started   ▶ delivery   ◆ speaking to persuade

▲ fundamentals   ∴ engaging your audience   ★ speaking occasions

■ content   ▼ speaking to inform   ✳ resources

Do: Audience Performs the Procedure

Unlike reporting new information about objects, people, and events, informative presentations about procedures often include a section where audience members are asked to *do* or at least try to do the procedure. Clearly, you can't ask an audience to ride a unicycle or play a bagpipe unless you're teaching a unicycle or bagpipe class. You can, however, ask audience members to create an aerodynamic paper airplane, try a yoga pose, or communicate a simple sentence with American Sign Language.

Here's an example of the way a Starbucks manager teaches new employees how to make a latte:[3]

1. *Tell.* The manager provides a written recipe and describes the procedure for making the latte.
2. *Show.* The manager demonstrates how to make a latte, one step at a time.
3. *Do.* The manager asks each employee to make a latte in accordance with the recipe.
4. *Respond.* The manager assesses how well employees are making the lattes and provides constructive feedback that will help them improve their performance.

Notice the addition of a fourth step: *respond.* When training people to perform a task they will be required to do well, it is essential to provide feedback. Coach them individually or as a group, ask and answer questions as they practice, and offer praise and suggestions for improvement. **AUDIENCE INTERACTION** can enhance interest, learning, and recall, especially when teaching a procedure.

277–78

Conclusion

Informative presentations that report new information can be demanding for both speakers and audience members alike. They compete with the overflow of facts and stories that bombard us every day. Whether you're touring the external anatomy of a fire ant or showing classmates how to sew on a button, your most important goal is to develop a compelling value step based on your purpose and thorough audience analysis. This strategy will help you choose relevant supporting material and organize your key points to increase audience attention and comprehension.

Reporting new information becomes even more challenging when demonstrating a procedure. The tell-show-do technique can help you navigate this difficult process. Make sure you *tell* and *show* at the same time, speak extemporaneously, and encourage questions during and after a demonstration. When you include the *do* step, your presentation becomes a collaborative undertaking that requires the full attention of everyone involved. As you watch audience members practice a procedure, seek and answer their questions and offer constructive criticism and praise. The way you respond to their attempts can turn a humdrum presentation into one your audience will remember for a long time.

6.3 Explaining Complex Ideas

Unlike reporting new information, informative presentations that **explain complex ideas** assume that audience members are aware of a given subject but lack a deep understanding of it. These presentations answer the questions *Why is this happening?*, *What does that mean?*, and *How does this work?* Consider the following questions and the extent to which you could explain the intricacies of each topic:

- Why do people yawn?
- What's the difference between stocks and bonds?
- What are the origins, basic principles, and contemporary applications of Islamic Sharia law?
- What is the scientific basis for claims about climate change?
- Why do so many people misunderstand the nature of gluten?

To be an excellent explanatory speaker, you need to understand why questions like these are difficult to answer and then create a presentation that overcomes those difficulties. Thanks to the insights in Katherine Rowan's **THEORY OF INFORMATIVE AND EXPLANATORY COMMUNICATION**, there are a number of strategies to guide you when explaining complex ideas.[1]

316–18

Rowan introduces three types of explanatory presentations that deepen audience understanding: ones that *clarify difficult terms*, ones that *describe a quasi-scientific phenomenon*, and ones that *overcome audience confusion and misunderstanding*. Although these strategies may overlap—for example, you may need to clarify a difficult term while describing a quasi-scientific phenomenon—we'll examine them as separate presentations to highlight the way they are used to achieve a particular informative purpose.

Clarifying Difficult Terms

238 ⁒

Unlike an object, person, event, or procedure, a difficult term is often **ABSTRACT**—rarely can you touch it, demonstrate it, or explain it with a short and simple definition. Try to explain *genome*, *quantum mechanics*, or the *electoral college* to someone and you'll see what we mean.

Presentations that **clarify difficult terms** explain what a difficult term means and, in some cases, what it doesn't mean. What, for example, is *rhetoric*? Many people think rhetoric refers to a speech that purposely deceives or misleads an audience rather than how speech is used as a means of legitimate persuasion. Clarifying the meaning of a term can explain the differences between commonly confused words, such as *validity* and *reliability*, or *ethos* and *ethics*. It can also help audience members understand the functions of biotechnology or the scope of Islamic Sharia law.

Clarifying a difficult term is just that—difficult. It is a challenge for both speakers and listeners. Katherine Rowan suggests the following strategies:[2]

- *Define the term's essential features.* What are the consistent qualities in every example of the term? For instance, what is a defining feature of a mammal? Only mammals have three middle ear bones.

- *Use a variety of examples.* What are different, yet typical, examples of the term? For instance, humans, gorillas, whales, and bats are all mammals.

- *Contrast examples and nonexamples.* Can you think of common misconceptions about the term or instances where it's incorrectly used? For example, whales live their lives in the sea but are not fish; bats can fly but are not birds.

- *Quiz the audience.* Pose questions and, if necessary, provide the answer yourself. For example: "True or false? Only mammals have backbones." (False: birds, fish, reptiles, and amphibians also have backbones.)

468–78 ★
You may also want to include a **QUESTION-AND-ANSWER SESSION** at the end of your presentation so the audience has an opportunity to request further clarification.

The following sample outline clarifies the meaning of the term *mammals* and explains, using the four recommended strategies, where and why humans are included in this class of animals:

TOPIC AREA: Humans as mammals

PURPOSE: To explain the essential features of animals identified as mammals

CENTRAL IDEA: Understanding the characteristics of mammals explains why humans are included in the classification.

VALUE STEP: Under the classification of mammals, humans share common characteristics and ancestors with 5,500 related animal species.

ORGANIZATION: **CATEGORICAL ARRANGEMENT** with question-and-answer session

138–39

KEY POINTS:

A. Essential features: All mammals have mammary glands for nursing young, hairs on their skin, and three inner ear bones.

B. Varied examples: Mammals are divided into three subclasses based on reproductive characteristics.

   1. Egg-laying monotremes: duck-billed platypus and spiny anteater

   2. External-pouch marsupials: kangaroos, koalas, opossums, and wombats

   3. Placentals: humans, whales, bats, cats, rats, elephants

C. Nonexamples

   1. Birds, fish, and reptiles have backbones, but are not mammals.

   2. Chickens, penguins, and platypuses lay eggs, but only platypuses are mammals.

   3. Bats and birds fly, but only bats are mammals.

D. Quiz the audience

1. True or false? All mammals have some form of hair. (True: young whales and porpoises have hair—and dolphins are born with small mustaches.)

2. True or false? Some mammals lay eggs. (True: the spiny anteater and duck-billed platypus lay eggs.)

In the above outline, each key point applies a different strategy in a specific order. Why provide nonexamples or quiz the audience at the end? Both help ensure audience members understand the term you're defining. You could, however, integrate some of the strategies into a single key point by, for example, encouraging listeners to ask questions throughout the presentation: "I've listed three identifying features of mammals. Does anyone know of others?" Since many people have mistaken ideas about what makes a mammal a mammal, addressing the issue in your first key point would make the rest of your presentation go more smoothly.

For an example of clarifying a term (*introverts*) by explaining its features, see Notable Speaker: Susan Cain, page 176.

Describing a Quasi-Scientific Phenomenon

The phrase *quasi-scientific phenomenon* may itself require some clarification. The key word is *quasi*, which means "resembling." Thus, when **describing a quasi-scientific phenomenon**, you're looking for ways to enhance audience understanding about a complex scientific idea without using unfamiliar scientific terms, sophisticated statistical methods, or the complicated graphs and charts printed in research journals. Instead, you're describing what something is *like* rather than what it *is*.

Consider, for example, an explanation of supply-and-demand economics from a scientific paper: "System dynamicists believe that the availability of a product, rather than its rate of production, affects the market price and demand. This means that the inventory of a product is a major determinant in setting price and regulating demand."[3] Would you use this language in a presentation to an audience unfamiliar with the topic? Most certainly not. What you need is a simpler and more listener-friendly explanation. For example, you could begin by noting that *supply* refers to the quantity of a product that's available, and *demand* refers to how many people want the product. Then you could describe what happens when supply and demand interact.

Unlike the challenge of clarifying a difficult term, describing a quasi-scientific phenomenon is both complex and multidimensional. Here, you are asking audience members to grasp something that may require specialized knowledge to understand. Perhaps the biggest challenge when giving this kind of presentation is identifying the "big picture" for the audience—that is, the most crucial components from a mass of potentially confusing ideas. Here are four recommendations that can help you describe the big picture to your audience:[4]

1. *Provide clear* **KEY POINTS** *and a variety of* **SUPPORTING MATERIAL** *that's organized well.* Explaining a scientific process usually uses a **CHRONOLOGICAL ORGANIZATIONAL** pattern or **CATEGORICAL ORGANIZATION**.

   133–36
   115–19
   139–40
   138–39
   247–48

2. *Use* **METAPHORS, SIMILES, AND ANALOGIES**. Compare the unfamiliar concept to something the audience already understands. For example, the term *blueprint* has been used to explain genetics. However, because a blueprint implies something that doesn't change, a better and easier-to-understand explanatory metaphor would be *baking bread*. Not only does it describe something that grows (yeast), it also describes a process that can result in a different product depending on the circumstances—such as baking on dry or humid days, or using different ovens.[5] Thus, despite the same recipe of *genes*, no two people are genetically the same (with the exception of some identical twins).

3. *Use* **PRESENTATION AIDS**. A diagram of our solar system, an enlarged illustration of a COVID-19 virus, or an animation of plant growth are

   282–305

only a few examples of presentation aids that may enhance your audience's interest in and ability to understand a challenging idea, theory, or process.

149–51

4. *Use* **TRANSITIONS, PREVIEWS, SUMMARIES, AND SIGNPOSTS**. The complexity of a scientific phenomenon often requires the skilled use of connective phrases that separate the discrete principles of a complex idea into digestible parts (for example, "First . . . second . . . third . . .").

In the following outline, a presentation about the complex weather patterns known as El Niño and La Niña[6] uses the aforementioned strategies to help audience members understand these two scientific phenomena. Unlike explanatory presentations that clarify terms or overcome confusion and misunderstanding, the key points do not correspond to individual strategies. Rather, all the strategies can be used to explain each key point.

TOPIC AREA:	El Niño and La Niña
PURPOSE:	To explain how El Niño and La Niña affect the earth's weather
CENTRAL IDEA:	El Niño and La Niña are two related weather patterns that raise and lower the temperature of water in the equatorial Pacific Ocean, thereby affecting weather and climate conditions in the United States and around the world.
VALUE STEP:	El Niño and La Niña can affect the weather where you live, sometimes in dangerous ways.

144–46

ORGANIZATION:	**COMPARE/CONTRAST** with presentation aids (for example, maps, animations, and photos of severe weather)
KEY POINTS:	A. What are El Niño and La Niña?
	1. El Niño (Spanish for "little boy," or "the Christ child" in Peru) warms the sea surface temperature in the Pacific Ocean near the equator.

2. La Niña (Spanish for "little girl") cools the sea surface temperature in the Pacific Ocean near the equator.

3. El Niño and La Niña are often "partners in a dance" in which subsequent weather and climate conditions vary depending on who is "leading."

B. When do they occur?

1. El Niño is a regularly occurring climate feature.

2. La Niña is less predictable and causes extremely cold water temperatures and frequently serious weather conditions.

3. As brother-sister events, El Niño and La Niña can interact or act independently.

C. How do they impact the United States?

1. El Niño's effects in North America

2. La Niña's effects in the United States

3. El Niño's and La Niña's lack of impact on climate change

Notice how all four strategies are integrated into each of the clear, well-organized key points. The metaphors of a little boy and little girl, dancing partners, and a brother-sister relationship are used throughout the presentation. Certainly, presentation aids would further enhance audience understanding of these phenomena. And although we haven't specified them in the outline, the presentation itself would include clear transitional phrases to separate the two characteristics, behavior, and impact of each weather phenomenon.

Overcoming Confusion and Misunderstanding

The third type of explanatory presentation seeks to **overcome confusion and misunderstanding**, a task that has grown increasingly important as false or misleading information has spread almost uncontrollably among ideological factions at home and abroad. Why, for example, do people believe vaccines cause autism or that Donald Trump won the 2020 presidential election? Because people cling to strongly held beliefs that reinforce a particular viewpoint, even when those beliefs are proven false. As a result, informative speakers often face an uphill battle to replace erroneous beliefs with ones based on legitimate facts.

At first, an informative presentation may not seem the best way to explain what is and is not a fact. Wouldn't a persuasive presentation be more appropriate? It all depends on your **PURPOSE**. Whereas a **PERSUASIVE PRESENTATION** tries to change people's opinions and/or behaviors, an informative presentation tries to set the record straight with facts based on the work of reputable researchers and objective experts.

87–101 ▲
349–50 ◆

To overcome confusion and misunderstanding, we recommend four strategies used in the following order:[7]

1. *State the misconception.* Phrase the misunderstood claim in neutral terms to make sure its goal is to inform, not persuade—and to avoid a negative reaction from your audience. "Some people believe the earth is flat" is an unbiased statement that is less inflammatory than "The Flat Earth Society is totally wrong."

2. *Acknowledge the misconception's believability and the reason(s) it is believed.* Explain why audience members may be confused or misinformed about their beliefs. Scientific and historic claims often change with new research. Advertisers often stretch or misrepresent a product's power. Social media allows falsehoods to spread unchecked.

120–30 ■
115–16 ■
117–18 ■
282–305 ⁖

3. *Create dissatisfaction with the misconception, or explain the misconception by providing contrary evidence.* Make sure you choose legitimate, well-recognized experts whose conclusions have been tested as **VALID**. Cite the experts' credentials in your presentation. Use **FACTS, STATISTICS, AND TESTIMONY**; **STORIES**; and, if appropriate, **PRESENTATION AIDS** to clarify the issue.

4. *State and explain the more acceptable or accurate belief or theory.* Phrase the corrected claim as accurately as you can. Instead of "The earth is round," say, "The earth is an irregularly shaped ellipsoid."

● getting started   ▶ delivery   ◆ speaking to persuade
▲ fundamentals   ⁖ engaging your audience   ★ speaking occasions
■ content   ▼ speaking to inform   ✳ resources

The following outline incorporates the above four steps to help a speaker develop and deliver a presentation that overcomes misconceptions about a particular vaccine:

TOPIC AREA: Vaccinating children for measles, mumps, and rubella (MMR)

PURPOSE: To explain common misconceptions about the risks of this vaccine

CENTRAL IDEA: Claims that the MMR vaccine is harmful and can cause autism have been disproven.

VALUE STEP: Confusion and misunderstanding about the MMR vaccine have put the health and lives of many children in jeopardy.

ORGANIZATION: PROBLEM-SOLUTION ARRANGEMENT

140–41

KEY POINTS:
A. Some parents refuse to vaccinate their children because they believe the MMR vaccine causes autism.

B. This belief is understandable given a published study by Dr. Andrew Wakefield in 1998 and subsequent media hype about the MMR vaccine causing autism in British children.

C. The study's link between the MMR vaccine and autism has been completely discredited by well-respected researchers and medical organizations. Dr. Wakefield lost his medical licenses and the paper was withdrawn by the journal that published it.

D. Vaccinated children are healthier and less likely to contract serious diseases and/or make other children sick.

Unlike a persuasive presentation that entreats parents to vaccinate their children against MMR, the above example clearly fits the purpose of informative presentations: to instruct, explain, enlighten, demonstrate, clarify, correct, remind, or describe. If it's successful, this presentation will encourage misinformed audience members to rethink what they believe about an issue.

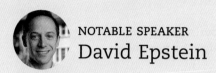

NOTABLE SPEAKER
David Epstein

A former senior writer at *Sports Illustrated*, David Epstein is a journalist whose work often focuses on the intersection of sports, medicine, and science. In 2014, he delivered a compelling TED talk based on his book *The Sports Gene: Inside the Science of Extraordinary Athletic Performance*. Epstein addresses the question of why contemporary athletes seem faster, better, and stronger than their historical counterparts. The large number and high production value of his presentation aids help him explain several complex ideas and misunderstood concepts about a variety of sports.

Search Terms
To locate a video of this presentation online, enter the following key words into a search engine: David Epstein athletes. The video is approximately 14:53 in length.

What to Watch For
Epstein uses numerous explanatory speaking strategies to achieve his goal of explaining why contemporary athletes are faster, better, and stronger than their historic counterparts.

- He clarifies an initially difficult concept by using multiple comparative examples, both obscure and well known (tall basketball players, small gymnasts, swimmers with long torsos, marathon runner with thin shins) accompanied by superb visuals, and by posing questions to the audience.

- He describes quasi-scientific phenomena using three key points, a clear organizational format, and effective transitions.

- He addresses and corrects misconceptions audience members may have about athletic ability by acknowledging what many people believe—that humans beings have evolved into better athletes over the last century—and then providing a more complicated explanation (but with clarity): that the improvements are largely due to technological innovations, specialized body types for different sports, and a more productive mindset in athletic training and competition.

[0:00–0:45] Epstein begins his talk with the Olympics motto: "*Citius, altius, fortius.* Faster, higher, stronger." He then displays his first slide showing that the 2012 Olympic marathon winner beat the 1904 winner by almost one and a half hours. "So what's going on here?" he asks. Epstein's challenge is to explain complex phenomena that require a scientific understanding and connect to frequently misunderstood beliefs about athletic abilities. He starts to meet this challenge by clearly identifying his central idea: "I want to take a look at what's really behind this march of athletic progress."

[1:12–2:53] Epstein's first extended example is a slide explaining that if Jesse Owens, winner of the 100-meter sprint at the 1936 Olympics, had propelled himself out of a block and run on a modern track, he would have been within a stride of beating Usain Bolt, considered the greatest sprinter of all time. Epstein uses this first example to preview his organizational structure and makes the first of his three key points: improved technology has improved athletic performance.

Every example he uses has its own recognizable structure, almost always accompanied by a slide. He introduces the examples and the differences between the pictured athletes— some famous, some not. Then he links the example to one of his key points—technology advancements, genetic differences, or athlete mindset—to explain differences in performance.

(NOTABLE SPEAKER CONTINUED)

[4:21–4:52] Epstein examines the 100-meter freestyle world record in swimming. He uses a slide to explain that although "the record is always trending downward . . . it's punctuated by these steep cliffs," all of which reflect technological advancements: the flip turn, pool gutters that reduce water turbulence, and low-friction swimsuits. He zooms in on each of the "cliffs," getting four slides out of one.

[7:05–7:56] Throughout his presentation, Epstein demonstrates the value of multiple presentation aids to support key points. When discussing how the height and weight of athletes has changed over time, he uses a scatter graph to illustrate what researchers call the Big Bang of Body Types—the splintering of athletes' body types into specialized shapes and sizes, depending on which sport they compete in.

[7:55–8:55] Epstein uses four slides to explain why the number of basketball players who are seven feet tall doubled in a short period of time. He begins by showing an image of a basketball player. He then switches to an image of ten dots, one of which is yellow. The yellow dot represents the one player in ten in the NBA today who is at least seven feet tall. Next, he adds several more rows of gray dots to illustrate how rare it is to find a man who is seven feet tall in the general population. Finally, he makes a slightly different but related point by showing six dots—one of which is a basketball. Even though seven-foot-tall men are extremely rare in the general population, for every six such men that you might find, one of those six will play in the NBA!

[10:00–10:30] When comparing and contrasting athletes with each other, Epstein uses images that show them side by side. Parts of his presentation generate audience laughter, as when he compares the bodies of six-foot-four swimmer Michael Phelps and five-foot-nine runner Hicham El Guerrouj.

[11:35–14:00] By the time he reaches his third key point—changing mindsets change athletic performance—his explanation is not as clear as the first two (changing technology and changing gene pool). The presentation becomes more abstract and the slides less instructive.

EXERCISE

After viewing Epstein's speech, reflect on these questions:

1. To what extent do you better understand why modern athletes are faster, higher, and stronger?

2. How did Epstein use the strategies recommended for explanatory presentations? Was it easy or difficult to identify the strategies? Were they obvious or subtle? Does it matter if the audience can identify them?

3. How many key points were there? How many subpoints/examples were under each key point? What were the transitions?

4. In your opinion, which presentation aids were the most and least effective? Explain.

5. Epstein used more than two dozen presentation aids. Should he have used more words and fewer visuals? Or did he get it just right? Explain.

6. In what ways, if any, could Epstein have improved the content and/or delivery of his presentation?

Conclusion

Informative presentations can take many forms. If you're a news anchor or tour guide, most of what you do is report new information. But what if instead of sharing a recipe for making bread, you explain how yeast works? Or if instead of providing a short biography of Mozart, you explain the reasons his works are significant today and unmatched by his contemporaries? The difference between these examples is your purpose. Your purpose determines whether you're clarifying a difficult term, describing a quasi-scientific phenomenon, or overcoming confusion or misunderstanding. (Your purpose will also determine if you're speaking to persuade rather than to inform.) We have provided strategies for developing each type of explanatory presentation. But keep in mind that in some rhetorical situations you may need to apply more than one set of explanatory strategies at different points in your presentation.

Part 7
Speaking to Persuade

Persuasion—the process of convincing people to change their opinions or behavior of their own free will—is a fact of our daily lives. Contemporary rhetorician Andrea Lunsford has gone so far as to claim that "everything's an argument"[1]—that even sharing a straightforward piece of information is an attempt to persuade your listeners that what you're saying is truthful, accurate, and worth knowing. The three chapters that follow are all about persuasive speaking. They provide you with essential PERSUASIVE STRATEGIES for making your presentations more believable, influential, and memorable, and they will also help you sharpen your critical thinking skills when considering your own and others' ARGUMENTS.

Speaking to Persuade

7.1 Understanding Persuasion

Persuasive messages bombard us from the time we wake up until the moment we end each day. Sometimes persuasion is obvious—a sales call, a political campaign speech, a plea for donations. At other times, it's more subtle—a sermon, an investment newsletter, a hint about a desired birthday present. Businesses use persuasion to sell products. Colleges use persuasion to recruit students and faculty. Even children use persuasive speaking to convince parents to let them stay up late or to buy them the newest toy. It's here, it's there, it's everywhere! So what, exactly, is persuasion?

The Purpose of Persuasion

Persuasion strives to change people's opinions (what they believe, think, or feel) and/or their behavior (what they do). Persuasive speaking is distinct from, but partly dependent on, informative speaking. Experienced speakers know that in order to persuade an audience, they must present information. For instance, if you are asking audience members to reduce the amount of meat they consume, you may include factual information about the negative health and environmental consequences of consuming meat products. In most rhetorical situations, applying basic principles of effective **INFORMATIVE SPEAKING** is critical to your success as a persuasive speaker. So how do these two types of speaking differ? The dividing line between informing and persuading is your **PURPOSE**.

310–16

87–101

319–32
333–46

Think of it this way: The primary goal of an informative presentation is *to tell your audience something important* by **REPORTING NEW INFORMATION**, clarifying difficult terms, **EXPLAINING COMPLEX IDEAS**, and/or correcting misunderstood information. In a persuasive presentation your primary goal is *to ask for something from your audience*—their agreement or a change in their opinions and/or behavior.

getting started   ▶ delivery   ◆ speaking to persuade
▲ fundamentals   ⁂ engaging your audience   ★ speaking occasions
▬ content   ▬ speaking to inform   ❋ resources

In general, it's easier to persuade audience members to change their opinions than it is to convince them to do something they wouldn't otherwise do. The following table shows how a persuasive presentation on a particular topic might ask the audience to change either their opinion or their behavior. Note the difference between the two goals.

Opinion	Behavior
Springy Shoes makes the best high-quality athletic shoes.	Buy Springy Shoes.
Your family is more important than your job.	Eat dinner with your family at least five times a week.
We need stricter drunk driving laws and punishments.	Write a letter to your state legislator supporting stricter drunk driving laws.
Chris has extreme views on almost every issue.	Vote for Fran, Chris's opponent.

Bear in mind that persuading people to change their opinion or belief is not necessarily going to lead to a change in their behavior. Changing audience opinions is already a challenge, even for experienced speakers, and sometimes it's the only realistic goal you can set for yourself in one presentation. If your goal is to change behavior, you'll first need to persuade your listeners that your opinion is reasonable, and then you'll need to motivate them to take some action as a result. It's a tall order, and in the rest of this chapter and the chapters that follow, we discuss some of the strategies you can use to make this happen. But first, let's consider the ethical implications of persuasive speaking.

The Ethics of Persuasion

Successful persuasive speakers demonstrate an impressive mastery of the art of speaking—they have learned how to bring people around to their way of thinking. Changing other people's attitudes, opinions, beliefs, and/or actions is, at its heart, an act of rhetorical power. But like all forms of power, persuasive power can be misused.

40–41

You might wonder, "Can I learn the skills and techniques needed to become a more persuasive speaker and still be an **ETHICAL SPEAKER**?" The

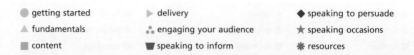

● getting started   ▶ delivery   ◆ speaking to persuade
▲ fundamentals   ∴ engaging your audience   ★ speaking occasions
■ content   ▼ speaking to inform   ✳ resources

answer is "Yes, but only if your purpose is ethical." Sadly, some of the most evil people in history have been highly effective persuasive speakers. Adolf Hitler, to cite an obvious example, was a very convincing speaker. But so were many extraordinarily ethical people. Abraham Lincoln, Mahatma Gandhi, and Martin Luther King Jr., for example, wielded just as much rhetorical power with their audiences as Hitler did with his. Whether evil or well intentioned, many persuasive speakers with impressive speaking skills are committed to achieving their purpose. So what's the difference between them?

The answer is, as it is with ethical behavior generally, that ethical persuasive speakers are committed to honorable **VALUES**—truthfulness, respect for people's rights, concern for the audience's well-being—and they are aware of and responsible for the consequences if they achieve their speaking goals. The act of persuading is not, all by itself, unethical. Certainly, it is ethical to persuade others to donate money to a legitimate charity or to urge listeners to stop engaging in dangerous behavior. On the other hand, if you persuade your audience to bully, intimidate, or harm people who hold different opinions from yours by distorting the truth, both your means and ultimate goal are unethical. Persuasion becomes unethical if you are trying to make people think, feel, or do something that does not benefit them or may hurt them, that misrepresents the truth, that serves your own or an organization's self-centered interests, or that violates the rights and freedom of others. As with all types of speaking situations, ethical persuasive speakers should commit themselves to following the **CREDO FOR ETHICAL COMMUNICATION** .

▲ 79–80

● 40–41

The Components of Persuasive Speaking: Claims and Appeals

What is the best way to understand the persuasive speaking process? Are there core principles and fundamental strategies you should learn and apply when developing a persuasive presentation? It may surprise you to know that there have been substantive answers to these questions for more than twenty-five hundred years. During the early fourth century BCE, the Greek philosopher Aristotle watched and listened to speakers in the courts and in the marketplaces of Athens. Based on his observations, he developed a multidimensional theory of persuasion in the *Rhetoric*—a book that continues to influence the way we think about persuasion today.

Aristotle's ideas about the general nature and particular features of persuasive speaking are complex and well worth reading in the original work, but for the purposes of this discussion we begin by introducing two major components that Aristotle believed set persuasion apart from other types of speaking: *claims* and *appeals*.

Persuasive Claims

A **claim** is the conclusion of a persuasive argument—it states what you want your audience to believe and/or do. Rhetoricians have classified persuasive claims into four basic types: *claims of fact*, *claims of conjecture*, *claims of value*, and *claims of policy*. Here's how to tell them apart:

Type of claim	Function	Examples
Fact	States that something is true, that an event occurred, that a cause can be identified, or that a theory correctly explains a phenomenon	• Viruses, not bacteria, cause the common cold. • Global carbon emissions fell by more than 15 percent in the first quarter of 2020.
Conjecture	Suggests that something will or will not happen in the future	• By 2045, non-Hispanic whites will become a minority group in the United States. • The new spending bill will result in lower taxes for all middle-class citizens.
Value	Asserts the worth of something—good or bad; right or wrong; best, average, or worst	• Plagiarism is unethical. • Denying Americans access to affordable quality health care is unconscionable and harmful.
Policy	Recommends a course of action or solution to a problem	• Our state should ban vaping in offices and public places. • All college students should take a communication course.

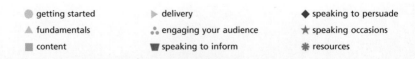

● getting started	▶ delivery	◆ speaking to persuade
▲ fundamentals	⁚• engaging your audience	★ speaking occasions
■ content	▼ speaking to inform	✳ resources

A **claim of fact** contends that a statement about people, objects, or events is true and verifiable. Claims of fact answer questions such as these: *Are more or fewer people migrating from Central America to the United States than ever before? Is marijuana an addictive drug? Does the measles vaccine cause autism?* When developing a legitimate claim of fact, use objective, verifiable **SUPPORTING MATERIAL** to substantiate your claim. Keep in mind that there are often competing claims made by others. If you claim *There is no scientific connection between vaccines and autism*, for example, you must be prepared to address audience members who disagree.

120–30

A **claim of conjecture** makes statements about the future. It's impossible to predict the future with perfect accuracy, but you can make well-informed assumptions based on strong, valid research and observable trends. Claims of conjecture answer questions such as these: *How will higher tariffs on goods from other countries affect the US economy? Will stricter enforcement and increased penalties for drunk driving decrease the number of motor vehicle accidents? Who will win the upcoming election (or tournament or celebrated prize)? Will there be another pandemic in the next five years?* Like claims of fact, claims of conjecture require supporting material based on expert opinions and valid data. They also require that you clearly describe the thought process you use to support your claim. Much like claims of fact, there can be competing claims of conjecture, such as the following two public assertions that were made in the first half of 2020: *The coronavirus is going to go away without a vaccine* and *The virus is going to continue until we develop an effective vaccine and administer it to most people.*

A **claim of value** identifies what is right or wrong in a particular situation. Claims of value can be challenging because audience members hold a variety of attitudes and beliefs. Here are some questions answered by claims of value: *Is forcing transgender people to use the bathroom of their birth sex right or wrong? Is banning immigrants from certain countries fair and justifiable? Is it unethical to knowingly share falsified or misleading messages via social media?* Claims of value should cite the most reliable and respected opinions and data you can find, but they also should explain how *your* point of view connects to your **AUDIENCE'S VALUES**. More than claims of fact or conjecture, claims of value require you to be in tune with your audience's beliefs and attitudes—to be an especially **AUDIENCE-CENTERED SPEAKER**.

79–80

70–72

Keep in mind that what you see as immoral or wrong may seem good and right by some audience members.

A **claim of policy** proposes a course of action. Here are a few examples: *We should ban hate speech on campus. The government should cancel student loan debt. The drinking age should be lowered to eighteen, the same age that people can enlist in the military.* As is the case with all claims, audience members may not support your proposed actions. Think of the wide range of opinions on issues such as gun control, abortion, immigration, freedom of speech, animal rights, and global climate change. Rarely can speakers advocate a position on any of these issues without considering and adapting to the disparate opinions of audience members.

Claims of policy usually require that you establish claims of fact, conjecture, and/or value as a basis for advocating a course of action. It is difficult to imagine a claim of policy that doesn't show that something is happening or will happen and that it has value-based implications. Once you've done that, you can persuade your audience that your recommended solution—the means by which you propose to change things—is the right one.

Consider a presentation about bicycle safety on a college campus: A significant number of students ride bikes on campus (fact). Increasing enrollment and the popularity of bicycles will increase bike traffic and accidents (conjecture). Irresponsible bike riders who defy and/or disregard traffic rules are endangering the safety of others (value). We should develop and enforce traffic and campus rules to improve bike safety (policy). Persuading an audience to support the enforcement of stricter bicycle traffic rules is all but impossible unless you explain why. Claims of fact, conjecture, and value provide the "why."

Persuasive Appeals

Like lawyers before a jury, persuasive speakers must prove their case. In *Rhetoric*, Aristotle identifies three major modes of persuasion—three types of *appeals* that speakers use to persuade an audience: *ethos, pathos,* and *logos.* According to Aristotle:

> Of the modes of persuasion furnished by the spoken word there are three kinds. The first kind depends on the personal character of the

speaker [ethos]; the second on putting the audience into a certain frame of mind [pathos]; the third on the proof, or apparent proof, provided by the words of the speech itself [logos].[2]

Ethos: Personal Appeals Aristotle and many contemporary rhetoricians claim that the speaker's personal character—their **ethos** (which we also call **SPEAKER CREDIBILITY**) is often the most fundamental and effective persuasive appeal. Consider how ethos operates in your everyday life. Do you believe what your favorite professors tell you? If, in your opinion, they are honorable, reliable, and experts in their field of study, you probably do. Do you trust what a respected member of the clergy says? Again, if you have faith in the integrity and goodwill of that person, you probably do. Ethos is a powerful appeal—but you have to *earn* it from your audience if you expect it to help you achieve your persuasive purpose.

▲ 57–66

Most speakers begin a presentation with some of their ethos already established in the audience's mind. This is called the speaker's **initial credibility**. A speaker's initial credibility may be quite low if the audience knows nothing about them (other than their physical appearance) before they speak; it may be high if the speaker's reputation for expertise and honesty precedes them; or it may be somewhere in between. Whether starting with low or high ethos, successful persuasive speakers work to *increase* or take advantage of their existing credibility over the course of a presentation.

The effect you have on an audience's perception of your ethos during a presentation is called **derived credibility**. Your derived credibility may wax and wane over the course of your presentation, based on many different factors: the quality and **ORGANIZATION** of your content, the nature and skill of your delivery, and the degree to which you convey **IMMEDIACY**, **LIKABILITY**, and **DYNAMISM**. Most of this book is devoted to helping you increase your derived credibility as you speak. However, in addition to the advice provided in other chapters, here are a few specific strategies you can use to enhance your ethos during your presentation:

■ 138–48
▶ 186
▲ 63–65
▲ 66

- *Identify with your audience.* Rhetorical scholar Kenneth Burke describes successful persuasion as **identification**, a process by which the speaker and audience recognize that they share attitudes, ideas, feelings, values, and experiences. According to Burke, you can persuade another person only insofar as you can talk someone's language through speech, gesture, tonality, order, image, and attitude, identifying your ways with theirs.[3] We refer to a similar strategy elsewhere in this book as seeking **COMMON GROUND**. When you acknowledge and share what you and your audience members have in common—when you identify with them and they with you—you are more likely to enhance your credibility.

71 ▲

- *Personalize your message.* To enhance your credibility early in your presentation, you might provide personal information about yourself and/or the reason you are speaking. Here's an example: *As I thought about the topics I might choose for this presentation, it occurred to me that because I am a nutrition major and grew up on a farm, I probably know more than most people about the food we eat. That's why I want to talk about the importance of healthy eating habits.* Or you might display a photograph of your college's nutrition lab and say, *Research done in our nutrition program where I work as an intern has found* . . . Even if you are not pictured in the photograph, showing the lab helps your audience imagine you in that setting, which of course provides a sense of credibility.

- *Use audience-centered supporting material.* Right from the beginning of your presentation, introduce strong supporting material that the audience is likely to believe and that demonstrates respect for their beliefs and values. Here's an example: *I know that you wouldn't be participating in this webinar unless you were worried about the closing of schools during the pandemic. And I wouldn't be here either. I also assume that you are familiar with the long-standing education research about "summer learning loss," when kids regress academically during their annual three-month vacation.*[4] *So let's think about what a twelve-month disruption could mean and what we can do about it.*

- *Demonstrate open mindedness.* Show your audience that you have considered significant research and viewpoints about your topic and that you understand the basis for such opinions: *For many years, I believed that fat was the big bad culprit in our diets. Only recently have I learned that salt and sugar may be more harmful than fat.*

- *Borrow other people's ethos.* You can enhance your credibility by quoting an expert with high credibility whose knowledge, research, or public reputation is well known to the audience. And if that person is in some way connected to you, you can use their ethos as a support for your own. For example, you might say, *Professor Grabowski, chairman of our nutrition department and everyone's favorite food expert, discovered this relationship three years ago.*

Finally, there is your **terminal credibility**—what audience members feel about you after you have finished your presentation. Even though your audience is the ultimate judge of your ethos, terminal credibility is, like derived credibility, partly the result of your actions and persona. How you **END YOUR PRESENTATION** and the manner in which you respond to **AUDIENCE QUESTIONS** and objections can have a significant effect on your terminal credibility. Although you may have earned credibility as you spoke, failure to lock it in as you conclude a presentation can affect— positively or negatively—what your audience remembers about you and your message.

■ 169–75
★ 468–78

Pathos: Emotional Appeals You may have seen the print and media ads by the American Society for the Prevention of Cruelty to Animals depicting a pitiful puppy, trembling chihuahua, or physically abused dog staring at you with big brown eyes. The copy may say, "Starved, abandoned, left to suffer," or "No food, no shelter, no love," with information on how to donate or adopt a pet. During the height of the COVID-19 pandemic, memes, photos, quotations, and videos of exhausted health care workers with red, teary eyes evoked a wide range of emotions—from awe and admiration to sadness and fear. Appeals like these stir various emotions—anger, desire, fear, pride, envy, joy, hate, jealousy, or pity. They can also target values such as justice, generosity, courage, forgiveness, and wisdom.

Aristotle referred to this mode of persuasion—the use of **emotional appeals**—as **pathos**. An emotional appeal can strengthen a persuasive presentation by causing audience members to *feel something* while listening to you and, in some cases, without being aware of it, modify their beliefs to reflect the emotions they feel. As psychological studies have since confirmed, and as Aristotle and his contemporaries knew intuitively, we are more likely to pay attention to, sympathize with, and remember arguments that (in addition to demonstrating the truth of something) stir strong emotional responses in us. Notice, for instance, how the following speaker uses emotional appeals to evoke audience sympathies and concerns about a scourge that has killed almost half a million Americans.[5]

> High school student Laurie Porter watched her mother cycle in and out of opioid addiction and rehab for years. Every time her mom promised to change and become part of Laurie's life again, Laurie knew it wouldn't happen. When she found a syringe in her mother's purse and two more in the dryer, she pleaded with her mother. "I cried, begged her to stop, but she was too out of it to care." What little money they had went to buying drugs. Sometimes Laurie would go without food so her sister could eat. Like thousands and thousands of other children, Laurie has become a member of Generation O: the children whose parents are opioid addicts.

Rather than relying only on evidence and statistics to demonstrate the significance of the opioid crisis (although she does do that in other parts of her presentation), the speaker tells the story of one young person's personal and heartbreaking experience with it. **STORIES** like this can evoke sympathy and fear. They can also help listeners understand that the same thing could happen to them or to someone they love. And, as a result, it becomes more likely that they will support a speaker's proposed action to address it.

253–67 ⋮

There is one emotion that deserves special attention in persuasive presentations. Of all the emotions a speaker can appeal to, fear may be the most powerful, most frequently used, and most researched. What explains the power of fear appeals? Many thinkers believe that fear is the most primal, basic emotion—one of the few that we share with the rest of the animal kingdom. Philosopher Martha Nussbaum describes fear as "the earliest emotion in human life. Whereas anger requires sophisticated thinking, fear only needs 'an awareness of danger.'"[6]

Think of how many public messages use fear appeals. Life insurance ads suggest that you invest not for yourself but for those you love. Political ads advise that you should vote for particular candidates because they will make the world safer for you, your children, and the generations that follow them (and that you will not be as safe if you vote for their opponent). Think about the extent to which fear appeals affect or have affected your attitudes, opinions, and behavior about the following actions:

- Your choice of where to live
- Your decision to acquire protective gear (a handgun, pepper spray, an alarm system) or learn self-defense skills (karate, boxing, krav maga)
- Your attitude and beliefs about immigrants and refugees seeking entrance into the United States
- Your willingness to travel abroad or visit a major US city
- Your decision on whether to get vaccinated

At some point, your decisions about these things (or things like them) were probably influenced by a persuasive fear appeal. As powerful as fear appeals can be, however, they are not always successful. Persuasion scholar Richard Perloff notes that it isn't easy to frighten people—or rather, to frighten most of the people you're attempting to persuade. And even if you succeed in scaring most of your listeners, your fear appeal may not produce a change in their attitude other than making them anxious and unsettled. However, when a fear appeal is well crafted and well delivered, and when it is used for a good reason (for example, to prevent your listeners from putting themselves or their loved ones in harm's way), it can be very effective. So how do you make successful fear appeals? Here are a few suggestions:[7]

- *You must scare the heck out of your audience.* Don't beat around the bush. Dramatic, high-fear messages are more effective than those that soften the dangers or dire outcomes. Use **VIVID LANGUAGE** to explain how your audience's current opinions or behavior can have dreadful consequences.   242
- *Audience members must believe that what is being threatened could happen to them or someone they care about.* If audience members have never had a car accident after drinking a lot of alcohol, it's time to tell them stories and show **VISUAL AIDS** of people who said the same thing the night before killing a family in a head-on collision. Other audience   289–90

members may be more concerned about what might happen to people they love than about what might happen to themselves. For this group, the best fear appeals tell listeners they ought to do something because if they don't, their loved ones will suffer horribly as a result.

- *Make sure that what scares you also scares your audience.* Consider the values and needs of your audience when considering what frightens them. Just because something terrifies you doesn't mean it terrifies *them.* Think of how many people were initially unafraid of contracting COVID-19 until someone they cared about suffered or died from the disease. Assess your assumptions about the audience's fears through **AUDIENCE ANALYSIS**.

72–80 ▲

- *Avoid overused threats.* The best fear appeals are novel. Just about every teenager ignores some of the overused threats parents make. The "Just say no" to drugs campaign didn't succeed. A mother who repeatedly threatens, "If you don't do well on this exam, you won't get into college," may be met with a teen's snarky reply: "Sure, Mom, I won't get into any school." Creative persuaders come up with appeals listeners have not considered before.

- *Discuss solutions.* This last piece of advice is key: Once you've scared audience members, tell them how to prevent the problem or minimize the danger. Drunk driving ads don't simply tell you not to drink. They tell you to "drink responsibly"—have a designated driver, leave your car at home, or call a cab. Think of it this way: you have made them sick with fear; now it's time to make them well.

Making an emotional appeal can be a justifiable and effective means of persuasion. But emotional appeals—and especially fear appeals—also have the potential to be used in malicious and unethical ways. Critical thinkers in an audience can analyze whether the emotions aroused by a speaker are applicable and appropriate to the occasion and the purpose,

42 ●

but it shouldn't be up to them. As an **ETHICAL SPEAKER**, you should make decisions that both achieve your persuasive purpose and do so in ways that serve your audience's best interests. Revving up fans at a pep rally or evoking sympathy by telling a sad story may be relevant and reasonable,

● getting started   ▶ delivery   ◆ speaking to persuade
▲ fundamentals   ⁂ engaging your audience   ★ speaking occasions
■ content   ▼ speaking to inform   ✳ resources

but stirring up emotions based on fabricated facts and doubtful inferences violates the values that every ethical speaker should uphold. The key is to use emotional appeals judiciously, wisely, and well.

Logos: Appeals to Reason The third mode of persuasion, **logos** (also referred to as **appeals to reason**), relies on well-crafted claims that are reasonable and sensible. The success of logical appeals depends on your and your audience's ability to think rationally and critically in order to arrive at a justified conclusion. Unlike ethos and pathos, logos does not rely on who you are or how well you arouse audience emotions. Instead, it depends on building clear and compelling arguments, supporting your claims with relevant and valid **SUPPORTING MATERIAL** (facts, statistics, testimony, definitions, analogies, examples, stories, and audio/visual aids), and then tying all these elements together with good reasoning.

 115–19

An effective appeal to reason meets four criteria:

1. The claims in your presentation are true and verifiable.
2. The supporting material you use to justify your claims is valid.
3. There is a strong connection between your claims and the supporting material that justifies them.
4. The content and sequence of claims in your presentation support and strengthen the argument.

As the most complex of appeals, the appeal to reason requires speakers to understand the nature and prerequisites for building strong arguments and to recognize and refute weak (or deliberately misleading) ones. The following chapter, **THINKING CRITICALLY ABOUT ARGUMENTS**, will go into more detail about how to recognize good and bad arguments.

363–81

For an example of a presentation using all three persuasive appeals (ethos, pathos, and logos), see Notable Speaker: Zach Wahls, page 83.

Conclusion

Persuasion affects everyone. In daily encounters with family members, friends, colleagues, and acquaintances—whether face-to-face or via some form of media—we cannot escape the constant stream of persuasive messages. We are asked to join, buy, salute, condemn, enjoy, participate, learn, and decide what is supposedly best for us and others. That is the goal of persuasion: to change people's opinions and/or their behavior.

When preparing a persuasive presentation, make sure you develop a series of strong claims and consider how (and in what combination) you will use the three main types of appeals: ethos (personal appeals), pathos (emotional appeals), and logos (appeals to reason).

Remember that your ethos is determined by your audience. Effective speakers do everything they can to enhance their ethos—from identifying with the audience, personalizing their message, and using audience-centered supporting material to demonstrating an open mind and enlisting the credibility of experts—but in the end, your ethos is determined by your audience.

Because audiences are more likely to pay attention to and remember arguments that stir strong emotions, pathos can be a highly effective mode of persuasion. But emotional appeals, and especially fear appeals, can be used either ethically or unethically to achieve a speaker's purpose. Arousing an audience's fear is justified when the threat is real and the speaker addresses the threat truthfully and offers reasonable remedies, but it can also cause listeners to abandon critical thinking and to embrace irresponsible, irrational, and/or harmful actions. Use pathos wisely.

Logos is, essentially, the basis for rational arguments—the justifiable ideas and content in your presentation and the words you use to express them, all tied together with sound reasoning. Logos—also called the appeal to reason—requires speakers to use valid evidence and legitimate reasoning to support their claims.

7.2 Thinking Critically about Arguments

When we use the word *argument* in our everyday lives, we often mean a heated disagreement, an angry quarrel, or a fight between people that concludes with one person feeling distressed and defeated and the other feeling dominant and victorious (and perhaps a little guilty). But that sort of argument is not what happens in good persuasive speaking. A persuasive argument—the kind we're discussing in this chapter—is an *alternative* to a fight. **Arguments** are composed of CLAIMS supported by evidence and reasons for accepting them. They attempt to persuade people to change their opinion or take an action of their own free will. Although your arguments may not achieve everything you hope for, they're still better than fighting.

◆ 352–54

A persuasive argument is more than a recitation of facts and statistics or a series of anecdotes and expert testimony assembled in a haphazard way. Look at the picture on the next page—a lithograph called *Waterfall* by the artist M. C. Escher. Do you see anything unusual about it?

The Escher structure *seems* to make sense, but when you look more closely, you see that it's just an illusion—water can't possibly flow through the structure in the upward manner depicted. Similarly, many presentations that initially appear to have well-constructed arguments are really only *illusions* of arguments. Telling the difference between arguments that are well reasoned and trustworthy and those that only appear reasonable and logical is the purpose of this chapter.

There are entire courses of study devoted to the process of thinking critically and logically about arguments, but for the purposes of persuasive speaking, we offer essential principles and analytical tools to help you evaluate the arguments you wish to make as well as those you read and hear. Let's start by looking more carefully at the principles and types of reasoning.

Waterfall by M. C. Escher, 1961.

Reasoning

The process of constructing and analyzing an argument is called **reasoning**. When our reasoning produces an argument that is worth believing (or confirms that someone else's argument is worth believing), it becomes a *well-reasoned argument*. Every well-reasoned argument offers a number of *statements* (sometimes called **premises**) that support and lead us to accept its *claim* (sometimes called its **conclusion**). There are two major types of reasoning: *deductive reasoning* and *inductive reasoning*.

Deductive Reasoning

Deductive reasoning has a strict requirement: if its initial statements (premises) are true, its claim (conclusion) will also be true. The most famous example of deductive reasoning is this:

All humans are mortal.

Socrates is a human.

Therefore, Socrates is mortal.

If the first two premises are true, so is the conclusion. The *structure* of this argument guarantees the truth of the concluding claim. Very few arguments in real life are deductive. In the real world of communication, listening to a deductive argument presented out loud can be a boring, even irritating, experience for listeners. Most persuasive speakers don't recite three-part deductive arguments. Instead, they might employ a deductive argument that's hidden below the surface, with some of its premises unspoken (for example, "All of us will eventually die. You will too."). Even if you believe that you've presented a bulletproof deductive argument in your presentation, do not rely on your argument's validity to persuade your audience. You should also enlist other argumentative strategies, even if all you're arguing is that Socrates was, indeed, mortal.

Inductive Reasoning

Whereas deductive reasoning moves from general reasons to a specific (and necessarily true) conclusion, **inductive reasoning** assembles a number of related observations that together lead to a general conclusion that *probably* explains something important about the observations. Inductive reasoning creates claims based on causality, generalizations, classifications, comparisons, and/or predictions based on incomplete information and/or statistical data.

Inductive reasoning is common in everyday life: "Whenever I see the clouds build up like that in the afternoon, it usually rains." It's also the sort of reasoning that drives scientific research and discovery.

The truth of a claim in an inductive argument is never 100 percent guaranteed; it can be judged only as more or less likely true, as relatively strong or weak. The strength of an inductive argument depends on the accuracy of observations and the explanation's level of probability. For instance, if you were to say, "All fifty dogs I saw at the local dog show had hair or fur," and then were to conclude, "Therefore all dogs have hair or fur," your argument would be a weak inductive argument because the **SAMPLE** you used to reach your conclusion simply isn't big enough for you

■ 128–29

to make a generalization about "all dogs." (As a matter of fact, you would be wrong. There are breeds of dog without hair or fur.) But if you were to conclude instead that "therefore *most* dogs have hair or fur," the simple change from "all" to "most" would make your argument a relatively strong inductive argument.

There are several types of inductive reasoning. Here are five examples related to the COVID-19 pandemic:

Type of inductive reasoning	Definition	Example
Cause	Actions or inactions that consistently give rise to a predictable effect—another action, phenomenon, or condition	In 2019, a mysterious new respiratory and vascular disease appeared in Wuhan, China. All the patients presenting with this disease were found to have a new coronavirus in their system. This coronavirus—soon named COVID-19—was identified as the cause of the disease.
Sign	Observations about a phenomenon that are linked so frequently that a particular effect is predictable. The sign does not cause the effect but is evidence of the effect.	Most confirmed COVID-19 patients experience some combination of the following symptoms: fever, dry cough, breathing difficulty, muscle aches, chills, tiredness, and loss of taste and smell.
Generalization	A series of examples that share characteristics or outcomes considered reliable as descriptions or predictions that are true in most situations	Contact tracers and public researchers report that many COVID-19 patients attended large indoor gatherings with people who weren't wearing masks or social distancing. Conversely, fewer people contracted COVID-19 if they were consistently isolated and masked.

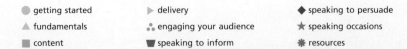

Type of inductive reasoning	Definition	Example
Classification	Grouping various objects on the basis of their commonly known properties; taking what is known to be true about a group of people, objects, events, and phenomena as true about an individual member of the group	Countries that instituted universal mask wearing, social distancing, business shutdowns, quarantines, and strict border control had the lowest COVID rates and deaths. New Zealand had one of the lowest rates of infection in the world, probably because it instituted all these actions.
Analogy	A comparison of two otherwise different things based on similar qualities, functions, and/or characteristics in order to conclude that what is true about one is likely to be true about the other	Wearing a mask to protect yourself and others from COVID-19 is like wearing a seat belt and not driving when drunk.

When you create and analyze inductive arguments, keep in mind that they are almost never 100 percent true. It is therefore imperative to employ critical thinking skills each time you encounter them. Begin this process by asking analytical questions: Is there a better conclusion based on your reasoning in the argument? Is a comparison between one thing and another (as in the case of an analogy or classification) both *real* and *relevant* to the conclusion? In short, if an alternative conclusion seems more likely than the one in an argument, or if comparisons don't seem real or relevant, the argument is weak. And if that is the case, modify or completely change your argument and reject someone else's argument accordingly.

Although inductive reasoning can seem very logical, it may rely too much on intuition, emotions, and snap judgments.[1] Persuading an audience to accept your conclusions can depend on **PERSONAL** and **EMOTIONAL APPEALS** (ethos and pathos) as much as it does on the apparent

◆ 355–57
◆ 357–61

reasonableness of your argument (logos). Even Aristotle noted that ethos and pathos can be more effective and powerful than logical arguments—and that they are not necessarily invalid or unethical means of persuasion. As an audience member, consider the degree to which an argument is based on one of these other appeals. Knowing the difference between the speaker's use of logos, ethos, and pathos in a persuasive presentation will sharpen your critical thinking about your own arguments and help you identify flawed arguments you read or hear.

Thinking Critically about Facts, Inferences, and Opinions

To think critically about the arguments in a presentation—yours or someone else's—you need to understand the differences among *facts*, *inferences*, and *opinions*. A **fact** is a statement about a person, object, or event that can be proven true or false. An **inference** goes beyond facts to reach a conclusion that may not be provable; inferences often add unproven information to an observation in order to make sense about what's happening. An **opinion** is a statement that evaluates or judges the facts and inferences in a situation. For example, the statement "Maia always turns her work in on time" can be a fact based on an instructor's records and observations. However, the claim "I'm sure Maia will continue to turn her work in on time" is an inference, and a personal judgment such as "Maia is a responsible and reliable person" is an opinion. As you can see, inferences and opinions have a great deal in common. What makes them different is the personal nature of opinions. The following table summarizes the ways that facts, inferences, and opinions differ:[2]

Facts	Inferences	Opinions
• Can be proven	• Can be made at any time	• Can be made at any time
• Stick with what is observed	• Go beyond what is observed	• Go beyond what is observed and/or inferred
• Are objective	• Are interpretations of facts	• Are value judgments about facts and inferences
• Seek truth		
	• Claim probability	• Seek justification and agreement

● getting started   ▶ delivery   ◆ speaking to persuade
▲ fundamentals   ∴ engaging your audience   ★ speaking occasions
■ content   ▼ speaking to inform   ✳ resources

Consider why the following edited paragraph from a newspaper editorial requires an understanding of how facts, inferences, and opinions are used to support a position:[3]

> [Opinion] It is a shameful distinction, but [Fact] Texas is the undisputed capital of capital punishment. [Inference] At a time when the rest of the country is having serious doubts about the death penalty, [Facts] as of November 2020 Texas has executed more than 569 people since the death penalty was reinstated in 1976. The state with the second-highest number of executions (113) was Virginia. That [Inference] gaping disparity provides further evidence that [Opinion] Texas's governor, legislature, courts, and votes should reassess their addiction to executions.

The Toulmin Model of Argument

When you create or analyze an argument, it helps to have a clear sense of its structure and components. There are many different models that help us look at and build strong, clear, well-reasoned arguments, but one in particular is especially useful for students of persuasive speaking. Developed in the 1950s by Stephen Toulmin, a philosopher and the author of *The Uses of Argument*, the Toulmin model of argument has become a mainstay in communication studies.[4]

The **Toulmin model of argument** explains that a complete argument requires three fundamental components: a *claim*, *evidence*, and a *warrant*. In many speaking situations, one or more of three additional components— *backing* for the warrant, *reservations*, and *qualifiers*—are also necessary.[5] Regardless of whether you are putting together an argument for a presentation or you are an audience member listening to a speaker make an argument, you should think critically about all of Toulmin's components to determine whether the message is worthy of belief.

Claim

In Toulmin's model, a **CLAIM** answers the question *What is the argument trying to prove?* A claim states the conclusion or position a speaker advocates in a presentation. It is the idea or opinion you want the audience to learn or believe as well as the action you want them to take. For example, a speaker could claim that "fasting is the best and safest way to diet" or that

◆ 352–54

"communication skills are the most important characteristics to look for when recruiting new employees" or that "capital punishment does not deter violent crimes." When developing or analyzing the validity of an argument, your first critical thinking task is to identify the claim.

Evidence

Evidence answers the question *How do you know that?* In a complete argument, you must support and justify a claim by providing evidence for its acceptance. Evidence consists of relevant, verified, and **VALID** facts and supporting material.

120–30 ■

Evidence strengthens and secures belief in an argument. If you claim that millions of Americans cannot afford adequate health insurance, statistics from a reputable source can help justify your claim. If you argue that responsible environmentalists support deer hunting, use reputable testimony and/or statistics to prove your point. If you are trying to demonstrate the benefits of an early diagnosis of diabetes, you may tell two contrasting stories—one about a person with an early diagnosis and one who wasn't diagnosed until the disease had ravaged their body.

Both speakers and audience members should think critically about the quality of evidence used to support a claim by asking five questions:

1. Is the evidence relevant, timely, and specific to this particular claim?
2. Is there enough evidence to justify the claim?
3. Is the evidence understandable to listeners?

121–22 ■

4. Is the source of evidence **IDENTIFIED, CREDIBLE, AND UNBIASED**?

124–26 ■

5. Is the evidence consistent with similar information from **OTHER CREDIBLE SOURCES**?

Thinking critically about the validity of the evidence you use and how audience members will judge the persuasiveness of your presentation can

57–66 ▲

also enhance your **CREDIBILITY** as an ethical speaker.

In addition to the above criteria, make sure your persuasive evidence is *compelling*. What makes evidence compelling? Three things: compelling evidence is *novel*, *believable*, and *dramatic*.

Novel Evidence Evidence that is already so well known that your audience is almost guaranteed to be aware of it often fails to persuade because it doesn't engage an audience's attention, interest, or critical thinking as effectively as new or not widely known evidence. This lesson is not lost on advertisers who change up their ads once a particular version becomes too familiar. Effective persuaders look for fresh new **SUPPORTING MATERIAL**—facts, examples, statistics, and testimony as well as new analogies and stories to engage their audience.

115–19

Believable Evidence If you suspect that audience members will doubt the truth of your evidence, you'll need to bolster its believability. Address the reasons why they may doubt the evidence, and explain its relevance, accuracy, and authority. Provide more examples and testimony. Establish the credibility of your evidence by identifying other respected sources that reach the same conclusion as your **PRIMARY SOURCE**. If the source of your evidence has high credibility, mention the source *before* presenting your evidence in your presentation.

122–23

Dramatic Evidence When using evidence, especially statistics, for a persuasive presentation, find ways to dramatize its importance. Instead of simply saying that your proposal will "save the organization $250,000" during the next year, you could make it sound more dramatic by saying that it will "save a quarter of a million dollars next year, the equivalent of the entire travel budgets of the three largest divisions of the company." Statistics are often more dramatic when they are used in attention-getting comparisons and examples like this one: "Motorists pay twice as much to repair cars damaged by potholes than our government spends to fix the same holes. Why not save motorists money by investing in better road repair?"

Warrant

A **warrant** answers the question *What gives you the right to make that claim based on that evidence?* The warrant explains why the evidence is relevant and how it supports the claim.

The nature of warrants differs in every argument, depending on the rhetorical situation. In some cases, your warrant will establish the credibility of the source of your evidence. In another case, it can explain how a study was conducted. Warrants can identify cause-and-effect relationships, connect signs or symptoms to a phenomenon, draw a connection between one example and other examples in the same class, establish the credibility of a source or speaker, and appeal to the motives, values, and emotions of the audience.

The following illustration shows how the "basic T" of the Toulmin model represents the three fundamental components—claim, evidence, and warrant—of an argument.

THE BASIC "T" OF THE TOULMIN MODEL

EVIDENCE　　　　　　　　　　　　　　　　　(Therefore) **CLAIM**

(Since) **WARRANT**

EXAMPLE OF THE TOULMIN MODEL

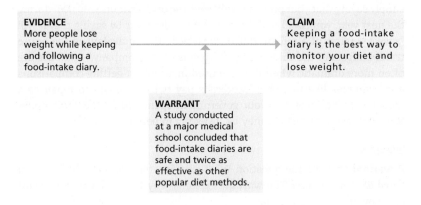

EVIDENCE
More people lose weight while keeping and following a food-intake diary.

CLAIM
Keeping a food-intake diary is the best way to monitor your diet and lose weight.

WARRANT
A study conducted at a major medical school concluded that food-intake diaries are safe and twice as effective as other popular diet methods.

Thus, an argument advocating food diaries might sound something like this:

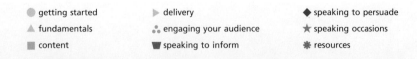

● getting started　　▶ delivery　　◆ speaking to persuade
▲ fundamentals　　⁝⁝ engaging your audience　　★ speaking occasions
■ content　　▼ speaking to inform　　✳ resources

[Evidence] Almost half of all Americans want to lose weight. [Claim] If you're among them, you should keep a food-intake diary. [Warrant] Dr. Nathan Carter, the lead researcher in a medical school study, has reported that patients who kept food-intake diaries were twice as likely to lose weight as were patients who used any other method.

Backing, Reservations, and Qualifiers

In addition to the three primary elements of an argument, there are three supplementary components of the Toulmin model: *backing* (what Toulmin called "support for the warrant"), *reservations*, and *qualifiers*.

Backing certifies the validity of the argument's warrant or provides more data and information justifying it. If audience members question why the warrant should be accepted as the link between the evidence and the claim, backing can be crucial. In the case of the food-intake diary example above, the backing could be in the form of more information about the credibility of the expert cited in the warrant; for example, "Dr. Nathan Carter and his colleagues received two national awards for their contributions to weight-loss research."

Not all claims are true all the time. The **reservation** component of the Toulmin model recognizes exceptions to an argument's claim or indicates that a claim may not be true under certain circumstances. When you acknowledge a reservation, you have anticipated reasonable questions or objections from audience members. Generally, a reservation is expressed by the word *unless*, as in "unless the diet isn't well calibrated or there are genetic or hormonal causes of obesity."

When an argument contains reservations, the speaker should qualify the claim. The **qualifier** states the degree to which a claim appears to be true. Qualifiers usually include the words *probably*, *possibly*, or *likely*. For example, consider this claim with a qualifier: "Unless there are medical reasons for seeking other therapies, using and following a food-intake diary calibrated to your own dietary goals is *probably* the best way to lose weight."

Speakers need qualifiers when the evidence or warrant is less than certain and when audience members are likely to have doubts. Qualifiers can make an argument more acceptable to a skeptical audience. They can also enhance your **CREDIBILITY** as an honest and ethical speaker.

▲ 57–66

The figure below illustrates a six-part model of an argument:

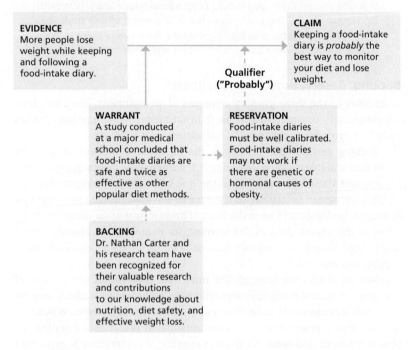

EVIDENCE
More people lose weight while keeping and following a food-intake diary.

CLAIM
Keeping a food-intake diary is *probably* the best way to monitor your diet and lose weight.

Qualifier
("Probably")

WARRANT
A study conducted at a major medical school concluded that food-intake diaries are safe and twice as effective as other popular diet methods.

RESERVATION
Food-intake diaries must be well calibrated. Food-intake diaries may not work if there are genetic or hormonal causes of obesity.

BACKING
Dr. Nathan Carter and his research team have been recognized for their valuable research and contributions to our knowledge about nutrition, diet safety, and effective weight loss.

For an example of arguments employing the components of Toulmin's model, see Notable Speaker: Yassmin Abdel-Magied, page 189.

The Fallacies of Argument

30–31

If you **LISTEN EFFECTIVELY** and think critically about presentations, you will encounter good and bad arguments. Skilled speakers and listeners recognize flawed arguments by identifying fallacies. A **fallacy** is an error in

● getting started
▲ fundamentals
■ content

▶ delivery
⁝ engaging your audience
▼ speaking to inform

◆ speaking to persuade
★ speaking occasions
✳ resources

thinking that has the potential to mislead or deceive others. Fallacies can be intentional or unintentional. However, when an unethical communicator misuses evidence or reasoning, or when a well-meaning speaker misinterprets evidence or draws erroneous conclusions, the result is still the same—inaccuracy and deception.

After you've learned to identify a variety of fallacies, don't be surprised if you begin noticing them everywhere—in television commercials and political campaigns, on social media and talk radio, in podcasts and on YouTube, and in everyday conversations. What, for example, is fallacious about an advertising claim that "no other aspirin is more effective for pain"? (All products labeled *aspirin* are the same; their active ingredient is acetylsalicylic acid.) What about "We're America's best pickup truck"? (Who says? What does "best" mean? Are foreign-brand pickup trucks better?) Is it fallacious when a politician calls an opponent a radical socialist or a corrupt capitalist? (What is meant by "socialist" and "capitalist"? Calling an opponent derogatory names is often used to avoid a discussion about real issues.) What follows are seven of the most common fallacies you'll encounter when reviewing your own arguments and listening to speakers support their claims.

Attacking the Person

The **attacking the person fallacy** has a Latin name—*ad hominem*—which means "against the man." An ad hominem argument makes irrelevant attacks against a person rather than against the content of a person's message. Responding to the claim "Property taxes should be increased in order to properly fund our schools" with "What would you know? You don't own a home!" attacks the person rather than the argument. Name-calling, malicious labeling, and attacking a person rather than the substance of an argument are unethical ad hominem fallacies. Political campaign ads are notorious for attacking candidates in personal ways rather than addressing important public issues. In some cases, such attacks may be justified to expose an opponent's unethical, immoral, and dishonest statements and behavior.

When a speaker is talking about a person's character, intelligence, or credibility in a critical way, you should ask yourself these questions:

- Does the person deserve this negative criticism?
- Is the personal attack a way of distracting the audience or avoiding a discussion of important issues, or is it a relevant critique of the person's credibility?
- How often does the speaker resort to attacking someone else rather than make a coherent argument?
- Is the attack appropriate or excessive?

Appeal to Authority

Expert opinion is often used to support arguments. However, when the supposed expert has no relevant experience on the issues being discussed, the **appeal to authority fallacy** occurs. For example, the advertising pitch "I'm not a doctor, but I play one on TV, and I recommend that you use Nick's Cough Syrup" is a fallacious appeal to authority, unless the actor has expert credentials on medical issues. You often see television and magazine advertisements in which celebrities praise the medicines they use, the companies that insure them, the financial institutions that manage their money, or the beauty products that make them look younger and more attractive. But their authority is only that they are well known, popular, and attractive—not that they bring any special expertise to their claims.

If a speaker is making an appeal to authority, you should ask yourself these questions:

- Does the speaker, or the person the speaker identifies as an authority, have the experience and qualifications to be an expert authority on the subject?
- Who benefits if you believe the authority—listeners or the so-called authority?
- Is the status of the authority a relevant criterion for accepting the argument's claims?

Appeal to Popularity

The **appeal to popularity fallacy**, sometimes also called the *bandwagon appeal*, claims that an action is acceptable or excusable because many people are doing it. Just because a lot of people hold a particular belief or engage in an action does not make it right. If lots of people believe that penicillin can cure your cold, should you ask your physician for a prescription? Instead, it may mean that a lot of people are wrong. A speaker might state or imply that audience members are "out of it," "behind the times," or "not in step" if they fail to join the majority and support a particular issue. If these examples all sound relatively harmless, the bandwagon appeal is also frequently used to justify and recruit people to join hate groups, unscrupulous financial schemes, and illegal actions.

When faced with an appeal based on what many people believe or do, ask yourself these questions:

- Is popularity a relevant criterion for making a decision?
- Is the appeal justified because it's popular?
- What are the disadvantages of following the crowd in this case?

Appeal to Emotions

The **appeal to emotions fallacy** happens when a speaker uses **PATHOS** inappropriately, arousing audience feelings in order to manipulate their attitudes and behaviors or to distract listeners from a bad or nonexistent argument. When appeals to emotions aren't consistent with facts and reasoning, but are a replacement for them, the speaker has unethically chosen to engage in the appeal to emotions fallacy. Obviously, an ethical speaker may arouse justifiable fear, pity, or joy when there *are* circumstances we should fear, tragic situations that arouse sympathy, and good news that elicits happiness. However, when speakers appeal to emotions in order to conceal faulty reasoning, deceive an audience, or provoke unwarranted hatred or violence, their claims should be rejected and condemned.

◆ 357–61

When a speaker makes an appeal to emotions, ask yourself the following questions:

- Are the facts, situations, or stories that arouse emotions true?
- Are the speaker's emotional examples unusual or rare?
- Beyond the emotional appeal, does the speaker include valid arguments with logical supporting evidence, warrants, and claims?
- Can the aroused emotions lead to attitudes, beliefs, and/or actions that harm innocent or trusting people?
- Do the emotional appeals serve the speaker's self-interests only?

Faulty Cause

"We are losing sales because our sales team is not working hard enough." This statement may overlook other causes for low sales, such as a competitor's superior product or a price increase that made the product less affordable. The **faulty cause fallacy** occurs when you claim that a particular situation or event is the cause of another event before ruling out other possible causes. Often this fallacy involves confusing a merely *chronological* sequence of events with a *cause* preceding an *effect*. Just because you catch a cold each year during cold-weather months doesn't mean that the cold weather caused your illness. (A virus is the cause of the common cold, and you are more likely to catch one when spending more time indoors.)

Unfortunately, faulty cause fallacies can be difficult to detect, in part because they're so common. When a speaker attempts to argue a cause-and-effect relationship, you should ask these questions:

- Has the speaker or sources of information identified the *real* cause?
- What else could explain why this happened?
- Are there multiple causes instead of just one?

Hasty Generalizations and Selected Instances

All it takes to commit a **hasty generalization fallacy** is to jump to a conclusion in an inductive argument based on too little evidence or too few experiences. This fallacy argues that if it is true for some, then it must be true for all. "Don't go to that restaurant; I went once, and the service was awful" is a hasty generalization. One negative experience does not mean that other visits to the restaurant would not be enjoyable.

When a speaker is making an inductive argument and generalizing from a set of specific instances, you should ask these questions:

- Is the conclusion based on **ENOUGH DATA** and/or typical **EXAMPLES**?
- Are there a significant number of exceptions to this conclusion?

128–29

117

The related **selected instances fallacy** is more sinister than the hasty generalization fallacy. It occurs when a speaker purposely picks atypical examples to prove an argument. Let's say that you are trying to convince a pro-environmental group that they should help elect a candidate to Congress. You know that the candidate whom you support has a record of voting against environment-friendly initiatives in the state legislature, yet you choose to tell the audience only about the one time their representative voted yes on a pro-environmental bill. In this case, you are using the fallacy of selected instances. Not only is your argument fallacious; it's also unethical.

When a speaker bases their arguments on a limited number of examples, ask yourself these questions:

- Are these rare or infrequent examples?
- How many times has the opposite occurred?
- Why did the speaker choose these particular stories or examples?

Begging the Question

The **begging the question fallacy** is a type of circular reasoning in which the evidence meant to support an argument assumes the claim is true, as in:

> Fortnite (by Epic Games) is the best video game because Epic Games makes the best games and Fortnite is their best game.

Notice that there is no warrant in this argument because the evidence and claim are the same and assumed true. This type of fallacy often shows up when a speaker merely restates a claim by rearranging the ideas—providing a mirror image of the claim itself. Here's another example: "Freedom of speech is one of the central values of open, democratic societies because open, democratic societies value freedom of speech." In *Begging the Question*, Douglas Walton writes that this fallacy uses "deceptive tactics to try to get a respondent to accept something as a legitimate premise that is really not, to slur over the omission, and to disguise the failure of any genuine proof."[6]

When a speaker is making an argument that seems circular, ask these questions:

- Does the argument assume that something unproven is true?
- Does evidence (and warrant, if there is one) sound like the claim itself?

As you think critically about possible fallacies in the arguments you hear or present, keep in mind that there is something known as the **fallacy fallacy**, which is the incorrect assumption that just because an argument is fallacious, its conclusion must be wrong. Even if a speaker has used flawed reasoning to reach a conclusion, there is always a possibility that the conclusion is true. Suppose a speaker claims you should reduce the amount of gluten in your diet because so many people are now buying gluten-free products. The basis for the conclusion is an appeal to popularity fallacy. The number of people "now buying gluten-free products" doesn't prove anything about health benefits. The conclusion, however—that we should consider reducing the amount of gluten in our diets—may be a good one for people with gluten-related sensitivity or ailments.

Conclusion

Developing and analyzing arguments is not an easy task. It requires critical thinking and can be time consuming. It also requires an open mind and a willingness to question both seemingly innocent and controversial claims. What really matters is that both speakers and listeners have the knowledge, skills, and desire to test and, when appropriate, challenge what others say. Understanding the basic types of arguments and the differences among facts, inferences, and opinions is a good first step in becoming an effective, ethical, and credible speaker.

getting started   ▶ delivery   ◆ speaking to persuade
▲ fundamentals   ⁘ engaging your audience   ★ speaking occasions
■ content   ◥ speaking to inform   ✳ resources

The Toulmin model of argument provides a way for speakers and audience members to understand the components of a sound argument—a claim, evidence, and a warrant—and identify arguments that fall short of being believable and valid. In some rhetorical situations, one or more of three additional components may be necessary: backing, reservations, and qualifiers.

Identifying flawed evidence and fallacious arguments may be difficult at first, but this skill is invaluable once you learn how to do so. Assessing the reasoning in your argument's warrant and identifying the need for other argumentative components can make the difference between an argument that achieves or fails to achieve its purpose—that of changing audience attitudes and behavior.

Most speakers and audience members are not unreasonable, even if they disagree. They do, however, owe one another a thoughtful response. Ultimately, your credibility and success as a persuasive speaker depend on your ability to think critically as you create, use, and analyze arguments.

7.3 Rhetorical Strategies for Persuasive Presentations

363–81 ◆

5–10 ●

As important as it is for a speaker to think critically and strategically about arguments, a rock-solid argument won't by itself persuade audience members to change their opinions or behavior. Successful persuasive speakers do more than present a series of **WELL-REASONED ARGUMENTS**. They succeed by strategically developing and organizing their arguments into a coherent persuasive message. This chapter is about how, specifically, to think about and strategically address a **RHETORICAL SITUATION** when your purpose is persuasion. We begin with the most important consideration: your audience.

Consider Your Audience

If you want to change audience members' opinions or behavior, you need to understand something fundamental about human psychology: most people, most of the time, resist change. Why don't we vote for a new candidate who asks for our support? Why don't we buy every product a celebrity or sports star recommends? Why don't most of us follow through on our New Year's resolutions? The answer is summed up with a single word: *inertia*. Most of us, most of the time, choose to stay the course—to do and believe what we've always done and believed. The best way to overcome inertia is through another single word: *desire*. Audience members rarely change their opinions or behavior just because what you've said is reasonable. They must *want* to change. Your job is to explain why the opinions and/or behaviors you advocate are more beneficial and attractive than the ones they currently hold or the actions they currently favor. So how can you accomplish this? Here are several strategies.

● getting started   ▶ delivery   ◆ speaking to persuade

▲ fundamentals   ⁘ engaging your audience   ★ speaking occasions

■ content   ◤ speaking to inform   ✳ resources

Set Reasonable Goals

Effective persuasive speakers seek incremental, achievable changes in audience attitudes and behavior. They rarely ask or expect people to make radical changes after hearing one presentation.

Think about who you were five or ten years ago. You probably held different attitudes than you do now. When did you change your viewpoints? Most likely not overnight. In fact, it probably took a long time. Would-be persuaders often make the mistake of believing they can successfully and significantly change an audience's opinion or behavior with one good presentation. Change often requires a campaign or a series of speeches. Thus, when you develop your arguments, don't try to get people to move from totally against something to totally for something, or vice versa. Instead, help them become less adamant about what they believe and more open to agreeing with you.

Present Two Sides of an Argument

As you plan a persuasive presentation, you may be tempted to tell your audience only your side of the story. After all, won't this keep your listeners focused on your persuasive purpose rather than being distracted by ideas and objections that oppose your arguments? It's a strong temptation, but you should resist it—both for ethical and strategic reasons.

Misleading an audience by presenting only one side of an argument is simply unethical. There may be good reasons that several members of your audience cannot or should not change their opinions or behavior. The wisest and fairest move—and part of the job of being an **ETHICAL SPEAKER**— is to acknowledge opposing sides of an issue.[1]

● 40–41

Does that mean you shouldn't vigorously defend your own perspective? No, of course not. Bringing up other points of view has the strategic value of strengthening the persuasiveness of your appeal. You might say, for instance, "Here is my position. . . . Others may tell you the opposite, so I want to explain why I think the other position is weaker and even unwise." When you acknowledge that legitimate differences of opinion exist, your audience is more likely to see you as trustworthy, convincing, and honest for recognizing other points of view. When your arguments are strong, a two-sided approach can enhance your **CREDIBILITY** and your persuasiveness.

▲ 57–66

Assume that your listeners know there is or must be another side. And yes, explicitly acknowledging that point of view and then arguing against it can be challenging. Effective persuaders meet that challenge head-on, acknowledge that dissenting points of view exist, and use valid 369–73 ◆ CLAIMS, EVIDENCE, AND WARRANTS to address differing opinions. They explain what opponents want you to believe and do and why their arguments and proposals are questionable or flawed. Not only will you be more persuasive by taking this approach, the process of figuring out what the other side might say will make *your* arguments stronger.

Focus on Benefits

Marketers and salespeople draw distinctions among the terms *features, functions,* and *benefits.* For these sales professionals, *features* perform *functions* that generate *benefits,* and *benefits* are what they try to sell.

Think about the image of a car you'd like to own. Like any car, it has four wheels, doors, an engine, and other parts—these are its features. Together, these features get you where you want to go—this is their function. But few people buy a particular car because it has those features and functions. Every car has them. Instead, what sells a car are its benefits. For one buyer, safety, affordability, and a minimal need for repairs might matter the most. For another, prestige, status, and performance might be most important. Smart marketers and salespeople emphasize how the features perform a distinctive function (for example, making the car more reliable or making it feel more luxurious) that produce unique benefits for the buyer.

Skilled persuasive speakers answer their listeners' most basic 77 ▲ question—WHAT'S IN IT FOR ME?—with a **benefits step**, an explicit explanation of how audience members will gain something important by accepting the argument or proposal. In contrast, inexperienced speakers (and unsuccessful salespeople) often spend too much time describing features and not enough time focusing audience attention on how their proposal will benefit them.

Avoid Strong Do and Don't Messages

How would you feel if a speaker got up and declared, "Listen up! I'm here to tell you that what you believe and do is wrong." This kind of statement

---

can trigger a defensive, protective response—"Oh yeah, go ahead and try!"—which makes it much more difficult for a speaker to persuade you to change your beliefs or behavior.

Psychological reactance theory explains why telling an audience what they must and must not do can produce the exact opposite reaction. The theory suggests that when you perceive a threat to your freedom to believe and behave as you wish, you may go out of your way to try the forbidden behavior or to rebel against the prohibiting authority.[2] During the COVID-19 pandemic, this dynamic was part of the reason some people refused to wear a face mask in public despite clear guidance and mandates from public health officials and respected medical experts.

After years of telling young people to "just say no," we have learned that preaching abstinence (from alcohol, drugs, premarital and unprotected sex, or junk food) doesn't work very well. Instead, we're better off recommending behaviors that reduce harms. Organizations devoted to addressing various social problems understand this principle very well. For example, messages advocating the use of designated drivers avoid saying, "Don't drink alcohol." Instead, they suggest that offering to be the sober driver who gets everyone home safely after a night of drinking is something that friends do for one another.

If you believe that your audience may react negatively to your arguments, consider the following strategies as a means of reducing the likelihood of a reactance response:

- Avoid strong, direct commands such as "Don't," "Stop," and "You must."

- Although **FEAR APPEALS** have their value, avoid extreme statements that describe terrible and unrealistic consequences such as "You will die," "You will fail," or "You will be punished."

◆ 357–61

- Avoid finger pointing—literally and figuratively. Don't single out specific audience members for condemnation or harsh criticism.

- Advocate a middle ground that preserves the audience's freedom and dignity while moving them toward attitudinal and/or behavioral change.

- Invite audience members to share their viewpoints and suggestions about a recognized problem so that both you—the speaker—and your listeners gain a better understanding of a complex issue.[3]

Keep in mind that the level of a threat and resulting negative reaction to a message will differ among audience members. However, the above strategies are more likely to produce a positive reaction from most audiences.

Take the Best Route

357–61 ◆
361 ◆
57–66 ▲

Which persuasive appeals are the most effective—those based on EMOTIONS, EVIDENCE AND LOGIC, or SPEAKER CREDIBILITY? The answer is . . . it depends on your audience. The **elaboration likelihood model of persuasion** claims that there are two distinct routes—*central* or *peripheral*—that listeners take when processing a persuasive message. As a speaker, you must decide which persuasive route to take based on an analysis of how willing and able audience members are to process your message.

363–81 ◆

When audience members are very interested and highly motivated to listen to your presentation and are likely to THINK CRITICALLY ABOUT YOUR ARGUMENT, you will be more persuasive if you take a **central route to persuasion**. When you take the central route to persuasion, use strong, valid, and believable evidence to support your claims, as well as acknowledging and arguing against opposing points of view. Highly motivated, critical thinkers tend to counterargue when listening to a persuader. For example, they may think, "I just read an article that proves the opposite" or "That may be fine in Arkansas, but it won't work in New Jersey." These listeners expect direct, reasonable responses to their internal objections.

When audience members are less interested, less motivated, and less likely to think critically, you're better off taking an indirect, **peripheral route to persuasion**. When you take the peripheral route, use evidence and rhetorical strategies that are more personal and less dependent on critical thinking. You should exemplify CONFIDENCE and LIKABILITY to build your credibility because these listeners are highly influenced by whether they like and believe you. Use vivid EXAMPLES and dramatic STORIES to support your arguments and rely on emotional appeals that MOTIVATE THEM TO CARE. You may even take an "everything but the kitchen sink" approach to your arguments when attempting to persuade less motivated, less critical listeners because they often interpret the quantity of a speaker's arguments as more persuasive than the quality of the reasoning.

184–85 ▶
63–65 ▲
117 ■
253–67 ⋰
397–99 ◆

Of course, many audiences are composed of listeners with varying levels of interest, motivation, and critical thinking ability. In such cases,

● getting started　　▶ delivery　　◆ speaking to persuade
▲ fundamentals　　⋰ engaging your audience　　★ speaking occasions
■ content　　▼ speaking to inform　　✳ resources

you're better off using appropriate central *and* peripheral strategies that appeal to a diverse audience—and you'll need to maintain a balance between them. Highly involved critical thinkers may become impatient with your peripheral strategies while less involved audience members may become lost, bored, or annoyed when you present a detailed argument. If possible, you may need to identify one or the other type of listener as your **TARGET AUDIENCE** and appeal primarily to them.

▲ 73

Adapt to Audience Attitudes

Among the many things **AUDIENCE ANALYSIS** can tell you about your listeners (for example, their demographic characteristics and their values), one of the most important is determining the extent to which the majority of members of your audience agrees or disagrees with you. Think about this aspect of your audience's opinions as a value along a continuum from "strongly agree with me" to "strongly disagree with me":

▲ 72–80

CONTINUUM OF AUDIENCE ATTITUDES

Strongly agree with me	Agree	Undecided	Disagree	Strongly disagree with me

When you understand where audience members stand on an issue, you can begin the process of adapting your message to the people you want to persuade.

Persuading Audience Members Who Agree with You People use the expression "preaching to the choir" to imply that there is no reason to persuade a friendly, supportive audience. If they already agree, why try to change their minds? Yet members of the clergy preach to the choir all the time in sermons that rely on shared beliefs. The reason is that the strength and survival of a religious institution and its values lie with faithful members—those who already believe. A good sermon or member's testimony can strengthen that bond by reassuring loyal members that their faith is well founded, encouraging them to stand by their religious beliefs. In much the same way, a persuasive presentation to an audience of "true believers" can build even stronger agreement with the speaker.

You can strengthen your agreeable audience's attitudes and encourage behavioral change by adopting the following strategies:

- *Present new information.* New information and evidence are more persuasive and memorable than old information and familiar evidence. A new piece of confirming data or a new study gives your audience even more confidence in their favorable opinion of your argument. Avoid, as much as you can, repeating what listeners have heard many times before. At best, the old stuff may simply bore them; at worst, you may undermine the strength of their support.

117–18
137–38
242
184

- *Excite your audience's emotions.* Use **EXAMPLES AND STORIES** related to your **CENTRAL IDEA** that stimulate your audience's feelings of attachment to you and your position. Use **VIVID LANGUAGE** and **EXPRESSIVE DELIVERY** to demonstrate that the opinions you share are not only justified but compelling and inspiring too.

- *Provide a personal role model.* Strengthen your credibility by telling your listeners what you have seen or done. Talk about the volunteer work you did for a nonprofit organization that landed you a permanent job, or how you've successfully saved and invested your earnings. Explain how you overcame a serious problem or personal hardship to become who you are today. Tell them how supporting a particular cause has made a positive difference in your life and the lives of others.

- *Advocate a course of action.* If your listeners agree with you in principle but haven't yet changed their behavior, explain why and how they should pursue a specific course of action (sign a petition, vote for a particular candidate, change their eating habits, volunteer at a food bank).

Finally, when speaking to listeners who already agree with you, consider giving them an **inoculation**. According to social psychologist William McGuire, protecting audience attitudes from counterpersuasion by the other side is like inoculating the body against disease.[4] You can build up audience resistance by exposing flaws in the arguments of the opposition and showing listeners how to refute those arguments. Researchers have documented the power of inoculation in many contexts—from opposing political attack messages to preventing youths from joining

● getting started   ▶ delivery   ◆ speaking to persuade
▲ fundamentals   ⁚• engaging your audience   ★ speaking occasions
■ content   ◥ speaking to inform   ✳ resources

gangs. Inoculation works best when audience members care about an issue because it makes them aware that their attitudes are vulnerable to attack, and then provides ammunition against or resistance to the attack.[5] It also creates a more enduring change in attitudes or behavior.

Persuading Audience Members Who Disagree with You Audiences that are likely to disagree with you won't necessarily be hostile or rude, but persuading them is a challenge. When audience members disagree with you, they have—at least in their own minds—good reasons for doing so. Understanding what those reasons are and how your listeners have come by those opinions is the first step in persuading them to consider a different point of view. Good **AUDIENCE ANALYSIS** will help you get there.

▲ 72–80

Generally, it's a good idea to start with points of agreement with your audience. Standing with your listeners on **COMMON GROUND**— a place where both you and your audience can agree—is often the key to persuading audience members who don't share your opinions, values, or beliefs. If you can get listeners to nod their heads early in your presentation, they will be predisposed to listen to your arguments when you get to points of disagreement. Savvy speakers often start their presentations by raising ideas and issues that get people saying yes. In persuasion research, this strategy is called the "foot-in-the-door method." Persuaders get listeners to agree to something minor, and then they get them to agree to something just a bit bigger, and so on until listeners are agreeing with a speaker's major claims. Charities are famous for using this strategy. Send a charity five dollars, and next time you'll be asked to give ten or fifteen dollars. Give ten dollars, and the charity will come back asking for twenty.

▲ 71

Here are some additional strategies for persuading audience members who may disagree with you:

- *Set achievable goals.* Do not expect listeners to change their opinions or behavior radically. Even a small step taken in your direction can eventually add up to a big change. Sometimes just getting an audience to listen to you is a victory.

- *Accept and adapt to differences of opinion.* Acknowledge the legitimacy of your audience's opinions and give them credit for defending their principles. Demonstrate respect for their viewpoint before asking them to respect yours. Use a two-sided message in which you explain or compare two viewpoints and also show the superiority of your position.

120–30 ■

- *Use fair and respected evidence.* Make sure your **SUPPORTING MATERIAL** is solid—true, verifiable, and unambiguous. Choose evidence from respected, unbiased sources.

57–66 ▲

- *Build your personal credibility.* Do everything you can to establish and build your **CREDIBILITY** over the course of your presentation. Positive feelings about you can transfer to positive feelings about your message.

Persuading Indecisive Audience Members Some indecisive audience members may not have an opinion about your topic because they are *uninformed*, *undecided*, or *unconcerned*. Whereas an **uninformed audience** is fairly easy to persuade because all they lack is strong, relevant information about an issue, an **undecided audience** has often given the issue a great deal of thought. They understand both sides of the issues and want to stay right where they are—in the middle. When speaking to an **unconcerned audience**, whose members, for whatever reason, aren't particularly interested in or don't appreciate the importance of an issue, you need to give them a reason to listen and care. Knowing which type of persuasive strategy to apply in each case depends on the reasons for indecision.

STRATEGIES FOR PERSUADING INDECISIVE AUDIENCE MEMBERS

For the uninformed	For the undecided	For the unconcerned
• Gain their attention and interest. • Present relevant and compelling information.	• Acknowledge the legitimacy of different viewpoints. • Provide new information or a different interpretation of familiar information. • Emphasize or reinforce the strength of arguments on one side of the issue.	• Gain their attention and interest. • Give them a personal reason to listen and care. Touch their emotions. • Present novel, believable, and dramatic information and evidence.

In the following example, a college student began her presentation on the importance of voting by getting the attention of unconcerned students and giving them a reason to pay attention:

> How many of you applied for some form of financial aid for college? [*More than half the class raised their hands.*] How many of you got the full amount you applied for or needed? [*Less than one-fourth of the class raised their hands.*] I have some bad news for you. Financial aid may be even more difficult to get in the future. But the good news is that there's something you can do about it.

In the real world of persuasive speaking, you will probably face audiences with some members who agree with your message, others who don't, and still others who are indecisive. In such cases, you can focus your persuasive efforts on just one group, your target audience—the largest, most influential, or easiest to persuade—or you can seek common ground among all three types of audiences.

Adapt to Culturally Diverse Audiences

If you are speaking to a culturally diverse audience, you should do your best to understand, respect, and **ADAPT** to the various ways your audience may respond. You can improve the likelihood of achieving the purpose of your persuasive presentation if you adapt the content and structure of your message to the different ways audiences process information.

▲ 80–82

The United States is the most individualistic culture in the world. Many audience members will value personal freedom and achievements—a "me" orientation—above all else. In collectivist, "we"-oriented cultures (traditionally, Asian and Latin American countries as well as some cocultures in the United States fall in this category), audience members are more likely to be persuaded by appeals that value group identity, selflessness, and collective action.[6] Whereas appeals that benefit "me"—personal wealth, personal success, personal health and fitness—may be highly persuasive in the United States, "we" appeals that benefit society and families may be more effective in collectivist cultures.

There is also a difference in how cultures interpret verbal and nonverbal messages. In the United States, the United Kingdom, Germany, Scandinavian

140–41 ■

countries, and Switzerland, for example, audiences generally expect and comprehend messages that are clear, factual, and objective. Words are valued and believed. For example, persuasive appeals in a highly verbal culture are often direct—do this, buy that, drink this, avoid that, just do it! In advertising, this would be termed a *hard-sell* approach to persuasion. The **PROBLEM-SOLUTION ORGANIZATIONAL PATTERN** characterizes this kind of thinking.

In contrast, audiences in China, Korea, Japan, other Asian countries, and most Latin American countries expect messages that are implied and situation specific. Nonverbal behavior is valued and believed more than words. Here, a soft-sell approach is a more appropriate persuasive strategy. When addressing this kind of audience, encourage listeners to draw their own conclusions. Demonstrate benefits and advantages rather than advocating or demanding action. Make sure that your verbal and nonverbal messages are consistent with each other. When addressing this kind of audience, a **COMPARATIVE ADVANTAGES** or **PERSUASIVE STORIES** organizational approach may be more persuasive.

394–95 ◆
396 ◆

Differences among cultures are very real. At the same time, be cautious about how you interpret and use this information. Are all Japanese listeners "we" focused and highly sensitive to nonverbal behavior? Of course not. Are all Americans aggressive "me" speakers? No. Also remember that within the United States, there are cocultures (Native Americans, African Americans, Hispanic/Latino Americans, Asian Americans, and various religious groups) whose members may be as sensitive to nonverbal messages as audience members from other countries.

Effective persuasive speakers devote extra time and energy investigating the attitudes, beliefs, values, and thinking patterns of a culture before speaking in order to ensure that they understand, respect, and do their best to adapt to their listeners.

Test Your Thinking on Others

At times, all of us have deluded ourselves about something we strongly believe. As speakers, we also make flawed decisions about presentations. We may believe that everyone in the audience will be glued to every word we say, exhibiting high levels of interest and agreement. Experienced speakers avoid such self-deception by testing and retesting their messages on others.

The members of a "test" audience, even if only one or two people, who read or listen to your presentation for the very first time may have simple but important **FEEDBACK**—observations and questions that can help improve your presentation. They may be confused by a complex or abstract idea, may be unwilling to accept a claim or argument you think is foolproof, may feel manipulated by an argument or proposal, or may be upset by an inappropriate example or word. If your test audience doesn't have an immediate reaction, ask questions. In their opinion, what was your **CENTRAL IDEA**? At what points were they the most interested, bored, supportive, or suspicious? Were there any words they didn't understand? How effective was your **DELIVERY**? How engaging were your **PRESENTATION AIDS**?

● 33–34

■ 137–38
▶ 184–86
•• 282–305

You don't have to adopt every suggestion or respond to every objection, but you should consider their reactions seriously. At the same time, you may be delighted to discover that you've made excellent strategic decisions and that your work in progress is ready to go.

Use Persuasive Organizational Patterns

No matter what sort of presentation you're delivering, clear, easy-to-follow **ORGANIZATION** is of paramount importance if you hope to achieve your **PURPOSE**. The strategic decisions you make about organizing your message will affect its persuasiveness. Here we describe several organizational patterns that are particularly effective in persuasive presentations: *problem-cause-solution, comparative advantages, refuting objections, persuasive stories,* and *Monroe's motivated sequence.*

■ 138–48
▲ 87–101

Problem-Cause-Solution

A speaker organizes a persuasive presentation in the **problem-cause-solution** pattern (which is similar to the **PROBLEM-SOLUTION ARRANGEMENT**) by first identifying a significant *problem*, then explaining why the problem exists or continues (the *cause*), and finally recommending a *solution*. This organizational pattern works best when you are proposing a specific course

■ 140–41

of action and need to justify why the solution you propose addresses the cause or causes of the problem. In the following outline, the speaker uses a problem-cause-solution organizational pattern to focus on the need for improving public education in the United States:[7]

Problem

A. American public school scores are falling behind those in other countries.
   1. The United States ranks 37th out of 79 countries in math and 18th in science.
   2. China, Hong Kong, Singapore, Poland, Canada, Estonia, Finland, Slovenia, and others consistently outperform the United States.

Causes

B. The United States lags behind for several reasons.
   1. American students spend fewer days and hours in school than students in other countries.
   2. US teacher training programs are inadequate, and teacher evaluation systems are ineffective.
   3. Inequality in US public schools stems from state variations in property tax bases and teacher salaries.

Solution

C. Rigorous, national education standards for students, teachers, and instructional resource levels can significantly improve public education.
   1. Similar plans work well in other modern countries.
   2. National education standards can improve the quality and equity of public schools.

Comparative Advantages

The **comparative advantage** pattern is useful when your audience already agrees there is a significant problem or unmet goal (for example, to improve health care, reduce childhood obesity, or minimize computer hacking). This type of organizational pattern first describes your plan and then shows that your proposal will do a better job solving the problem or achieving a goal than other plans. It also shows that when compared to other plans, there are more advantages than disadvantages to your plan.

getting started   ▶ delivery   ◆ speaking to persuade
▲ fundamentals   ∴ engaging your audience   ★ speaking occasions
■ content   ▼ speaking to inform   ❋ resources

In the following outline, a speaker contends that an extended hunting season is a more advantageous way of reducing the serious problems caused by the growing deer population. After presenting a plan to reduce the deer population, each subpoint in the second key point explains how the plan will achieve the goal of reducing the deer population better than the regulations and laws that are currently in place.

A. There is a plan that will help reduce the deer population.   *Plan*

   1. The deer-hunting season should be extended.

   2. States should allow hunters to kill more female deer.

B. This plan will reduce the severity of the problem.   *Comparative Advantages*

   1. It will save millions of dollars now lost from crop, garden, and forest seedling damage.

   2. It will reduce the number of deer ticks carrying Lyme disease.

   3. It will reduce the number of automobile deaths and injuries caused by deer crossing highways.

Refuting Objections

Sometimes audience members agree there is a problem or difficult-to-make decision but are reluctant to do anything about it because they view your proposal as objectionable, risky, expensive, or difficult to do. Other audience members may come prepared to reject your persuasive message before hearing it because they are adamantly opposed, uninformed, or misinformed about the situation. The **refuting objections** pattern addresses these concerns and doubts by structuring a presentation that explicitly refutes or overcomes beliefs and attitudes that stand in opposition to your purpose.

This organizational pattern begins by framing the problem: *Why don't (or won't) many people . . . wear a protective face mask during an epidemic / visit a foreign country / vote for [name of candidate]?* Then it spells out the most common objections that prevent people from taking the desired action. The final section refutes the objections with strong, vivid evidence. In the following example, the speaker uses the refuting objections organizational pattern to encourage listeners to donate blood:

Problem —○ A. People should give blood but often don't.

    1. Most people think that giving blood is a good idea.

    2. Most people don't give blood.

Objections —○ B. There are several reasons people don't give blood.

    1. They're afraid of pain and needles.

    2. They're afraid that they could get a disease from giving blood.

    3. They claim that they don't have time or know where to give blood.

Refutation —○ C. These reasons should not deter you from giving blood.

    1. There is little or no pain in giving blood.

    2. You can't *get* a disease by *giving* blood.

    3. The Red Cross makes it easy and convenient to give the gift of life by scheduling blood donation clinics in many locations.

Persuasive Stories

253–67 ..
133–36 ■

357–61 ◆

STORIES capture and hold an audience's interest and can serve as a form of persuasive proof. Stories can also be used as the **KEY POINTS** in a persuasive presentation. When using the **persuasive stories** organizational pattern, you rely on **EMOTIONAL PROOF** to show how people, events, and objects are affected by the change you are seeking. This organizational pattern can be an effective way to present a persuasive speech to neutral audience members who are uninformed or are unable or unwilling to listen critically.

The following speaker uses a series of stories as the key points to convince an audience to support programs designed to help political refugees:

Stories —○ A. The stories of three refugee families demonstrate the need for and the value of migration ministries.

    1. Story of Letai Teku and her family (Cambodia)

    2. Story of Peter Musooli and his sister (Ethiopia)

    3. Story of Naser Rugova and his family (Kosovo)

Outcome —○ B. More support for migration ministries can save even more families who are fleeing foreign tyranny and persecution.

● getting started   ▶ delivery   ◆ speaking to persuade

▲ fundamentals   .. engaging your audience   ★ speaking occasions

■ content   ▼ speaking to inform   ✳ resources

Monroe's Motivated Sequence

In the mid-1930s, communication professor Alan Monroe at Purdue University took the basic steps of a sales pitch and transformed them into a method for organizing persuasive presentations. This five-step pattern soon became known as **Monroe's motivated sequence**.[8] Although Monroe's model incorporates aspects of the previously described organizational patterns, it specifically emphasizes the importance of motivating an audience to do something that will benefit them—and perhaps others. This organizational pattern has five sequential steps: *attention, need, satisfaction, visualization,* and *action*.

1. *Attention.* You gain audience attention and interest by using one or more of the methods recommended in previous chapters for creating effective **INTRODUCTIONS** to a presentation and **ENGAGING YOUR AUDIENCE**. This step is also an opportunity to build your **CREDIBILITY**.

2. *Need.* You describe a serious problem that needs to be solved or minimized. Most importantly, explain how this situation affects your audience. This is also a good place to put in a **VALUE STEP**. Frequently used in informative presentations, a value step explains why a particular problem or issue should matter to your listeners, why they should care about how it affects others, and how solving it could lead to greater well-being and success. Use the words *you* and *your* throughout this section. Emphasize the negative consequences of what will happen if the problem isn't solved.

3. *Satisfaction.* You propose a plan that will solve or minimize the problem you described in the need step. Explain why your plan is realistic, relevant, and workable, as well as why it is better than alternative plans. In some cases, you may need to address objections the audience has to your proposal.

4. *Visualization.* You help listeners envision the positive outcome of accepting the plan or recommendations you described in the satisfaction step. Visualization is unique to Monroe's motivated sequence. Ask the audience to picture what their future will be like with—and without—your proposed solution. Use

161–69
235–305
57–66

311–13

242
357–61

VIVID LANGUAGE and powerful **EMOTIONAL APPEALS** as well as inclusive pronouns (*you*, *your*, *we*, and *us*) to help listeners see themselves in the community of people enjoying the benefits of your proposal in the future. The visualization step makes this organizational pattern particularly useful for audience members who are uninformed, unconcerned, and unmotivated to listen or for listeners who are skeptical of or opposed to the proposed course of actions.

5. *Action.* Always end with a **call for action**. Tell the audience exactly what to do. Remind your listeners why this action is necessary and how it will affect them in positive ways. A call to action should be concrete, achievable, and memorable, not wishy-washy or theoretical. Calls to action can ask an audience to donate money, sign a petition, raise their hands in agreement, join a club, register to vote, eat less salt, or tell someone else what they've just heard. A poor call-to-action dilutes the power of a persuasive presentation; a great call-to-action stirs your audience to act enthusiastically and to remember you and your message. End your call for action with an inspiring, compelling, and memorable **CONCLUSION**.

169–75

In the following example, a speaker uses Monroe's motivated sequence to organize the key points of a presentation about the devastating effects of worldwide pollution and climate change by beginning with a description of the slow destruction of the Great Barrier Reef in Australia, expanding it to similar problems closer to home, and concluding with a concrete and specific call to action.

Attention　　A. Stories, examples, statistics, and testimony about Australia's Great Barrier Reef

　　　1. My amazing trip to the Great Barrier Reef
　　　2. Descriptions of corals, marine life, and water quality
　　　3. Examples of similar sites near where the audience lives

Need　　B. Pollution and climate change are destroying beautiful and precious natural wonders.

　　　1. The Great Barrier Reef is being destroyed at a rapid pace.

⬤ getting started　　▶ delivery　　◆ speaking to persuade
▲ fundamentals　　∴ engaging your audience　　★ speaking occasions
■ content　　◥ speaking to inform　　✳ resources

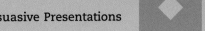

   2. Other natural wonders are being destroyed.
   3. Our cities and towns, homes, national and state parks, lakes and seashores, farmland, and natural wildlife are in imminent danger.

C. What can you do to reduce pollution and climate change?   *Satisfaction*

   1. Reduce your carbon footprint and reliance on fossil fuels.
   2. Ride a bike or walk rather than driving short distances.
   3. Donate money or your time to organizations dedicated to saving the planet from pollution and climate change.
   4. Support candidates and elected officials who promise to protect the environment from pollution and climate change.

D. Imagine a world with less pollution and decreasing climate change.   *Visualization*

   1. Envision the Great Barrier Reef as well as forests, public parks, productive farmland, and clean rivers and lakes in all their beauty.
   2. Picture clean beaches, reduced forest fires, new national and state parks, fewer droughts and floods, and secure, healthy food supplies.
   3. Foresee generations of children swimming with Nemo and the turtles on a preserved reef.

E. Act now to make our world less polluted and less devastated by climate change.   *Action*

   1. Do at least one small thing every day to reduce environmental damage. Tell your family, friends, and coworkers to do the same.
   2. Join and support organizations dedicated to the cause. Write letters to the editors of news agencies and informational websites.
   3. Contact candidates and elected officials and urge them to enact laws and regulations that will significantly decrease the negative effects of pollution and climate change.

NOTABLE SPEAKER
Ron Finley

In 2010, Ron Finley decided to do something about the "food desert" (a neighborhood with insufficient access to nutritious food) in his South Central Los Angeles community. He began by planting a garden in an unused patch of dirt, the parkway between the sidewalk of his house and the road. When the city of Los Angeles fined him for improper use of the parkway, which is owned by the city and not Finley, he fought back and began his journey toward activism on a grander scale. In 2013, he shared his urban gardening experience on the TED stage. Shortly thereafter, he launched the Ron Finley Project with a focus on community gardening and rejuvenation. With the support of several natural foods companies, the project's goal is to create communities "where gardening is gangsta, where cool kids know their nutrition and where communities embrace the act of growing, knowing and sharing the best of the earth's fresh-grown food."[9]

Search Terms

To locate a video of this presentation online, enter the following key words into a search engine: Ron Finley TED talk. The video is approximately 10:45 in length.

What to Watch For

Finley uses several persuasive speaking strategies to address his audience. Initially, most audience members know very little about him or the project he champions. He also knows that his audience isn't going to rise up and join his movement with seeds and shovels in hand. But they and the millions of people who watch his TED talk might become supporters of his cause—which is his primary purpose.

Finley's success depends in large part on his ethos. He exhibits confidence, trustworthiness, likability, and dynamism—the hallmarks of credibility. He uses many kinds of evidence—enhanced by powerful presentation aids—that are novel, believable, and dramatic. His language makes his talk memorable: "food desert"; "gangsta gardener"; "growing your own food is like printing money."

Finley's presentation is also an example of how Monroe's motivated sequence can stimulate, inspire, and persuade an audience. His final call to action combines clear, oral, rhetorical, and eloquent language that brings the audience to its feet in an ovation.

[0:00–1:00] Finley begins his talk with a powerful introduction, a model of persuasion in itself, that puts him right in the middle of the story: "I live in South Central," he says, and then shows and describes three slides: "liquor stores, fast food, vacant lots." He explains that an attempt to change the name of South Central to South Los Angeles will look the same: "liquor stores, fast food, vacant lots." Then he cites a statistic also shown on a large slide: "Just like 26.5 million other Americans, I live in a food desert. South Central Los Angeles, home of the drive-through and the drive-by." His short sentences, ironic use of slides, and stand-out statistics gain attention, set the mood, connect to his audience, and announce his topic.

[1:00–1:49] Finley highlights the gravity of the situation by explaining that drive-throughs are killing more people than drive-bys: the food options available to his neighbors have led to an obesity rate (which correlates with public health issues such as diabetes and heart disease) in his neighborhood that is five times higher than it is in wealthy Beverly Hills. His claims rely on dramatic evidence that shows how different life can be for people who live no more than ten miles apart from one another.

(NOTABLE SPEAKER CONTINUED)

[1:40–2:07] Finley expresses his frustration at seeing the health effects of poor nutrition on his community. He evokes audience emotions by expressing his dismay about how wheelchairs are bought and sold like used cars. Rather than relying solely on statistics, he describes the situation using pathos and powerful examples. He then says, "This has to stop. So I figured that the problem is the solution." [A slide appears: Food is the problem and the solution.] Then he repeats: "Food is the problem and food is the solution." There is no mistaking his claim.

[2:07–3:39] Finley's ethos is rooted in his personal experience with urban farming. "So what I did," he says, "I planted a food forest in the front of my house. It was on a strip of land that we call a parkway." He shows two before-and-after slides to clarify what he means. He then tells the story of fighting city government, which first issued a citation and then a warrant for gardening on city-owned land. He won the fight, received media recognition, and garnered the support of a councilman in the process.

[3:40–7:28] Within his story about fighting the city government, he explains that the city owns the equivalent of twenty Central Parks in vacant lots, which is enough space to plant 725 million tomato plants. "Why the hell would they not okay this?" he asks. Finley skillfully uses facts, stories, examples, definitions, statistics, presentation aids, analogies, and metaphors ("I'm an artist. Gardening is my graffiti. I grow my art.") to support his arguments.

[7:28–8:37] Turning his attention to the benefits of what he calls "gangsta gardening," he says, "Growing your own food is like printing your own money." Finley notes that kids eat kale when they grow kale, and eating food that they grow helps them to understand the impact that food has on the mind and body. Beyond being able to eat what they grow, Finley explains that gardening gives kids an opportunity to take over their communities and to live a sustainable life. The ultimate benefit might just be that the next George Washington Carver will be produced out of kids who are gangsta gardeners—a benefit that would reach beyond Finley's immediate community.

EXERCISE

After viewing Finley's speech, reflect on these questions:

1. What does Finley do to enhance his credibility? Does he succeed? To what extent does his credibility function as a persuasive appeal?

2. Identify examples of how and where Finley uses emotional appeals in his presentation.

3. In what ways does Finley focus on the benefits of his project for people in South Central and/or benefits for the audience?

4. Which elaboration likelihood model route to persuasion does Finley use? Is it the "best route"?

5. How successfully does Finley use the sequential steps of Monroe's motivated sequence? Identify where they occur in his presentation.

6. Do you think Finley's audience will modify their opinions and/or behavior as a result listening to his presentation? Why or why not?

7. In what ways, if any, could Finley have improved the content and delivery of his presentation?

Conclusion

Persuasive speaking is a challenging and consequential task. Great speeches have changed people's minds and behaviors in significant ways. They have motivated people to support political candidates and deepen their faith in a religion or cause, and they have rallied citizens and troops in times of war and public emergencies. Most persuasive presentations do not seek or achieve such lofty goals. But they *can* modify thinking and make significant, beneficial changes in the daily lives of many people.

Because your success as a persuasive speaker depends on whether or not members of your audience change their opinions or behavior in response to your presentation, your work should begin with careful analysis and adaptation to your audience. Many audience-centered persuasive speaking strategies apply in all rhetorical situations: having a clear persuasive purpose, setting reasonable goals, and acknowledging opposing points of view. Other decisions will depend on what your audience analysis tells you about your listeners' attitudes (whether they agree or disagree with you) and their level of interest, engagement, and critical listening ability. Whatever you learn about your audience, persuasion begins with knowing what they currently believe and then adapting your presentation to that reality in order to achieve a realistic persuasive goal.

Another key consideration for persuasive speakers is organization. In addition to the commonly used organizational patterns that apply to all sorts of speaking occasions, there are several formats that are particularly well suited for persuasive presentations. As you analyze all aspects of the rhetorical situation, consider whether or which of the following patterns can help you achieve your purpose: problem-cause-solution, comparative advantages, refuting objections, persuasive stories, and Monroe's motivated sequence.

Regardless of how you organize your persuasive presentation, remember that the basic principles of organization apply to all types of speeches: identify your key points and central idea; choose an appropriate organizational pattern; sequence your key points strategically; connect your key points to help your audience follow, understand, and remember your message; and deliver your presentation in a manner that demonstrates expressiveness, confidence, stage presence, and immediacy.

● getting started　▶ delivery　◆ speaking to persuade
▲ fundamentals　∴ engaging your audience　★ speaking occasions
■ content　▼ speaking to inform　✳ resources

Part 8

Special Speaking Occasions

Every presentation occurs at a specific *time* and *place* using a particular *medium*, and there is always one or more *reasons* why an audience assembles to hear it. These four factors constitute the presentation's *occasion*. The audience on certain occasions will have specific expectations about what you will say and how you should say it. Being aware of and adapting to these expectations is essential to your success as a speaker. The chapters that follow describe the key features of ten special speaking occasions and suggest helpful guidelines and tips that are specific to each one.

Special Speaking Occasions

8.1 Impromptu Speeches

Impromptu speeches—presentations for which a speaker has little or no preparation or practice time—are common. In some cases, they are so informal and casual you may not recognize them as a presentation. When you've just returned from a vacation and your friend says, "Tell me about your trip!," you're being asked to speak impromptu. How will you answer? By focusing on three highlights? By describing the trip day by day? Or maybe by explaining *why* you wanted to take the trip in the first place? However you approach your answer, you have only a few moments to decide what you will say and how you will say it.

Now imagine yourself at a public meeting or rally. You disagree with one of the speakers, and the floor is opened for audience comments. How will you explain and express your disagreement? What's your purpose and central idea? And can you make these decisions right before or as you are beginning to speak?

In each of these situations and many others—being asked by your professor to share your opinion in class, or by your boss to summarize a sales report with no advance warning, or by a panel of interviewers to describe your career accomplishments, to name just a few—the response you make will be an impromptu speech.

Key Features

Impromptu Speeches Require Quick Thinking

The major difference between impromptu speeches and other kinds of presentations is that you have little or no time to prepare and practice an impromptu speech. You must quickly determine what you will say. More than anything else, you should determine your **PURPOSE** and **CENTRAL IDEA**—what do you want your audience to know, believe, or do as a result

▲ 87–101
■ 137–38

● getting started   ▶ delivery   ◆ speaking to persuade
▲ fundamentals   ∴ engaging your audience   ★ speaking occasions
■ content   ▼ speaking to inform   ✳ resources

of listening to you speak? This kind of critical quick thinking continues throughout your impromptu speech until you've said your final word.

Impromptu Speeches Can Significantly Enhance Your Credibility

57–66 ▲

Impromptu speaking situations can be challenging and stressful, but they also provide opportunities to build your **CREDIBILITY**. If your impromptu speech demonstrates you are competent, trustworthy, likable, and dynamic, your listeners will not only be impressed and persuaded in the moment, but they will also be more willing to accept and remember your message if you speak to them in the future.

Impromptu Speeches Don't Need to Be Polished or Perfect, but They Should Be Personal

186 ▶

Impromptu speaking works best when a speaker's delivery is **IMMEDIATE**, friendly, and genuine. Your audience won't expect a polished or professional delivery (in fact, they might distrust an impromptu speaker who seems too polished), but they will appreciate (and you will benefit) if your delivery is focused on making a genuine personal connection with them.

A Brief Guide to Impromptu Speaking

Consider the Rhetorical Situation

5–6 ●

OCCASION Impromptu speaking occurs in response to an on-the-spot prompt or question from someone: a teacher may ask you to explain your answer to a discussion question, your boss may request a quick summary of your department's work on a project, or your friends may ask you to tell a story about an adventure you had. Your response needs to be immediate (that is, you're being asked to speak *right now*) and generally should be brief.

55–69 ▲
307–46 ▼
253–67 ∴
235–305 ∴

SPEAKER Consider your speaking strengths. Are you most comfortable and confident when **PRESENTING FACTS AND INFORMATION**? Telling **STORIES**? Sharing quotations or summarizing other people's expert opinions? **ENGAGING AUDIENCE MEMBERS**? Whatever your particular strengths might

● getting started   ▶ delivery   ◆ speaking to persuade
▲ fundamentals   ∴ engaging your audience   ★ speaking occasions
■ content   ▼ speaking to inform   ✳ resources

be, lean on them. An effective impromptu speech rests on a foundation of **CONFIDENCE**. Sticking to what you know and what you do well is the best way to build that foundation.

▶ 184–85

AUDIENCE Because you will have no time to prepare and practice, adapting an impromptu speech to your audience happens in real time, right before and as you are speaking. If your listeners are colleagues, classmates, or friends whom you already know, you may do a quick **AUDIENCE ANALYSIS**, reminding yourself of what you already know about their characteristics, attitudes, beliefs, and values. But mostly, you will need to use your senses and your judgment to gauge how your listeners are responding while you speak. Observe and listen to them carefully before and while you are speaking, and try to adapt to their **FEEDBACK**.

▲ 70–86

▲ 72–80

● 33–34

▲ 87–101

PURPOSE Unlike other sorts of presentations for which you have time to prepare and practice, determining the purpose of an impromptu speech must happen immediately. It all boils down to answering this question: *What do I want my audience to learn, believe, or do as a result of this speech?* It might help to frame your purpose as a phrase or slogan you can say and repeat with ease. For example, if you oppose the construction of a 300-foot-tall condominium in a community of small homes, your purpose may be "to persuade audience members that the proposed 300-foot-tall condominium is too darn high." The phrase "too darn high" could then be used throughout your presentation: as a warning that traffic will increase because it's too darn high, that it will ruin the open skyline because it's too darn high, and that it sets a bad precedent because it's too darn high.

CONTENT Once you have decided on your purpose, spend the few seconds (or, if you're lucky, minutes) you have before speaking to identify **KEY POINTS** and **SUPPORTING MATERIAL** that will bolster your purpose. Use a simple organizational format (there are a few suggested below) to arrange your ideas. Consider beginning with a **STORY** you know well that will engage audience interest and/or emotions.

■ 103–79

■ 133–36

■ 115–19

⁂ 253–67

DELIVERY The qualities of effective delivery (expressiveness, confidence, stage presence, and immediacy) apply to impromptu speaking just as much

▶ 181–33

as they do to any other type of rhetorical situation. But don't worry—most audiences do not expect you to be polished when speaking impromptu. Most important is to maintain frequent **EYE CONTACT** with your listeners and adopt a relaxed, **OPEN POSTURE** while speaking so you connect with them and are sensitive to their responses as you speak.

210–12
216–17

Anticipate Impromptu Speaking Situations

In some rhetorical situations, you might know in advance that you could be called on to speak impromptu. If you see that happening, take time, to think about what you might say. If, at an upcoming staff meeting, you may be asked to bring everyone up to date about a project you're managing, consider how you could organize the content of your answer. If you attend a public meeting where a controversial issue will be discussed, think about how you would express your opinion if given the opportunity to speak. Be ready to talk about ideas and information you already know about the topic. Are there facts, examples, stories, memorized quotations, or other **SUPPORTING MATERIALS** you can use? Can you share what you've learned from a book, news or social media site, or a friend? A couple of examples and a good story may be all you need to support your **CENTRAL IDEA** in an impromptu speech.

115–19
137–38

Apply a Ready-to-Use Organizational Pattern

A clear, easy-to-follow **ORGANIZATION** is indispensable to an effective impromptu speech. Although you don't have much time to think about how to organize your presentation, you might consider one of the following simple organizational patterns.

138–48

Past, Present, Future This pattern uses **TIME ARRANGEMENT** as its organizing principle. For example, if someone were to ask you to speak impromptu about the value of a college education, you might begin by explaining that at the turn of the twentieth century, a college education was not necessary for most jobs and was something only the rich and gifted could afford to pursue. However, by the end of the last century, jobs that once required only a high-school diploma required at least a college degree. In this century and beyond, our best hope for prosperity in a more competitive world

139–40

● getting started   ▶ delivery   ◆ speaking to persuade
▲ fundamentals   ∴ engaging your audience   ★ speaking occasions
■ content   ▼ speaking to inform   ✳ resources

is a college-educated work force. Time arrangement can be as focused as yesterday, today, and tomorrow or as far reaching as from the Stone Age to the post-pandemic era.

Me, My Friend, and You In this pattern, you begin by explaining how the topic affects or has affected you, tell how it affects or has affected another person, and conclude with how it can affect your audience. For example, if you're advocating the importance of a college education, you can start with your own story—why you went to college, what you have gained from your experience, and why you like or liked it. Then you can tell a story about someone else who did or didn't go to college. Finally, you can draw general conclusions about the importance of a college education for the members of this audience. The key in this pattern is moving from your personal experiences to establishing **COMMON GROUND** with your audience.

▲ 71

State It, Prove It, Relate It, Conclude It In this pattern, you follow four steps: (1) here's my **CLAIM**, (2) here's evidence that justifies the claim, (3) here are examples demonstrating the relevance of this claim to the audience, and (4) here's a summary of why listeners should believe this claim. You may state that, in your opinion, a college education is valuable. Next, offer reasons supported by examples that relate to the audience: a college education can prepare you for a career (examples of various careers), inspire you to become a lifelong learner (examples of respected and learned people), and help you meet interesting people who will be your good friends for the rest of your life (examples of your best friends). Finally, summarize why the members of this audience should pursue a college education.

◆ 352–54

Use Your Thought Speed

Time is precious to an impromptu speaker. If you're lucky, you may have a minute to jot down a few ideas before speaking. In most cases, though, you will have only a few seconds to prepare. The key to managing this time is to take advantage of your **THOUGHT SPEED**—your brain's ability to think faster (sometimes hundreds of words per minute faster) than you speak. If you worry that thought speed is a special talent, just think about times

● 32–33

when you've had a fast-paced, low-stakes conversation with friends. Was your mind filled with a lot of things you could say? Probably. Were you concerned about how you looked or sounded? Probably not. Instead, you were focused on contributing to the conversation.

Thought speed isn't a special skill you need to learn—it's how your mind works when you're communicating unselfconsciously. Even so, you need to practice using it if you expect it to work when you're speaking. Used efficiently and effectively, thought speed gives you time—whether you're aware of it or not—to think about what you want to say.

Keep in Mind . . .

There Is No Time for Anxiety With so much going on just before and while delivering an impromptu speech, there is almost no time for **SPEAKING ANXIETY** to creep into the process. Consider this: After students conclude a major presentation assignment in class, a classmate or the instructor may ask a question. Usually without more than a second's hesitation, most students answer the question with ease. They're not thinking about stage fright; they're thinking about their answer.

Buy Extra Time In the few seconds between the time you're asked to make impromptu remarks and the moment when you start speaking, you have to come up with a plan for your presentation. You can stretch those seconds by following a few suggestions: *Pause thoughtfully.* Give yourself a few seconds to think before you speak. Your audience may appreciate that you are carefully considering what you want to say rather than scrambling for ideas. If asked a question, *rephrase it.* Repeat the meaning of the question in your own words. In addition to ensuring you heard and understood the question or topic for comment, it also gives you more time.

Use All-Purpose Quotations and Stories Most of us know a few quotations by heart—from a treasured book, a favorite writer or poet, song lyrics, or tag lines in famous commercials. Try memorizing a few all-purpose quotations you can apply to almost any speaking situation. Not only does quoting someone make you sound intelligent, but it also gives you a little extra time to think about what you want to say. The same is true of stories.

15–27

Build a store of engaging personal stories or stories you've heard or read about that relate to your purpose or the topic.

Practice Impromptu Speaking When you are alone, with no pressures from an audience, practice impromptu speaking. Pick a news headline and create an impromptu speech in which you describe its importance and implications. Google famous quotations and randomly choose one as the basis for impromptu remarks. As you practice, tap into your thought speed: one part of your thinking should focus on what you are saying and another part should focus on what you will say next. Make sure to practice aloud—you won't become comfortable using this technique any other way.

If you need more help

See 1.2, SPEAKING ANXIETY, to review methods for decreasing your speaking anxiety in impromptu situations where the lack of preparation time can make you more nervous. See 1.3, LISTENING, to learn more about effective listening methods and using your thought speed. See 4.4, PRACTICING YOUR DELIVERY, to review the difference between impromptu speaking and extemporaneous speaking. See 7.1, UNDERSTANDING PERSUASION, to review the main types of claims you might make.

15–27

28–38
220–33

349–62

8.2 Introducing a Speaker

When **introducing a speaker**, you are the warm-up act for the presenter you introduce. Your purpose is to motivate audience members to listen to and value the speaker and the speaker's message. Done well, a good introduction of a speaker will give your listeners reasons to pay attention and admire and respect the presenter before they step up to speak.

Consider the following presentation that introduced a speaker at a national meeting of humanities scholars and educators. In this case, most audience members at this event knew Dr. Alicia Juarrero was a former member of the National Council of the National Endowment for the Humanities, but they knew very little about her as an educator and advocate. Here's how one of the authors of this book introduced her:

> I am delighted to introduce Dr. Alicia Juarrero, our distinguished keynote speaker. You can read about her impressive background, honors, publications, and service to higher education in your program. But your program does not do justice to her work as an educator and advocate.
>
> If Alicia had lived during the Golden Age of Greece and had been a male citizen of Athens, I have no doubt that she would have founded the Academy—well before it was barely a gleam in Plato's eye. Because, first and foremost, Dr. Juarrero is a teacher. When her college created its Faculty Excellence Award, no one doubted that Alicia would be the first recipient. Her distinguished résumé cannot capture the dedicated hours and effort she's spent helping educators and supporting working women in Cuba.
>
> At the beginning of each semester, Dr. Juarrero shares a statement by Plato with her students: "Thinking is the talking of the soul with itself." To that Alicia adds, "I welcome only thinkers to my classes." And rest assured, if they don't come into her class as thinkers, they have plenty to think about by the time they leave.

● getting started   ▶ delivery   ◆ speaking to persuade
▲ fundamentals   ∴ engaging your audience   ★ speaking occasions
■ content   ◤ speaking to inform   ✳ resources

Key Features

Speaker Introductions Are Not about You

Successful speaker introductions focus an audience's attention on the next speaker, not the present one (you). It's not necessary or even desirable to spend any speaking time building your credibility or enhancing your immediacy—your listeners only want to learn about the person you're introducing. At concerts, warm-up bands shouldn't overshadow the main act. In introductions, the introducer should not compete for attention with the person they're introducing.

Speaker Introductions Are Highly Focused

Effective speaker introductions are information-rich and focused. They don't stray from the point. Audience members should be too busy listening to relevant and interesting information about the speaker to wonder, "Where is this going?" or "When will this end?"

Speaker Introductions Motivate Audience Interest

At their best, speaker introductions not only inform the audience about the speaker's qualifications and characteristics, but they also persuade the audience that the speaker is admirable and trustworthy—someone well worth listening to.

Speaker Introductions Find the Right Balance

A good speaker introduction avoids overly exaggerated praise while still complimenting the speaker's legitimate achievements. It also doesn't go on longer than necessary or pile on more information than is required to achieve its purpose. It interests audience members without giving away what the speaker will say. In short, it walks the ideal line between too little and too much.

A Brief Guide to Introducing a Speaker

Consider the Rhetorical Situation

OCCASION The reason for a speech of introduction is clear: a particular speaker needs to be introduced to a particular audience by someone who is already familiar (or at least more familiar) to the audience. Generally,

 5–6

speaker introductions are (and should be) brief, and they always precede the speaker's presentation. Although they occur in many different locations, the introducer is usually familiar with the place—an office, an organization's headquarters, a school, or other institution in which the introducer is a member of the community.

55–69 ▲

57–66 ▲

SPEAKER Why are *you* introducing this speaker? Is there something about your relationship with the speaker that makes you the ideal person to introduce them? Or is your **CREDIBILITY** with the audience the reason you were asked to introduce the speaker? Remember your introduction is not about you—it should focus audience attention on the speaker and should bolster their credibility, not (necessarily) yours. But don't ignore the fact that your own credibility can influence whether or not your introduction persuades your listeners that the speaker is someone worth listening to.

70–86 ▲

71 ▲

AUDIENCE What do your listeners already know about the speaker? What do they need to know? Given what you know (or learn) about the audience, what do you think will convince them to pay attention and/or care about this speaker? Look for at least one thing that will make the speaker especially interesting to this particular audience. If you have a sense that the speaker's values complement the audience's, is there a way to mention the **COMMON GROUND** they share?

87–101 ▲

355 ◆

58–61 ▲

61–62 ▲

63–65 ▲

PURPOSE Your general purpose is clear: to introduce a distinctive presenter to a particular audience in a specific rhetorical situation. Based on what you know about the speaker and the audience, your purpose may vary. If, for example, the speaker is unknown to the audience, your purpose may be establishing the speaker's **INITIAL CREDIBILITY**. If the presenter's topic or reputation is controversial, your purpose may be to acknowledge that fact and encourage the audience to listen with an open mind. Ask yourself: What can I say that will impress *this particular* audience about *this particular* presenter's **COMPETENCE**, **TRUSTWORTHINESS**, and **LIKABILITY**?

103–79 ■

133–36 ■

CONTENT Determine the **KEY POINTS** that will help you build a well-organized introduction. Look for and include the most relevant and

● getting started   ▶ delivery   ◆ speaking to persuade
▲ fundamentals   ∴ engaging your audience   ★ speaking occasions
■ content   ♥ speaking to inform   ❋ resources

interesting information about the person you're introducing—without over-doing it. Ask yourself: What do I know or what have I learned about the speaker that will help achieve the purpose of this introduction? Avoid sharing a random collection of unrelated comments. Include a **VALUE STEP** that explains why the speaker's message is applicable to audience members and how it can affect their well-being and success.

311–13

DELIVERY It may seem a small matter, but the most important aspect of delivery to consider when introducing a speaker is this: Are you certain about how to pronounce the speaker's name? If you aren't sure, ask! As with many other presentations, **EXTEMPORANEOUS DELIVERY** works well for a speaker introduction if you can keep the information about the speaker clear in your mind with minimal notes. If you decide to use a **MANUSCRIPT**, practice your delivery in order to maximize **EYE CONTACT** instead of read-ing it word for word. Some speakers memorize the first few lines of an introduction and are skilled enough to modify what they say if needed. Although it's fine to turn and address the speaker when telling a story or emphasizing an achievement, you should spend most of the introduction looking at the audience, not at the speaker.

181–233

221–22

222–23
210–12

Interview the Speaker Beforehand

Introducing a speaker requires that you know more about them than the audience can learn by reading about them online or in a flyer. The best way to do so is by talking with the speaker beforehand. But before you do, make sure to do research about the speaker on your own; this will enable you to ask better questions. Here are some questions to get your conversa-tion started:

- What do you hope to achieve by addressing this audience? Is there some way my introduction can help you do that?
- Here's a summary of what I know about you. . . . What else should I know or consider sharing with the audience?
- How and why did you first become involved in this subject? Why is it personally important to you?

- What are the most important things you want this audience to know about you and/or your topic before you begin your presentation?

- Are there some people I should contact to learn more about you and your work or achievements? Is there a news story or article you'd recommend or something you've written that I should read?

In some cases, a professional speaker or someone who frequently speaks to various groups will have a sample introduction you can use. It will cover what, in the speaker's opinion, are the most important ideas and information to emphasize in your introduction. Unfortunately, if all you do is read the introduction, it won't sound like you and won't stress things you know about the speaker and audience. You can use the information provided by the speaker, but make the presentation your own.

Introducing Yourself

In some rhetorical situations, the audience may not know who you are. In fact, you may be introduced by someone else as the person who will be introducing the speaker. If you and the audience are not acquainted and you are not introduced by someone else, begin by introducing yourself and establishing quickly and directly your connection to the speaker: "My name is _____ and I have taken—and passed—three philosophy classes taught by Dr. Alicia Juarrero. She is my favorite professor. I believe you will understand why I feel this way during and after her presentation."

Keep in Mind . . .

Repeat the Presenter's Name Mention the speaker's name several times during the introduction unless the audience knows the speaker well.

249

Avoid Clichés Trite, overused, and unoriginal, CLICHÉS undermine the unique impression of the speaker you're attempting to leave with the audience. Instead of an overused phrase such as "Tonight's speaker needs no introduction," simply tell your audience something they don't already know about this otherwise well-known person. If you're at a loss about how to end, don't resort to a tired phrase such as

---

- getting started
- fundamentals
- content
- delivery
- engaging your audience
- speaking to inform
- speaking to persuade
- speaking occasions
- resources

"without further ado." Instead, simply say, "Please join me in welcoming _____" or "I am honored to introduce _____," and then step aside.

Adapt to the Setting In some cases, you may be the only person who can make sure the facilities and equipment are prepared and ready for use by the speaker. In other situations, you may be the organizer and the introducer. Make sure you are prepared to adapt to the setting, both for your own and for the speaker's sake.

Begin the Applause At the end of your introduction, begin applauding until the speaker reaches the lectern or podium. This cues your audience to applaud. If appropriate, shake hands with the speaker. Then, when the speaker begins the presentation, **LISTEN** closely. You might have to respond to a thank-you for a great introduction.

30–31

If you need more help

See **2.2, AUDIENCE**, if you need guidelines for understanding and adapting to the audience, and **3.4, INTRODUCTIONS AND CONCLUSIONS**, for some good advice about effective ways to begin and end a presentation—advice that can be easily adapted to this special type of introduction.

70–86
160–79

NOTABLE SPEAKERS
Dr. Ronald A. Crutcher and Courtney Britt

Search Terms
To locate a video of this presentation online, enter the following key words into a search engine: University of Richmond 2016 Commencement Courtney Britt. The video is approximately 4:56 in length.

Introducing a Speaker:
Commencement Address
At the 2016 Commencement at the University of Richmond, the university president, Dr. Ronald A. Crutcher, introduced Courtney Britt, a graduating student who would then introduce the commencement speaker. Crutcher lists many of Britt's accomplishments as well as her service to the university. Crutcher's speaking style is relaxed and very likable even as he reads prepared remarks. His less-than-a-minute introduction is just enough to establish her credibility without taking time from Britt's introduction or the commencement speaker's address.

described in the commencement program. She uses a chronological organizational pattern moving from Hunter-Gault's childhood and college integration experience to her prestigious journalism career. Britt then lists many of the commencement speaker's awards and honors. The conclusion is more personal: both Britt and Hunter-Gault are members of the same sorority, Delta Sigma Theta, which is committed to sisterhood, social justice, and public service. Britt reads her introduction from a manuscript that—if you look carefully—is typed in large, readable letters. For this formal commencement speaker introduction, the script is carefully written and read.

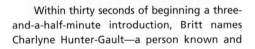

Within thirty seconds of beginning a three-and-a-half-minute introduction, Britt names Charlyne Hunter-Gault—a person known and

Do you think Britt did a good job inspiring audience interest in Hunter-Gault? How might she have improved her introduction?

8.3 Welcome Remarks

A common but underappreciated type of presentation, **welcome remarks** are often delivered when a group of people visit or join a school, company, or organization or to kick off special events or occasions. Some examples include:

- A college president, professor, student, or admissions officer welcomes high-school students and their parents to a campus visit.
- A youth group leader welcomes teenagers to a religious retreat.
- A corporate executive welcomes new employees to the firm's orientation week.
- The director of a living-history site welcomes visitors and explains what their experience at the facility will be like.

Although they may seem simple, welcome remarks require preparation and **PRACTICE**, just like any other form of presentation speaking. They also require careful attention to your audience, who should be the focus of your greeting. In addition to helping an audience look forward to whatever will follow, the best welcome remarks make an audience feel the speaker knows who they are and why they are there.

▶ 228–33

The following excerpt is the beginning of a welcome speech delivered by Kristen Bub, an advanced doctoral student, to the incoming 2007 class at Harvard University's Graduate School of Education. Ms. Bub addressed the students about what to expect at the school and what she has learned along the way. Notice how her remarks connect the speaker, the university, and the audience.

> Good morning and welcome to the Harvard Graduate School of Education. It is both an honor and a privilege to stand before you today

and welcome you to this amazing community. If you are anything like I was when I started, you are sitting there feeling a million different emotions and asking yourself a million different questions. "Did I make the right choice?" (*without a doubt*); "Is this worth the sacrifices I have made to get here?" (*absolutely*); and perhaps as you have already heard, you are not the admissions mistake. In fact, I can assure each and every one of you that you are here because you deserve to be, and because you can bring something new and exciting to this diverse learning community. So welcome![1]

Key Features

Welcome Remarks Connect Your Audience to the Organization or Event

The very name of this type of speaking occasion depicts its purpose: your job is to make your audience feel welcome. You should help your listeners understand how they fit in and how they can benefit from the session, tour, or experience they're about to have.

Welcome Remarks Are Not about You

Although you may be the chosen representative of an organization and the first person audience members encounter, you are not what it's all about. Unlike someone doing a **TOAST** or a **EULOGY**, your listeners don't need to feel a personal connection to you—so, other than your title or relationship to the organization, there isn't much more your audience needs to know about you.

442–48 ⭐
449–55 ⭐

Welcome Remarks Highlight Your Organization

Your presentation should make a positive impression on the audience about the organization you represent (for example, "When I give campus tours, I am always amazed by this campus—the buildings, the grounds, and even the professors"). If your listeners feel comfortable, eager, and interested in the event or organization as a result of your remarks, you will enhance your organization's **CREDIBILITY**, and you will have created a positive communication climate that benefits everyone.

57–66 ▲

- ⬤ getting started
- ▲ fundamentals
- ■ content

- ▶ delivery
- ⸪ engaging your audience
- ▆ speaking to inform

- ◆ speaking to persuade
- ★ speaking occasions
- ✺ resources

Welcome Remarks Are Brief (but Not Too Brief)

Welcome remarks should be more than a simple "Hello, here's what will happen; enjoy!" But they shouldn't be much longer than Kristen Bub's on page 421. In most situations, you should give only enough detail to make it clear you know something specific about the audience and to make them comfortable in their new environment, but once you've done that, your job is done.

A Brief Guide to Welcome Remarks

Consider the Rhetorical Situation

OCCASION A group of visitors or guests have arrived at a school, a company, or an organization and need someone to make them feel welcome and to familiarize them with the reasons and agenda for their visit. Welcome remarks are very brief and occur on or near the site where the visit or tour is happening.

5–6

SPEAKER Audience members simply need to know who you are and why you are welcoming them—your job title or position in the organization may be all that's needed to make this clear to them. If, like Kristen Bub, you were once in the same position as your listeners, you might say something to make this clear, but remember to keep this aspect of your remarks brief.

55–69

AUDIENCE Do some **AUDIENCE ANALYSIS** to look for characteristics, concerns, interests, experiences, and expectations your audience shares with the organization you represent. What do you know about your listeners' personal goals and history? Connecting their characteristics, beliefs, or values to your organization in some way will increase their interest and sense of connection to it.

70–86
72–80

PURPOSE Your overarching purpose is to make your audience feel they are welcome. If this is the beginning of a long-term relationship (for instance, an orientation for new students or employees), you should link your audience's goals and aspirations to the organization and help your listeners

87–101

feel they belong. If this is a onetime event (a guided tour of a factory or museum, for example), your purpose is to generate interest and enthusiasm for the event by making it clear how they will benefit from it.

103–79

CONTENT Welcome remarks should be brief, friendly, inclusive, and positive. Ask yourself: What can I say in a short amount of time that will

138–48

engage the audience and highlight the reason for or the importance of the

161–69

event? Use a simple **ORGANIZATIONAL PATTERN** that features an engaging

169–75

INTRODUCTION and memorable **CONCLUSION**.

181–233

DELIVERY Welcome remarks should be natural and friendly and should

186

establish **IMMEDIACY** with your listeners. **EXTEMPORANEOUS DELIVERY** is

221–22

best, but if you've written down your remarks, practice them enough so you don't (or rarely) need to consult your notes.

Linking Your Audience and Your Organization

71

With welcome remarks, the **COMMON GROUND** you're looking for isn't about you; it's about finding common ground shared by your audience and the organization you represent. Answering the following questions can help you connect the group you represent to members of the visiting audience:

- How much does the audience know about your organization?
- Why is the audience attending this event, and why is your organization hosting it?
- What is the visiting group's mission, goals, and reputation? How is it similar to or different from your organization's mission, goals, and reputation?
- Are the characteristics, attitudes, beliefs, values, and goals of audience members similar to those in your organization? Is there a meaningful organizational slogan, motto, or mission statement you can share?
- What are the expectations of your guests for the event and your organization?

Organizing Welcome Remarks

As with any presentation, there are numerous ways to organize the content of a welcome. The following **OUTLINE** depicts a more typical, bare-bones template for a welcome:[2]

152–53

I. Introduction

    A. Introduce yourself (and your title or function) to the audience.

    B. Welcome the audience (and, if applicable, their organization) to the occasion or name of the event and to the host/sponsor, and thank the audience for coming.

    C. Provide a brief description of the host/sponsor (the business, organization, agency) and the occasion/event.

II. Body

    A. Preview highlights of the event or occasion.

    B. Explain how audience members can benefit by attending and/or participating.

    C. Welcome and answer questions.

III. Conclusion

    A. Briefly review the agenda/schedule and make any announcements, if needed.

    B. Introduce the next speaker, if appropriate.

    C. Conclude by generating enthusiasm and appreciation for what's to come.

Keep in Mind . . .

Adapt Your Speaking Style to Your Audience If you and the audience are already acquainted and share common characteristics and attitudes, you can use a casual, conversational speaking style. If you and the audience are new to one another, you might want to use a more formal style to demonstrate professionalism and respect for your listeners.

Highlight Benefits Emphasize important ("you won't want to miss") features that will occur during the event or during your listeners' time as members of the organization and how audience members can benefit from them.

Acknowledge Important Individuals Recognize the visiting group's leader or other important audience members by name somewhere in your welcoming remarks. Make sure you correctly pronounce their names (and the name of the group you are welcoming).

Stick Around after You Finish Speaking Don't rush out the door. Someone may have a question or need your help. Even if you do nothing more than stand at the back of the room for a few minutes, you will be further extending the goodwill created by your welcome.

If you need more help

70–86
268–79

See 2.2, **AUDIENCE**, to help you understand, respect, and adapt to the audience. See 5.3 **GENERATING INTEREST**, to transform a humdrum welcome into one that overcomes audience disinterest, uses humor and stories, and cultivates audience participation.

● getting started	▶ delivery	◆ speaking to persuade
▲ fundamentals	⁝ engaging your audience	★ speaking occasions
■ content	▼ speaking to inform	✳ resources

8.4 Presenting an Award

Whether large or small, corporate or nonprofit, local or international, organizations of all sorts—from a small-town high school to the international Nobel Prize committee—hold awards ceremonies for similar reasons: to recognize individual or group excellence, to motivate others to strive for higher goals, and to publicly call attention to the organization and its good work.

There are two central figures in every awards ceremony: the person who presents the award and the person who accepts the award. **Presenting an award** and accepting an award are obviously related, but they are different in terms of presentation strategies. In this chapter, we focus on the central principles, strategies, and skills of the presenter.

Here's an excerpt from a famous award presentation by Egil Aarvik, chairman of the Norwegian Nobel Committee, presenting the Nobel Peace Prize to Elie Wiesel in 1986:

> I doubt whether any other individual, through the use of such quiet speech, has achieved more or been more widely heard. The words are not big, and the voice which speaks them is low. It is a voice of peace we hear. But the power is intense. Truly, the little spark will not be put out, but will become a burning torch for our common belief in the future. Truly, prisoner number A 7713 has become a human being once again—a human being dedicated to humanity. . . .
>
> It is in recognition of this particular human spirit's victory over the powers of death and degradation, and as a support to the rebellion of good against the evil in the world, that the Norwegian Nobel Committee today presents the Nobel Peace Prize to Elie Wiesel. We do this on behalf of millions—from all peoples and races. We do it in deep reverence for the memory of the dead, but also with the deep-felt hope that the prize will be a small contribution which will forward the cause which is the greatest of all humanity's concerns—the cause of peace.[1]

Key Features

Presenting an Award Is Not about You

It is, of course, an honor to be chosen to represent an organization giving an award, but you should remember that you are not what the occasion is all about. Successful award presentations focus an audience's attention on the award and the recipient. It's not necessary or even desirable to spend any speaking time building your credibility or enhancing your immediacy—the audience wants only to join you in celebrating an achievement.

Your Remarks Depend on What the Audience Knows

During some award presentations, the audience knows who the winner is but doesn't know very much about the award (an example might be a popular celebrity receiving an award from a small nonprofit organization). During others, the audience knows something about the award but not much about the person receiving it (for example, an up-and-coming musician, writer, or artist receiving a MacArthur Foundation "Genius" Award). A successful award presentation ensures that by its conclusion, the audience understands what the award is and why the recipient deserves it.

Your Remarks Can Be Brief or Lengthy

The rhetorical situation and tradition often dictate the length of an award presentation. The presentations of Nobel Prizes are long because they do more than celebrate a particular winner or winners. They also explain the significance of the award. Consider the last sentence of the Nobel Peace Prize presentation to Elie Wiesel: the award is presented "with the deep-felt hope that the prize will be a small contribution which will forward the cause which is the greatest of all humanity's concerns—the cause of peace." However, in an informal setting where everyone knows who the nominees are and why they are finalists for this award, there may be little to say other than praising all the nominees and then announcing the winner.

A Brief Guide to Presenting an Award

Consider the Rhetorical Situation

OCCASION The reason for an award presentation is reflected in its name: someone is being honored with a gift or award in recognition of a specific achievement or overall excellence. The presenter describes the award and its importance and also identifies the recipient and explains why the recipient is being honored. The timing of an award presentation is determined by the organization hosting the event where the award will be given and can range from a few minutes to a longer, formal presentation. Award presentations often occur at celebratory events, and the logistical details about the timing are usually choreographed and planned with great care. The settings of award presentations can vary but are usually chosen and laid out by the organization giving the award.

● 5–6

SPEAKER An award presentation should focus audience attention on the award winner and its sponsor. You might want to clarify for the audience why you are presenting the award—your position in or relationship to the organization giving the award, for instance—but beyond that, you should keep the focus off yourself. One way to do this is to ensure you are comfortable and **CONFIDENT** delivering the presentation. A nervous, scattered presenter will distract attention from the award and its recipient. So play to your strengths as a speaker, stay in your comfort zone, and use your skills to honor the recipient.

▲ 55–69

▶ 184–85

AUDIENCE Award audiences differ in every rhetorical situation. Ask yourself: What do the listeners already know about the award recipient? What do they *need* to know? Why should they pay attention and/or care about this award? How can I demonstrate the importance and benefits of the award and its significance to the audience? Answering these questions requires **AUDIENCE ANALYSIS** to determine what your audience knows, believes, wants, and expects.

▲ 70–86

▲ 72–80

PURPOSE Your purpose is clear: to present an award to a worthy recipient. Depending on what you learn about the audience's awareness and

▲ 87–101

knowledge of the recipient and the award, your purpose can vary. If, for example, the audience doesn't know very much about the winner, you should focus on the person's background, achievements, and **CREDIBILITY**. If they know the recipient but not much about the award, you'll want to make sure to explain its significance.

CONTENT Learn as much as you can about the award recipient (including, and most important, the pronunciation of their full name if you are unsure of it!) and the significance of the award. Research the person's background, achievements, personal characteristics, and opinions. Begin

with an attention-getting **INTRODUCTION**. Use **STORIES** and examples to stimulate the audience's interest and feelings. Provide a clear and vivid description of the winner's accomplishments. Identify the values, virtues, and benefits of the award. If appropriate, mention past award winners.

Pay particular attention to the **SPEAKING STYLES** and strategies you use. Whereas eloquence may be appropriate and expected for conferring a prestigious, international prize, a clear conversational style may be better suited

for a local club award presentation. Finish with a heartfelt **CONCLUSION**.

DELIVERY An award presentation is not an occasion for impromptu speaking. **EXTEMPORANEOUS DELIVERY**—which allows you to maximize eye contact and seem spontaneous but also well prepared—is more appropriate.

When an award winner has a long list of accomplishments, or you want to read something the winner has said or written, a **MANUSCRIPT** may be needed. If you decide to use a manuscript, practice your delivery so you can maintain eye contact with your audience rather than reading most of it word for word. If you recognize the winner at the beginning of your presentation, look directly at the audience and occasionally at the winner (regardless of whether that person is seated on stage or still in the audience). If you reveal the winner at the end, look at the audience up until the moment you announce the winner.

Revealing the Winner

In some cases, award recipients and audience members know who will be honored at the event. Presenters can prepare their remarks in advance. In other situations, the name of the winner is a secret and known only

---

● getting started   ▶ delivery   ◆ speaking to persuade
▲ fundamentals   ⁙ engaging your audience   ★ speaking occasions
■ content   ◣ speaking to inform   ✳ resources

to a few people. Nobel Prize winners know in advance; major book award winners do not. Nor do most local recipients of "best athlete" or "best pizza" prizes.

When neither the award winner nor the audience knows who will win the award, you have an important decision to make: Should you surprise the award winner and audience at the end of your presentation, or should you identify the award winner at the beginning? Although it may be fun to keep the nominees and audience guessing, identifying the person at the beginning may be the better choice, particularly if audience members don't know the recipient very well or at all. That is not the case for the Academy Awards or college football's Heisman Trophy. If you recognize the winner at the beginning of your presentation, you can invite the person to join you at the front of the room or on the stage. If you reveal the winner at the end of your presentation, invite the person to come forward and join you. Some of these decisions may be determined by the traditions of the organization. Make sure to ask the organizers if they have a preference.

Keep in Mind . . .

Enlist Language Strategies to Achieve Your Purpose Take another look at Egil Aarvik's eloquent Nobel Peace Prize presentation (p. 427). What lifts his presentation to a higher stature is his language. Aarvik's words are clear and brief—as are most of his sentences, as in "The words [Wiesel's] are not big, and the voice which speaks them is low. It is a voice of peace we hear. But the power is intense." He contrasts big and small, peace and power, and repeats the simple word "is" in three sentences. Writing this kind of presentation is not easy because every carefully chosen word and phrase contributes to achieving its purpose.

Pay Attention to the Nature of the Occasion and the Logistics of the Setting How formal is the award ceremony? How formal should your presentation be? If other members of the organization will be assisting in the award presentation in any way (for instance, coming onstage with a trophy or other object to be presented to the recipient), talk to them beforehand to coordinate what will happen when. Make sure the facilities and equipment are prepared and ready for use.

Introduce Yourself, but Keep It Simple If most audience members don't know who you are and you are not introduced by someone else, begin by introducing yourself: "My name is _____, and I chaired this year's selection committee" or "As president of _____, I'm delighted to recognize, honor, and present this year's award winner with _____."

Perfect the Handoff If you are handing someone an object or envelope, present the award with your left hand and shake the person's right hand. Practice this gesture at home before the event—it's worth the effort! This is the moment for photographs, so you'll want to avoid an awkward handoff. Once you've handed the award to the recipient, step aside so the winner is the center of attention.

Make Sure They Don't Remember You Most audience members remember the recipients of awards, particularly if it's someone they know or the award is highly prestigious, but if the presentation of the award is done well, they will rarely remember who presented the award. Unfortunately, when audiences *do* remember who presented the award, it is almost always for the wrong reason—namely, because the presenter has done something to call attention to themselves, diminishing the specialness of the event and the honor for the recipient. If you achieve your purpose, motivating your listeners to appreciate the winner's achievement and the significance of the award, you will not be remembered. Strive to not be remembered!

If you need more help

87–101 ▲
220–33 ▶
237–52 ⁝

See 2.3, **PURPOSE**, to help you determine your primary purpose in your presentation and achieve general speaking goals. See 4.4, **PRACTICING YOUR DELIVERY**, so you can deliver your presentation sincerely and naturally. See 5.1, **USING LANGUAGE**, to understand how your language choices can enhance the value of an award and the merits of the winner.

● getting started   ▶ delivery   ◆ speaking to persuade
▲ fundamentals   ⁝ engaging your audience   ★ speaking occasions
■ content   ◥ speaking to inform   ✳ resources

8.5 Accepting an Award

Obviously, presenting an award and accepting an award are connected. They literally go hand to hand—the speaker hands an award to a recipient who accepts it. But they are not the same kind of presentation. The rhetorical situation for the recipient is different from that of the presenter—even though they occur one right after another. **Accepting an award**—the subject of this chapter—involves expressing your gratitude for whatever honor you're receiving and acknowledging its significance. It is also an occasion to praise the organization or group that sponsors the award and hosts the event. It may even be an opportunity for you to raise awareness about a cause or principle you believe in.

The logistics of awards ceremonies vary. Some, such as the Academy Awards or the Nobel Prize ceremony, are carefully choreographed. The majority of awards ceremonies, however, are smaller events occurring in less formal settings, such as schools, offices, community organizations, corporations, city halls, houses of worship, and summer camps. Although these different settings bring specific expectations with them (level of formality and type of dress, time limits, traditions concerning what is said and how it is said), there are some features all acceptance speeches share.

Key Features

Acceptances Often Follow Rules and Traditions

Many awards ceremonies have become traditions with a rich history and established customs and conventions. Although famous recipients may flout or simply be unaware of the conventions of such ceremonies, it is generally expected that recipients will have some familiarity with the cultural norms of the event and will shape their acceptance to conform to them.

Acceptances Express Gratitude First and Foremost

An award or honor presentation bestows on a recipient the respect and acknowledgment of an entire community. It is a significant public gesture, even in small, intimate, and informal settings. As such, it merits a respectful and gracious response. The most successful acceptance speeches usually begin and end with a sincere expression of gratitude.

Acceptances Often Praise the Award Giver

In addition to expressing personal thanks to individuals, acceptance speakers usually praise the organization or group granting the award—for the work they do, for the principles they profess, and/or for the causes they support. Successful acceptance speeches support the beliefs, values, and commitments of the organization giving the award and its members (who may represent the majority of audience members).

Acceptances May Advocate a Related Cause

For better or worse, some award winners use acceptance speeches to promote a public or personal cause. Generally, it is inappropriate and even offensive to advocate an unrelated or unpopular cause. However, a supportive statement within the context of the rhetorical situation can raise the quality and impact of the honoree's remarks, especially if the cause is closely aligned with the values of the organization giving the award. For example, in his acceptance speech for the Academy Award for Best Actor in the film *The Reverent*, Leonardo DiCaprio said, "Climate change is real, it is happening right now. It is the most urgent threat facing our entire species, and we need to work collectively together and stop procrastinating."[1]

A Brief Guide to Accepting an Award

Consider the Rhetorical Situation

5–6 ●

OCCASION The reason for an award acceptance is as straightforward as the act of presenting one: someone (you—congratulations!) is being honored with a gift or award in recognition of a specific achievement or overall excellence and is invited to say a few words in gratitude. The occasion,

---

● getting started   ▶ delivery   ◆ speaking to persuade
▲ fundamentals   ∴ engaging your audience   ★ speaking occasions
■ content   ▼ speaking to inform   ✳ resources

timing, and planning of an awards ceremony is determined and managed by the event organizers. Potential or pre-announced award recipients are given directions about when to rise, where to go, what to wear, and how long to speak. Depending on the formality and significance of the award, accepting an award can be an informal, brief thank-you or a longer, scripted address at a public event.

SPEAKER Your **INITIAL CREDIBILITY** will be high because you are being honored, even more so if the person presenting the award to you does a good job of explaining who you are and why you are receiving the award. Even so, a poor acceptance speech can change how the audience feels about you. Don't squander your credibility. If you know you will be receiving an award, develop an appropriate and meaningful acceptance speech based on the advice in this chapter. If the award is a surprise to you, use **IMPROMPTU SPEAKING** skills to produce an effective and meaningful presentation that will enhance your credibility and gratify the people and/or organization you thank.

▲ 55–69
◆ 355

★ 407–13

AUDIENCE Audience members will have heard many wonderful things about you. Your role is to **CONNECT** with them. Justify their good feelings and the respect they've bestowed on you with their attendance, attention, and applause. Remember: most of your listeners are representatives of, or at least affiliated with, the organization or group that has honored you. Show them you are grateful, delighted, and honored by the award. Tell them you revere their work and their values.

▲ 70–86
▲ 55–57

PURPOSE Accepting an award has two purposes: first, to thank those who sponsor and give the award as well as the people who helped you earn it, and second, and maybe more important, to explain the value of the organization and its mission. In some cases, if appropriate, you may advocate a related worthy cause that reflects their mission.

▲ 87–101

CONTENT The first and perhaps last words out of your mouth should be an expression of gratitude. Make a list of those you want to thank, and bring it with you so you don't forget someone. Explain why the award means a great deal to you. You may also tell a brief personal **STORY** related to the work you've done to earn the award and use a bit of **SELF-EFFACING HUMOR**.

■ 103–79

⁂ 253–67
⁂ 273–74

Praise the other nominees if they are known. Use some of your time to emphasize the importance of the cause for which you are being honored. End with an inspirational **CONCLUSION**. If you're having difficulty finding the right words, use a quotation by someone who captures your feelings.

169–75

DELIVERY If you know in advance that you will receive an award, prepare and **PRACTICE** what you will say. **EXTEMPORANEOUS DELIVERY** is best; the most memorable acceptance speakers use very few or no notes at all—other than having the names of people or organizations that must be thanked and perhaps a brief list of **KEY POINTS**. Unless the awards ceremony is formal, significant, and public, avoid reading from a manuscript because it can detract from your **EXPRESSIVENESS, CONFIDENCE, STAGE PRESENCE, AND IMMEDIACY**. Maintain as much eye contact as possible and zero in on some of the important people in your audience as you thank them or praise their work. And smile!

181–233
228–33
221–22
133–36
184–86

Know What's Expected, Just in Case

If you know you will be receiving an award and have never attended the event, find out what is expected of recipients. Make sure you can answer the following questions: Should you acknowledge the presenter? Whom should you thank? If known, are you expected to acknowledge the other nominees by name or as a group? What is the time limit?

Many award ceremonies do not announce the winner(s) in advance. Some identify the finalists but wait for the event to crown the victor. So what should you do if you're a nominee? If you are one of a limited number of nominees or finalists, you should prepare and practice remarks—just in case. Some of the worst awards ceremonies have been marred by winners who could have but didn't prepare in advance.

Apply Impromptu Speaking Strategies if You're Caught Off-Guard

If you are totally surprised when you hear your name as the winner of an award or recipient of an honor, use **IMPROMPTU SPEAKING** strategies and skills to see you through. As you walk to the front of the room or onto a stage, think about what you want to say and the people you need to thank.

407–13 ★

getting started • delivery ▶ speaking to persuade ◆
fundamentals ▲ engaging your audience ⁘ speaking occasions ★
content ■ speaking to inform ◤ resources ✳

Apply a ready-to-use impromptu speaking format, such as "past, present, future" or "me, my friend, and you" to organize your remarks. And make sure you emphasize the importance of the award and its purpose.

Use Appropriate Language Styles

Consider which of the four **CORE SPEAKING STYLES**—clear, oral, rhetorical, and eloquent—are most appropriate. The **LANGUAGE** used in acceptance speeches range from casual and colloquial to eloquent and inspirational. Your analysis of the rhetorical situation should help you make informed choices about the language you use when accepting an award. Consider the following remarks made by two different speakers accepting prestigious prizes:

239–45
237–52

> Hi guys. My name is on here [*gestures to the award plaque*]. I'm not gonna lie, I'm pretty shook right now. I'm just trying to think of something funny to say, but it's hard because I might vomit any time. If that happens, don't worry. I think someone in my group has Altoids. You got Altoids?[2]

This is how Nana Kwame Adjei-Brenyah opened his 2019 acceptance speech when he won the PEN/Jean Stein Book Award for *Friday Black*, a book of short stories. The award recognizes works that break new ground, reshape boundaries, and have the potential for a lasting influence.

Now read the opening sentences of Elie Wiesel's acceptance speech when he won the 1986 Nobel Peace Prize. He was a celebrated writer, revered international spokesperson, and a Jewish survivor of the Auschwitz and Buchenwald concentration camps.

> It is with a profound sense of humility that I accept the honor you have chosen to bestow upon me. I know: your choice transcends me. This both frightens and pleases me. It frightens me because I wonder: do I have the right to represent the multitudes who have perished? Do I have the right to accept this great honor on their behalf? . . . I do not. That would be presumptuous. No one may speak for the dead, no one may interpret their mutilated dreams and visions. It pleases me because I may say that this honor belongs to all the survivors and their children, and through us, to the Jewish people with whose destiny I have always identified.[3]

Although the language style in the first example may seem inappropriate for a prestigious awards ceremony, the speaker's surprise and unsophisticated response was an impromptu beginning to an acceptance speech in which he went on to say he had wanted his stories to be out in the world: "I felt like maybe they could help somebody feel seen. Maybe they could push the conversation in a direction that mattered. I thought maybe if I imagined a world a little bit worse than ours, maybe collectively we could imagine a world that's much better."[4]

Adjei-Brenyah varied his language style over the course of his acceptance speech. It resonated with a "voice" that readers who know his work would recognize and find familiar. His authentic use of language made the speech a memorable success.

Wiesel's award was not a surprise, and he was not limited to a few minutes. The profound significance of the Nobel Peace Prize called for a manuscript speech that was finely crafted and eloquent, and Wiesel achieved this by employing a model of language strategies that lifted his presentation to classic heights.

Keep in Mind . . .

Limit the Number of Thank-Yous Don't overwhelm the audience with a long thank-you list. Name the key people who were most influential in supporting you and the mission of your work as well as key sponsors. If appropriate, you may also thank the presenter of the award.

Honor the Time Limit If you are given a time limit, honor it. If you are not given a time limit, resist the temptation to talk more than a couple of minutes unless you know for certain that your audience expects something longer. Prepare and practice your remarks in advance so you know you can say what's important in the time you have.

Speak from the Heart Go beyond the expected words of thanks. Share how you feel at this moment and why the award has value for both you and the audience. Speak authentically and with feeling.

Speak with Few or No Notes If you know in advance that you will be expected to speak when accepting an award and that you will only have a limited amount of time, consider memorizing your presentation, but bring your notes or manuscript with you in case you need them. When the award is a complete surprise, you won't have any notes, but you can bring the program (if there is a written program) with you to the podium to make sure you thank the sponsors and, perhaps, other nominees.

If you need more help

See 4.1, THE IMPORTANCE OF DELIVERY, to help you develop expressiveness, confidence, stage presence, and immediacy, and 5.1, USING LANGUAGE, to use a variety of language styles and strategies that are appropriate for you, the audience, and your purpose.

183–93
237–52

NOTABLE SPEAKER
Berta Cáceres

Search Terms
To locate a video of this presentation online, enter the following key words into a search engine: Berta Cáceres Goldman Prize acceptance speech 2015. The video is approximately 3:00 minutes in length.

Acceptance Speech: 2015 Goldman Prize

In 2015, Berta Cáceres received the prestigious Goldman Environmental Prize, which honors the achievements and leadership of grassroots environmental activists from around the world. Cáceres cofounded COPINH (the National Council of Popular and Indigenous Organizations of Honduras). Among many other efforts, she led a grassroots campaign against Sinohydro, the world's largest dam developer, to terminate its contract for construction of the Agua Zarca hydroelectric dams project in Indigenous Lenca people territory. Challenging such a powerful transnational corporation cost Cáceres her life. She was murdered in March 2016. In 2018, seven men who had been hired by the company constructing the dam were convicted of her murder and sentenced to thirty to fifty years.[5]

Other than beginning with "Gracias, Buenos noches," Cáceres does not repeat the word "gracias" (thank you) until the very end of her speech. Nor does she explain the importance of the award. The audience knew why she'd won. They were there to thank *her*. Her final full sentence recognizes and dedicates the award to people "who gave their lives" to the struggle. And then she ends with "muchas gracias" (thank you very much).

Cáceres uses a manuscript—as do most speakers accepting highly prestigious and visible awards. Her vocal and physical delivery animates her message, emphasizes critical sentences, and reveals her uncompromising and emotional dedication to a cause.

Cáceres speaks in Spanish. Even if you don't understand Spanish, watch and listen to how she emphasizes what seem to be powerful phrases and the way her voice and movements highlight her devotion and fearlessness to a cause. What follows is the translation. If you know Spanish, you will appreciate the strength, resolve, and marvel of her message. For readers who do not know Spanish or need a translation to ensure better comprehension, the translation captures her skillful use of stylistic devices (repetition, alliteration, metaphor, and the rule of three). Consider the power of "¡Despertemos! ¡Despertemos Humanidad! Ya no hay tiempo." (Let us wake up! Let us wake up, humanity! We're out of time.) Her heroic call is similar to Greta Thunburg's entreaties about climate change.

> In our world-views, we are beings who come from the Earth, from the water, and from corn. The Lenca people are ancestral guardians of the rivers, in turn protected by the spirits of young girls, who teach us that giving our lives in various ways for the protection of the rivers is giving our lives for the well-being of humanity and of this planet.
>
> COPINH, walking alongside people struggling for their emancipation, validates this commitment to continue protecting our waters, the rivers, our shared resources and nature in general, as well as our rights as a people. Let us wake up! Let us wake up, humankind! We're out of time.
>
> We must shake our conscience free of the rapacious capitalism, racism and patriarchy that will only assure our own self destruction. The Gualcarque River has called upon us, as have other gravely threatened rivers. We must answer their call.
>
> Our Mother Earth—militarized, fenced in, poisoned, a place where basic rights are systematically violated—demands that we take action. Let us build societies that are able to coexist in a dignified way . . . in a way that protects life. Let us come together and remain hopeful as we defend and care for the blood of this earth and of its spirits.
>
> I dedicate this award to all the rebels out there, to my mother, to the Lenca people, to Rio Blanco and to the martyrs who gave their lives in the struggle to defend our natural resources. Thank you very much.[6]

8.6 Toasts

Toasts are celebratory rituals where a group of people are invited to raise their glasses and drink together to honor a person, a couple, a group, an occasion, or an accomplishment. The term *toast* comes from an old English tradition of putting a spiced piece of toast in an alcoholic drink to add more flavor. Toasts bring attention to something special—they "spice up" and add flavor to a celebration.

If you have attended a wedding, a special birthday party, a retirement dinner, or a company banquet, you've probably lifted your glass and toasted the newlyweds, family members, guest of honor, retiree, or employee. Toasts can also celebrate a shared milestone: Our tenth anniversary in business! The opening of our new Fine Arts building! Our soccer team's victory! Sometimes toasts are spontaneous and unplanned; for instance, you may be moved to make a spontaneous toast to good friends sharing a meal. Others are longer, well-planned tributes, spoken at a brother's wedding, for example, or at a retirement dinner for a respected longtime company manager. Most of us, at some point in our lives, will give a toast.

A toast can be as solemn as a prayer or as risqué as a wedding-night joke. It can remind an audience why they are attending a special celebration. Because toasts are supposed to make everyone feel good, they can be more emotional, inspiring, and joyful than other types of presentations.

Brief toasts can be fun to write yourself, but you can also find examples online or in books devoted solely to toasts. Here are a few examples:

- "May you always work like you don't need the money; may you always love like you've never been hurt; and may you always dance like there's nobody watching." (Jack Canfield, coauthor, *Chicken Soup for the Soul*)

- "As I toast this beautiful and blissfully happy couple, I know that 'wherever they go, there is Eden.'" (Adapted from Mark Twain, *Eve's Diary*)
- "May the saddest day of your future be no worse than the happiest day of your past." (Traditional)
- "Here's to friends and family who know us well but love us just the same." (Traditional)

Although a one-line salute may be appropriate when several people are making toasts, the best toasts have more to say. They demonstrate you've taken time to create a personal gift for a beloved person or couple, a tribute to an esteemed honoree, or a heartfelt thank-you to gracious hosts.

Key Features

Toasts Are a Personal Gift

Toasts are a gift to the audience in need of some **ENTERTAINMENT** and **ENGAGEMENT**. Guests perk up and quiet down when they see someone pick up microphone with a drink in their hand. A toast gives you a few privileged minutes to bestow a personal gift on someone or a couple you love or a group you admire. It also honors your relationship with a person or group by demonstrating how pleased and proud you are to have them in your life. A well-thought-out toast can also create or reinforce a bond among the attendees who now have a basis for interacting with one another.

▲ 93–94
∴ 235–305

Toasts Often Have a "Hook"

A hook (much like the shiny fishing hooks that attract and catch fish) is something that captures audience attention. It can be a famous birthday or historical event that occurs on the toast day or a little-known **STORY** about the person being toasted. A hook can also be a related joke, an impressive fact, or an inspiring story. The best hooks make an audience want to hear more. Look at how the following statements can hook an audience depending on how you complete each sentence: "Tonight you will learn why

∴ 253–67

Spencer _____ (is called Hawk)" or "Do you know the story about Chris _____ (and the alligator in a children's playground)?"

Toasts Should Be Prepared Well in Advance

Admittedly, some so-called toasts are spontaneous remarks made in the company of others. They can be a simple "Congratulations!" or a rambling set of stories ending with "Bottoms up!" Given their spur-of-the-moment qualities, these toasts are rarely worth remembering. The best and most meaningful toasts—the toasts everyone remembers and treasures—require days of preparation and multiple PRACTICE sessions to reach their potential and impress an audience.

228–33 ▷

A Brief Guide to Making a Toast

Consider the Rhetorical Situation

5–6 ●

OCCASION The reason for a toast is to honor a person, a couple, a group, an occasion, or an accomplishment in a social, celebratory manner. The timing of a toast may be determined by the organizers of the event where the toast occurs (for example, a wedding reception may start with a social/cocktail hour, a meal, and then a toast or toasts), or it may be a spontaneous event. Toasts can be (and often are) very brief, but some are longer—a few minutes or more. Toasts occur in many locations, from bars and restaurants to workplaces and other institutional settings.

55–69 ▲

SPEAKER Why are you making this toast on this occasion? Do you need to explain your relationship to the person, people, or event? If you are very close to the person or people you are toasting, consider what you know, feel, and are willing to share with others. Many toasts reveal as much about your feelings and experiences as they do about the object of the toast. But don't get carried away by making yourself the main character in the story.

70–86 ▲
80–82 ▲

AUDIENCE How will you ADAPT to what listeners already know and feel about the person(s) or occasion honored by the toast? In some cases,

---

● getting started   ▷ delivery   ◆ speaking to persuade

▲ fundamentals   ∴ engaging your audience   ★ speaking occasions

■ content   ▼ speaking to inform   ✳ resources

you will need to share background information or something they don't know. What do they expect to hear in the toast, and how can you meet those expectations? Although toasts are often humorous, they should not offend audience members who might consider the content inappropriate.

PURPOSE The primary purpose of a toast is to celebrate a person, couple, group, or occasion and to draw in the audience to feel a bond with one another. Ask yourself: How can I celebrate the person or group I'm toasting and help the audience join in the celebration? Give audience members who don't know one another a reason to talk to other guests as well as the motivation to talk to the person(s) you toasted.

▲ 87–101

CONTENT Celebrate the person, couple, group, or occasion with special stories, accomplishments, personal experiences, and more. If you decide to use a quotation from another source (book, poem, song lyric, well-known story), make sure it is relevant and meaningful. Despite what you may have seen in comic TV shows and films, don't offend or embarrass the person you're toasting or the audience. Many toasts include humorous stories— usually in the first half—to engage audience attention and emotions. But if you wonder whether the **HUMOR** is appropriate or might not appeal to all, think twice about your choices. More sincere statements should be shared closer to the end.

■ 103–79

⁘ 272–75

DELIVERY How formal is the occasion, and how formal should the toast be? Whether formal or informal, try to project a spontaneous and natural speaking style. Rehearse the toast long enough and well enough to speak **CONFIDENTLY**, **EXPRESSIVELY**, and **FLUENTLY** with limited or no notes. Do not read your toast word for word. When you read a toast, your **CREDIBILITY** diminishes, the audience will quickly lose interest, and your message may not seem genuine. But if, for some reason, you must use a manuscript, practice it repeatedly so you can look at your listeners rather than burying your head and muffling your voice in a pile of wrinkled pages you have trouble reading. The best toasts seem spontaneous and inspired because they are well prepared and skillfully rehearsed.

▶ 181–233

▶ 184–85
▶ 184
▶ 205–6
▲ 57–66

Organizing a Toast

Most toasts do not need a formal or complex organizational pattern, particularly if they are brief. But if your toast is longer than a few sentences, put your ideas in a strategic order. For example, consider a past, current, and future format, or expand on three words that describe the person(s) or occasion. Consider a simple organizational structure: begin with a hook, share brief background information, tell a good **STORY**, and conclude with personal observations.

253–67

Enriching a Toast

239–45

Use an appropriate **SPEAKING STYLE** that suits the rhetorical situation and generates audience interest and engagement. Avoid overused adjectives (nice, funny, great, cool) that can lose their power and importance in a toast. Instead, tell a brief story that demonstrates someone's kindness or how the person's sense of humor defused an uncomfortable situation. Also avoid clichés. Would this person really give a stranger the shirt off his back? Would or even could this person really bend over backward to be there for a friend? A brief story is a better way to visualize someone's admirable characteristics. Rather than telling a "this happened, then this happened" story, use **INTENSE, VIVID, AND POWERFUL LANGUAGE** that helps audience members see, hear, and feel what's going on.

242–43

Keep in Mind . . .

Be Direct and Brief Your job is to say what everyone else is feeling. Try to capture those feelings in your toast without losing your focus or getting sidetracked. If possible, keep the toast short and simple. Listeners are unlikely to want or remember a long-winded toast. Don't let audience members get tired of holding their glasses up in the air.

210–12

Adjust Your Delivery Make direct **EYE CONTACT** with audience members and at the person(s) or group you are toasting. Stand up in a place where everyone can see and hear you. If you are nervous, slow down. Remember, meaningful pauses create anticipation. If there is a microphone available, use it. Without a microphone, you may need to project your voice to command attention and reach everyone. Smile!

- ● getting started
- ▲ fundamentals
- ■ content
- ▶ delivery
- ⁙ engaging your audience
- ◣ speaking to inform
- ◆ speaking to persuade
- ★ speaking occasions
- ✻ resources

Drink First Conclude by raising your glass, smiling, and extending an invitation to everyone in attendance: "Now please join me in a toast to _____." You may want to clink the honored person's glass or "air clink." Then sip your drink, and everyone will sip with you.

If you need more help

See 4.4, **PRACTICING YOUR DELIVERY**, if you need guidance on choosing a delivery mode and practice techniques. See 5.2, **TELLING STORIES**, if you want to develop and tell a good story. See 5.3, **GENERATING INTEREST**, if you want to generate interest, use humor, and actively involve audience members.

▶ 220–33
∴ 253–67
∴ 268–79

NOTABLE SPEAKER
Bill Nighy

Search Terms
To locate a video of this presentation online, enter the following key words into a search engine: Bill Nighy About Time best man speech. The video is approximately 1:05 in length.

A Toast: From *About Time*
In the 2013 British film *About Time*, a father (played by Bill Nighy), offers a 127-word wedding toast that lasts sixty-three seconds. That is a very slow rate of speaking, but given the father's role, his message, and his evident feelings, this toast works. So much so that the clip is one of the most watched and favorite examples of a wedding toast.

Before watching the toast, read it. It's not many words. As a text, it's a bit odd. But the father hooks and involves his audience in his first sentence with a subtle and amusing statement about this son's "failures as a man and as a table tennis player." When he playfully lists the only three men he has ever loved, his son is the final person named. Then he makes a transition to saying something meaningful and sincere about his son. The toast is delivered beautifully by a talented actor using words written by a screenwriter. Even so, it is a model of a fine, meaningful, and poignant toast.

> Later on, I may tell you about Tim's many failings as a man and as a table tennis player. But important first is to say the one—big thing. I've only loved three men in my life. My dad was a frosty bugger so that only leaves dear Uncle Desmond, um, B. B. King—obviously—and this young man here. I'd only give one piece of advice to anyone marrying. We're all quite similar in the end. We all get old and tell the same tales too many times. But try and marry someone—kind. And this is a kind man, with a good heart. I'm not particularly proud of many things in my life. But I am very proud to be the father of my son.

8.7 Eulogies

Eulogies are tributes that praise the dead and celebrate their lives. Most people think of a eulogy as a speech delivered shortly after a person's death. Some eulogies, however, are delivered years later to commemorate the anniversary of a death or to celebrate an important person's historical achievements.

A eulogy is one of the most challenging presentations to create and deliver. You are talking to an audience of bereaved people and are probably feeling the loss of someone who mattered to you. Despite the weight of this challenge, each eulogy is an opportunity to celebrate someone's life. It offers closure and comfort to the person's friends and loved ones. Despite their differences in content, note how the following excerpts from three eulogies honor the memory of the deceased.

- "She had a luminous quality—a combination of wistfulness, radiance, yearning—to set her apart and yet make everyone wish to be a part of it, to share in the childish naiveté which was so shy and yet so vibrant." Lee Strasberg, famous teacher of the "method" acting style, speaking about Marilyn Monroe[1]

- "The thing about John's life was the amazing sweep of it. From a tiny prison cell in Vietnam to the floor of the United States Senate. From troublemaking plebe to presidential candidate. Wherever John passed throughout the world, people immediately knew there was a leader in their midst. In one epic life was written the courage and greatness of our country." Former US president George W. Bush, speaking about Senator John McCain[2]

- "I was so privileged . . . to witness the magnitude of talent of this singer's singer, this musician's musician. And let me add for you that behind her God-given, natural talent, was the drive of a total perfectionist. After we decided on the material for an ensuing album, she would go into Aretha mode and privately rehearse, practice, and prepare. By the time she came into the studio, she literally owned the song. Everyone in the studio would be in awe of her mastery when she stepped up to the microphone." Clive Davis, founder of Arista Records, speaking about Aretha Franklin[3]

Key Features

Eulogies Focus on the Deceased

As nervous as speakers may be before and while delivering a eulogy, they should always understand that the presentation isn't about them. Rather, it pays tribute, says farewell, and evokes cherished memories of the person who has passed away.

Eulogies Create a Comforting, Shared Experience

Eulogies offer comfort and a sense of commonality that everyone in attendance can share. Rather than being mournful, a eulogy can be enriching and inspiring. Notable eulogies capture the essence of the person—what made the person special. Addressing audience members by name or by affiliations (family, friends, coworkers) creates a distinctive and memorable shared experience.

Authenticity Is More Important Than Anything Else

Eulogies that are remembered and appreciated express ideas and emotions that are genuine and truthful: in other words, they are authentic. Lack of eloquence, awkward moments, and minor mistakes that could mar another type of speech are usually forgiven by an audience when they sense the speaker is speaking authentically.

A Brief Guide to Giving a Eulogy

Consider the Rhetorical Situation

5–6

OCCASION The reason for a eulogy is clear: a person has died, and that person's friends, associates, and loved ones want to honor their life and

---

● getting started   ▶ delivery   ◆ speaking to persuade

▲ fundamentals   ∴ engaging your audience   ★ speaking occasions

■ content   ▼ speaking to inform   ✳ resources

share in a comforting social ceremony to express their grief. The timing of a eulogy is determined first, of course, by the deceased's passing, but then also by the wishes of the family or other people close to the deceased who have planned the memorial service or ceremony. The setting for eulogies may be a building or location that is considered by at least some attendees as a sacred or revered space—a house of worship, for example, or the grounds of a cemetery—or it may be another space that has been set up for the purpose, such as a funeral home, a relative or friend's home, or a familiar and appropriate workplace room or auditorium. In some cases, a eulogy addresses a major tragedy, as in presidential eulogies for the victims of mass shootings, terrorism, insurgencies, and natural disasters.

SPEAKER Make sure you know why *you* are doing this eulogy for this person at this time and place. If some audience members do not know who you are or your relationship to the person you are eulogizing, briefly explain why you are speaking. Remember that a eulogy is not about you. It is all about the person you are honoring—a gift to those who knew and cared about the person.

▲ 55–69

AUDIENCE What was the audience's relationship to the deceased person? What do your listeners already know and feel about the deceased person? In some cases, you may need to provide biographical information about the person. In other cases, you can assume that everyone knew the person well. Also consider the audience's expectations and frame of mind. Is a humorous story appropriate or inappropriate? Does the audience expect a formal or informal presentation?

▲ 70–86

PURPOSE A eulogy has two related goals: to comfort those who grieve and to honor the deceased person. How can you celebrate the values and accomplishments of the person and adapt to the emotional context? The most effective eulogies are simple and straightforward. Remember your goals, and craft your eulogy around them.

▲ 87–101

CONTENT Use your relationship with the deceased person to guide your choice of content. If, for example, you are speaking as the person's work colleague, supervisor, or even athletic teammate, your content will be

■ 103–79

253–67
different from that of a close friend or family member. What **STORIES** will you tell to highlight the person's achievements, values, or personal qualities? Are there meaningful quotations you can use if your own words seem inadequate? Choose an organizational pattern that matches your purpose, the audience, and your selected content. Make the eulogy brief, typically no more than four minutes.

181–233
201–3
DELIVERY Rehearse the eulogy, and try to keep your voice steady and loud enough to be heard by your audience. Can you speak at an appropriate **RATE** and pause to signal thoughtfulness and importance? Is your eulogy an appropriate length—brief rather than long winded? Although notes allow

210–12
more **EYE CONTACT** and connections with the audience, a manuscript may be necessary to help you through a highly emotional eulogy.

Organizing a Eulogy

138–48
139–40
144
Most eulogies use a simple **ORGANIZATIONAL PATTERN**. Two common methods for organizing a eulogy are **CHRONOLOGICAL** and **STORY-BASED PATTERNS**. You may, for example, follow the person's development and achievements chronologically from an early age or from when you became acquainted. Or you may prefer to share a series of stories that personify someone's beliefs, values, and/or personality traits. You may even consider using a creative organizational pattern: you could write a final letter to the deceased person or review the person's favorite TV shows or films and describe famous scenes that capture an emotional moment or personality trait.

161–69
The most important thing to do at the **BEGINNING** of a eulogy is to make sure people know who you are and why you are speaking: "My name is Emma, and I was Sofia's college roommate for four years and

169–75
her faithful friend since then," for example. The **ENDING** of a eulogy can take different forms, but the most powerful endings connect the deceased person's life to the lives of the people assembled to honor that person. "Sofia will always be an inspiration to me. I am, and I believe everyone in this room is, a better person because of her. How blessed we are to have known her."

● getting started   ▶ delivery   ◆ speaking to persuade

▲ fundamentals   ⁛ engaging your audience   ★ speaking occasions

■ content   ◤ speaking to inform   ✳ resources

Keep in Mind . . .

Celebrate Small Truths Your job is not to talk about everything the person has done. Instead, focus on a theme that, in your mind, defines the person— a great parent, a wonderfully funny neighbor or colleague, a gifted sailor, a brilliant teacher. Then reflect back on a few vivid details or examples of that defining characteristic. "He drove people crazy with those mismatched pairs of socks. But that was just who he was: a fantastical nonconformist with a fabulous sense of humor."

Name the Deceased Person's Virtues Consider using the traditional language of the classical "virtues" to describe the deceased person's qualities of character, such as *courage, compassion, loyalty, honesty, humility, patience, generosity, empathy, kindness, tolerance, fairness, a sense of humor*, among others. These words are widely understood, and the qualities they identify are widely admired. Think carefully about which ones apply to the deceased, and use them sparingly, so these descriptors feel (and are) specifically appropriate to the person being honored.

Listen to the Eulogies That Precede Yours Frequently, more than one person will offer a eulogy. Family members and friends may stand up and share remembrances. **LISTEN** carefully to what they say. You don't want to repeat the same story. When it's your turn, connect your eulogy to what has been said before if you can.

30–31

A Eulogy Doesn't Need to Be Perfect It's okay to look, sound, and feel nervous, emotional, and grief-stricken. Many speakers find it difficult to maintain their composure while delivering a eulogy. No one in the audience will think less of you if you cannot finish a eulogy or if you falter in its delivery. They will, however, think a great deal more of you if you handle this difficult speaking task with serenity and skill.

Avoid Presumptions or Trite Statements Don't tell audience members you know what they are going through, that they should be happy the suffering is finally over, or that they will be fine in a few weeks. Even if such statements are well meant, audience members want and need to go through their own grieving process.

Use Language That Inspires and Consoles Great eulogies often use 237–52 **LANGUAGE** that is eloquent, expressive, and even poetic. They rise above everyday language to make the occasion feel as special as the person being honored. Of course, if eloquence doesn't feel natural to you, don't force yourself to use language in this way. Above all, use language that authentically expresses your feelings.

Consider Laughter Most of today's memorial services are celebrations. It's okay to tell a funny story about the deceased. A little laughter takes the 272–75 tension of sadness away. Obviously, your **HUMOR** must be in good taste.

Talk to Who Matters You have two audiences when delivering a eulogy: the immediate loved ones of the deceased and the larger audience of 210–12 friends and acquaintances. Make **EYE CONTACT** with the immediate family at various points in the eulogy, offering them comfort for their loss. At other points, be sure to acknowledge the grief and shared memories of all others present.

Prepare a Manuscript Family members often ask speakers for copies of their eulogies, so make sure your words are the ones you want preserved for posterity. If you suspect that may be the case, prepare your 222–23 eulogy in **MANUSCRIPT FORM**, but practice it many times so your delivery 221–22 seems **EXTEMPORANEOUS**.

If you need more help

15–27
70–86
253–67 See 1.2, **SPEAKING ANXIETY**, if you need advice about managing your nervousness. See 2.2, **AUDIENCE**, to help you think carefully about the emotions and needs of your listeners. See 5.2, **TELLING STORIES**, to learn more about how to enhance your eulogy with a personal story.

- ● getting started
- ▲ fundamentals
- ■ content
- ▶ delivery
- ⁂ engaging your audience
- ▼ speaking to inform
- ◆ speaking to persuade
- ★ speaking occasions
- ✳ resources

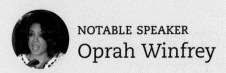

NOTABLE SPEAKER
Oprah Winfrey

Search Terms
To locate a video of this presentation online, enter the following key words into a search engine: Oprah Winfrey Rosa Parks eulogy. The video is approximately 4:10 in length.

Eulogy for Rosa Parks
In October 2005, the activist Rosa Parks, whom the United States Congress in 1999 had honored as "the first lady of civil rights," died at the age of ninety-two. A week after her death, a memorial service at the African Methodist Episcopal Church in Washington, DC, was held in her honor. Tributes were paid to her legacy by politicians, activists, personal acquaintances, and celebrities, including one of the most respected individuals in American media, Oprah Winfrey. Here's an excerpt from her moving eulogy, a video of which is widely available online:[4]

I grew up in the South, and Rosa Parks was a hero to me long before I recognized and understood the power and impact that her life embodied. I remember my father telling me about this colored woman who had refused to give up her seat. And in my child's mind, I thought, "She must be really big." I thought she must be at least a hundred feet tall. I imagined her being stalwart and strong and carrying a shield to hold back the white folks. And then I grew up and had the esteemed honor of meeting her. And wasn't that a surprise. Here was this petite, almost delicate lady who was the personification of grace and goodness. And I thanked her then. I said, "Thank you," for myself and for every colored girl, every colored boy, who didn't have heroes who were celebrated. I thanked her then. And after our first meeting I realized that God uses good people to do great things. And I'm here today to say a final thank you, Sister Rosa, for being a great woman who used your life to serve, to serve us all. That day that you refused to give up your seat on the bus, you, Sister Rosa, changed the trajectory of my life and the lives of so many other people in the world. I would not be standing here today nor standing where I stand every day had she not chosen to sit down. I know that. I know that. I know that. I know that, and I honor that. Had she not chosen to say we shall not—we shall not be moved.

8.8 Team Presentations and Public Group Discussions

Previous chapters in this book have focused on your role as a solo speaker presenting to an audience. The ability to speak for and by yourself is an important life skill, but working and communicating with others is no less important. Success in today's complex world often depends on your ability to communicate in groups.

Everyone works and speaks in groups—at school and on the job; with family members, friends, and coworkers; in diverse locations from sports fields and battlefields to courtrooms and classrooms. Much of this group communication is conducted without an audience present: every person who attends a closed-door work-team meeting, for example, is an active participant and may be asked to speak. Because this is a book on presentation speaking, this chapter focuses on the strategies and skills needed to communicate effectively *to an audience* within a group, on behalf of a group, or by an entire group. Specifically, we examine two types of presentational group communication: *team presentations* and *public group discussions*. Let's look at each one separately.

Team Presentations

Team presentations occur when the members of a cohesive group work together to prepare and deliver a well-coordinated presentation to achieve a specific, agreed-upon **group goal**.[1] Organizations as diverse as nonprofit agencies and global corporations rely on team presentations to make proposals, compete for major contracts, and request funding.

Team presentations can demonstrate whether a group or company is competent enough to perform a task or take on a major responsibility. For

● getting started   ▶ delivery   ◆ speaking to persuade
▲ fundamentals   ∴ engaging your audience ★ speaking occasions
■ content   ♥ speaking to inform   ❋ resources

that reason, team presentations often have high stakes.[2] Here are some examples:[3]

- A software start-up makes the "short list" of businesses being considered for a contract to retool a Fortune 500 company's inventory and customer-service management systems. A team consisting of the CEO, the director of sales, and the director of product development deliver an hour-long presentation and demonstration to the relevant management group of a prospective company in a bid to win the contract.

- In an attempt to increase government funding of a public university, a college president asks a team consisting of an administrator, a professor, a staff member, and a student government representative to deliver a presentation to the state legislature's appropriations committee. The legislature gives the team twenty minutes to make its case.

- A professional football team seeks backing for a new stadium by bringing a well-rehearsed group of executives and star players to a public meeting at which they explain how the stadium will enhance the economic development and prestige of the community without adversely affecting the surrounding neighborhoods.

Key Features

Team Presentations Have an Agreed-upon Group Goal

Having a common goal is the single most important factor that separates successful from unsuccessful team presentations.[4] Much like a solo speaker's **PURPOSE**, a group's agreed-upon goal will determine the communication strategies and skills needed to achieve that goal.

▲ 87–101

Team Presentations Are a Group Product

A team presentation is not a random collection of individual, independent speeches; it is a team product. Team presentations are the ultimate group challenge because they require efficient and effective decision making as well as coordinated performances.

Team Presentations Balance Structure and Spontaneity

An effective team presentation needs a balanced approach: it should be carefully organized and rehearsed *but also* flexible and adaptable. Team members must be well prepared with their own presentations *and* prepared to adapt to listeners' questions. They must be able to tactfully correct a team member's misstep *and* support a needed adaptation during the presentation. Members should also be prepared to address logistical problems (such as a technological issue with presentation aids) *and* adapt to an unexpected shortening or lengthening of their time limit.

A Brief Guide to Team Presentations

Consider the Rhetorical Situation

5–6 ●

OCCASION   Team presentations occur because a working group has been created and tasked with informing and/or persuading a specific audience to achieve a common goal, such as winning a valuable contract, proposing a new project, or updating students on a new campus initiative. They occur whenever the need arises to use a team's shared expertise and speaking skills to achieve a rhetorical purpose. Depending on the occasion and because a team consists of multiple participants, the resulting team presentation can be of moderate length (fifteen to twenty minutes) or, if a detailed, multimediated presentation is called for, may last as 468–78 ★ long as an hour—often followed up with a **QUESTION-AND-ANSWER SESSION**. Team presentations can happen anywhere—in school, in public, in a work setting—and are often held in a place that may be unfamiliar to the team beforehand (for example, in another company's corporate offices).

55–69 ▲

SPEAKER   The "speaker" in a team presentation is the team as a whole. The team must demonstrate its overall competence, trustworthiness, likability, and dynamism. Consider the composition of your team: What is each team member's greatest strength? What can they speak about most competently and confidently? Use team members strategically; capitalize on 57–66 ▲ their strengths. One weak link can jeopardize an entire team's **CREDIBILITY**.

● getting started　　　▶ delivery　　　　　　　　◆ speaking to persuade

▲ fundamentals　　　∴ engaging your audience　　★ speaking occasions

■ content　　　　　　♥ speaking to inform　　　　✳ resources

AUDIENCE Learn as much as you can about your listeners using **AUDIENCE ANALYSIS**. Who will be there? What are their characteristics, interests, attitudes, and values? Do you have a clear sense of their respective status, responsibilities, and influence? If there is a primary decision maker in the audience, you should consider that person your **TARGET AUDIENCE** and adapt to what you learn about the person's background and beliefs. Finally, if your audience is entirely made up of members of a specific organization (for example, a government entity or community association), make sure your message addresses the values and needs of that organization.

▲ 70–86
▲ 72–80

▲ 73

PURPOSE Develop a shared goal that is specific, relevant, and achievable. Make sure every member understands, fully supports, and is well prepared to achieve that goal. Each team member should know the purpose of their particular portion of the presentation and make sure it supports the shared goal. It helps to think of the shared goal as similar to the purpose of a solo presentation and each team member's purpose is a key supporting point.

▲ 87–101

CONTENT Research and select ideas and **SUPPORTING MATERIALS** that are relevant, varied, and persuasive. Make sure that all **ARGUMENTS** include at least a claim, evidence, and warrant and, if needed, backing for the warrant. Make sure the overall organization of the team presentation is clear and that the individual presentations logically flow from one to the other. Link each presentation to the next with effective transitions.

■ 103–79
■ 115–19
◆ 369–74

DELIVERY Practice the entire presentation several times. Because you're working as a team, offer feedback and adjust individual presentations and the group presentation as a whole after every practice session. Use well-prepared, coordinated, professional-caliber **PRESENTATIONS AIDS**, if needed.

▶ 228–33

∴ 282–305

Coordinating a Team Presentation

Every team presentation should have a leader who launches the presentation and serves as the link between the other presenters. The leader tells listeners how the team's presentation is organized, introduces the

66 ▲
184–85 ▶

presenters, directs questions to appropriate members, and wraps up the entire presentation with a well-crafted, well-delivered conclusion.[5] Ideally, this responsibility should be given to your most **DYNAMIC** and **CONFIDENT** speaker, but sometimes the most senior member of the team assumes this mantle, regardless of their speaking skills. When this happens, it is the responsibility of every team member during practice sessions to provide feedback and advice that enhances the team leader's performance. If nothing improves, consider inviting two or three associates to offer a critique—which is not a bad idea for any team presentation. And, if possible, make sure one of them has more authority or rank than the team leader.

Team presentations require a great deal of preparation time, effort, and resources—so they need to be very carefully coordinated and choreographed. Marjorie Brody, the author of *Speaking Your Way to the Top*, puts it this way:

> To be effective, team presentations must be meticulously planned and executed. They must be like a ballet, in which each dancer knows exactly where to stand, when to move, and when to exit from the stage. . . . If a team works like a smooth, well-oiled machine, if one member's presentation flows into the next presentation, and if all members present themselves professionally and intelligently, the impression left is one of confidence and competence.[6]

Keep in Mind . . .

Focus on Every Detail Every team member should know *every* detail of the team's presentation. Don't just focus on your own part.

Emphasize a Theme In addition to the group goal, consider developing a theme, slogan, or metaphor for your team presentation that is repeated and woven into each member's presentation.

Use Your Time Wisely Get the most out of each minute. If you have been given thirty minutes for a team presentation, time your group and make sure it's no longer than twenty-five minutes. Despite your best efforts to plan every second of a team presentation, it usually will take more time

⬤ getting started   ▶ delivery   ◆ speaking to persuade
▲ fundamentals   ⁜ engaging your audience   ★ speaking occasions
■ content   ◥ speaking to inform   ✳ resources

in front of an audience, especially if team members make minor changes to adapt to audience feedback.

Assume Leadership Functions If You Don't Have a Team Leader In the absence of a designated leader, each team member can introduce the next team speaker, preview the importance of the topic, and bolster the speaker's credibility. In addition to giving the speaker's credentials, a brief relevant story about the person can give the audience another reason to listen.[7]

Don't Contradict Your Teammates Although you may at times need to tactfully correct a teammate's error, you should nevertheless present a united front. Your audience will notice if one team member repeatedly disagrees with or contradicts what another member says.

Only One Person Answers Each Question Sometimes everyone on the team feels the need to chime in, but when an audience member asks a question, only the person with the most knowledge of the issue should answer. More than one response takes extra time and often adds little value.

Pay Attention to Your Teammates as They Speak When one person is speaking, it's not uncommon to see their teammates staring into space, reading or writing notes, or even whispering to other team members—behaviors that will distract listeners from the presentation. Be a model of **EFFECTIVE LISTENING**. It's important to demonstrate the level of engagement you'd like to see from your audience. Every team member should look at and, where appropriate, nod as their teammate is speaking.

30–31

Research the Setting, if Possible Get to the location early to make sure the setup and equipment meet the team's needs. Lack of requested equipment may require changes to the team's plan. A last-minute request from a key audience member may require adjustments to the speaking order or a slight change in the focus of a team member's presentation.

Chat with Audience Members If possible, the team should spend time with audience members before the presentation and adapt their presentation to what they've learned from these informal chats.

Public Group Discussions

Public group discussions occur when a group of selected people speak in front of and for the benefit of an audience about a predetermined topic. Group discussions are less tightly coordinated than team presentations, and although the members of the group generally follow an agenda and stay focused on a particular topic, they may not coordinate their respective presentations with one another to achieve a common group goal. Although presenters in a public group discussion may share a general goal—for example, three student government association members might make individual presentations opposing a proposed tuition increase at the monthly public meeting of the college's board of trustees—they don't typically choreograph their efforts. The most common types of group discussions are *panel discussions, symposiums, forums,* and *governance groups.*

Panel Discussions

A **panel discussion** occurs when several participants—who may or may not know one another in advance—discuss a common topic for the benefit of an audience. Panel discussions are common on television and radio, on podcasts, at professional organizations' conventions, and during special events hosted by colleges and universities, houses of worship, art and culture festivals, public libraries, and other public institutions. The participants in such discussions talk with one another in order to educate, influence, or entertain an audience. A moderator typically controls the flow of communication.

Symposiums

In a **symposium**, group members—again, who may or may not know one another in advance—present short, uninterrupted presentations to an audience on different aspects of a topic. For example, a university may sponsor a symposium on the state of the US economy where an elected official, an economist, a union officer, and a small business owner each give uninterrupted talks about ways to protect and bolster the economy. Although symposium members may not agree with one another, their collective goal is to educate audience members by sharing their expertise and perspectives and perhaps to persuade listeners that their perspectives on the topic are valuable.

Forums

A **forum** often follows a panel discussion or symposium and gives audience members the opportunity to comment or **ASK QUESTIONS**. Some forums invite open discussions, letting audience members share their concerns about a specific issue. Other forums give the public an opportunity to ask questions of and express concerns to elected officials and experts. In some cases, members of the group may ask questions of one another. A conscientious moderator tries to give audience members and group members the opportunity to interact.

★ 476–78

Governance Groups

A **governance group** makes public policy decisions, usually in public settings open to public audiences. State legislatures, city and county councils, and the governing boards of public agencies and educational institutions must conduct most of their meetings in public. At colleges and universities, student government and other student associations often invite the entire campus community to attend their meetings. In the United States, perhaps the most visible and most public governance group of all is the US Congress. With only a few exceptions (for example, national security briefings), Congress cannot deny the public access to its deliberations, many of which are broadcast on the C-SPAN network. The decisions made by a governance group are often partisan and sometimes controversial, and they are generally determined by a vote of its members. These votes, along with the comments each member makes during deliberations, become part of the public record.

Key Features

Group Discussions Follow an Agenda, Not a Single Group Goal

An **agenda** is an outline of the topics to be discussed in a group meeting. They are indispensable in, but not limited to, private staff and executive group meetings. Public governance groups use agendas to make sure they get through critical and legally required topics of public interest. Panel discussions use them for the same reason but may be more flexible if a particular topic engages the audience more than others. Even a symposium may give participants an agenda that designates how much time they have for their own presentations as well as the time the moderator needs to introduce the participants and topic—and the time being set aside for a public forum.

Group Discussions Require the Cooperation and Respect of All Members

Although the individual participants of a public group discussion may not share the same goals or opinions, they do share a common interest in ensuring the discussion benefits the audience. Participants should respect the agenda and rules of the discussion, and show respect for other speakers, even if they don't agree with them. If individual members disrespect their fellow presenters (for example, by showing visible irritation or boredom when they speak), the audience may question the credibility of the entire group and the legitimacy of the event overall.

Group Discussions Can Mix Different Formats

Features of panel discussions, symposiums, forums, and governance groups may be included in a public group discussion. Near the end of a symposium, a moderator may conduct a panel discussion among participants to discuss the topic as a whole. That may be followed by an audience forum. A governance group may interrupt its deliberations to hear a short symposium from members of a constituent group with a particular point of view. And, particularly at local government and public board meetings, there may be

468–78 ★

open time for a **QUESTION-AND-ANSWER SESSION**.

A Brief Guide to Group Discussions

Consider the Rhetorical Situation

5–6 ●

OCCASION Public group discussions occur for many different reasons. The main thing to determine or identify is the kind of group discussion—panel discussion, symposium, forum, or governance group—you are participating

● getting started	▶ delivery	◆ speaking to persuade
▲ fundamentals	∴ engaging your audience	★ speaking occasions
■ content	▼ speaking to inform	✳ resources

in, on which topic, and with what goal. These multiple factors define the "reason" for the group discussion and your contributions. The time, duration, and place of the discussion will be determined by the organizers of the discussion, which of course may include you, as a member of the organization or group that will be convening the discussion. In some of these groups—particularly the symposium—there will be rules about how much time is allotted to each speaker and to the discussion as a whole, but others will be more open-ended.

SPEAKER Establish both the group's and each participant's **CREDIBILITY** by sharing members' credentials and relevant experiences with the audience. Accept your responsibilities to the public audience and to an outside group or organization you may be representing. Unless absolutely necessary or expected, do not assume the role of rebellious member.

▲ 55–69
▲ 57–66

AUDIENCE As with any presentation, research the audience's characteristics and attitudes using **AUDIENCE ANALYSIS**. Consider and respect the audience's needs and expectations as well as their **FEEDBACK** during or after the group presentation. In some cases, other group members may be an equally important audience you want to inform and/or influence.

▲ 70–86
▲ 72–80
● 33–34

PURPOSE The common purpose of any public group discussion is to **BENEFIT THE AUDIENCE IN SOME WAY**—to educate them about a topic, to deliberate and make a decision that benefits them, to give them the opportunity to voice their concerns and ask questions. Acknowledge that the goals of individual members and the group may differ. Ask yourself: Are those differences compatible or conflicting? If there is disagreement among group members, strive to keep the presentations objective and civil.

▲ 87–101
▲ 77

CONTENT Include appropriate, interesting, and memorable content that is clear and well organized. Avoid repeating what other members have said unless it's to state that you agree or disagree with them or need to add more information. Use a clear, listener-friendly **ORGANIZATIONAL PATTERN** in your presentations with a limited number of **KEY POINTS**. Stick to time limits so every member has an equal say.

■ 103–79

■ 138–48
■ 133–36

181–233 ▶
228–33 ▶
282–305 ∴

DELIVERY Plan and **PRACTICE** your delivery in the style you will give it: standing or sitting, with or without a microphone or notes, speaking formally or informally, using **PRESENTATION AIDS** (if appropriate), and so on. Dress appropriately and be courteous. When participating in a public discussion, remember you are "onstage" all the time, even when you aren't speaking. Even if you disagree with what other members say, look at and respect other members when they speak—and hope they will do the same for you.[8]

Moderating a Public Discussion Group

468–78 ★

421–26 ★

Many public group discussions include a designated moderator who controls the flow of participation and, in the case of a forum or **QUESTION-AND-ANSWER SESSION**, gives audience members an equal opportunity to participate. At the beginning of a group discussion, a moderator may **WELCOME** the audience and explain the event's purpose and topic. Depending on the type of group and the occasion, a moderator may also provide an overview of the event's agenda, introduce the speakers, and indicate whether there will be time for member interaction and audience questions. From then on, the moderator looks and listens to both the speakers and audience members to ensure the session achieves its purpose. As is also the case with controlling vehicle traffic, the moderator explains and enforces the "rules of the road" for the discussion. Here are some general guidelines to use if you are serving as the moderator:

30–31 ●

- Keep track of the time, and enforce time limits. This task requires tact, **EFFECTIVE LISTENING**, and a respect for the needs of speakers *and* audience members.

- Be prepared to interrupt members who drift from the topic, engage in inappropriate behavior, rudely interrupt others, and/or break agreed-upon rules.

- Protect the rights of group and audience members by guaranteeing their right to speak when appropriate.

- Guarantee the rights of group and audience members to speak on different sides of an issue by balancing participation between frequent and infrequent contributors as well as between members who support and those who oppose a proposal.

Keep in Mind . . .

Public Group Discussions Require Significant Planning Group discussions usually involve more time and preparation than simply scheduling a single speaker. The event must be well planned in terms of the choice of a place, the selection and preparation of participants, the logistics, and (in many cases) the publicity needed to attract an audience.

People Problems May Arise Some members may be well prepared and energized. Other may rarely contribute because they are unprepared or want to avoid conflict and extra work. Strong, dominating members can put pressure on others that stifles dissent. Although no one wants to work with difficult or unpleasant members, you may have no choice. A good moderator should intervene to resolve problems and control levels of participation. In some cases, if there is no moderator, another member can interrupt someone who is speaking longer than the time limit or is behaving inappropriately. Even the audience may react negatively to a problem member and call for fairness and civility.

If you need more help

See 5.3, GENERATING INTEREST, to capture audience attention and heighten audience involvement. See 5.4, PRESENTATION AIDS, to produce uniform, professional-quality presentation aids. See 7.3, RHETORICAL STRATEGIES FOR PERSUASIVE PRESENTATIONS, to develop and present well-justified persuasive arguments. See 8.9, QUESTION-AND-ANSWER SESSIONS, to conduct a productive question-and-answer session.

268–79
282–305
382–404

468–78

8.9 Question-and-Answer Sessions

407–13 ★

The **question-and-answer session**, often called a Q&A, is a series of brief **IMPROMPTU PRESENTATIONS** guided by questions from the audience. Although its informality may lead some speakers to think of it more as a casual conversation than a speaking occasion, a Q&A should be approached with the same level of seriousness as any other type of presentation.

A Q&A can be a stand-alone event, as is the case of a coach or sports director answering questions from the media after a sporting event, or it can follow a presentation, as in the case of a developer's proposal at a city council meeting to build a new apartment complex—after which the developer, the architect, and other members of the developer's team take questions from the public and council members. Some occasions—debates, public hearings, sales presentations, and group presentations—have Q&As all but built into the process. Many everyday presentations—to a class, a group of colleagues, or trainees at a new job—depend on questions and answers to achieve their purpose.

184–85 ▶

Audience members often report liking Q&As better than the presentations that precede them. Why? Because speakers often talk and move more naturally and with more **CONFIDENCE** while answering questions than they do when giving a formal speech. They stop thinking about how they sound and look and instead focus on addressing a specific listener with a specific question.

57–66 ▲

Q&A sessions give audience members the opportunity to interact directly with a speaker after remaining quiet and attentive during a presentation, to hear what others in the audience are thinking, and to evaluate a speaker's **CREDIBILITY** based on how well they respond to audience questions and concerns.

Effective speakers prepare for every Q&A session by anticipating possible questions and keeping additional ideas, information, and arguments in mind for possible use during a Q&A.

- ● getting started
- ▲ fundamentals
- ■ content
- ▶ delivery
- ⁘ engaging your audience
- ▼ speaking to inform
- ◆ speaking to persuade
- ★ speaking occasions
- ✳ resources

In April 2004, a reporter asked President George W. Bush about his biggest mistake as president. Here are several excerpts from Bush's answer:

> I wish you'd have given me this written question ahead of time so I could plan for it. John, I'm sure historians will look back say, gosh, he could've done it better this way or that way. You know I just—I'm sure something will pop into my head here in the midst of this press conference, with all the pressure of trying to come up with an answer, but it hasn't yet. . . . I hope—I don't want to sound like I've made no mistakes. I'm confident I have. I just haven't—you just put me under the spot here, and maybe I'm not as quick on my feet as I should be in coming up with one.[1]

Bush wasn't prepared for the question. His "near inability to respond to this question was the lead story on the news the following morning. His fumble received more attention in many media outlets than did his formal statement."[2] Fortunately, there are a variety of ways for you to prepare for and excel at this unique type of speaking situation.

Key Features

Q&As Should Answer Audience Questions

Three words constitute the most important piece of advice for a speaker in a Q&A session: *answer the question.* This may seem self-evident, but how often have you witnessed a politician—to give just one example—evade a question and do everything *but* answer it? Most audience members know and don't like a speaker who won't answer the question, fakes an answer, or changes the subject. Unless the question is highly technical and demands a long response, your answer should be clear, brief, truthful, and to the point.

Q&As Require Good Questions

Just as a speaker is responsible for answering audience questions competently and honestly, audience members are responsible for the quality and relevance of the questions they ask. Skillful questioners should ask questions based on what they want or need to know and whether they believe it's important to further support or challenge a speaker's claims.

Q&As Benefit from Active Listening

30–31

For a Q&A to go well—to benefit both the speaker(s) and listeners—speakers and audience members should use their **LISTENING SKILLS** to make sure they fully understand the meaning, purpose, and tone of each question and answer. Both parties should consider whether a question and answer is clear or confusing, supportive or antagonistic, personal or impersonal.

36

They also should "listen" to the questioner's and speaker's **NONVERBAL BEHAVIOR** to accurately interpret their emotional meaning. If a questioner's voice and posture are unfriendly, tense, or combative, an effective speaker will pick up on the questioner's hostility and try to answer the question as diplomatically as possible. If, after a challenging question, a speaker's

61–62

response is aggressive and nasty, the audience may question the speak-

63–65

er's **TRUSTWORTHINESS**, **LIKABILITY**, and overall temperament.

A Brief Guide to Question-and-Answer Sessions

Consider the Rhetorical Situation

5–6

OCCASION Q&A sessions occur in response to anticipated or actual questions posed by an audience. A Q&A may be planned in advance for the end of a presentation, or unplanned, after a presentation that ends early enough to field requested audience questions. A freestanding Q&A may be held to address a particular topic, crisis, or event that has made the session necessary. When a Q&A is part of a presentation, it usually follows the presentation itself, unless the speaker encourages audience members to ask questions during the presentation. Some Q&As, whether freestanding or part of a presentation, can be brief or quite lengthy—depending on the planning and significance of the issues being addressed. Q&As are held in all sorts of locations and settings—from classrooms to presidential debates.

55–69
57–66

SPEAKER Although all four dimensions of **SPEAKER CREDIBILITY** (competence, trustworthiness, likability, and dynamism) are relevant to a Q&A session, three are particularly important when answering audience questions. If you fail to answer a legitimate question or your answer is unsatisfactory or inaccurate, the audience will question your **COMPETENCE**. If audience members believe that your answers are fair, honest, and reliable, they are more likely to interpret your responses as **TRUSTWORTHY**.[3] And if you are seen as **LIKABLE**—friendly, warm, and empathetic—when listening to and answering audience questions, audience members will see your answers as audience-centered and true to who you are. Remember that your perceived honesty, integrity, and good character reflect your commitment to being an **ETHICAL SPEAKER**. If you answer questions well, you may enhance people's perceptions of your credibility.

58–61
61–62
63–65
41–47

AUDIENCE If you have **ANALYZED YOUR AUDIENCE** prior to the Q&A session, your responses to questions should reflect what you've learned about your listeners and will better serve their interests and needs. Most audiences enjoy Q&A sessions as long as they are controlled, time limited, and fair.

70–86
72–80

Because Q&As open up the floor to any audience member with a question, you may encounter some questioners who do not represent the attitudes, knowledge, traits, or values of the audience as a whole. Some of these questioners are grandstanding or "trolling." They ask questions to attract attention, show off, impress the audience, and/or intimidate the speaker. (A common annoying version of this kind of question is frequently phrased "This isn't a question so much as a comment . . .") Most audience members have little patience with such self-centered questioners. If you have a clear sense of the attitudes, values, and needs of the majority of your listeners, you can deflect attempts by grandstanders to disrupt or hijack a Q&A by appealing to your audience for support. They may be grateful if you interrupt such a questioner by saying, "Excuse me and thank you for your comments, but there are other people in the audience waiting to ask questions."

PURPOSE If a Q&A session follows your presentation, your purpose should be the same as your presentation's. It gives you the opportunity to share more information, clarify misunderstandings, define difficult terms, provide better explanations of complex ideas, extend persuasive arguments, inspire an audience to action, and further enhance your credibility. If a Q&A stands on its own, your purpose is to answer your audience's questions and

87–101

address their concerns as directly, thoroughly, and concisely as possible, which will enhance your own credibility as a result.

103–79

CONTENT The key to making a Q&A session a positive experience for both you and your audience is preparation. You should predict possible questions in advance, practice the **KEY POINTS** you believe will be most important to your audience, and have a pre-prepared **CONCLUSION** memorized to graciously end the Q&A. Also be prepared with additional supporting material—interesting **STATISTICS**, **STORIES**, **EXAMPLES**, and **TESTIMONIES**—to support your claims and purpose. When you get a question and don't want to repeat what you've said in your presentation, you can share this new information with ease if you have prepared for it in advance.[4]

133–36
169–75

115
117–18
117
116

184–86

DELIVERY The four qualities of delivery—expressiveness, confidence, stage presence, and immediacy—are just as important in a Q&A session as they are in any other presentation. In some ways, your delivery style may be even more important when answering questions because audiences expect a more relaxed, authentic, and immediate *you*. We've noticed that when students answer questions about their topic after a graded presentation, they are more relaxed, speak in an informal oral style, and behave more like their audience and less like a "speaker." Also pay attention to your **PHYSICAL DELIVERY**. Looking bored, annoyed, impatient, or condescending while a questioner is speaking sends a negative message. If the questioner or audience senses your negative response, your credibility may diminish. Remember, you are making an impression as you listen. Establish and maintain full eye contact, smile, and lean toward the questioner.

210–19

Encouraging Questioners

What should you do at the beginning of a Q&A session if no one asks a question? Should you say "Great!" and sprint off the stage? No! Effective speakers use a variety of techniques to encourage audience members to ask questions:

- Do not open a Q&A session with "Are there any questions?" At first, no one may respond. They may need a little time to prepare their question or hope that someone else will break the ice. Instead, assume there *are* questions, and ask, "What are your questions?" or "Who has the first question?"

- If no one poses a question right away, pause and wait. Inexperienced speakers often feel uncomfortable waiting the several seconds it takes for audience members to come up with questions. Even a five-second pause can seem like five minutes. Think about this challenge from the audience's perspective. Just as you may need a moment to organize your thoughts for an answer, audience members may need time to frame their questions.

- If after a significant amount of time has passed and you still don't get any questions, offer some of your own. Some possibilities include: "One of the questions I often hear after my presentation is . . ." or "If I were in the audience, I'd want to know . . ."

- Once an audience member asks the first question, you may face the opposite situation: an overwhelming number of questions and not enough time to answer them. As you near the end of your allotted time, or when you determine the Q&A has gone on long enough, bring the questioning to an end by saying, "I have time for two more questions." Then do just that: answer two more questions, then thank the audience for their participation. If necessary or convenient, you may want to invite audience members to continue the conversation in another location. In this way, other audience members can ask their questions after you've cleared the stage or room for other speakers and activities.

Respecting Questioners

Most questioners are good people seeking answers to genuine questions. Even if they don't phrase their questions well, you will sense what they want to know. A few questioners, however, fall into a different category. They can be highly opinionated or difficult to comprehend. Nevertheless, you should treat all your questioners respectfully. The following suggestions can help you give questioners the respect they deserve:

- *Don't embarrass a questioner.* Most people don't ask questions they know to be stupid, even if they preface it with a statement like, "This may be dumb, but . . ." Always begin by assuming their question is sincere, and do your best to answer it with the same seriousness as any other question, even if you think the answer is obvious. Your audience will appreciate your generosity.

15–27

- *Assist a nervous questioner.* Like speakers, audience members often experience **SPEECH ANXIETY** when they ask questions. Help them through their nerve-racking moment in the spotlight. Encourage, praise, and thank them.

- *Help a questioner stay focused.* An overexcited questioner may try to give a speech rather than ask a question. Once it becomes evident this is what's happening, try to interrupt politely and ask, "What's your question?" If they keep going, you may find audience members supporting you by vocalizing their wish that the questioner stop talking.

Handling Hostile Questions

Depending on your topic and the people in your audience, you may be faced with one or more hostile questions. If this happens, don't panic. Even when an audience doesn't agree with what you've said, they will usually be sympathetic and supportive if one of their members starts to badger you. They wouldn't want to be in your shoes and therefore may become your best allies. Fortunately, there are strategies to help you deal with a hostile question from an antagonistic audience member:

- *Listen carefully, and don't strike back.* The last thing you want is to get drawn into an argument with one person. Taking a few seconds to think can help you stay calm and avoid an embarrassing response. Hostile questioners are trying to provoke you. Don't let them. Be diplomatic and keep your cool. Audience members may become just as tired of listening to a harangue as you are. When a questioner is being abusive, offensive, or threatening, it's often effective to suggest the person talk to you after the presentation and then to quickly move on to the next person who has a question without allowing time for them to follow up.

- Look for **COMMON GROUND**, *an area on which you and the questioner agree, and build your answer from there.* For example, "Then we both agree customers are waiting far too long in line with their purchases. We just differ on how to speed up the checkout process." In addition, use fair and respected **EVIDENCE** to support the answer to a question. It's important to accept differences of opinion while remaining true to your purpose. Work to build personal credibility by treating your audience with respect and by answering their questions as specifically as you can.

▲ 71

◆ 370–71

Keep in Mind . . .

Pounce or Pause before Answering In some cases, you may need to respond immediately to a question, particularly if a simple yes or no response is called for. But unless you believe an instant response is appropriate, you should reflect on the question. Audience members respect speakers who give visible, thoughtful consideration to their questions. Pausing also gives you time to think and develop a response—much as you would in an **IMPROMPTU SPEECH**.

★ 407–13

Thank Commendable Questioners When an audience member asks a particularly good question or something that supports your **PURPOSE**, you can thank them for their question and then demonstrate its value in your response. Avoid insincere flattery. Savvy audience members will know your compliments are not sincere. Even the most polite speaker may not want to thank every questioner at a Q&A.

▲ 87–101

Repeat or Rephrase the Question If some audience members can't hear the question, repeat it for them. Even better, rephrase it and ask, "Did I get that right?" The last thing you want to do is answer the wrong question. Not only can you make the question easier to answer if you put it in your own words, but you may also be able to replace negative phrases with positive or neutral ones. For example, instead of repeating, "Why does our PR office do such a lousy job publicizing our achievements?" you could paraphrase the question as "What can our PR office do to better publicize our achievements?"[5]

Expect Follow-up Questions or Objections In some cases, you will answer someone's question and the person will ask you a second question based on your answer to the first ("If that were so, then wouldn't . . ."). If you can answer the follow-up question well, your listeners will know you are well prepared. But don't let the follow-ups become a conversation between you and one questioner. You can invite the questioner to talk to you later and/ or indicate that other people who may have questions should be given the chance to ask them.

Prepare Concluding Remarks in Advance When audience questions begin winding down or when it's time to stop the Q&A, make sure you've considered or prepared your concluding remarks. Saying "thank you" is polite, but it doesn't take advantage of the opportunity to end with a memorable statement. Instead, return to your **CENTRAL IDEA**, make references to the **CONCLUSION** of your presentation, or talk about the future. You could also refer to the audience's questions and how they helped emphasize the importance of your message. Even if your concluding statement is brief, it can neatly and professionally wrap things up.

137–38 ■
169–75 ■

If You Can't Answer a Question Sometimes people will ask you a question you don't know how to respond to. If that happens, don't pretend you have an answer or you'll lose **CREDIBILITY**. Instead, try two things: First, admit you don't know and see if someone in the audience has an answer. Second, promise to find the answer and get back to the questioner—then make sure you follow up.

57–66 ▲

How to Ask a Speaker a Good Question

You've probably attended a Q&A where members of the audience asked excellent questions that clarified an idea or challenged a conclusion or opinion. You've probably also heard audience members ask ill-informed, confusing, or rude questions. You may have even seen someone give their own miniature speech rather than ask a question, merely standing up to stand out and listen to their own voice. Sometimes a disappointing Q&A is as much the fault of the questioners as it is the shortcomings of the speaker's answers.

● getting started   ▶ delivery   ◆ speaking to persuade
▲ fundamentals   ⁝ engaging your audience   ★ speaking occasions
■ content   ♥ speaking to inform   ✳ resources

Just as a speaker is responsible for answering audience questions respectfully, honestly, and competently, **GOOD AUDIENCE MEMBERS** are responsible for the quality and relevance of the questions they ask. There is a popular concept called WAIT, which stands for "Why am I talking?" Before you ask a question or raise an objection, start by asking yourself that question. Then consider the fundament elements of the **RHETORICAL SPEECHMAKING PROCESS** and ask yourself:

47–48

3–14

- How credible am I?
- Will the audience appreciate my question?
- What's my purpose for asking a question?
- How will my question relate to the speaker's message?
- How will I deliver my question?

Once you've decided to ask a question, how do you come up with something productive and meaningful? Skillful questioners choose one of several types of questions based on what they want or need to know and whether they believe it's important to point out an error or question the speaker's claims. Here are some prompts that can help you ask a good question:[6]

- Could you expand or further explain what you mean by . . . ?
- Here's how I'd summarize what you said . . . Is that correct? Have I misunderstood the point you're trying to make?
- I understand your views, but I also know most scientific studies disagree with your perspective. How do you answer . . . ?
- The study you quoted used only university students [or only men, or wealthy people, or a small number of people] as subjects. Do your findings apply beyond that group?
- What evidence did you rely on to make your claims about . . . ? What's the source of your evidence? How does your evidence warrant your conclusion?
- What's the big picture here? How do your conclusions apply to other situations, such as . . . ?

Once you've finished your question, listen to the speaker's answer respectfully. If you ask an important and well-constructed question, audience members may later thank you for helping them clarify, more fully understand, or challenge a critical issue or the speaker's central idea.

If you need more help

28–38 See 1.3, LISTENING, to help you, as a speaker or listener, accurately hear, understand, recall, interpret, evaluate, and respond when asking and answering questions.
39–51 See 1.4, ETHICS AND FREEDOM OF SPEECH, to defend and respect a speaker's
114–32 and listener's right to ask and answer questions. See 3.2, RESEARCH AND SUPPORTING MATERIAL, for making sure the supporting material you use in a question or answer is valid.

8.10 Online Presentations

Are you one of the world's two billion YouTube users? Have you watched TED talks? Perhaps you've listened to some of the thirty million episodes on 850,000 active podcasts.[1] Maybe you've been interviewed for a job via a platform such as Skype or Zoom. If you have seen or done any of these things, you've experienced **online presentations**—recorded or live presentations that are uploaded onto various platforms on the internet.

As a student during the COVID-19 pandemic, you may have experienced your classes virtually, watching your instructors' lectures or participating in class discussions online. You may have submitted on-screen presentations to fulfill the requirements of a course. During the pandemic, a huge percentage of the professional workforce was driven online too—forcing workers to use teleconferences and videoconferences to communicate with colleagues who were working remotely. Although they were quite common prior to the pandemic, 2020 was the year nearly *everyone* became familiar with online presentations.

An online presentation is more than *just* a mediated speech. It is a special speaking occasion that has a distinct reason (why it is online), time (real or delayed), and place (cyberspace and screen). And as is the case with other special occasion presentations, you may have less control over why, when, and where the presentation occurs. The key is to understand which aspects of the online speaking situation are within your control and to prepare accordingly.

Key Features

Online Presentations Are Contained within a Frame

Unlike in-person presentations where you are "framed" by the room you're speaking in and where your audience sees not only you but also one another and the entire setting in a full panoramic view, online presentations are by necessity and design narrowly framed in the rectangular "window" of a computer or any large, standalone screen.

Online presentations have both advantages and disadvantages. On the one hand, you can usually control the way online audiences see you—the framing is up to you. Also, an online presentation can be managed and delivered in ways that minimize distractions within the presentational space.

On the other hand, being in a frame, even if you set up your camera at a distance, means that your ability to freely move around—if that's the mode of delivery that makes you most comfortable and confident—is severely restricted. If you present in the most common framing—a head-and-shoulders perspective—even your hand gestures will be limited (or will be off-screen).

Because your audience will have only your framing rectangle to look at during your presentation, and because you may not be able to control or adapt to the distractions in each viewer's own setting, the likelihood of your audience being distracted from your presentation is high.

Before giving an online presentation, decide the most effective background that will fit within the camera's frame.

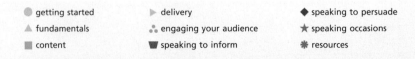

⬤ getting started

▶ delivery

◆ speaking to persuade

▲ fundamentals

⁖ engaging your audience

★ speaking occasions

■ content

🛒 speaking to inform

✳ resources

Online Presentations Focus Attention on the Speaker's Face

As film directors and viewers know, the screen has a way of concentrating our viewing attention on the faces of the actors performing in movies and TV. Film acting demands that actors give special attention to their **FACIAL EXPRESSIONS** and **GESTURES** . In online presentations, even when the frame isn't quite as tight as an extreme close-up in a film or television show, the audience will be very attentive to your face—even more so than in live, in-person presentations.

▶ 212–13
▶ 213–15

Online Presentations Require Modified Delivery Skills

Because most online presentations focus audience attention on your face and upper body—regardless of whether you are standing or sitting—they restrict your freedom of movement and range of gestures during a presentation. Being heard isn't a problem if your microphone's volume level and sensitivity are properly set. However, **VOCAL QUALITIES** such as rate, pitch, inflection, and fluency, as well as the clarity and correctness of the words you use, are amplified and more noticeable online. They also become a permanent record of how well you deliver your message.

▶ 196–206

Online Presentations Permit Real-Time or Recorded Speaking

Online presentations can occur live and in real time, or they can be recorded for viewing later—in other words, they can be either *synchronous* or *asynchronous*. **Synchronous communication** occurs when you present and/or interact with your audience in the same digital space and time. During **asynchronous communication**—the sort of communication that YouTube, podcast platforms, and other recorded media enable—you and your audience are not communicating with one another at the same time. There are advantages and disadvantages of each mode of presenting online.

A Brief Guide to Online Presentations

Consider the Rhetorical Situation

OCCASION In online presentations, your "location" is an obvious and significant aspect of the rhetorical situation. No matter where you are located, the camera is focused on you, and no matter where audience members are,

● 5–6

they are somewhere other than your location. Just as a speaker should do everything to scope out and manage the location of an in-person presentation, successful online presenters are keenly aware of their presentation's "place." They may have to learn the particular technical details of a video-conferencing platform; understand the basics of framing, lighting, and audio for the camera; and/or keep in mind how their audience will be experiencing their presentations. The time for an online presentation consists of either a definite start time for synchronous speaking or a deadline for submitting a recorded, asynchronous presentation. The length of online presentations and the reasons for them vary widely.

55–69 ▲
186 ▶

57–66 ▲
268–79 ⁛
210–12 ▶

SPEAKER Given the mediated nature of an online presentation, successful online speakers focus on establishing **IMMEDIACY** in different ways than they would in person. Without face-to-face interaction, how can you enhance your **CREDIBILITY**, **GENERATE AUDIENCE INTEREST**, and motivate your listeners to engage with your online presentation? One way is to make sure you maintain **EYE CONTACT** with the camera for a greater period of time than you would do when talking to an audience in person. While long periods of unbroken eye contact in the real world would be inappropriate or even creepy (imagine, for example, if you were to lock eyes with one member of your audience while giving an in-person presentation and stay focused only on them!), the majority of the time you present online should be spent maintaining direct eye contact with the camera. Another bit of advice: make sure you're attentive to your facial expressions. Your face should reflect the feelings your words convey. But don't follow this advice too far—don't "act out" facial expressions if they're not natural to you. More than anything, be authentically yourself, and don't force yourself to play a role that isn't genuine. Most audiences—even when listening to an audio-only program—can detect insincerity and playacting.

70–86 ▲
70–72 ▲
72–80 ▲

AUDIENCE Being an **AUDIENCE-CENTERED** online speaker involves the same decisions and principles that apply to any other speaking situation. Doing a thorough **AUDIENCE ANALYSIS** well ahead of your presentation is essential. Because you won't have as much (or the same kind of) in-the-moment feedback from your audience as when you're speaking online, you

---

● getting started   ▶ delivery   ◆ speaking to persuade

▲ fundamentals   ⁛ engaging your audience   ★ speaking occasions

■ content   ▼ speaking to inform   ✳ resources

should always keep your **TARGET AUDIENCE** in mind as you prepare and deliver your presentation. Consider why you enjoy a particular podcast or YouTube video. Is it because you like the speaker, the content, the production style? Focus on the kinds of listeners who, in your opinion, will like or be interested in your online presentation. Involve them. Use polls, chat, and breakout rooms. Use audience members' names when appropriate. Give them a reason to listen. Ask **WIIFT**: What's in it for them? Keep in mind that the online medium may seem less intimate and immediate to your audience. Adapt **IMMEDIACY STRATEGIES** to enhance your delivery. Use inclusive language to establish that you care about your audience's interests and needs and to signal that you and they are standing together on **COMMON GROUND**. Look directly into the camera lens, smile, and use a warm and expressive voice, a relaxed posture, and a direct face-to-face body orientation. Speak as though you're having a personal conversation with each member of your audience.

▲ 73

▲ 77

▶ 186

▲ 71

PURPOSE Think about your purpose as carefully and seriously for an online presentation as you would for an in-person presentation. Make sure you know what you want to say before you develop and start recording or participating, and keep it firmly in mind as you speak. As is the case with all presentations, develop a specific, achievable, and relevant **PURPOSE STATEMENT** that can guide every decision you make about an online presentation.

▲ 87–101

▲ 95–97

CONTENT The basics of selecting and organizing your content for online presentations are the same as in-person presentations: you should use your purpose statement to identify the main ideas and **SUPPORTING MATERIALS** you want to include in your presentation. The criteria you apply to selecting content—making sure it is up to date, accurate, relevant, and valid—become even more relevant in an online presentation, because an incorrect statement, manipulated fact, biased source, or poorly explained concept will become part of a permanent audio or video record of your presentation and may damage your long-term **CREDIBILITY**. When organizing your content, formulate a **CENTRAL IDEA** that summarizes your **KEY POINTS** and forms the basis for your presentation's organization. In addition to the

■ 103–79

■ 115–19

▲ 57–66

■ 137–38

■ 133–36

282–305 ⁞⁞
words you say, put the **PRESENTATION AIDS**—illustrations, slides, demonstrations, and sound effects—exactly where you will use them as you plan and organize the content of your message.

181–233 ▶
DELIVERY Online presentations require adjustments to your vocal and physical delivery because the space you have available to you is constrained to the window in which your image is recorded and because your voice is recorded by a microphone. Successful online presenters focus on being expressive and immediate with their face and upper body (as long as it feels natural and authentic). They also adjust their audio equipment so that their optimal presentational voice is picked up by the microphone clearly and without distortion. Maintaining steady eye contact with the camera is a must. If you break eye contact frequently, looking to your left and right or up and down, viewers will wonder what is going on in those directions. Although some video recording technologies let you to see your image in a corner of the screen, don't look at it. It can distract both you and your audience.

221–22 ▶
407–13 ★
Depending on the type and topic of online presentation, try to use an **EXTEMPORANEOUS** speaking style. If you speak **IMPROMPTU**, you may sound hesitant, appear disorganized, and seem to lack coherence. However, reading a script word for word can be dull and robotic. An extemporaneous style is more likely to sound and look authentic and audience centered. Even though extemporaneous speaking doesn't require a manuscript, you may have brief notes so you stay on track.

Adapt to the Logistics

In an online speaking environment, the setting, your appearance, the lighting, the video-recording equipment, and the sound-recording equipment may require as much attention as the presentation itself.

Setting Online presentations are delivered in many different settings ranging from fully equipped studios to dorm rooms. But whatever the setting you use to record or deliver an online presentation, your audience will experience it within the narrow confines of a screen. Remember: you are in control of the frame. Make sure your setting enhances the value and impact of your message. Take a critical look at the background for your video. If you are speaking about something historical, an appropriate backdrop might be a bookcase, a map, or a historic site (either inside or outside). If you are recording in a room at home, in a dorm, or at work, make sure the background is uncluttered. Get rid of anything that could distract or disturb viewers. Ask friends and family member to stay quiet and out of view as you are presenting. If you can't find a good backdrop or can't do much about the backdrop as it is, find a way to cast a virtual background behind you. Common videoconferencing platforms like Zoom or Microsoft Teams offer various virtual background options. Make sure the background matches the message. For example, don't put up a background of an exotic beach resort if you're talking about poverty. If you're recording video, consider hanging a solid color sheet or cloth behind you or buy a portable green screen (this will require editing software) to insert a digital background before releasing the video.

If you present or record inside, use a room that is as soundproof as possible. Rooms with carpet are better than rooms with hardwood floors. If you can, shut the door to keep out friends, pets, and little children. Or put a sign on the door: recording in progress—do not enter. If you're speaking outside, try to avoid noisy areas. Consider possible interruptions such as people talking and moving in the background without knowing a video is being recorded.

Before you begin recording, switch off distracting audible computer and phone notifications. Eliminate ambient noises—the fan from an air-conditioning unit, the television in another room.

Appearance Your appearance matters as much in online presentations as in in-person speeches. Make sure to dress appropriately for the occasion. If it's a business presentation, dress professionally. If it's an assignment for class, dress as you would if presenting in a physical classroom. Test your wardrobe on camera before your presentation to see if there's anything distracting about your clothing. Because of how much attention online presentations direct to your face, make sure you're well groomed, and don't wear makeup or accessories that will distract your audience from your facial expressions and words.

Lighting Lighting the place where you will be speaking affects the quality of your video. The most effective lighting setup reduces shadows and extreme contrasts, giving your face an evenly illuminated appearance. The best way to do this is to make use of two sources of light: a *key light* and a *fill light*. Fortunately, you don't need to buy professional lighting equipment. You can use desk lamps or clamp lights or a window with natural light coming through it. The key light is the strongest light you have available and should be placed on one side of the camera and angled either up or down at you. The fill light should be placed on the other side of the camera, opposite the key light. The goal of the fill light is to fill in the shadows that a key light alone will cast on your face. It may take adjusting to get the fill light positioned at just the right angle to achieve a pleasing effect.

TWO DIFFERENT DEGREES OF FILL LIGHT

On the left, the key light is strong, and there is a relatively weak fill light, leaving one side of the presenter's face darker than the other. On the right, the key light and fill light are relatively equal in strength, which results in even lighting of both sides of the speaker's face.

If you have only one light available to you, set it up in a more or less front-lit position. There are many relatively inexpensive "ring" lights available for this purpose that provide a bright and diffuse light. In general, it's best not to speak with a window behind you in bright daylight. You will appear dark and in the shadows. However, if you must give an online presentation in a room with strong natural light coming in through a window, simply set yourself up so that you are facing that window, and if you have another light source, use it to fill in whatever shadows the natural light is casting on your face. If you're recording outside, find a location that softens shadows while still providing a strong, even light on your face.

LIGHTING WITH A SINGLE SOURCE

If you have only one light source—whether natural or artificial—try to situate it so that it is illuminating the front of your face. Ring lights are a good option for front lighting. They produce a bright but somewhat diffuse illumination, as you can see here.

Video Recording Check the camera angles to get a straight-on view of yourself. You don't want viewers looking at your chin, the ceiling, or the top of your head. Close-ups can be too close and shots from a distance make it hard to see details. If you're using the camera on a computer, iPad, or smartphone, make sure your camera lens is a bit higher than eye level. If you have a stand-alone camera, you can use and adjust a tripod to achieve the right level—even a low-cost model will stabilize the shot.

Although high-end, high-definition professional cameras will produce professional-looking shots, many newer smartphones and computers have excellent cameras capable of recording quality video footage, so you'll find there's probably no need to purchase an expensive camera to record your presentation. If you're using a smartphone to record your presentation, place it on a tripod if you can and remember to turn it horizontally. This will create a widescreen video, which creates a more friendly viewing experience for your audience.

Sound Recording While camera quality is very high on many smartphones and computers, the audio may not be as good as when using a separate, dedicated microphone. Filmmakers have long known that audio quality is at least as important to a viewer's experience and engagement as the video quality. If you have the budget to do so, consider buying a separate microphone that best suits your setting and your optimal vocal style.

Keep in Mind . . .

228–33 ▶
Practice! It is as essential to **PRACTICE** for online presentations as for any other type. Because they've seen countless examples of slick online productions and presentations, audience members may expect an online presentation to be more professional and engaging than an in-person presentation. The key to getting it right is to record your practice sessions as they will be presented—with the same lighting, same audio equipment, same setting, same clothing, and so forth. You will quickly see if your presentation needs more work or is ready to go.

Involve the Audience during Synchronous Presentations If you are doing a synchronous presentation, try to maximize your audience's involvement (within reason and while recognizing the limitations of the medium). Ask people to answer questions or share their experiences; audience members' opinions can be gauged by a simple show of hands. Involving audience members is an opportunity to test whether they understand, like, and accept your message.

282–305 ∴
Adjust and Upgrade Presentation Aids If you intend to use **PRESENTATION AIDS**—whether images, objects, graphics, or sounds—make sure you know exactly how you will bring them into your audience's view. Slides and other

---

onscreen aids will be visible and effective only if you know how to shift between views of your face and the sharing of your screen. Unless you are showing a full-screen presentation aid, physical objects, whiteboards, drawings, and other visual aids should be visible and legible in the frame while not crowding you out of it. Remember: you are your presentation's most important visual aid. Don't fill your presentation with so many aids that your audience can't connect with you.

If you need more help

See 2.2, AUDIENCE, to learn how an analysis of audience characteristics and attitudes can guide how you develop and deliver online presentations. See 4.1, THE IMPORTANCE OF DELIVERY, to learn more about enhancing immediacy. See 4.2, VOCAL DELIVERY, to review recommendation for improving vocal delivery skills. See 5.4, PRESENTATION AIDS, to adapt strategies for creating and using presentations aids in an online presentation.

70–86
183–93

194–209
282–305

Part 9

Resources

As you now know, a presentation is most effective when you and your audience connect in a meaningful way. You also know that a well-organized presentation helps audience members understand and make informed decisions about your message, while helping you—the speaker—achieve your purpose. The two chapters that follow provide, as promised in previous chapters, detailed instructions for how to use specialized devices—**AUDIENCE SURVEYS** and **PRESENTATION OUTLINES**— to learn more about your audience and organize your content.

Resources

9.1 How to Survey an Audience

A presentation is effective only when you and your audience connect in a meaningful way. To make that connection, you need to know as much as you can about them. Who are they? Why are they here? What do they know? What are their interests? What are their attitudes? And what are their values?

Answering questions like these requires thorough **AUDIENCE ANALYSIS**. This process can range from brief observations made right before or during your presentation to using sophisticated survey research. How much audience analysis you do depends on how much time, skill, and energy you devote to the task.

▲ 72–80

In many speaking situations, such as classrooms or the workplace, you may already know a lot about your audience. As you plan your presentation, think about who will be attending, their likes and dislikes, their knowledge and experience, and so on.

If you're unfamiliar with your audience, however, there are systematic ways to analyze who they are and how you might create an effective and meaningful presentation. This chapter focuses on several survey techniques you can use to research, analyze, and then **ADAPT** to your audience as you prepare and deliver your presentation. We describe basic survey guidelines, types of survey questions, and protocols for conducting and administering a survey, as well as how to ask questions in one-on-one interviews and face-to-face focus groups. To that we add techniques for informally surveying your audience *during* a presentation and then making appropriate adjustments *as* you speak.

▲ 80–82

● getting started   ▶ delivery   ◆ speaking to persuade

▲ fundamentals   ⁑ engaging your audience   ★ speaking occasions

■ content   ▼ speaking to inform   ✳ resources

Audience Surveys

Probably everyone has completed a **survey**, a common research method that uses a set of questions to obtain useful information and insights about the characteristics, knowledge, attitudes, beliefs, and behaviors of a predetermined group of people. There are several ways to collect data: (1) paper-and-pencil surveys, (2) website surveys, (3) telephone surveys, and (4) face-to-face surveys in the form of interviews and focus groups.[1]

Surveys ask about products, preferences, candidates running for office, and customer service experiences. Politicians rely on voter surveys, known as polls, to design campaigns ads and craft public addresses. Corporations rely on consumer surveys to develop new products and improve existing ones. Television networks use viewer surveys to determine which shows will live or die. So how do you use this method to prepare for a presentation?

There are hundreds of books, websites, and articles devoted to developing, administering, and analyzing survey research. We've distilled much of that advice here. Although we can't teach you everything there is to know about survey methods, we can recommend strategies that will help you design an effective, efficient, and ETHICAL pre-presentation survey of your audience. A good survey should be

43

- Focused on what you need to know
- Fair
- Neutral
- Confidential
- Relevant
- Brief and simple
- Pretested
- Professional looking

Need to Know

A good survey should tell you something you don't already know about your audience. Avoid questions with obvious or predictable answers, such as "Should the United States oppose terrorism?" or "Do you want to earn more money?" Neither is likely to elicit a response different from what you would expect.

A good survey should also give you information you can use. When drafting questions, always start with your **PURPOSE**. What is your goal, and what do you need to know about your audience in order to achieve it? Once you know the kinds of information you hope to gather, make sure your questions are phrased to produce useful responses. For example, the question "Do you exercise regularly?" does not tell you whether *regularly* means twice a day, week, or month. An open-ended question such as "Why do you support Robin Brown for mayor?" could give you a useless answer: "Because she is the best candidate" or "I voted for her last time." Let's look at alternative approaches to the same question:

87–101

POOR QUESTION:	Why do you support Robin Brown for mayor?
GOOD QUESTION:	List three reasons why Robin Brown is the best candidate for mayor.

POOR QUESTION:	Do you exercise regularly? _____ yes _____ no
GOOD QUESTION:	How often do you do exercise for more than 20 uninterrupted minutes?

_____ Rarely or never

_____ Once or twice a month

_____ Once or more a week

_____ Daily (when possible)

Fairness

A good survey should be fair. If you don't phrase your questions fairly, you won't get an accurate picture of your audience. Don't ask questions that "force survey respondents to choose an answer that doesn't reflect their opinion, thereby making your data unreliable."[2] Yes-or-no questions are often unfair to audience members who don't like either option or are undecided. Questions such as "Are you against gun control?" or "Do you favor the legalization of marijuana?" don't leave room for answers such as "It depends on the circumstances," "I can think of other options," or "I haven't made up my mind."

Neutrality

Avoid asking questions that all but force people to respond in ways that favor the survey taker's position. For example, in a Pew Research survey, 51 percent of respondents said they favored "making it legal to give terminally ill patients the means to end their lives," but only 44 percent said they favored "making it legal for doctors to assist terminally ill patients to commit suicide."[3] The first statement is neutral, whereas the second is biased because of the negative **CONNOTATIONS** of *suicide*, leading some respondents to an unfavorable opinion.

237–38

Political campaigns often distribute "push polls," or surveys filled with questions seeking predetermined or self-serving responses. For example, one congressional candidate's questionnaire asked, "Do you favor the socialist medical plan advocated by Bernie Sanders? Yes or no." The use of "socialist" is meant to provoke a particular response: if you think socialism is bad, then Bernie Sanders's medical plan must be bad. The question also neglects to provide details about the plan itself, further skewing the results to a desired conclusion. Ethical survey researchers avoid questions that evoke only the opinions they want responders to agree with.

Confidentiality

A good survey is confidential. Respondents are more likely to give you honest information about themselves, their opinions, and their behavior if you don't ask for their names or other identifying information. Respect your audience's privacy. In a familiar speaking situation (a college class, business/organization, social service club, or house of worship), you may already know your audience will be predominantly female, or African American, or under thirty years old. Avoid survey questions that make it easy to identify the few members who are different.

Relevance

108–10
87–101

Only ask questions that are relevant to your **TOPIC** and **PURPOSE**. Why ask questions about religion or sexual identity when you are speaking about the newest technologies NASA is using in space? If, however, you are talking about a religious mission you took last summer, then it might be important to understand how audience members feel about religion generally—or your religion specifically. If you are speaking about gravity or space exploration, then it might be valuable to learn more about your audience's scientific background.

Brevity and Simplicity

Most people don't like taking the time to answer a long questionnaire. If you ask a very long list of questions, respondents may become tired of answering them and quit taking the survey. Use simple, concrete, and grammatically correct language, and steer clear of **CLICHÉS**, abbreviations, and jargon. Avoid giving away too much information about your presentation in the survey because it can ruin the effect you are trying to achieve. If your questions use words or express opinions similar to those in your presentation, respondents may feel as though you are priming them to agree with you.

•• 249

Pretesting

Every legitimate survey company pretests questions to find out if respondents are interpreting their meaning as intended. If you don't have access to audience members, test your questions on friends, family members, or coworkers. You may discover your questions are vague or that the questions you want to use don't gather the kind of information you need. If necessary, make changes to your questionnaire—and be sure to pretest the revision as well. You may discover you have too many questions, which may tire or frustrate respondents, or too few to get the kind of data you need to analyze and then adapt to your audience.

Professional Appearance

A good survey looks professional. It should be formatted consistently, easy to read, and include a clear set of instructions. Audience members are more likely to give serious thought to a professional-looking survey than to one that has been scribbled down and slapped together at the last minute.

Types of Survey Questions

87–101 ▲

There are two broad types of survey questions: open ended and close ended. When choosing which to use, consider your **PURPOSE** as well as the kind of information you think will be most useful when preparing your presentation. Whenever possible, use more than one type of question. If your survey looks repetitive, respondents may not take your questions seriously—or may ignore them entirely. The types of survey questions that follow are especially useful when analyzing an audience.

Open-Ended Questions

Open-ended questions allow audience members to provide detailed answers. They often begin with phrases, such as "What do you like most about . . . ," "Please explain why . . . ," and "What do you know about . . ." Here are a few examples:

- If you have never donated blood, please explain the reason or reasons why you haven't.
- What are two characteristics you like most about your favorite professor?
- What are the most important qualities you look for in a new employee?
- Explain why you voted for _____.
- What religious beliefs, if any, are shared by Christians, Muslims, and Jews?

The answers to open-ended question are very valuable, but be careful not to overuse them. Some surveys put open-ended questions near the end of a questionnaire so respondents have had time to think about the topic, while others ask them early so respondents aren't influenced by previous survey questions.

A quick rule: one or two good open-ended questions is enough—but don't put them back-to-back. Open-ended questions require more time and effort to answer. When there are several in a row, respondents may experience survey fatigue and fail to answer more than the first question conscientiously, or they may not respond to those that follow.

● getting started   ▶ delivery   ◆ speaking to persuade

▲ fundamentals   ⁘ engaging your audience   ★ speaking occasions

■ content   ▼ speaking to inform   ✳ resources

Close-Ended Questions

Close-ended questions force audience members to choose an answer from a limited list. As a student and consumer, you are probably familiar with the following four general types of close-ended questions, each of which can address different purposes.

Multiple-Choice Questions Everyone knows what a multiple-choice question is. They are the go-to question type on most exams and achievement tests. And as a survey question, they are the most popular because they provide the clearest results. There are two variations of multiple-choice questions. The first example below asks for a single answer. The second example—also called a checklist—allows a fixed or unfixed number of multiple answers.

In your opinion, what percentage of your daily communicating time do you spend listening?

_____ More than 70 percent

_____ 40–70 percent

_____ 20–39 percent

_____ 10–19 percent

_____ Less than 10 percent

Which beliefs and values are *most important* to you? You may check one or more answers.

_____ Individuality and self-interest take precedence over group interests.

_____ All forms of authority, including government, should be viewed with suspicion.

_____ Your personal success depends on acceptance among your peers.

_____ You should belong to an organized religious institution.

_____ All human beings are equal.

_____ America is a symbol of progress.

_____ Protecting our environment is a moral and survival issue.

Ratings Ratings questions—often called an agree-disagree scale or a Likert scale—ask audience members to specify their level of agreement or disagreement about a series of statements. There are two types of rating scales that tap different traits—thinking and feeling. The first example asks respondents to think about the importance of specific speaking skills. The second example surveys audience feelings about speaking in various contexts.

How would you rate the following items in terms of their importance to you in becoming a more effective speaker? Circle one of the numbers for each of the four items that represent how important or unimportant it is as a presentation speaking skill.

	Extremely important	Very important	Somewhat important	Not very important	Not at all important
1. Organizing a presentation	5	4	3	2	1
2. Adapting to an audience	5	4	3	2	1
3. Speaking impromptu	5	4	3	2	1
4. Persuading an audience	5	4	3	2	1

Indicate the degree to which each statement applies to you by marking whether you (1) strongly agree, (2) agree, (3) are undecided, (4) disagree, or (5) strongly disagree.[4]

_____ 1. I have no fear of speaking up in conversations.

_____ 2. My thoughts become confused when I give a speech.

_____ 3. I dislike participating in group discussions.

Rank Ordering Ranking questions ask audience members to put answer options in a preferred order. In addition to tapping how someone reacts to each option, these questions help you understand each option's popularity relative to the audience as a whole. Keep in mind that this kind of question takes longer to answer because survey takers may reorder their options several times. The first example below asks you to rank the features of a physical product. The second wants you to rank the quality of customer service in five fast-food chains.

> Which of the following features of your fitness tracker do you like the most? Order the features from highest (5, the feature you like most) to lowest (1, the feature you like least).
>
> _____ Measuring sleep time and quality
>
> _____ Setting fitness goals
>
> _____ Tracking number of steps per day
>
> _____ Monitoring active minutes
>
> _____ Recording calories consumed

> Which of the following fast-food chains provide the best customer service? Order them from best (5, the best customer service) to worst (1, the customer service you like the least). Do not rate the food.
>
> _____ McDonald's
>
> _____ Burger King
>
> _____ Chipotle
>
> _____ Chick-fil-A
>
> _____ Wendy's

Demographic Questions Demographic survey questions collect information about audience demographics such as age, gender, race, marital status, religion, income, and occupation. These answers can help you segment your audience based on who they are and what they do. Demographic questions are often used to gather information about an audience's political viewpoints.

To which generation do you belong?

____ Greatest Generation (born 1901–27)

____ Silent Generation (1928–45)

____ Baby Boomers (1946–64)

____ Generation X (1965–80)

____ Millennials or Generation Y (1981–96)

____ Generation Z or Zoomers (1997–2012)

How would you describe your political viewpoint?[5]

____ Very liberal

____ Slightly liberal

____ Slightly conservative

____ Very conservative

____ Prefer not to say

How to Use Demographic Data

When surveying an audience, be careful about asking respondents for demographic data. Some people may be reluctant to answer questions about their age, gender, ethnicity, religion, income, occupation, marital status, and more because they don't want to box themselves into a category. They also may want to keep that sort of information private. Consider this example: if audience members are predominantly white and middle aged, and someone checks African American and eighteen to twenty-four years old, it may be easy to identify the respondent in what is supposed to be an anonymous survey. However, the answers to such questions can sometimes be very valuable. They can help you identify factors that may influence how people will respond to your presentation. They also let you compare and contrast the responses of various subgroups. For example, the age of audience members can tell you a great deal about their knowledge and experience with modern technology, as well as their familiarity with historical events and popular pastimes.

When asking about demographic information, make sure the answer options adapt to probable characteristics of your audience. Remember that

getting started   ▶ delivery   ◆ speaking to persuade
▲ fundamentals   ⁌ engaging your audience   ★ speaking occasions
◼ content   ◤ speaking to inform   ✳ resources

the words *male* and *female* refer to biological classifications rather than identity. When asking about gender, you should provide a variety of answer options, including male, female, transgender, nonbinary, other, and prefer not to answer. If sexual orientation is relevant to your **TOPIC** and **PURPOSE**, try to include a wide range of answer choices: for example, heterosexual, homosexual, bisexual, asexual, and pansexual. Alternatively, you could use an open-ended question, but the results would be more difficult to tabulate and summarize.[6]

■ 108–10

▲ 87–101

When asking about race, remember that many people are of mixed races and that the US Census now identifies Hispanic and Latino (which is the largest minority group in the United States) as an ethnicity, not a race. You can adapt to changes in race and ethnicity designations by combining the categories into a single question that alphabetizes all but the last three options:

Which of the following categories best describes you?

____ Asian or Pacific Islander

____ Black or African American

____ Hispanic or Latino

____ Native American or Alaskan Native

____ White or Caucasian

____ Multiracial or biracial

____ My race/ethnicity is not listed here.

____ I prefer to not answer this question.

Try to be inclusive and avoid upsetting members who are left off a demographic checklist when asking audience members questions about, for example, their religion. Don't restrict yourself to Christian, Jewish, Muslim, and other unless it's appropriate for the content and context of your presentation. The Pew Research Center uses a standard religion question, "What is your present religion, if any?" The list of possible responses includes twelve different religious designations that begin with the most common US affiliations: "Are you Protestant; Roman Catholic; Mormon; Orthodox, such as Greek or Russian Orthodox; Jewish; Muslim; Buddhist; Hindu; atheist; agnostic; something else; or nothing in particular?" Even this question leaves out Armenian Orthodox, Coptic Christians, Jainism, Sikhism, Shinto, and more.

5–10
The way you ask and use the answers to demographic questions can vary depending on the **RHETORICAL SITUATION** and whether you really need to know the answers. And remember this important survey guideline: Do you really need to know the answer to this question in order to understand and adapt to your audience?

Survey Administration

Once you have developed and prepared a survey, determine the best way to distribute and collect your questionnaires. If you are speaking to a classroom audience, you should hand out and collect your survey several days before the date of your presentation. Alternatively, your instructor may set aside part of one class period for this process.

It is more difficult and time consuming to distribute and collect a survey outside a classroom setting. You may first need the permission and cooperation of the group or organization you will be addressing, and then you'll need to distribute and collect the responses and set aside enough time to analyze the results.

There was a time when surveys were mailed to respondents—in fact, the US Census Bureau still relies on initial mail-in questionnaires. To do this, you'd have to provide stamped, preaddressed return envelopes so respondents can, with little effort, return their questionnaires directly to you. Even so, response rates for mailed surveys unfortunately tend to be quite low.

The good news is that online tools such as SurveyMonkey, Google Forms, SurveyLegend, Typeform, Qualtrics, Survey Planet, Snap Surveys, and others have made it much easier to create, distribute, and process the results of a survey. In most cases, they provide only a shell for your questions. You still need to write valid questions and send them to a list of recipients you've compiled. Even if you've followed survey-making guidelines and chosen appropriate types of questions, a poorly written or biased set of survey questions will produce bad and/or useless results. And remember, depending on the likely audience, some members may not be confident, willing, or able to answer online questions.

If you don't have time to survey your audience, you may look for general answers to research questions about an audience. For example, the Gallup polling organization's website (www.gallup.com) provides detailed information about many population characteristics—from product preferences and social interests to audience knowledge of and opinions about political issues and candidates. However, as interesting as these studies may be, your audience may not conform to general poll results. Every audience is different in its own way. Search for and honor those differences.

If you need more help

See 2.2, **AUDIENCE**, to learn more about audience analysis.

70–86

Interviews and Focus Groups

If you want to survey your audience, a questionnaire isn't your only option. One alternative is scheduling an interview with one or two people who know the audience better than you do. Another option is conducting a focus group with people who are part of—or similar to—the audience you expect to address.

Interviews and focus groups offer the opportunity to pretest your questions and identify the ones that require revisions. They also allow you to discuss the answers with respondents. For example, you could ask someone why they answered a close-ended question in a particular way. By directly interacting with the participants, you may discover critical issues your questionnaire overlooked.

Interviews

There are several ways an **interview**—a private one-on-one conversation between you and an audience member either in person or via media—can provide detailed, valuable information to help you prepare for a presentation. For example, you may be able to interview the person who invited you to speak or someone else who knows the audience better than you do. Begin by asking general questions: "What should I know about this audience?" "Do you think they'll be attentive and interested in my topic?" "What, if anything, does the audience know about me? What do you think they *should* know?" "Should I schedule time for audience questions?" Then you can test some of your survey questions: "What's the average age of the audience?" "What issues related to my topic are important to them?" "Do they know a lot about this topic, or will it be new to most of them?" "Are there 'toxic' topics I should avoid?" In some cases, you may be able to interview a few audience members in advance. Listen for common characteristics as well as information about their opinions and behaviors, but stay focused on

87–101

your **PURPOSE**. Demonstrate that your goal is to learn as much as you can in order to tailor your presentation to their interests and needs.

When using an interview to gather audience information, there are some things to keep in mind. What you learn from a handful of interviews may not be representative of the audience as a whole. And the people you interview may be unwilling to give you honest answers—or they may give you the answers they think you want to hear.[7] Consider what you know and/or have learned about your audience using other methods to process and adapt to interview responses. If necessary, ask them to explain their answers in more detail.

Focus Groups

A **focus group** is an exploratory, qualitative research method where people discuss a series of carefully selected questions guided by a moderator—who may be a hired consultant, a psychologist, or you (the speaker). As with any survey, your job is to gather information that will be useful when preparing your presentation. Like in an interview, you have the chance to hear and observe what participants think and feel in real time.[8] Focus groups may take some effort, but they can be just as valuable as a good survey if planned and conducted with care. Here are some basic guidelines for conducting a productive focus group.

Develop Appropriate Survey Questions The questions you use in a focus group are not necessarily the same questions you would ask in a written survey. If nothing else, there are fewer questions, and they should be ranked in order of importance. The strength of focus groups is that you can ask group members to explain why they chose a particular answer and observe how they respond to other group members who chose different answers. Although you may be tempted to ask the exact same questions you put in a survey, "focus group questions should be less specific and allow participants to provide longer answers." Broader questions are particularly helpful in finding out what audience members "understand about a topic area and how [they] interpret questions (in particular, how framing a topic or question in different ways might affect responses)." Ask questions that will "elicit unedited reactions from the group members, and then ask more specific follow-up questions."[9]

Select Your Participants Carefully If possible, choose people who represent the demographics, attitudes, and behaviors of your TARGET AUDIENCE. If the topic is controversial, research potential participants and invite people who agree, disagree, and are UNDECIDED. In some cases, you may need permission and help to conduct a focus group. Check with the organization or person who invited you to speak before developing questions and contacting potential participants. An alternative is to ask a group of friends to take on the characteristics and roles of a representative group. At least you'll get some feedback on the questions you ask.

▲ 73

◆ 390–91

Pretest Your Questions Pretesting is just as important with focus groups as it with written surveys. You can do the same with a couple of friends or classmates who are typical of the audience you will address. You can also test your open-ended questions to find out which answers are most common and then develop closed-ended questions that include those responses as answer choices.[10]

Bring an Agenda Although it's important to be flexible when conducting a focus group, an agenda will help you stay on track and use your time wisely. Start by asking participants their names and for an explanation of why they might attend a presentation like the one you're preparing. Then ask questions that probe deeper than a written survey could. Ask *why* and *how* questions to better understand how people think and feel about the topic. Use **EFFECTIVE LISTENING** skills and **CLEAR** and **ORAL SPEAKING STYLES**, and pay attention to **NONVERBAL BEHAVIOR**.

Facilitate Conversation Make sure you include everyone in the discussion— and pay special attention to those who speak less, seem unwilling to participate, or are hesitant to disagree with other members. Don't accept an idea expressed by the most vocal and articulate participant unless it's well represented by others and confirmed with other audience analysis findings. At its best, a focus group gives you a sense of how the full audience might react, but keep in mind that it may not be a highly representative **SAMPLE** of the audience population.

Midpresentation Surveys and Adaptations

We have, so far, defined surveys as questionnaires, interviews, or focus groups. But in a broader sense, surveys involve looking at and listening carefully to people in order to gain information about them, regardless of when, where, or how you do it. Surveying, analyzing, and adapting to an audience does not end when you begin your presentation. It can and should continue as you speak.

If you are speaking to an audience you know well or are talking about a topic you care about and have had previous success with, you may not need to survey your audience in advance. Instead, you'll need to engage in a midpresentation survey that analyzes audience reactions and justifies modifications to your message. This is particularly true if your audience or their reactions are not what you expected.

If an audience of engineers or top executives unexpectedly brings their spouses or families to your presentation, should you ignore them or acknowledge and adapt to them? If the CEO shows up at a training workshop for clerical workers, should you continue the presentation you planned, or do you adjust it so participants feel more comfortable in the presence of their boss? If your carefully researched and well-organized presentation doesn't seem to be working, or if your audience members seem restless, bored, or hostile, how can you adjust to that negative feedback?

● getting started   ▶ delivery   ◆ speaking to persuade

▲ fundamentals   ⁑ engaging your audience   ★ speaking occasions

■ content   ◤ speaking to inform   ✳ resources

And if they are fully engaged, eager, and wanting more, what can you do to lift your presentation to a higher level that fully connects with *their* expectations? (In fact, with video software like Zoom, you can conduct polls at any point in your presentation to get information about how your audience is reacting. The answers you receive can shape how you continue your presentation.)

Here's a famous example of midpresentation adaptation in a speech that many people assume was fully prepared in advance. While Martin Luther King Jr. was delivering what is now called the "I Have a Dream" speech, he began making changes to the phrasing in his manuscript that seemed awkward or didn't connect with the audience. But it was the great gospel singer Mahalia Jackson (who often accompanied King at rallies and had heard many of his sermons) who changed the course of his address. As he was delivering an already excellent speech, Jackson cried out, "Tell them about the dream, Martin! Tell them about the dream!" King took notice and began speaking **EXTEMPORANEOUSLY** based on what he'd said about "the dream" in previous speeches and sermons. His body language transformed from lecturer to preacher. Clarence B. Jones, one of King's advisers and speechwriters, described what happened after Jackson's call out: "I have never seen him speak the way I saw him on that day. It was as if some cosmic transcendental force came down and occupied his body. It was the same body, the same voice, but the voice had something I had never heard before."[11]

▶ 221–22

We are *not* suggesting that midpresentation observations and analysis will require you to abandon a well-prepared speech. We are recommending that by observing audience responses as you speak, you may modify—substantially or modestly—what you're saying in ways that help you achieve your purpose. If your audience seems to be losing interest, try to figure out why and adapt. Are you going into too much detail or speaking too long? Are you repeating what they already seem to know? Do they appear to disagree with your claims? Are they tired? How you respond to such questions and then modify your presentation accordingly is the difference between getting out what *you* want to say and truly connecting with audience needs, interests, and concerns. It is the difference between making a speech and achieving your **PURPOSE**.

▲ 87–101

Regardless of whether you conduct a sophisticated survey or use other audience analysis methods, the confidence to make sudden changes depends on good advance preparation. If you have analyzed your audience, prepared well, and practiced your presentation, you should be able to deviate from your plan with little trouble. Remember that one of the ways presentations differ from written communication is in the presenter's ability to adapt to a living, breathing audience on the spot. Speakers who stubbornly stick to their outlines or manuscripts and refuse to adapt to their audience will rarely be successful. Depending on what you see, hear, and sense as you speak, trust your level of preparation and your ability to modify your content and delivery.

A presentation is effective only when you and your audience connect in a meaningful way. Your success or failure is determined by the quality of that relationship and by the extent to which you and your audience share an understanding of your message.

● getting started   ▶ delivery   ◆ speaking to persuade
▲ fundamentals   ⁑ engaging your audience   ★ speaking occasions
■ content   ▼ speaking to inform   ✳ resources

9.2 How to Outline a Presentation

In addition to using **CHUNKING**, **MIND MAPPING**, **THE SPEECH FRAMER**, or an **ORGANIZATIONAL PATTERN** to structure your presentation, an outline can help you brainstorm ideas, choose materials to support those ideas, determine your key points, and arrange everything in a strategic order. Outlining also allows you to modify the content and organization of a presentation with ease. Once finished, an outline—like the speech framer—provides a road map to keep you on topic if you get lost along the way.

134

134–36

153–55

138–48

The Basics of Outlining

You may have learned how to outline in other courses and textbooks. Those methods also apply to presentations, with a few exceptions. Here we offer three basic outlining rules that also apply to presentation speaking:

1. Use numbers, letters, and indentations.
2. Divide your subpoints logically.
3. Keep the outline consistent.

Use Numbers, Letters, and Indentations

All parts of an outline should be systematically numbered, lettered, and indented to signal the hierarchy of ideas in your presentation. Roman numerals (I, II, III, and so on) signify the largest major divisions at the top of the hierarchy. We recommend using a roman numeral I for your **INTRODUCTION**, roman numeral II for the body, and roman numeral III for the **CONCLUSION**. This suggestion breaks a rule you may encounter in writing textbooks: to leave the introduction and conclusion out of the outline.

161–69

169–75

However, when speaking to a group of people, these sections are so vital to a presentation's structure and success that we recommend including them.

After using roman numerals to establish the major sections of your presentation, you should follow standard outlining rules about letters, numbers, and indentation.

133–36 ▪
- Indented capital letters (A, B, C, and so on) are used to subdivide the introduction, body, and conclusion into small sections. For example, capital letters should designate the **KEY POINTS** within the body of your presentation.

352–54 ◆
- Further indented arabic numbers (1, 2, 3, and so on) indicate the next level down in the hierarchy of your outline. They are used to identify the **CLAIMS** and **SUPPORTING MATERIAL** for each key point.

115–19 ▪
371–73 ◆
373–74 ◆
- If you need a fourth level—for example, for the **WARRANT** or **BACKING** of an argument—you would indent even further and use lowercase letters (a, b, c, and so on).

Divide Your Subpoints Logically

Each section of your outline should include at least two subsections indented underneath—or none at all. In other words, if there is a point A, there must be, at the least, a point B; for every subpoint 1, there must be a subpoint 2. Why? Because you cannot logically divide something into only one part.

WRONG: I.
          A.
    II.

RIGHT: I.
          A.
          B.
    II.

● getting started	▶ delivery	◆ speaking to persuade
▲ fundamentals	∴ engaging your audience	★ speaking occasions
▪ content	▼ speaking to inform	✳ resources

Keep the Outline Consistent

Use a word, phrase, or full sentence for each key point (A, B, C) in your outline rather than mixing styles. When you get to the arabic-number level (1, 2, 3), you may need more than a word or a phrase to record supporting material, but whatever style you chose, try to be consistent at each level of the outline.

It's also important to be consistent grammatically. If you begin a subpoint with a verb, the subpoints that follow should also start with a verb. Consistency will not only make your outline easier to read, but it will also force you to find precise language for each section.

WRONG: I. Consistent style

II. Use a consistent grammatical form.

RIGHT: I. Keep the outline consistent in style.

II. Use a consistent grammatical form.

RIGHT: I. Consistent style

II. Consistent grammatical form

These rules can help you create a clear and useful outline. With consistent headings, style, and grammar, your outline will provide a dependable structure for organizing—and in some cases delivering—your presentation.

Types of Outlines

Outlines give you a logical framework on which to hang your ideas and supporting material. In this section, we describe three types of outlines—*preliminary outlines, speaking notes outlines,* and *full-sentence outlines*—that speakers use to organize their presentations during different phases of the preparation process.

Keep in mind that every outline will be different based on the topic, the rhetorical situation, and the type of organizational pattern you choose. For example, the key points and supporting material in a **STORIES AND EXAMPLES**

■ 144

144–46 ■

395–96 ◆
397–99 ◆

organizational pattern will be very different from a **COMPARISON-ONTRAST** organizational pattern. In a persuasive presentation, the key points and supporting material in **REFUTING OBJECTIONS ORDER** will be organized differently than if you were using **MONROE'S MOTIVATED SEQUENCE**.

The Preliminary Outline

Outlines are not born fully formed, with every detail and subpoint in place. They begin with a few basic building blocks and grow from there. A **preliminary outline** puts the major sections of your presentation into a clear and logical order, allowing you to fill in the ideas and information you intend to use. In its simplest form, a preliminary outline looks like this:

I. Introduction

    A. Attention getter: _____

    B. Central idea: _____

    C. Preview of key points: _____

II. Body of presentation

    A. Key point 1: _____

        1. Supporting material: _____

        2. Supporting material: _____

    B. Key point 2: _____

        1. Supporting material: _____

        2. Supporting material: _____

    C. Key point 3: _____

        1. Supporting material: _____

        2. Supporting material: _____

III. Conclusion

A preliminary outline can be used to organize almost any presentation; you can literally fill in the blanks for each section. Depending on the topic and the rhetorical situation, you could easily modify this template by changing the number of key points and amount of supporting material you decide to include for each point.

Unless you already know your topic really well, it may take some time to draft your preliminary outline. The process begins in earnest only after you have formulated an initial **PURPOSE**, analyzed your **AUDIENCE**, begun researching your **TOPIC**, and collected appropriate **SUPPORTING MATERIAL**. You may then use **CHUNKING**, **MIND MAPPING**, or the above template to identify and sort your key points. A preliminary outline is just that—preliminary—built from an initial set of ideas that are likely to change as you develop your presentation.

89–91
72–80
111–12
115–19
134
134–36

The following preliminary outline is a bare-bones plan for organizing the content of a presentation about anger:

Preliminary Outline: Anger

I. Introduction

    A. Attention getter: Defining anger

    B. Central idea: Understanding and dealing with anger

    C. Preview of key points: Understanding anger myths, expressing anger, responding to anger

II. Body of presentation

    A. Key point 1: Understanding anger myths

        1. Supporting material: Believing that anger is good

        2. Supporting material: Believing that anger is caused by others

    B. Key point 2: Expressing anger

        1. Supporting material: Acknowledging your anger

        2. Supporting material: Avoiding personal attacks

    C. Key point 3: Responding to anger from others

        1. Supporting material: Identifying the source of anger

        2. Supporting material: Seeking resolution

III. Conclusion

The Speaking Notes Outline

221–22 ▶

You can further develop your preliminary outline by creating a speaking notes outline. A **speaking notes outline** supports an **EXTEMPORANEOUS DELIVERY STYLE** and produces a clear, more detailed organizational structure. The example below expands the preliminary outline about anger by adding more content. As you'll see, there are new subpoints as well as more supporting material and questions for the audience. These kinds of changes naturally happen during the speech preparation process as you incorporate more substantive material.

115–19 ▪

Notice the various forms of **SUPPORTING MATERIALS** (definition, facts, quotations, examples, story, research) *and* how the outline does not follow every outlining rule. What matters is that the presentation is organized and functions as an effective set of speaking notes. Keep in mind that the following example is only one possible version of a presentation about anger. Assuming you are well prepared and well rehearsed, you may need only a hint to remember some sections, such as "[Ask for student examples]" or "[Tell the story about Ruth]."

Speaking Notes Outline: Why and How to Deal with Anger[1]

I. Introduction

Ask the audience: "Have you ever been angry?" Everyone feels anger at some time. It's a natural, human reaction.

A. Attention getter: What is anger? "Emotional response to unmet expectations."

Examples: Expecting friends to tell the truth and discovering they've been dishonest; expecting but not receiving praise for good work; expecting an A on an exam but getting a C. [Ask for additional audience examples.]

B. Central idea: Understanding the causes and consequences of anger can help you avoid, manage, and respond appropriately to anger and threatening situations.

Quote Aristotle: "Anybody can become angry—that is easy; but to be angry with the right person, and to the right degree, and at the right time, and for the right purpose, and in the right way—that is not within everybody's power and is not easy."

C. Preview: Dispelling anger myths, expressing anger, responding to anger from others

II. Body of presentation

    A. Key point 1: Understanding anger myths [Eifert et al.]

        1. Myth: Anger can be helpful. Fact: Other than warning you of danger, it can make things worse—including your health.

        2. Myth: Anger is caused by others. Fact: How you react to an unmet expectation is *your* choice, which is not dependent on what other people do.

    [Example: A rumor that a trusted colleague spreads about you]

    B. Key point 2: Expressing anger

        1. Explain why you are angry without yelling.

        2. Don't attack the other person.

        3. Describe how you *feel* by using "I" statements.

    C. Key point 3: Responding to anger from others

        1. Acknowledge the other person's anger: "I understand how angry you are."

        2. Identify the source and intensity of anger: "I don't think I said I'd write the report."

        3. Seek a collaborative resolution approach: "Let's work it out together."

III. Conclusion

    A. Summarize key points: Understanding anger myths, expressing anger, and responding to anger

    B. Quote from Carol Tavris, a highly respected social psychologist: Anger "requires an awareness of choice and an embrace of reason. It is knowing when to become angry—'this is wrong, this I will protest'—and when to make peace; when to take action, and when to keep silent; knowing the likely causes of one's anger and not berating the blameless."

The Full-Sentence Outline

Some speakers (and students required to do so by their communication instructors) take the outlining process one step further. They expand their preliminary outline into a full-sentence outline. A **full-sentence outline** is a comprehensive framework that follows established outlining conventions concerning content and format.

222–23 ▶
221–22 ▶

Depending on how detailed you make a full-sentence outline, it may resemble a complete manuscript of your presentation. Using a full-sentence outline can share the disadvantages of **MANUSCRIPT DELIVERY**, particularly if you are required, expected, or want to use **EXTEMPORANEOUS DELIVERY**. On the other hand, key points, explanations, and significant supporting materials should be easy to find. Full quotations, important statistics, and examples are written out to ensure accuracy. And, as its name implies, most of the content is written in full sentences.

In general, we do not recommend a comprehensive, full-sentence outline if it is little more than a manuscript speech cut into pieces and shoved into an outline. The full-sentence outline can, however, be useful when you

333–46 ▼

plan to read long quotations, **EXPLAIN COMPLEX IDEAS**, or share a list of examples or statistics. Whatever the rationale, make sure your delivery is more than a recitation.

In some cases, a comprehensive, full-sentence outline may serve you better than a manuscript because it clearly separates the major parts of a presentation into concise sections. Creating a full-sentence outline requires a great deal of time and effort, including multiple revisions during which you may discover sections that have either too much material or too little.

What follows is a full-sentence outline on the topic of anger. It includes almost all of the presentation's content as well as organizational markers (shown in bold), so you always know exactly where you are as you speak. There is also a bibliography at the end. It follows the conventions of *The Chicago Manual of Style*, but if your instructor asks you to submit one, you should confirm which style and format they prefer.

Full-Sentence Outline: Why and How to Deal with Anger

I. **Introduction**

    A. **Attention getter:** "Have you ever been angry or enraged?" All of us have. Everyone feels anger at some time—it's a natural, but often distressing, human reaction.

    B. **Central idea:** In order to deal with the causes and consequences of anger, begin by fact-checking your beliefs about anger, adopting constructive ways to express your anger, and learning how to respond respectfully and civilly to anger expressed by someone else. Before I recommend methods for dealing with anger, let's begin by understanding what anger is.

    C. **Definition of anger:** Anger is "an emotional response to unmet expectations." Here are some examples: expecting friends to tell the truth but discovering they've told a falsehood; expecting but not receiving praise for good work; expecting an A on an exam but getting a C; receiving unfair treatment or criticism. [Ask the audience for additional examples that exemplify the definition.]

    Transition: With this definition in mind, I hope you'll understand why what seems to be a simple definition can help you comprehend the nature, causes, and consequences of expressing and responding to anger responsibly.

II. **Body of presentation**

    A. **Key point 1:** Many of us believe several myths about anger that prevent us from effectively dealing with our own and someone else's anger. [Eifert et al.] Consider the follow claims:

        1. **True or false?** Anger can be helpful because it lets you vent your feelings, particularly if you feel threatened. The answer is true *and* false. True: In some cases, anger can be a warning of imminent danger. But false: Anger is rarely helpful. It can escalate and make things worse. And it is certainly bad for your health, particularly your heart. If you're quick to anger, you may regret it later.

2. **True or false?** Anger is caused when something bad happens unexpectedly or when someone says or does something that upsets or hurts you. False: It's easy and quite common to blame events and other people for your anger. However, you are the source of anger. If you blame others, you don't have to change how you behave—and you stay angry. [Example: Reacting angrily to an unreasonable request from your boss.]

3. **True or false?** Venting your anger lets you blow off steam. False: People who explode in anger usually become angrier. And those who must endure their anger are more likely to become angry.

Transition: In addition to understanding the nature of anger, it's just as important to express anger appropriately and in a way that avoids making things worse.

B. **Key point 2:** Learn how to manage your anger appropriately and effectively.

Identifying the causes and consequences of anger can help you respond appropriately to anger and threatening situations. To paraphrase Aristotle: Anybody can become angry—that is easy; but to be angry with the right person, and to the right degree, and at the right time, and for the right purpose, and in the right way—that is not within everybody's power and is not easy. [Aristotle]

Here are three ways of following Aristotle's wise advice [Wilmot and Hocker]:

1. **State that you are angry.** Don't shout. Control your nonverbal behavior, such as frowning or sneering, clenching a fist, or moving too close to the other person. Calmly state why you are angry. [Tell the story about working with Ruth on a project.]

2. **Explain why you are angry.** "I promised the group we'd complete this report by Tuesday, but I still don't have your section."

3. **Avoid personal attacks.** Don't resort to name-calling. Describe the problem as objectively as you can rather than ranting and raging at someone.

⬤ getting started　　▶ delivery　　◆ speaking to persuade

▲ fundamentals　　∴ engaging your audience　　★ speaking occasions

▪ content　　🥃 speaking to inform　　✳ resources

4. **Use "I" statements instead of "you" statements.** Describe your personal feelings rather than the bad things the other person did to you. Say, "I expected you to . . ." instead of "Because you screwed up, everything's a mess."

    Transition: Learning to express your anger appropriately is only half the equation for dealing with anger. In addition to managing your own anger, try to temper your response when someone is angry with you.

 C. **Key point 3:** Learn how to respond constructively to someone else's anger. [Wilmot and Hocker]

    1. **Acknowledge why the other person is angry.** "I understand how angry you are. Given that the report is due next week, I think I'd be just as upset if I were you."

    2. **Identify the issue or source of the anger.** "I don't think I said I'd write the report. As I remember, I said I'd give you my notes from the meeting."

    3. **Seek a collaborative approach to resolution.** "We've had a good working relationship. Perhaps we can sit down and work out how solve the problem."

III. **Conclusion**

 A. **Summarize key points.** Before letting anger take control of you and others, remember that erroneous beliefs may prevent you from dealing with it effectively. Then think about the situation and answer two questions: How can I express my anger in a way that may resolve the problem? And how should I react to someone else's anger in a way that won't make matters worse?

 B. **Conclude.** Take responsibility for your feelings and behavior when you face an unmet expectation or disappointment that's triggering. I'll leave you with another quotation worth remembering. Carol Tavris, author of *Anger: The Misunderstood Emotion*, wrote: Anger "requires an awareness of choice and an embrace of reason. It is knowing when to become angry—'this is wrong, this I will protest'—and when to make peace; when to take action, and when to keep silent; knowing the likely causes of one's anger without berating the blameless."

Bibliography

Aristotle, *Nicomanchean Ethics*, translated by W. D. Ross; revised by J. O. Urmson. In *The Complete Works of Aristotle: The Revised Oxford Translation*, edited by Jonathan Barnes, Bollingen Series, 2:1751. Princeton, NJ: Princeton University Press, 1984. Bekker number (keyed to the original Greek) is in Book II, 1109a.26. Note: The paraphrase of Aristotle quotation is a simplified version of his writing, but this other version is most frequently quoted in most quotation books and websites. What follows is part of the translation in Barnes: "Anyone can get angry—that is easy . . . ; but to do this to the right person, to the right extent, at the right time, with the right aim, and in the right way, *that* is not for everyone, nor is it easy."

Cahn, Dudley D., and Ruth Anna Abigail. *Managing Conflict through Communication*. 5th ed. Boston: Pearson, 2014, 187–98.

Canary, Daniel J., and Sandra Lakey. *Strategic Conflict*. New York: Routledge, 2013, 56–59.

Eifert, Georg H., Matthew McKay, and John P. Forsyth. *ACT on Life Not on Anger: The New Acceptance & Commitment Therapy Guide to Problem Anger*. Oakland, CA: New Harbinger, 2006, 15, 16, 19, 20, 21.

Svitil, Kathy A. *Calming the Anger Storm*. New York: Alpha, 2005, 14–15.

Tavris, Carol. *Anger: The Misunderstood Emotion*. New York: Simon & Schuster, 1982, 253.

Wilmot, William W., and Joyce L. Hocker. *Interpersonal Conflict*. 6th ed. Boston: McGraw-Hill, 2001, 251–53.

Additional Tips for Outlining

There are four additional outlining guidelines that can help you prepare and deliver a well-organized presentation, regardless of the type of outline you plan to use:

1. Write a headline.
2. Insert time markers.
3. Use manuscript cues.
4. Add a bibliography or references.

getting started   ▶ delivery   ◆ speaking to persuade

▲ fundamentals   ⁂ engaging your audience   ★ speaking occasions

■ content   ▼ speaking to inform   ✱ resources

Write a Headline

As with **PRESENTATION AIDS**, give your outline a title that reflects your 297–98
PURPOSE. Not only will it remind you of your overriding goal, but also it will 87–101
provide a way to describe your presentation to others. For example, there
is a big difference between a presentation titled "Anger as a Basic Human
Emotion" and one titled "Why and How to Deal with Anger."

Insert Time Markers

Whenever you practice with your outline, record the time it takes you to
deliver each section of your presentation. Then make sure the total adds
up to the assigned (or desired) time limit. If it doesn't, you will need to cut
some content or, in a few cases, add more. Once you are satisfied, mark
your final outline with those times. As you continue practicing, make sure
you are completing each section close to its allotted time length. If you're
exceeding your intended time, you may need to speak faster, cut material
in upcoming sections, or even drop a key point.

All presentations are subject to unexpected changes or disruptions.
If an audience member interrupts with an important question, it may be
wise to use some of your time to answer it. If you experience a technology
failure, you may have to discard a presentation aid or a story you want to
tell. And if, right before you speak, you find out that your time has been
shortened or expanded, you can look at your time markers to decide where
to accommodate those changes.

Use Manuscript Cues

When preparing your outline, it may be helpful to revisit the **MANUSCRIPT** 225–28
SPEAKING GUIDELINES. Use large double-spaced type. Mark up your outline
with delivery cues that tell you which words or phrases to emphasize with
changes in volume, rate, pitch, inflection, and fluency, as well as when
to pause and when to gesture and move. In addition to symbols such as
< for speak louder, /// for big pause, and ☺ for smile, you can use **bold**,
<u>underlining</u>, and ALL CAPS to emphasize an important word or phrase. And
if your outline is more than two pages, number the pages and consider
putting the outline in a binder.

Add a Bibliography or References

Depending on your expertise, topic, and the rhetorical situation, add a set of references to your outline. In some cases (such as a communication course), you may be required to turn in both your outline and a bibliography. But there's another reason to have your references close at hand: In a **QUESTION-AND-ANSWER SESSION** an audience member may ask about your data or the background of someone you quoted. Another listener may ask how to learn more about the topic. In both cases, having a list of references will allow you to share them verbally. And if someone wants a copy of your outline, you're doing them a favor by including the references you used to prepare the presentation.

468–78 ★

Glossary / Index

A

Aarvik, Egil, as speaker, 427, 431

Abdel-Magied, Yassmin, as speaker, 13, 189–93, 271, 304, 374

About Time (film), 448

abstract word, 238 A word that refers to an idea or concept that cannot be observed or touched and therefore may not have the same meaning for everyone. *See also* concrete word

accent, 208–9 A way of pronouncing words shaped by a combination of geography, social class, education, ethnicity, and first-language influences.

accepting an award, 433–41 A speaking OCCA-SION where the recipient expresses gratitude for receiving an award and acknowledges the award's significance. *See also* presenting an award
  example, 440–41
  guidelines, 434–39
  key features, 433–34

acoustics, 198 The properties or qualities of a room that affect how sound is transmitted as determined by the shape of the room, the extent of noise-absorbing materials, the height of the ceiling, and the number of people in the AUDIENCE.

active voice, 238–39 When the subject of a sentence performs the action of the verb: *The student read the* Iliad. *See also* passive voice

ad hominem fallacy, 375–76 *See* attacking the person fallacy

Adjei-Brenyah, Nana Kwame, as speaker, 437–38

agenda, 463–64, 507–8 An outline of the topics to be discussed both at a PUBLIC GROUP DISCUSSION and in private group meetings.

alliteration, 246–47 A STYLISTIC DEVICE in which a SPEAKER uses a series of words (or words placed closely together) that begin with the same sound: *The dictator of Iraq is not disarming. To the contrary, he is deceiving.*

analogy, 116–17, 248, 337, 367t A STYLISTIC DEVICE that compares two different things to highlight some point of similarity. Analogies expand SIMILES and METAPHORS and serve as SUPPORTING MATERIAL.

Note: This glossary / index defines key terms and concepts and directs you to pages in the book where you can find specific information on these and other topics. The words set in SMALL CAPITAL LETTERS are themselves defined in the glossary / index. Page references followed by an italicized "*f*" refer to figures; page references followed by an italicized "*t*" refer to tables.

attacks against a person rather the addressing the CONTENT of that person's MESSAGE. Also called an *ad hominem argument*.

audience, 70 The people a SPEAKER addresses in a variety of RHETORICAL SITUATIONS.
  Audience Bill of Rights, 34–35
  encouraging participation, 276–79
  ethical considerations, 43, 47–48
  importance of, 70–72
  listening responsibilities, 31–33, 35–38
  questions to ask, 7

audience analysis, 72–80 The work a SPEAKER does to research, understand, respect, and adapt to listeners before and during a presentation.
  adapting your message, 80–82
  attitudes and values, 77–80, 107–8, 387–91
  characteristics and motivations, 73–75, 360
  ethical considerations, 43
  examples of use, 80–85, 459
  knowledge and interests, 76–77
  and topic choice, 108–10
  for value step, 312–13

audience attitudes, 77–78, 387–91 The various OPINIONS held by AUDIENCE members in terms of whether and how strongly they agree or disagree with what a SPEAKER is saying and/or whether they are undecided.

Audience Bill of Rights, 34–35

audience-centered speaker, 70–72, 282–83, 353–54, 482–83 A SPEAKER who strives to understand, respect, and adapt to AUDIENCE characteristics and interests; thinks critically about listeners' points of view; and empathizes with listeners' motivations and needs.

audience survey. *See* survey
award
  accepting, 433–41
  presenting, 427–32

B

backing, 373–74 A supplementary component of the TOULMIN MODEL OF ARGUMENT that certifies the validity of the argument's WARRANT or provides more data and information justifying it.

Bacon, Francis, 173

bandwagon appeal, 377 *See* appeal to popularity fallacy

bar graph, 285–86, 285f A GRAPH that presents numerical data as rectangles of equal width but varying height or length.

begging the question fallacy, 379–80 A FALLACY in which the speaker's EVIDENCE is, essentially, the same as the argument's CLAIM.

Begging the Question (Walton), 380

benefits step, 384 A speaker's explanation of how AUDIENCE members will gain something important by accepting the speaker's ARGUMENT; used frequently in PERSUASIVE PRESENTATION.

topic. The conclusion of a PERSUASIVE PRESENTATION stating what the speaker wants the AUDIENCE to believe and/or do. There are four types of claims, all of which may be included in a single presentation: CLAIM OF FACT, CLAIM OF CONJECTURE, CLAIM OF VALUE, and CLAIM OF POLICY.

claim of conjecture, 352–53 A CLAIM stating that something will or will not happen in the future.

claim of fact, 352–53 A CLAIM stating that something is true, that an event occurred, that a cause can be identified, or that a theory correctly explains a phenomenon.

claim of policy, 352, 354 A CLAIM recommending a specific course of action or solution to a problem.

claim of value, 352–54 A CLAIM stating that something is worthwhile—good or bad; right or wrong; best, average, or worst.

clarify difficult terms, 334–36 The goal of a segment or an entire INFORMATIVE PRESENTATION that explains the meaning of a difficult word, phrase, or concept or describes the differences between commonly misunderstood words.

clear style, 239–40 A fundamental CORE SPEAKING STYLE in which a SPEAKER uses plain language, short, simple, and CONCRETE WORDS, as well as an ACTIVE VOICE.

cliché, 249, 418–19 A trite or tired expression that has lost its originality or force through overuse: *crystal clear, better late than never.*

close-ended question, 499–502 A type of SURVEY question that forces the AUDIENCE to choose one or more answers from a list. Examples include multiple-choice questions, ratings (agree-disagree and Likert scales), rank ordering, and demographic questions. *See also* open-ended question

code-switching, 208–9 The act of modifying your verbal and nonverbal communication based on various cultural contexts.

cognitive restructuring, 20 A technique for decreasing SPEAKING ANXIETY that involves challenging and changing unrealistic thinking into realistic expectations.

common ground, 71, 355–56, 389, 424, 475 The attitudes, values, beliefs, and behaviors that a SPEAKER shares with an AUDIENCE.

communication apprehension, 15 *See* speaking anxiety

comparative advantage arrangement, 394–95 An ORGANIZATIONAL PATTERN for a PERSUASIVE PRESENTATION in which the SPEAKER first describes a proposed plan and then shows how it will do a better job of solving a problem or achieving a goal compared to current or other suggested plans.

comparison-contrast arrangement, 144–46, 338 An ORGANIZATIONAL PATTERN that examines ideas or objects that are similar to or different from one another.

competence, 58–61, 66t A major dimension of SPEAKER CREDIBILITY that refers to whether AUDIENCE members perceive a SPEAKER as knowledgeable, qualified, and experienced about a given TOPIC. *See also* dynamism; likability; trustworthiness

conclusions, 169–75
    effective endings, 171–74
    example, 176–78
    goals, 169–70
    tips for, 174–75

concrete word, 238 A word that refers to a specific thing that can be perceived by our senses. *See also* abstract word

confidence, 184–85 A quality of effective DELIVERY that reflects AUDIENCE perceptions about whether a SPEAKER is self-assured and strongly believes in the importance and benefits of their MESSAGE. *See also* expressiveness; immediacy; stage presence

confusion and misunderstanding, 339–41

connectives, 149–51, 338 Phrases that link one part of a presentation to another, clarify how one idea relates to another, and/or identify how SUPPORTING MATERIAL bolsters a KEY POINT. Examples include INTERNAL PREVIEWS, INTERNAL SUMMARIES, TRANSITIONS, and SIGNPOSTS.

connotation, 237–38, 496 The feelings that specific words arouse in a person who reads, hears, or speaks them. *See also* denotation

content, 103–77 The generation, synthesis, and organization of ideas and information in a presentation's MESSAGE, communicated verbally and nonverbally to an AUDIENCE.

choosing a topic, 105–13
ethical considerations, 44–47
organizing. *See* organizing content
questions to ask, 8–9
research and supporting material, 114–32

context, information out of, 124
Conway, Kellyanne, 120

CORE speaking styles, 239–45, 437–38 Four fundamental SPEAKING STYLES used in PRESENTATION SPEAKING: CLEAR STYLE, ORAL STYLE, RHETORICAL STYLE, and ELOQUENT STYLE. Elements of each are often found in a single presentation.

core values of speakers, 55–57
credibility, speaker. *See* speaker credibility
Credo for Ethical Communication, 40–41, 351
Crutcher, Ronald A., as speaker, 420
cultural bias, 251–52
cultural differences, 7, 391–92. *See also* cultural values
cultural values, 79–80. *See also* cultural differences
Cuomo, Andrew, as speaker, 243

D

Davis, Clive, as speaker, 449–50

deductive reasoning, 364–65 A type of REASONING where if the initial statements (PREMISES) are true, the conclusion (CLAIM) is also true. *See also* inductive reasoning

defamation, 50 A false statement that damages a person's reputation, either through writing and pictures (libel) or through speech (slander).

defensive listening, 29 A poor LISTENING habit in which AUDIENCE members assume that a SPEAKER's controversial or critical statements are personal or unjust attacks. Rather than trying to understand the speaker's MESSAGE, defensive listeners focus only on how to challenge the speaker's position.

definition, 116 A type of SUPPORTING MATERIAL that explains or clarifies the meaning or meanings of a word, phrase, or concept.

delivery, 181–233 The ways in which SPEAKERS use their voice and body during a presentation. Key Features: CONFIDENCE • EXPRESSIVENESS • IMMEDIACY • STAGE PRESENCE
   competence and, 61
   components of effective, 187–88
   ethical considerations, 47, 188
   example, 189–93
   forms of, 220–25
   listening and, 29–30
   in mediated speaking, 481, 484
   physical. *See* physical delivery
   practicing, 220–33, 413
   presentation aids and, 302–5
   qualities of effective, 184–86, 275–76
   questions to ask, 10
   transitions, 151
   vocal. *See* vocal delivery

demographic information Information gathered through AUDIENCE ANALYSIS that includes, but is not limited to, race, age, gender, ethnicity, nationality, religion, citizen status, occupation, place and type of residence, income, educational level, political perspective, organizational affiliation, and social standing.

in audience analysis, 73–75
in audience survey, 501–4

demonstration speech, 328–30 A type of INFORMATIVE PRESENTATION that shows AUDIENCE members how to do a procedure, accompanied by verbal instructions and, in some cases, responses to audience FEEDBACK. *See also* tell-show-do

denotation, 237 The objective, literal meaning or meanings of words. *See also* connotation

derived credibility, 355–57 The varying effects a SPEAKER has on an AUDIENCE's perceptions of the speaker's credibility during a presentation. *See also* initial credibility; terminal credibility

describe a quasi-scientific phenomenon, 336–39 The goal of an explanatory INFORMATIVE PRESENTATION that enhances AUDIENCE understanding about a complex scientific idea or process without using unfamiliar terms, sophisticated statistical methods, or complicated visual aids.

diagram, 287–88, 288f A type of PRESENTATION AID that shows how things work in two dimensions.

DiCaprio, Leonardo, as speaker, 434

diction, 206 *See* articulation

digital presentation aid, 296–302 A type of PRESENTATION AID that is created, viewed, and/ or heard, distributed, modified, and preserved

E

fact, 115, 368–69 A type of SUPPORTING MATERIAL that refers to a verifiable observation, experience, or event.

fallacy, 374–80 An invalid ARGUMENT, error in thinking, or misleading statement that can—intentionally or unintentionally—deceive an AUDIENCE.
    defined, 374–75
    types of, 375–80

fallacy fallacy, 380 The incorrect assumption that just because an ARGUMENT is fallacious, its conclusion must be wrong.

Fauci, Anthony, as speaker, 239

faulty cause fallacy, 378 A FALLACY in which a SPEAKER inaccurately CLAIMS that a particular situation or event is caused by an event or action that preceded it.

fear appeal, 357–61, 385–86 A powerful and frequently used EMOTIONAL APPEAL that scares listeners as a way of persuading them to change their opinions and/or behavior.
    effective strategies, 359–60
    ethics of, 360–61
    as primal emotion, 358
    feeble intensifiers, 242

feedback, 33–34, 56, 71–72, 392–93 The verbal and nonverbal responses made by AUDIENCE members as they interpret and evaluate the meaning and DELIVERY of a presentation.

fidgets, 214–15, 219 Small, repetitive MOVEMENTS that function like physical FILLER PHRASES.

figures of speech. *See* stylistic devices

filler phrases, 205–6, 242 The various verbal interruptions, blunders, restarted sentences, and repeated words that fill space while you search for the next meaningful part of the sentence you're speaking, including "um" and "uh."

Finley, Ron, as speaker, 205, 305, 400–403

fluency, 205–6 A component of vocal quality that describes your ability to speak smoothly without tripping over words or pausing at awkward moments. *See also* pitch; projection; rate; volume

focus group, 506–8 An exploratory, qualitative RESEARCH method where people discuss a series of carefully selected questions in real time guided by a moderator.

Forni, P. M., *Choosing Civility*, 37

forum, 463–67 A type of PUBLIC GROUP DISCUSSION that often follows a PANEL DISCUSSION or SYMPOSIUM and gives AUDIENCE members the opportunity to comment or ask questions.

Franklin, Aretha, 449–50
Franklin, Robert M., as speaker, 173–74

free speech, 48–50, 51, 57 The right, as guaranteed in the US Constitution's First Amendment, to express your ideas and opinions without government prohibitions. Exceptions include libel and slander, incitement to violence and rebellion, and other circumstances.
    ethical considerations, 32, 48–51, 57

arrange your KEY POINTS and SUPPORTING MATERIAL into a sketch of your presentation.

premise, 364–65 A statement within an ARGUMENT that leads to a conclusion (or CLAIM) when connected by sound REASONING.

presentation aids, 118–19, 282–305 The supplementary audio, visual, and hands-on resources available for presenting and highlighting KEY POINTS and SUPPORTING MATERIAL in a presentation.

    and audience interest, 269–70
    benefits of, 282–83
    charts, graphs, and tables, 284–87
    delivery, 302–5, 488–89
    diagrams and models, 287–89
    digital aids, 296–302
    handouts, 290–92
    maps, 290
    photographs and illustrations, 289–90
    selection for purpose, 293–96
    sound effects and music, 292
    video and animation, 293

The Presentation Design Book (Rabb), 287

presentation speaking, 4–5 Any time a SPEAKER generates meaning using verbal and nonverbal MESSAGES and establishes a relationship with AUDIENCE members in a variety of contexts.

    limiting length, 268–69
    public speaking comparison, 3–4

presenting an award, 427–32 A speaking OCCASION where the presenter describes an award that someone has or will receive, focusing AUDIENCE attention on both the award and the recipient. *See also* accepting an award

    guidelines, 429–32
    key features, 428

primacy effect, 161 A tendency for AUDIENCE members to recall the introduction or beginning of a presentation more than the body of the speech. *See also* recency effect

primary source, 122–23 The document, TESTIMONY, or publication in which a piece of data, information, or a CLAIM first appears. *See also* secondary source

private goal, 90–91 A speaker's personal goal that differs from the overall PURPOSE of a presentation.

probability, 365–66

problem-cause-solution, 393–94 An ORGANIZATIONAL PATTERN often used in a PERSUASIVE PRESENTATION in which the SPEAKER first identifies a significant problem, then explains why the problem exists or continues, and finally recommends a solution.

problem-solution arrangement, 140–41, 341 An ORGANIZATIONAL PATTERN in which the SPEAKER describes a harmful or difficult situation and identifies a way to solve it.

procedures, informing about,
    327–32
progressive disclosure, 299

rate, 201–3 A component of vocal quality that describes the number of words per minute a SPEAKER says, which varies based on CONTENT, the speaker's DELIVERY style, and AUDIENCE expectations. *See also* fluency; pitch; projection; volume

reasoning, 364–68 The process of constructing and analyzing the validity of an argument.

recency effect, 170 The tendency of AUDIENCE members to recall the conclusion or last major point in a presentation more than the body of the speech. *See also* primacy effect

refuting objections, 395–96 An ORGANIZATIONAL PATTERN, often used in PERSUASIVE PRESENTATIONS, that helps overcome AUDIENCE ATTITUDES and beliefs that stand in opposition to the speaker's PURPOSE.

remembering, 31 A components of the HURIER model of EFFECTIVE LISTENING that describes your ability to retain and recall information you have heard. *See also* evaluating; hearing; interpreting; responding; understanding

repetition, 246 A STYLISTIC DEVICE that repeats important words, phrases, and sentences as a means of helping listeners remember the MESSAGE.

report new information, 316–18, 319–32 A type of INFORMATIVE PRESENTATION in which a SPEAKER reports unfamiliar information in order to create or increase AUDIENCE awareness about an object, person, event, or procedure.

research A systematic search or investigation—in books, articles, online sources,

INTERVIEWS, SURVEYS, and/or personal experiences—designed to find useful and appropriate SUPPORTING MATERIAL related to your TOPIC and PURPOSE. *See also* supporting material

> and competence, 58–59
> for topic, 111–13

reservation, 373–74 A supplementary component of the TOULMIN MODEL OF ARGUMENT that acknowledges exceptions to an argument's CLAIM or indicates why a claim may not be true under certain circumstances.

responding, 31 A component of the HURIER model of EFFECTIVE LISTENING that describes your ability to give appropriate and meaningful FEEDBACK that signals you have or have not heard and understood the SPEAKER. *See also* evaluating; hearing; interpreting; remembering; understanding

rhetoric, 5 The art of influencing the thinking, feelings, and behavior of an AUDIENCE.

Rhetoric (Aristotle), 5, 57, 351–52, 354–55

rhetorical situation, 4–10 The particular circumstance in which you speak to influence what your listeners know, believe, feel, and/or do. Key Features: AUDIENCE • CONTENT • DELIVERY • OCCASION • PURPOSE • SPEAKER

> Audience Bill of Rights, 34–35
> elements of, 5–10

rhetorical speechmaking process, 3–14 A complex process in which SPEAKERS make strategic and adaptive decisions appropriate for a RHETORICAL SITUATION.

> example, 10–13
> rhetorical situation, 4–10, 34–35
> terminology, 3–4

rhetorical style, 241–43 A fundamental CORE SPEAKING STYLE in which a SPEAKER uses VIVID LANGUAGE, LANGUAGE INTENSITY, and POWERFUL WORDS to persuade and motivate AUDIENCE members.

Rowan, Katherine, on informative communication, 316–18, 319–20, 333–46

rule of three, 136 AUDIENCES are more likely to understand and remember three KEY POINTS (as well as three words, phrases, or items in a row) instead of two, four, or more.

> for key points, 136, 315
> as stylistic device, 248–49, 258–59

S

sample, 128–29 A representative group of people, objects, items, or phenomena selected from a population as a whole for a statistical study.

sampling bias, 128–29 Some categories within an overall population in a statistical study that are intentionally or inadvertently excluded from the SAMPLE.

scientific method arrangement, 143–44 An ORGANIZATIONAL PATTERN that follows the well-established steps prescribed for conducting RESEARCH and publishing results in journals.

secondary source, 122–23 A document or publication that describes, reports, repeats, or summarizes information from primary sources and other secondary sources. *See also* primary source

selected instances fallacy, 379 A FALLACY in which the SPEAKER purposely picks atypical EXAMPLES to support an ARGUMENT.

selective listening, 29 A poor LISTENING habit in which AUDIENCE members pay attention only to MESSAGES they like or agree with, or avoid complex, unfamiliar information that contradicts or challenges OPINIONS they already hold.

self-centered interests, 76–77 Subjects that interest AUDIENCE members because there is something they can gain or lose by not paying attention. *See also* topic-centered interests

self-effacing humor, 273–74 The ability to direct humor at yourself.

sensory images, 315–16

setting, 5–6 The time and place where a presentation occurs.
    online presentation, 484–85

SIFT, 125–26 A method for evaluating the credibility and accuracy of messages you find online. SIFT stands for "Stop, Investigate, Find, and Trace."

signpost, 151 A type of CONNECTIVE that uses short, often numerical, references that

tell or remind listeners where you are in a presentation and how far you have to go.

simile, 247–48, 337 A STYLISTIC DEVICE that compares two things or ideas using words such as *like* or *as*. *See also* analogy; metaphor

Skype. *See* online presentation
Smith, Joe, as speaker, 280–81, 305, 330
Soneji, Mileha, as speaker, 108, 323–25
sound effects and music, in presentation
    aids, 292
sound recording, for online presentation,
    488
source credibility, 121–22

space arrangement, 140, 321 An ORGANIZATIONAL PATTERN that divides information based on location.

speaker, 55–69 The knowledge, personal characteristics, attitudes, values, skills, and ethics of a person who develops and delivers a presentation.
    core values, 55–57

speaker credibility, 57–69 The extent to which an AUDIENCE trusts, likes, and believes what a SPEAKER says. Key Features: COMPETENCE • DYNAMISM • LIKABILITY • TRUSTWORTHINESS. *See also* personal appeals
    competence, 58–61
    dynamism, 66
    example, 67–68
    fidgeting and, 214–15
    likability, 63–65
    in Q&A session, 470–71
    trustworthiness, 61–62, 383–84

something that did happen, is happening, or could happen.

    as examples and supporting material, 117–18

    hypothetical, 118

    as an introduction or conclusion, 162, 170

    as organizational pattern, 144, 358, 392, 396, 452

    telling. *See* storytelling

    why stories work, 264–267

stories and examples arrangement, 144, 322, 392, 452 An ORGANIZATIONAL FORMAT that relies on a series of STORIES or EXAMPLES as KEY POINTS.

story-building chart, 259t, 262t–64t A template that poses questions and recommends strategies that help structure and organize all the components of a story.

story fidelity, 265 The extent to which a story connects with the AUDIENCE and seems believable, logical, and truthful.

story probability, 264–65 The extent to which a story follows its own internal logic, could really happen, makes sense, and is consistent and coherent.

story truths, 265–67 Accepted principles in stories that communicate meaning and value to the AUDIENCE, OCCASION, PURPOSE, and SPEAKER.

storytelling, 253–67

    examples, 117–18, 260–62

    finding stories, 254–57

    shaping stories, 259–64

    story-building chart, 259t, 262t–64t

    strategies for, 257–59

    success factors, 264–67

Strasberg, Lee, as speaker, 449

stylistic devices, 245–49 A variety of LANGUAGE-based strategies that make a MESSAGE more effective, engaging, and memorable.

superficial listening, 29 A poor LISTENING habit in which AUDIENCE members pay more attention to a speaker's APPEARANCE and VOCAL DELIVERY than they do to what the SPEAKER has to say. Superficial listeners often draw conclusions about a speaker and their MESSAGE before the presentation is finished.

supporting material, 114–32 The FACTS, OPINIONS, STATISTICS, TESTIMONY, DEFINITIONS, ANALOGIES, EXAMPLES, STORIES, PRESENTATION AIDS, and other resources you use to advance your PURPOSE and KEY POINTS.

    and audience interest, 269–70

    evaluating statistics, 126–30

    example, 67–68

    in persuasion, 356, 361

    testing, 120–26

    types of, 115–20

survey, 493–510 A RESEARCH method that relies on a set of questions to obtain useful information about the characteristics, knowledge, attitudes, beliefs, and behaviors of AUDIENCE members.

    characteristics of, 494–97

    demographic data in, 502–4

symposium, 462–67 A common type of PUB-
LIC GROUP DISCUSSION where participants—
who may or may not know one another
in advance—present short, uninterrupted
presentations to an AUDIENCE on different
aspects of a TOPIC.

synchronous communication, 481, 488 When
the SPEAKER and AUDIENCE members interact
with each other in the same digital space at
the same time. *See also* asynchronous communication

T

table, 287, 294t, 302t–3t A PRESENTATION
AID that summarizes and compares data
or information, such as lists of EVIDENCE or
KEY POINTS, by arranging them into rows and
columns.

target audience, 73 The most important,
influential, or receptive members of your
AUDIENCE as determined by AUDIENCE
ANALYSIS.

team presentation, 456–61 A speaking OCCA-
SION where members of a cohesive group
work together to prepare and deliver a
well-coordinated presentation to achieve a
GROUP GOAL.

tell-show-do, 327–32 An instructional technique used in INFORMATIVE PRESENTATIONS to
teach a procedure that involves describing,
demonstrating, and finally asking AUDIENCE
members to perform the procedure with
supervision from the SPEAKER.

terminal credibility, 357 The SPEAKER CRED-
IBILITY you earn by the end of a presentation. *See also* derived credibility; initial
credibility

testimony, 116 A type of SUPPORTING MATE-
RIAL that refers to statements or OPINIONS
that someone has said or written.

**theory of informative communication, 316–18,
319–20, 333–46** A set of guidelines for making strategic decisions about the CONTENT
and structure of an INFORMATIVE PRESENTA-
TION, by focusing on the differences between
presentations that REPORT NEW INFORMATION
and those that EXPLAIN COMPLEX IDEAS.

thesis statement, 137–38, 163 *See* central
idea

thought speed, 32–33 The speed at which
you can think as opposed to the speed at
which you speak.

Thunberg, Greta, as speaker, xxix–xxx, xxxiii–xxxiv, 40

time arrangement, 139–40, 328, 330, 410–11 An ORGANIZATIONAL PATTERN that places KEY POINTS in a series of sequenced steps or points in time.

time markers, for outlines, 522, 523

toast, 5–6, 442–48 A speaking OCCASION where the SPEAKER honors a person, couple, group, event, or accomplishment and invites the AUDIENCE to raise their glasses and drink in celebration.
    example, 448
    guidelines, 444–47
    key features, 443–44

Todd, Chuck, on alternative facts, 120

topic, 105 The subject of your presentation. *See also* topic, choosing
    audience analysis and, 72

topic-centered interests, 77 Subjects AUDIENCE members enjoy LISTENING to and learning about, such as hobbies, sports or pastimes, or subjects loaded with intrigue and mystery. *See also* self-centered interests

topic, choosing, 105–13
    audience and, 108–10
    early research, 111–13
    examples, 106–8, 110–11, 112
    scope and, 110–11
    speaker and, 105–8

Toulmin model of argument, 369–74 A model for creating and evaluating the elements of a complete argument. Key Features: CLAIM • EVIDENCE • WARRANT • BACKING • RESERVATIONS • QUALIFIERS

Toulmin, Stephen, Toulmin model, 369

toxic topics, 109 Subjects to be avoided because they have the potential to turn an AUDIENCE against you and your MESSAGE.

transition, 149–51 A type of CONNECTIVE that uses words, numbers, brief phrases, or sentences to help guide your AUDIENCE from one KEY POINT or section to the next.

Trump, Melania, as speaker, 46

trustworthiness, 61–62, 66t A major dimension of SPEAKER CREDIBILITY that refers to whether AUDIENCE members perceive the SPEAKER as honest, reliable, and ethical. *See also* competence; dynamism; likability

Truth, Sojourner, as speaker, xxxi–xxxii
Twain, Mark, toast, 443

U

unconcerned audience, 390–91 An AUDIENCE whose members, for whatever reason, aren't particularly interested in a speaker's TOPIC.

undecided audience, 390–91 An AUDIENCE whose members have thought about a TOPIC but have not taken a position on it.

understanding, 30–31, 32 A component of the HURIER model of EFFECTIVE LISTENING that refers to your ability to grasp the intended meaning of a speaker's MESSAGE. *See also*

Notes

Preface

1. Isa Engleberg, Susan M. Ward, Lynn M. Disbrow, James A. Katt, Scott A. Myers, and Patricia O'Keefe, "The Development of a Set of Core Communication Competencies for Introductory Communication Courses," *Communication Education* 66, no. 1 (2017): 1–18.

Introduction: Your Voice Matters

1. Greta Thunberg, Full speech delivered at the UN Climate Change COP24 Conference (Katowice, Poland, December 15, 2018), uploaded by Connect4Climate with written transcript, YouTube, December 15, 2018, https://www.youtube.com/watch?v=VFkQSGyeCWg.

2. Greta Thunberg, Full speech at the EU Parliament in Strasbourg (Strasbourg, Germany, April 16, 2019), uploaded by FridaysForFuture, YouTube, April 21, 2019, https://www.youtube.com/watch?v=cJAcuQEVxTY. For written transcript, see "Greta Thunberg: 'Our House Is Falling Apart, and We Are Rapidly Running Out of Time,' speech to EU Parliament—2019," Speakola, April 16, 2019, https://speakola.com/ideas/greta-thunberg-speech-to-eu-parliament-2019.

3. During the early days of planning and drafting *The Norton Field Guide to Speaking*, Deanna Dannels generously hosted two separate gatherings at her home institution, North Carolina State University (NCSU), for the team to brainstorm and flesh out the scope of this book. Those who know Deanna know that she is a fierce advocate for student voices and a passionate scholar of teaching

practices, and her own voice in those early meetings at NCSU was instrumental in shaping this book. Although the rest of this book's chapters were written by the two authors, this introduction was partly drafted by, and its spirit and emphases largely determined by, Deanna. The authors extend their gratitude and appreciation for Deanna's contributions to this book and to the field of communication.

4. Greta Thunberg, "Transcript: Greta Thunberg's Speech at the U.N. Climate Action Summit," NPR, September 23, 2019, https://www.npr.org/2019/09/23/763452863/transcript-greta-thunbergs-speech-at-the-u-n-climate-action-summit.

5. Greta Thunberg, "The Disarming Case to Act Right Now on Climate Change," TEDx Stockholm, accessed April 20, 2021, https://www.ted.com/talks/greta_thunberg_the_disarming_case_to_act_right_now_on_climate_change/transcript.

1.1 The Rhetorical Speechmaking Process

1. "What Is Communication?," National Communication Association, accessed February 20, 2020, https://www.natcom.org/about-nca/what-communication.

1.2 Speaking Anxiety

1. "America's Top Fears 2018," Chapman University Survey of American Fears, October 16, 2018, https://blogs.chapman.edu/wilkinson/2018/10/16/americas-top-fears-2018.

2. Virginia P. Richmond, Jason S. Wrench, and James C. McCroskey, *Communication Apprehension, Avoidance, and Effectiveness*, 6th ed. (Boston: Pearson, 2013).

3. Lori J. Carrell and S. Clay Willmington, "The Relationship between Self-Report Measures of Communication Apprehension and Trained Observers' Ratings of Communication Competence," *Communication Reports* 11, no. 1 (1998): 87–95.

4. Michael T. Motley, *Overcoming Your Fear of Public Speaking: A Proven Method* (Boston: Houghton Mifflin, 1997), 27.

5. Thomas Gilovich and Kenneth Savitsky, "The Spotlight Effect and the Illusion of Transparency," *Current Directions in Psychological Science* 8, no. 6 (1999): 165–68.

6. John A. Daly, Anita L. Vangelisti, and David J. Weber, "Speech Anxiety Affects How People Prepare Speeches: A Protocol Analysis of the Preparation Process of Speaking," *Communication Monographs* 62, no. 1 (December 1995): 383–97.

1.3 Listening

1. Judi Brownell, *Listening: Attitudes, Principles, and Skills*, 6th ed. (New York: Routledge/Taylor & Francis, 2018), 14–18.

2. Ralph G. Nichols, "Ten Bad Listening Habits," *Supervisor's Notebook* 22, no. 1 (New York: Scott Foresman, Spring 1960), https://www.millersville.edu/gened/files/pdfs-faculty-handbook/15-ten-bad-listening-habits.pdf.

3. Ralph G. Nichols, "Listening Is a 10-Part Skill," *Nation's Business* 75 (September 1987): 40.

4. Pam A. Mueller and Daniel M. Oppenheimer, "The Pen Is Mightier than the Keyboard: Advantages of Longhand over Laptop Note Taking,"

Psychological Science 25, no. 6 (April 23, 2014): 1159–68, https://doi.org/10.1177/0956797614524581 (2018 correction: "Corrigendum: The Pen Is Mightier than the Keyboard: Advantages of Longhand over Laptop Note Taking," *Psychological Science* 29, no. 9 [July 31, 2018]: 1565–68, https://doi.org/10.1177/0956797618781773).

5. Inspired by the Audience's Bill of Rights in Gene Zelazny, *Say It with Presentations*, rev. and expanded ed. (New York: McGraw-Hill, 2006), 4–6.

6. P. M. Forni, *Choosing Civility: The Twenty-Five Rules of Considerate Conduct* (New York: St. Martin's Press, 2002), 9.

1.4 Ethics and Freedom of Speech

1. Quintilian, *Institutes of Oratory*, in *The Rhetorical Tradition: Readings from Classical Times to the Present*, ed. Patricia Bizzell and Bruce Herzberg (Boston: Bedford/St. Martin's, 2001), 418.

2. The Credo for Ethical Communication was developed at the 1999 Communication Ethics Credo Conference sponsored by the NCA. It was adopted and endorsed by the Legislative Council of the NCA in November 1999 and is available on the NCA website, https://www.natcom.org/sites/default/files/pages/1999_Public_Statements_NCA_Credo_for_Ethical_Communication_November.pdf. In 2017, the Credo was re-endorsed by the NCA, see https://www.natcom.org/sites/default/files/Public_Statement_Credo_for_Ethical_Communication_2017.pdf.

3. Judi Brownell, *Listening: Attitudes, Principles, and Skills*, 6th ed. (New York: Routledge/Taylor & Francis, 2018), 408–9.

4. E. A. Gjelten, "Does the First Amendment Protect Hate Speech?" Lawyers.com, 2020,

https://www.lawyers.com/legal-info/criminal/does-the-first-amendment-protect-hate-speech.html.

5. Legal Dictionary, Law.com, https://dictionary.law.com/Default.aspx?searched=defamation&type=1. Based on Gerald N. Hill and Kathleen Thompson Hill, *The People's Law Dictionary: Taking the Mystery out of Legal Language* (New York: Fine Communications, 2002).

6. Ronald C. Arnett, "The Practical Philosophy of Communication Ethics and Free Speech as the Foundation for Speech Communication," *Communication Quarterly* 38, no. 3 (1990): 216.

2.1 Speaker

1. John A. Daly and Madeleine H. Redlick, "Handling Questions and Objections Affects Audience Judgments of Speakers," *Communication Education* 65, no. 2 (2016): 164–81.

2. Alison Wood Brooks and Leslie K. John, "The Surprising Power of Questions," *Harvard Business Review*, May–June 2018, 60–67, https://hbr.org/2018/05/the-surprising-power-of-questions.html.

3. "Text: Obama's Re-election Victory Speech in Chicago," Reuters, November 7, 2012, https://www.reuters.com/article/usa-election-obama-speech-text/text-obamas-re-election-victory-speech-in-chicago-idINDEE8A60BA20121107.

2.2 Audience

1. Composite list of universal human values based on several sources: "The Six Pillars of Character," Resources: Making Ethical Decisions, Josephson Institute, 2002, https://josephsoninstitute.org/med-introtoc; Shalom H. Schwartz, Jan Cieciuch, Michele Vecchione, et al., "Refining the Theory of Basic Individual Values," *Journal of Personality and Social Psychology* 103, no. 4 (2012): 663–88; Shalom H. Schwartz, "An Overview of the Schwartz Theory of Basic Values," *Online Readings in Psychology and Culture* 2, no. 1 (2012), https://doi.org/10.9707/2307-0919.1116; and Kofi Annan, "Do We Still Have Universal Values?" (speech, Tübingen University, Tübingen, Germany, December 12, 2003), https://www.un.org/press/en/2003/sgsm9076.doc.htm.

2. Some of these early research efforts include Geert Hofstede, Gert Jan Hofstede, and Michael Minkov, *Culture and Organizations: Software of the Mind*, 3rd ed. (New York: McGraw-Hill, 2010); Geert Hofstede, *Culture's Consequences: Comparing Values, Behaviors, Institutions and Organizations across Nations*, 2nd ed. (Thousand Oaks, CA: Sage, 2001); Edward T. Hall, *The Silent Language* (Greenwich, CT: Fawcett, 1959); and Edward T. Hall, *Beyond Culture* (Garden City, NY: Anchor, 1997).

3.2 Research and Supporting Material

1. General David Petraeus, "Opening Statement at the U.S. Senate ISAF Confirmation Hearing," American Rhetoric: Online Speech Bank, June 29, 2010, https://www.americanrhetoric.com/speeches/davidpetraeusisafconfirmation.htm.

2. Nick Jonas, "Diabetes Awareness" (speech, National Press Club, Washington, DC, August 24, 2009), https://www.c-span.org/video/?288515-1/nick-jonas-diabetes.

3. The information cited in this speech is adapted from Lonnie Hanauer, letter to the editor, *New York Times*, March 2, 2019, A20.

4. Adapted from Steven D. Levitt and Stephen J. Dubner, *Freakonomics: A Rogue Economist Explores the Hidden Side of Everything* (New York: William Morrow, 2005), 55–56.

5. *Meet the Press*, transcript, NBC News, January 22, 2017, http://www.nbcnews.com/meet-the-press/meet-press-01-22-17-n710491.

6. Robert N. Proctor, "The History of the Discovery of the Cigarette–Lung Cancer Link: Evidentiary Traditions, Corporate Denial, Global Toll," *Tobacco Control* 21 (2012): 87–91, http://dx.doi.org/10.1136/tobaccocontrol-2011-050338 (January 1, 2013, correction: http://dx.doi.org/10.1136/tobaccocontrol-2011-050338corr1).

7. Emma Brown et al., "U.S. Deaths Soared in Early Weeks of Pandemic, Far Exceeding Number Attributed to Covid-19," *Washington Post*, April 27, 2020, https://www.washingtonpost.com/investigations/2020/04/27/covid-19-death-toll-undercounted.

8. Joe Concha, "AP Deletes Tweet on Trump's 'Animals' Comment: 'It Wasn't Made Clear He Was Speaking' about MS-13," *Hill*, May 17, 2018, https://thehill.com/homenews/media/388183-ap-deletes-tweet-on-trumps-animals-comment-it-wasnt-made-clear-he-was-speaking.

9. Matthew S. McGlone, "Contextomy: The Art of Quoting out of Context," *Media Culture and Society* 27, no. 4 (2005): 511–22.

10. Charlie Warzel, "Don't Go Down the Rabbit Hole," *New York Times*, February 18, 2021, https://www.nytimes.com/2021/02/18/opinion/fake-news-media-attention.html?referringSource=articleShare.

11. Andrea Baer and Dan Kipnis, "Evaluating Online Sources: Simple Strategies for Complex Thinking," Campbell Library, Rowan University, December 2, 2020, https://libguides.rowan.edu/EvaluatingOnlineSources.

12. Baer and Kipnis. See also Michael A. Caulfield, *Web Literacy for Student Fact Checkers . . . and Other People Who Care about Facts*, PressBooks, 2017, streamlined 2021. This work is licensed under a Creative Commons Attribution 4.0 Internal License.

13. "Vaccines and Autism," Children's Hospital of Philadelphia, Vaccine Education Center, May 7, 2018, https://www.chop.edu/centers-programs/vaccine-education-center/vaccines-and-other-conditions/vaccines-autism.

14. "How Does the Gallup US Poll Work?" Gallup, accessed November 7, 2019, https://www.gallup.com/224855/gallup-poll-work.aspx.

15. Jonathan Rothbaum and Ashley Edwards, "U.S. Median Household Income Was $63,179 in 2018, Not Significantly Different from 2017," United States Census Bureau, September 10, 2019, https://www.census.gov/library/stories/2019/09/us-median-household-income-not-significantly-different-from-2017.html.

16. Maurie Backman, "Are You Well-Paid? Compare Your Income to the Average," *Ascent*, February 18, 2020, https://www.fool.com/the-ascent/research/average-us-income.

3.3 Organizing Content

1. Michael J. Gelb, *Present Yourself! Capture Your Audience with Great Presentation* (Rolling Hills Estates, CA: Jalmar Press, 1988), 10–15.

2. Georg H. Eifert, Matthew McKay, and John P. Forsyth, *ACT on Life Not on Anger: The New Acceptance and Commitment Therapy Guide to Problem Anger* (Oakland, CA: New Harbinger, 2006), 14.

3. See Marie Winn, "The Trouble with Television," in *Taking Sides: Clashing Views on Controversial Issues in*

Mass Media and Society, 5th ed., ed. Alison Alexander and Jarice Hanson (Guilford, CT: Duskin /McGraw-Hill, 1999), 22–28.

4. See the chapters on reading and writing quantitative and qualitative research reports in Joann Keyton, *Communication Research: Asking Questions, Finding Answers* (Boston: McGraw-Hill, 2001), 314–45.

5. Richard Bullock, *The Norton Field Guide to Writing*, 5th ed. (New York: W. W. Norton, 2019), 425–27.

6. Dorothy Leeds, *Power Speak: Engage, Inspire, and Stimulate Your Audience* (Franklin Lakes, NJ: Career Press, 2003), 122–23.

7. Thomas Leech, *How to Prepare, Stage, and Deliver Winning Presentations* (New York: AMACOM, 1993), 97.

8. The speech framer was developed by Isa N. Engleberg as an alternative or supplement to outlining. See Isa N. Engleberg and John A. Daly, *Presentations in Everyday Life*, 3rd ed. (Boston: Pearson, 2009), 217–18.

9. Michael M. Klepper with Robert E. Gunther, *I'd Rather Die Than Give a Speech* (Burr Ridge, IL: Irwin, 1994), 6.

3.4 Introductions and Conclusions

1. Susan Cain, "The Power of Introverts," TED2012, March 2012, https://www.ted.com/talks/susan_cain _the_power_of_introverts/transcript?language=en.

2. Margaret Muller, "'I Have Down Syndrome': Student's Speech Proves Value of Hard Work," *Washington Post*, September 14, 1999, Health, 9.

3. Ronald W. Reagan, "Explosion of the Space Shuttle *Challenger* Address to the Nation," NASA History

Office, January 28, 1986, https://history.nasa.gov /reagan12886.html.

4. Marge Anderson, "Looking through Our Window: The Value of Indian Culture," *Vital Speeches of the Day* 65, no. 20 (1999): 633–34.

5. Muller, "'I Have Down Syndrome,'" 9.

6. Robert M. Franklin, "The Soul of Morehouse and the Future of the Mystique" (speech, President's Town Meeting, Morehouse College, Atlanta, April 21, 2009), https://web.archive.org/web/20130601050137 /http://giving.morehouse.edu/Document.Doc?id=37.

4.1 The Importance of Delivery

1. Brian Cutler, Steven D. Penrod, and Thomas E. Stuve, "Juror Decision Making in Eyewitness Identification Cases," *Law and Human Behavior* 12, no. 1 (1988): 41–55; and Bonnie Erickson, Allan E. Lind, Bruce C. Johnson, and William M. O'Barr, "Speech Style and Impression Formation in a Court Setting: The Effects of 'Powerful' and 'Powerless' Speech," *Journal of Experimental Social Psychology* 14, no. 3 (1978): 266–79.

2. Kathy Tyner, "Stage Presence: What It Means, Why It Matters, and How to Improve It," KD Conservatory, https://kdstudio.com/tag/stage-presence/.

3. Based on authors' observations as well as descriptions in Carmine Gallo, *The Presentation Secrets of Steve Jobs: How to Be Insanely Great in Front of Any Audience* (New York: McGraw-Hill, 2010).

4. Peter Andersen, "Immediacy," in *Encyclopedia of Communication Theory*, ed. Stephen W. Littlejohn and Karen A. Foss (Los Angeles: Sage, 2009), 501.

5. Judee K. Burgoon and Aaron E. Bacue, "Nonverbal Communication Skills," in *Handbook of*

Communication and Social Interaction Skills, ed. John O. Greene and Brant R. Burleson, (Mahwah, NJ: Lawrence Erlbaum, 2003), 195–96; and James Kennedy, Paul Baxter, and Tony Belpaeme, "Nonverbal Immediacy as a Characterisation of Social Behaviour for Human–Robot Interaction," *International Journal of Social Robotics* 9, no. 1 (2017): 109–28.

4.2 Vocal Delivery

1. Ofer Amir and Reut Levine-Yundof, "Listeners' Attitude toward People with Dysphonia," *Journal of Voice* 27, no. 4 (July 2013): 524.

2. Nina-Jo Moore, Mark Hickson III, and Don W. Stacks, *Nonverbal Communication: Studies and Applications*, 6th ed. (New York: Oxford University Press, 2014), 265–67.

3. Lyle V. Mayer, *Fundamentals of Voice and Articulation*, 13th ed. (Boston: McGraw-Hill, 2004), 55.

4. Mayer, *Fundamentals*, 66.

5. Richard L. Street Jr., Robert M. Brady, and William B. Putnam, "The Influence of Speech Rate Stereotypes and Rate Similarity on Listeners' Evaluations of Speakers," *Journal of Language and Social Psychology* 2, no. 1 (1993): 37–56; Norman Miller, Geoffrey Maruyama, Rex Julian Beaber, and Keith Valone, "Speed of Speech and Persuasion," *Journal of Personality and Social Psychology* 34, no. 4 (1976): 615–24, https://pdfs.semanticscholar.org/3231 /eb72791766c5c9e86a180c00f918984e5f90.pdf.

6. Roy F. Baumeister and Brad J. Bushman, *Social Psychology and Human Nature* (Boston: Cengage Learning, 2021), 275; Stephen M. Smith and David R. Shaffer, "Celerity and Cajolery: Rapid Speech May Promote or Inhibit Persuasion through Its Impact on Message Elaboration," *Personality and Social Psychology Bulletin* 17, no. 6 (1991): 663–69.

7. Susan D. Miller, *Be Heard the First Time: A Woman's Guide to Powerful Speaking* (Herndon, VA: Capital Books, 2006), 100.

8. Nagesh Belludi, "How to Speak Persuasively and Influence Others," *Right Attitudes: Ideas for Impact*, July 22, 2016, https://www.rightattitudes.com /2016/07/22/how-to-speak-persuasively.

9. Hilda B. Fisher, *Improving Voice and Articulation* (Boston: Houghton Mifflin, 1966), 172.

10. Michael Powell, "Deliberative in a Manic Game: Barack Obama," *New York Times*, June 4, 2008, A18.

11. Michael Erard, *Um: Slips, Stumbles, and Verbal Blunders, and What They Mean* (New York: Pantheon Books, 2007), 243–44.

12. National Geographic for AP Special Features, "The 'Um' Factor: What People Say between Thoughts," *Baltimore Sun*, September 28, 1992, 1D and 3D.

13. Erard, *Um*, 96.

14. Roberto Rey Agudo, "Everyone Has an Accent," *New York Times*, July 14, 2018, https://www.nytimes .com/2018/07/14/opinion/sunday/everyone-has-an -accent.html.

15. John McWorter, *Word on the Street: Debunking the Myth of a "Pure" Standard English* (Cambridge, MA: Perseus, 1998), 143, 145–46.

4.3 Physical Delivery

1. Roxanne Bauer, "The Impact of Making Eye Contact around the World," World Economic Forum, February 26, 2015, https://www.weforum.org

/agenda/2015/02/the-impact-of-making-eye
-contact-around-the-world.

2. Mark L. Knapp, Judith A. Hall, and Terrence G.
Hogan, *Nonverbal Communication in Human Interaction*, 8th ed. (Boston: Cengage, 2014), 258.

3. Carl Zimmer, "More to a Smile than Lips and
Teeth," *New York Times*, January 24, 2011, http://
www.nytimes.com/2011/01/25/science/25smile.html.

4. Everett M. Rogers and Thomas M. Steinfatt, *Intercultural Communication* (Prospect Heights, IL: Waveland, 1999), 174.

5. David Neiwert, "Is That an OK Sign? A White
Power Symbol? Or Just a Right-Wing Troll?" *Hatewatch*,
Southern Poverty Law Center, September 18, 2018,
https://www.splcenter.org/hatewatch/2018/09/18/ok
-sign-white-power-symbol-or-just-right-wing-troll.

6. Rogers and Steinfatt, *Intercultural Communication*,
172; and Guo-Ming Chen and William J. Starosta,
Foundations of Intercultural Communication (Boston:
Allyn & Bacon, 1998), 81–92.

7. Ron Hoff, *I Can See You Naked* (Kansas City, MO:
Andrews McMeel, 1992), 83.

4.4 Practicing Your Delivery

1. "How Does a Presidential Teleprompter Work?,"
Neil Tanner, Inc., December 17, 2013, https://www
.neiltanner.com/presidential-teleprompter; and "Using
Teleprompters to Your Advantage," metroConnections, June 12, 2013, https://www.metroconnections
.com/conference-services/meeting-management
/using-teleprompters-to-your-advantage.

5.1 Using Language

1. S. I. Hayakawa and Alan R. Hayakawa, *Language
and Thought in Action*, 5th ed. (San Diego, CA:
Harcourt Brace Jovanovich, 1990), 43.

2. Peter Nicholas and Ed Young, "Fauci: 'Bizarre'
White House Behavior Only Hurts the President,"
Atlantic, July 15, 2020, https://www.theatlantic.com
/politics/archive/2020/07/trump-fauci-coronavirus
-pandemic-oppo/614224.

3. Lani Arredondo, *The McGraw-Hill 36-Hour Course:
Business Presentations* (New York: McGraw-Hill,
1994), 147.

4. Robert H. Gass and John S. Seiter, *Persuasion,
Social Influence, and Compliance Gaining*, 6th ed.
(New York: Routledge, 2018), 175.

5. Gass and Seiter, 177; James Price Dillard and
Linda J. Marshall, "Persuasion as a Social Skill,"
in *Handbook of Communication and Social Interaction
Skills*, ed. John O. Greene and Brant R. Burleson
(Mahwah, NJ: Lawrence Erlbaum, 2003), 505–6; and
Richard M. Perloff, *The Dynamics of Persuasion*, 5th
ed. (New York: Routledge, 2014), 281–83.

6. Andrew M. Cuomo, "Audio & Rush Transcript:
Governor Cuomo Addresses President Trump's Threat
to Defund New York City and the Federal Government's Failure in the Ongoing COVID-19 Crisis,"
New York State COVID-19 Updates, September 3,
2020, https://www.governor.ny.gov/news/audio-rush
-transcript-governor-cuomo-addresses-president
-trumps-threat-defund-new-york-city-and.

7. Kathleen Hall Jamieson, *Eloquence in an Electronic
Age: The Transformation of Political Speechmaking* (New
York: Oxford University Press, 1988).

8. "Text of Obama's Speech: A More Perfect Union,"
Washington Wire, March 18, 2008, http://blogs.wsj
.com/washwire/2008/03/18/text-of-obamas-speech
-a-more-perfect-union. For a video of Obama's
speech, see "Barack Obama: 'A More Perfect
Union' (Full Speech)," https://www.youtube.com
/watch?v=zrp-v2tHaDo.

9. "Winston Churchill's Inspiring Wartime Speeches in Parliament," BBC News, May 8, 2020, https://www.bbc.com/news/uk-politics-52588148.

10. Adam Rosenberg, "An 11-year-old Student Shook March for Our Lives with Her Powerful Message," March 25, 2018 (video and transcript), Mashable, https://mashable.com/2018/03/25/naomi-wadler-march-for-our-lives-speech.

11. George W. Bush, State of the Union, White House, Office of the Press Secretary, January 28, 2003, https://georgewbush-whitehouse.archives.gov/news/releases/2003/01/20030128-19.html.

12. William Jefferson Clinton, "Democratic Presidential Nomination Acceptance Address," American Rhetoric: Online Speech Bank, July 16, 1992, https://www.americanrhetoric.com/speeches/wjclinton1992dnc.htm.

13. Max Atkinson, *Lend Me Your Ears* (New York: Oxford University Press, 2005), 221.

14. R. L. Trask, *Language: The Basics*, 2nd ed. (London: Routledge, 1995), 128.

15. Ronald H. Carpenter, *Choosing Powerful Words* (Boston: Allyn & Bacon, 1999), 109–11.

16. Atkinson, *Lend Me Your Ears*, 224.

17. Mickey Ciokajlo, "Hospital Layoffs Put on Hold," *Chicago Tribune*, June 6, 2007, https://www.chicagotribune.com/news/ct-xpm-2007-06-06-0706051099-story.html.

18. Amy Crawford and Jennifer Reeger, "First Ladies Honor Flight 93 Heroes," TribLive, September 12, 2010, https://archive.triblive.com/news/first-ladies-honor-flight-93-heroes. For video, see "September 11 Remembrance Ceremony for Flight 93," C-SPAN, September 11, 2010, https://www.c-span.org/video/?295418-1/september-11-remembrance-ceremony-flight-93.

19. Diana Hacker, *The Bedford Handbook*, 5th ed. (Boston: Bedford, 1998), 279.

20. Owen Peterson, *Representative American Speeches, 1989–1990* (New York: H. W. Wilson, 1991), 163–68.

5.2 Telling Stories

1. Steve Jobs, "You've Got to Find What You Love," *Stanford News*, June 14, 2005, https://news.stanford.edu/2005/06/14/jobs-061505.

2. Annette Simmons, *Whoever Tells the Best Story Wins* (New York: AMACOM, 2007), 19.

3. Matt Blitz, "How a Dirty Old Waffle Iron Became Nike's Holy Grail," *Popular Mechanics*, July 15, 2016, https://www.popularmechanics.com/technology/gadgets/a21841/nike-waffle-iron.

4. Rives Collins and Pamela J. Cooper, *The Power of Story: Teaching through Storytelling*, 2nd ed. (Boston: Allyn & Bacon, 1997), 24–28.

5. Based on Joanna Slan, *Using Stories and Humor: Grab Your Audience* (Boston: Allyn & Bacon, 1998), 89–95 and 116.

6. Walter R. Fisher, *Human Communication as Narration: Toward a Philosophy of Reason, Value, and Action* (Columbia: University of South Carolina Press, 1987), 47–49, 68–69.

7. Peter Guber, "The Four Truths of the Storyteller," *Harvard Business Review*, December 2007, https://hbr.org/2007/12/the-four-truths-of-the-storyteller.

8. "Read Oprah Winfrey's Rousing Golden Globes Speech," CNN, January 10, 2018, https://www.cnn

.com/2018/01/08/entertainment/oprah-globes
-speech-transcript/index.html.

5.3 Generating Interest

1. John A. Daly and Isa N. Engleberg, *Presentations in Everyday Life* (Boston: Houghton Mifflin, 2001), 3–4 and 21.

2. Granville N. Toogood, *The Articulate Executive: Learn to Look, Act, and Sound Like a Leader* (New York: McGraw-Hill, 2010), 83.

3. Marla Tabaka, "How to Give the Speech of a Lifetime," *Inc.*, March 3, 2014, https://www.inc.com/marla-tabaka/how-to-give-the-speech-of-a-lifetime-in-18-minutes-or-less.html.

4. Laura Lynch, "How Long Should Videos Be for E-Learning," *Learn Dash*, January 17, 2019, https://www.learndash.com/how-long-should-videos-be-for-e-learning.

5. Alan M. Perlman, *Writing Great Speeches: Professional Techniques You Can Use* (Boston: Allyn & Bacon, 1998), 52.

6. "Jacinda Ardern's Speech at Christchurch Memorial—Full Transcript," *Guardian*, March 28, 2019, https://www.theguardian.com/world/2019/mar/29/jacinda-arderns-speech-at-christchurch-memorial-full-transcript.

7. "Read the Full Transcript of Obama's Eulogy for John Lewis," *New York Times*, July 30, 2020, updated Aug. 19, 2020, https://www.nytimes.com/2020/07/30/us/obama-eulogy-john-lewis-full-transcript.html.

8. Ronald Reagan, "Remarks at the Annual Convention of the United States Jaycees in San Antonio, Texas," American Presidency Project, June 24, 1981, https://www.presidency.ucsb.edu/documents/remarks-the-annual-convention-the-united-states-jaycees-san-antonio-texas.

9. George W. Bush, "Bullhorn Address to Ground Zero Rescue Workers," American Rhetoric: Rhetoric of 9–11, September 14, 2001, https://www.americanrhetoric.com/speeches/gwbush911groundzerobullhorn.htm.

5.4 Presentation Aids

1. Gene Zelazny, *The Say It with Charts Complete Toolkit* (New York: McGraw-Hill, 2007), 28.

2. Zelazny, *Say It with Charts*, 28–29.

3. Kevin Mercadante, "Gender Pay Gap in 2021: The Long and Winding Road to Parity," *Money under 30*, December 28, 2020, https://www.moneyunder30.com/the-gender-pay-gap-in-the-21st-century

4. Margaret Y. Rabb, *The Presentation Design Book: Tips, Techniques & Advice for Creating Effective, Attractive Slides, Overheads, Screen Shows, Multimedia & More*, 2nd ed. (Chapel Hill, NC: Ventana Press, 1993), 154.

5. Stephen M. Kosslyn, *Clear and to the Point: 8 Psychological Principles for Compelling PowerPoint® Presentations* (New York: Oxford University Press, 2007), 184.

6. Kosslyn, *Clear and to the Point*, 210.

7. *PowerPoint Tutorial*, Module #3 (Boston: Houghton Mifflin, 2005).

8. "The Advantages and Disadvantages of PowerPoint," Boundless.com, accessed April 21, 2021. http://oer2go.org/mods/en-boundless/www.boundless.com/communications/textbooks/boundless-communications-textbook/preparing-and-using-visual-aids-16/using-powerpoint-and-alternatives-successfully-85

/the-advantages-and-disadvantages-of-powerpoint
-323-5654/index.html.

9. Zelazny, *Say It with Charts*, 18–19.

10. Robin Williams, *The Non-Designer's Presentation Book: Principle for Effective Presentation *Design* (Berkeley, CA: Peachpit Press, 2010), 41 and 137.

6.1 Understanding Informative Speaking

1. Katherine E. Rowan, "A New Pedagogy for Explanatory Public Speaking: Why Arrangement Should Not Substitute for Invention," *Communication Education* 44 (1995): 236–50; and Katherine E. Rowan, "Informing and Explaining Skills: Theory and Research on Informative Communication," in *Handbook of Communication and Social Interaction Skills*, ed. John O. Greene and Brant R. Burleson (Mahwah, NJ: Lawrence Erlbaum, 2003), 403–38.

2. Rowan, "A New Pedagogy," 242–43; and Rowan, "Informing and Explaining Skills," 419–420.

6.2 Reporting New Information

1. Katherine E. Rowan, "Informing and Explaining Skills: Theory and Research on Informative Communication," in *Handbook of Communication and Social Interaction Skills*, ed. John O. Greene and Brant R. Burleson (Mahwah, NJ: Lawrence Erlbaum, 2003), 412–19.

2. David K. Farkas, "The Logical and Rhetorical Construction of Procedural Discourse," *Technical Communication* (February 1999): 42–43, https://citeseerx.ist.psu.edu/viewdoc/download?doi=10.1.1.586.4894&rep=rep1&type=pdf; and Michael Steehouder and Hans van der Meij, "Designing and Evaluating Procedural Instructions with the Four Components Model," *2005 IEEE International Professional Communication Conference Proceedings*,

797–801, https://core.ac.uk/download/pdf/11460265.pdf

3. Ashley Chiasson, "Terminology Tuesday: Tell, Show, Do" *Ashley Chiasson*, April 5, 2016, http://ashleychiasson.com/blog/terminology-tuesday-tell-show-do.

6.3 Explaining Complex Ideas

1. Katherine E. Rowan, "Informing and Explaining Skills: Theory and Research on Informative Communication," in *Handbook of Communication and Social Interaction Skills*, ed. John O. Greene and Brant R. Burleson (Mahwah, NJ: Lawrence Erlbaum, 2003), 403–38; and Katherine E. Rowan, "A New Pedagogy for Explanatory Public Speaking: Why Arrangement Should Not Substitute for Invention," *Communication Education* 44 (1995): 236–50.

2. Rowan, "Informing and Explaining Skills," 420–22; and Rowan, "A New Pedagogy," 243.

3. Joseph Welan and Kamil Msefer, "Economic Supply and Demand," MIT System Dynamics in Education Project, January 14, 1996, https://ocw.mit.edu/courses/sloan-school-of-management/15-988-system-dynamics-self-study-fall-1998-spring-1999/readings/economics.pdf

4. Rowan, "Informing and Explaining Skills," 422–24.

5. Barbara Katz Rothman, *The Book of Life: A Personal and Ethical Guide to Race, Normality and the Human Gene Study* (Boston: Beacon Press, 2001), 23. See also Cynthia Taylor and Bryan M. Dewsbury, "On the Problem and Promise of Metaphor Use in Science and Science Communication," *Journal of Microbiology & Biology Education* 19, no. 1 (2018), https://www.ncbi.nlm.nih.gov/pmc/articles/PMC5969428.

6. Matt Rosenberg, "An Overview of El Nino and La Nina," ThoughtCo., August 27, 2020, thoughtco.com/el-nino-and-la-nina-overview-1434943; National

Oceanic and Atmospheric Administration, "What Are El Nino and La Nina?" National Ocean Service, accessed February 19, 2021, https://oceanservice.noaa.gov/facts/ninonina.html; "What Are El Niño and La Niña?" American Geosciences Institute, https://www.americangeosciences.org/critical-issues/faq/what-are-el-nino-and-la-nina; and David Funkhouser, "El Niño: The Basics," *State of the Planet*, Earth Institute/Columbia University, July 2, 2014, https://blogs.ei.columbia.edu/2014/07/02/el-nino-the-basics.

7. Rowan, "Informing and Explaining Skills," 424–26.

7.1 Understanding Persuasion

1. Andrea Lunsford and John R. Ruszkiewicz, *Everything's an Argument*, 8th ed. (Boston: Bedford/St. Martin's, 2018).

2. Aristotle, *The Complete Works of Aristotle: The Revised Oxford Translation*, ed. Jonathan Barnes, Bollingen Series (Princeton, NJ: Princeton University Press, 1983), 1:2155.

3. Kenneth Burke, *A Rhetoric of Motives* (Berkeley: University of California Press, 1969), 55.

4. Matthew Yglesias, "Prolonged School Closures Could Be Very Costly for America's Students," Vox, April 21, 2020, https://www.vox.com/2020/4/21/21223585/school-closure-impact-students-children.

5. This example is based on Dan Levin, "'Become My Mom Again': What It's Like to Grow Up amid the Opioid Crisis," *New York Times*, May 31, 2019, https://www.nytimes.com/2019/05/31/us/opioid-children-addiction.html.

6. Martha C. Nussbaum, *The Monarch of Fear: A Philosopher Looks at Our Political Crisis* (New York: Simon & Schuster, 2018), 24.

7. Richard M. Perloff, *The Dynamics of Persuasion: Communication and Attitudes in the 21st Century*, 7th ed. (New York: Routledge, 2020), 353–54.

7.2 Thinking Critically about Arguments

1. Hugo Mercier, "Reasoning Is More Intuitive than We Think," *Psychology Today*, August 17, 2011, https://www.psychologytoday.com/us/blog/social-design/201108/reasoning-is-more-intuitive-we-think.

2. Based on Judi Brownell, *Listening: Attitudes, Principles, and Skills*, 6th ed. (New York: Routledge, 2017), 257–259.

3. Based on editorial, "State without Pity," *New York Times*, December 27, 2006, A26.

4. Jay Verlinden, *Critical Thinking and Everyday Argument* (Belmont, CA: Wadsworth Thomson Learning, 2005), 79.

5. Stephen E. Toulmin, *The Uses of Argument* (London: Cambridge University Press, 1958); and Stephen Toulmin, Richard Rieke, and Allan Janik, *An Introduction to Reasoning* (New York: Macmillan, 1979).

6. Douglas N. Walton, *Begging the Question: Circular Reasoning as a Tactic of Argumentation* (Westport, CT: Greenwood Press, 1991), 285.

7.3 Rhetorical Strategies for Persuasive Presentations

1. Robert H. Gass and John S. Seiter, *Persuasion: Social Influence and Compliance Gaining*, 6th ed. (New York: Routledge, 2018), 224–25.

2. Jack W. Brehm, *A Theory of Psychological Reactance* (New York: Academic Press, 1966).

3. Sonja K. Foss and Karen A. Foss, *Inviting Transformation: Presentational Speaking in a Changing World*, 4th ed. (Long Grove, IL: Waveland, 2019), 11.

4. William J. McGuire, "Inducing Resistance to Persuasion: Some Contemporary Approaches," in *Advances in Experimental Psychology*, ed. Leonard Berkowitz (New York: Academic Press, 1964), 192–229.

5. Gass and Seiter, *Persuasion*, 221–23.

6. Sharon Shavitt and Michelle R. Nelson, "The Role of Attitude Functions in Persuasion and Social Judgment," in *The Persuasion Handbook: Developments in Theory and Practice*, ed. James Price Dillard and Michael Pfau (Thousand Oaks, CA: Sage, 2002), 150.

7. Moriah Balingit and Andrew Van Dam, "U.S. Students Continue to Lag behind Peers in East Asia and Europe in Reading, Math and Science, Exams Show," *Washington Post*, December 3, 2019, https://www.washingtonpost.com/local /education/us-students-continue-to-lag-behind -peers-in-east-asia-and-europe-in-reading-math -and-science-exams-show/2019/12/02/e9e3b37c -153d-11ea-9110-3b34ce1d92b1_story.html.

8. Alan H. Monroe, *Principles and Types of Speech* (Chicago: Scott, Foresman, 1935).

9. The Ron Finley Project, https://ronfinley.com.

8.3 Welcome Remarks

1. Kristen Bub, "Welcome Speech to 2007's Incoming Class" (Harvard Graduate School of Education, Cambridge, MA, September 11, 2007), https://www .gse.harvard.edu/news/07/09/welcome-speech -2007s-incoming-class.

2. Susan Dugdale, "How to Give a Great Welcome Speech," Write-out-loud.com, September 10, 2019, https://www.write-out-loud.com/welcome-speech .html.

8.4 Presenting an Award

1. Egil Aarvik, "Award Ceremony Speech" (Nobel Peace Prize presentation speech to Elie Wiesel, 1986), Nobel Prize, accessed April 21, 2021, https://www.nobelprize.org/prizes/peace/1986 /ceremony-speech.

8.5 Accepting an Award

1. Deirdre Durkan, Oscars: "10 Winners and Presenters Who Dedicated Their Speeches to a Cause," *Hollywood Reporter*, February 13, 2018, https://www.hollywoodreporter.com/lists/oscars -10-winners-presenters-who-dedicated-speeches-a -cause-1083819.

2. Nana Kwame Adjei-Brenyah's acceptance speech, both video and transcript, for the 2019 PEN/Jean Stein Book Award for *Friday Black* can be found on "Winners' Speeches from the 2019 Literary Awards Ceremony," Pen America, 2019, https://pen .org/2019-literary-awards-transcripts.

3. Elie Wiesel, "Elie Wiesel—Acceptance Speech" (Nobel Peace Prize acceptance speech, 1986), Nobel Prize, accessed April 21, 2021, https://www .nobelprize.org/prizes/peace/1986/wiesel/26054 -elie-wiesel-acceptance-speech-1986/

4. Wiesel, "Acceptance Speech."

5. Kelle Louaillier, "The Women Who Blazed the Trail for Social Justice," *Corporate Accountability*, March 31, 2017, https://www.corporateaccountability.org/blog /women-blazed-trail-social-justice/?gclid=Cj0KCQjwyN -DBhCDARIsAFOELTneZED0seCA-JWACSM2 -nq89rWemtu7JkiIiaqCH8soIDnoaID0Me8aAteGEALw _wcB; Denise Graveline and Becky Ham, "Famous Speech Friday: Berta Cáceres's 2015 Goldman Prize

Speech," DeniseGraveline.org, June 24, 2016, https://denisegraveline.org/2016/06/famous-speech -friday-berta-caceres.html; "Case History: Berta Cáceres," Front Line Defenders, accessed April 16, 2021, https://www.frontlinedefenders.org/en/case /case-history-berta-c%C3%A1ceres.

6. https://course-building.s3-us-west-2 .amazonaws.com/Public_Speaking/transcripts /BertaCaceresAcceptanceSpeech2015_transcript.txt.

8.7 Eulogies

1. Lee Strasberg, "Marilyn Monroe's Eulogy," Funeralwise, accessed April 21, 2021, https:// www.funeralwise.com/celebration-of-life/ceremony /eulogy/monroe.

2. "Read George W. Bush's Eulogy for John McCain," *New York Times*, September 1, 2018, https://www .nytimes.com/2018/09/01/us/politics/george-w-bush -john-mccain-eulogy.html.

3. Shirley Halperin, "Aretha Franklin Funeral: Read Clive Davis' Eulogy to the Queen of Soul," *Variety*, August 31, 2018, https://variety.com/2018/music /news/aretha-franklin-funeral-clive-davis -eulogy-1202923282.

4. "Oprah Winfrey, Eulogy for Rosa Parks," American Rhetoric: Online Speech Bank, October 31, 2005, https://www.americanrhetoric.com/speeches /oprahwinfreyonrosaparks.htm.

8.8 Team Presentations and Public Group Discussions

1. Isa N. Engleberg and Dianna R. Wynn, *Working in Groups: Communication Principles and Strategies*, 7th ed. (New York: Pearson, 2017), 224.

2. Thomas Leech, *How to Prepare, Stage, and Deliver Winning Presentations* (New York: AMACOM, 1993), 278.

3. Engleberg and Wynn, *Working in Groups*, 224.

4. Carl E. Larson and Frank M. J. LaFasto, *TeamWork: What Must Go Right/What Can Go Wrong* (Newbury, CA: Sage, 1989), 27.

5. PowerSpeaking, Inc., "Strategies for Terrific Team Presentations," *PowerSpeaking*, April 27, 2016, https://blog.powerspeaking.com/strategies_for _terrific_team_presentations.

6. Marjorie Brody, *Speaking Your Way to the Top: Making Powerful Business Presentations* (Boston: Allyn & Bacon, 1998), 81.

7. Judith Filek, "Tips for Seamless Team Presentations—A Baker's Dozen" (presentation blog post), Impact Communications, Inc., June 1, 2014, https://www.impactcommunicationsinc.com /presentation-communication-skills/tips-for -seamless-team-presentations-a-bakers-dozen/.

8. Engleberg and Wynn, *Working in Groups*, 224.

8.9 Question-and-Answer Sessions

1. "Text of President Bush's Press Conference," *New York Times*, April 13, 2004, https://www.nytimes .com/2004/04/13/politics/text-of-president-bushs -press-conference.html.

2. John A. Daly and Madeleine H. Redlick, "Handling Questions and Objections Affects Audience Judgments of Speakers," *Communication Education* 65, no. 2 (2016): 166.

3. Daly and Redlick, 164–81.

4. Tim Calkins, "How to Nail the Q&A Portion of Your Presentation," Quartz at Work, Quartz, September 20, 2018, https://qz.com/work/1397156 /how-to-manage-questions-after-a-presentation.

5. J. A. Daly and E. Glowacki, "Empowering Questions Affect How People Construe Their Behavior: Why How You Ask Matters in Self-Attributions for Physical Exercise and Healthy Eating, *Journal of Language and Social Psychology* 36, no. 5 (2016): 568–84.

6. Based on Laura Sangha, "Asking Questions of Speakers: Top Tips," *The Many Headed-Monster*, February 23, 2017, https://manyheadedmonster. wordpress.com/2017/02/23/asking-questions-of -speakers-top-tips.

8.10 Online Presentations

1. Ying Lin, "10 Powerful Podcast Statistics You Need to Know," *Oberlo*, June 7, 2020, https:// www.oberlo.com/blog/podcast-Summary%3A %20Podcast%20Statistics,-Here's %20a%20 summary&text=There%20are%20currently %20850%2C000%20active,of%2012%20listen %20to%20podcasts.

9.1 How to Survey an Audience

1. "What Is a Survey?" Qualtrics, accessed April 11, 2021, https://www.qualtrics.com/experience -management/research/survey-basics.

2. Sophia Bernazzani, "How to Write Good (Even Great!) Survey Questions," HubSpot, updated July 31, 2019, https://blog.hubspot.com/service /survey-questions.

3. "Questionnaire Design," Pew Research Center, accessed April 11, 2021, https://www.pewresearch .org/methods/u-s-survey-research/questionnaire -design.

4. Excerpt from Personal Report of Communication Apprehension-24 (PRCA-24), in *Communication Apprehension, Avoidance, and Effectiveness*, 6th ed., ed.

Virginia P. Richmond, Jason S. Wrench, and James C. McCroskey (Boston: Pearson, 2013), 123–25.

5. Clint Fontanella, "The 14 Best Demographic Questions to Use in Surveys," HubSpot, updated March 17, 2021, https://blog.hubspot.com/service /survey-demographic-questions.

6. Laura Wronski, "Why (and How!) to Ask Survey Questions on Sexual Orientation and Gender Identity," *Curiosity at Work*, SurveyMonkey, accessed April 11, 2021, https://www.surveymonkey.com /curiosity/ask-survey-questions-sexual-orientation -gender-identity.

7. "5.3: Conducting Audience Analysis," *Stand Up, Speak Out: The Practice and Ethics of Public Speaking* (Minneapolis: University of Minnesota Libraries Publishing, 2016), https://open.lib.umn.edu /publicspeaking/chapter/5-3-conducting-audience -analysis.

8. Isa N. Engleberg and Marlene C. Cohen, "Focus Group Research in the Community College," *Community Junior College Research Quarterly of Research and Practice* 13, no. 2 (1989): 101–8.

9. "Questionnaire Design."

10. "Questionnaire Design."

11. Emily Crockett, "The Woman Who Inspired Martin Luther King's 'I Have a Dream' Speech," Vox, January 16, 2017, https://www.vox.com /2016/1/18/10785882/martin-luther-king-dream -mahalia-jackson. See also "Mahalia Jackson, the Queen of Gospel, puts her stamp on the March on Washington," *History*, November 13, 2009, updated March 16, 2021, https://www.history.com/this-day -in-history/mahalia-jackson-the-queen-of-gospel -puts-her-stamp-on-the-march-on-washington; and a *Wall Street Journal* video interview with King's

adviser and speechwriter, Clarence B. Jones, in *How Martin Luther King Went Off Script in "I Have a Dream,"* uploaded by Wall Street Journal, YouTube, August 24, 2013, https://www.youtube.com /watch?v=KxlOlynG6FY.

9.2 How to Outline a Presentation

1. Kathy A. Svitil, *Calming the Anger Storm* (New York: Alpha, 2005), 14–15; Georg H. Eifert, Matthew McKay, and John P. Forsyth, *ACT on Life Not on Anger* (Oakland, CA: New Harbinger, 2006), 15, 16, 19, 20, 21; Dudley D. Cahn and Ruth Anna Abigail, *Managing Conflict through Communication*, 5th ed. (Boston: Pearson, 2014), 187–98; Carol Tavris, *Anger: The Misunderstood Emotion* (New York: Simon & Schuster, 1982), 253; Daniel J. Canary and Sandra Lakey, *Strategic Conflict* (New York: Routledge, 2013), 56–59; and William W. Wilmot and Joyce L. Hocker, *Interpersonal Conflict*, 6th ed. (Boston: McGraw-Hill, 2001), 251–53.

Credits

Photos

Pictures; **p. 455 (top):** AP Photo/Manuel Balce Ceneta; **p. 455 (bottom):** Metropolitan AME Church; **p. 480:** W. W. Norton & Company; **pp. 486–87:** W. W. Norton & Company.

Line Art

Page 286: "Median wages: 22–29 years of age" from Daniel A. Carroll and Amy Higgins, "A College Education Saddles Young Households with Debt, but Still Pays Off," *Economic Trends*, Federal Reserve Bank of Cleveland, July 16, 2014. Reproduced with permission of the Federal Reserve Bank of Cleveland; **p. 288:** "The Anatomy of a Flower" image copyright ducu59us/Shutterstock; **p. 291:** "Some College, No Degree by State" from Libby Nelson, "7 charts that show what happened to 31 million American college dropouts," Vox, July 30, 2014. Based on data from the American Community Survey. Reprinted with permission of Vox Media, LLC. https://www.vox.com/2014/7/30/5949139/americas-31-million-college-dropouts-in-7-charts; **p. 298:** "Share of Profits, by Region" republished with permission of McGraw-Hill LLC, from Sara Roche, Steve Sakson, and Gene Zelazny, *The Say It with Charts Complete Toolkit*, 2007. Permission conveyed through Copyright Clearance Center, Inc.

Text

Anderson, Marge: Excerpts from "Looking through Our Window: The Value of Indian Culture," *Vital Speeches of the Day* 65, no. 20 (1999):

633–34. Reprinted courtesy of the Estate of Marge Anderson.

Cáceres, Berta: Speech accepting 2015 Goldman Environmental Prize. https://youtu.be/AR1kwx8b0ms. Reprinted by permission of Goldman Environmental Prize.

McCroskey, James C.: Excerpt from Figure 3.1 Personal Report of Communication Apprehension (PRCA-24) in *Introduction to Rhetorical Communication*, 9th ed. (Routledge, 2016). Copyright © 2006, 2001, 1997, 1993, 1986, 1982, 1978, 1972, 1968 Taylor & Francis. All rights reserved. Reproduced with permission of the Licensor through PLSclear.

Muller, Margaret: Excerpts from "I Have Down Syndrome," *Washington Post*, September 14, 1999. Reprinted courtesy of Margaret Muller.

National Communication Association: "NCA Credo for Ethical Communications." Reprinted with the permission of the National Communication Association. All rights reserved.

Wadler, Naomi: Excerpt from speech at 2018 March for Our Lives Rally, Washington, DC, March 24, 2018. Mashable. https://mashable.com/2018/03/25/naomi-wadler-march-for-our-lives-speech/. Reprinted by permission of the author.

Winfrey, Oprah: Excerpt from eulogy for Rosa Parks, delivered October 31, 2005, Metropolitan AME Church, Washington, DC. Copyright © 2005 by Oprah Winfrey. Reused with permission.